# THE POLITICS OF
# ISLAMIC REVIVALISM

**Indiana Series in Arab and Islamic Studies**
Salih J. Altoma, Iliya Harik, and Mark Tessler, general editors

# THE
# POLITICS OF
# ISLAMIC REVIVALISM

## Diversity and Unity

EDITED BY

SHIREEN T. HUNTER

Published in association with the Center for
Strategic and International Studies, Washington, D.C.

INDIANA UNIVERSITY PRESS
*Bloomington and Indianapolis*

**Library of Congress Cataloging-in-Publication Data**

The Politics of Islamic revivalism.

(Indiana series in Arab and Islamic studies)
Bibliography: p.
Includes index.
1. Islam—20th century.  2. Islam and politics.
3. Islamic countries—Politics and government.
I. Hunter, Shireen.  II. Series.
BP60.P65   1988      297'.09'04      87-21380
ISBN 0-253-34549-9
ISBN 0-253-20466-6 (pbk.)
1 2 3 4 5 92 91 90 89 88

# CONTENTS

**Part IV**
**Islamic Revivalism in Africa**

**Part V**
**Islamic Revivalism in Asia**

**Part VI**

# FOREWORD

Western perceptions of Islam and Muslim societies are marked by an astonishing degree of immaturity. They oscillate between excessive alarm and equally excessive neglect. This study is designed to put some light, and hopefully balance, into the equation.

One of the most significant social and political developments of the past decade has been a growing revivalist wave throughout the Muslim world, a development that has captured the attention of the Western and Soviet publics and their political leaders. The revivalist wave, often misleadingly labeled "fundamentalist," has been expressed mostly in social and cultural terms and has resulted in increased popular demands for stricter application of Islamic law and code of ethics, the elimination of foreign cultural influences viewed as un-Islamic, and, in general, a growing willingness on the part of individual Muslims to apply Islamic principles in their daily lives.

The Muslim revivalist movement has not been limited to social and cultural spheres. Rather, it has had very significant political and economic dimensions. The more active and vocal revivalist groups have forcefully pressed for dramatic changes in the economic and social structures of Muslim societies along what they view as an authentic Islamic model. Indeed, in many countries these groups have had considerable success.

Yet, important as these developments are from an academic perspective, they do not per se account for, or justify, the West's preoccupation with this movement. After all, the West maintains friendly relations with a number of countries whose societies are essentially organized along Islamic legal and moral principles.

What has been very disturbing to the West, and indeed has been at the root of its preoccupation with the revivalist wave, is that the movement entails a militant fringe that is bent on bringing about sudden political change through violent means.

The militant components of the revivalist movement are very anti-Western, but also basically anti-Soviet. They maintain views of the outside world and the dynamics of international life that are incompatible not only with those of the West but also with those of the socialist world. The United States is the Western superpower and is in many ways the representative of Western civilization. Thus, in the militants' eyes it is the embodiment of everything that is wrong with this civilization and is therefore particularly targeted by them.

In view of the foregoing, it is obvious that the West cannot look upon a potential victory of militant revivalism with complacency. Indeed, the implications of such a victory were clearly demonstrated by the Iranian revolution of 1979 and many aspects of the still-unfolding Lebanese crisis.

Therefore, it is vital that the West—and the United States in particular—through appropriate policies, do whatever possible to prevent the further radicalization of the revivalist movement and to check the influence of its existing militant fringe.

To develop sound policies, the West needs a deeper understanding of the nature of the movement, its causes, and its complexities. It should avoid falling into the trap of simplistic and sweeping explications. Similarly, while remaining alert to the evolution of the movement, it should not exaggerate the potential threat of the movement—including its militant brand—to the West's interests, or the chances of the militants to gain power.

Failure to do so runs the risk of leading the West to overreaction, inaction, or a combination of both that could irremediably damage the West's relations with 900 million Muslims for a long time to come.

Given that the mission of the Center for Strategic and International Studies (CSIS) is to serve as a bridge between the world of ideas and the world of action, the importance of a deep understanding of the revivalist movement did not escape its attention. Thus, the Center's Middle East Program in 1985 organized a study group, which met at quarterly intervals for eighteen months, made up of foremost American and Muslim experts in the field to study the revivalist movement. The current volume is largely the result of the labors and deliberations of this group. It is our hope that it will help the reader toward a better understanding of the revivalist movement, and thus make a significant contribution to the development of sound Western responses to the challenge of Islamic revivalism and to the West's relations with the Islamic world.

ROBERT G. NEUMANN
Senior Adviser, Director of
Middle East Program, CSIS

# INTRODUCTION

## Shireen T. Hunter

Since February 1979, when a popular revolution led by the Ayatullah Ruhullah Khumaini toppled the Pahlavi monarchy and established an Islamic republic in Iran, Islam's political force and revolutionary appeal as a comprehensive ideology has fascinated and perplexed Western observers and academics. The tendencies of the more militant revivalists—anti-Western and especially anti-American—have at times been expressed in acts of violence against Western nationals. Thus the militant Islam popularly known as "Islamic fundamentalism" has been perceived as the greatest danger to Western interests throughout the Muslim world.

Consequently, during the last few years, Islam has become a favorite subject of study, whereas only ten years ago most political scientists and development experts dismissed it as largely irrelevant to the Muslim world's social and political development. In fact, partly to compensate for past neglect, many of these experts now project Islam as the most—if not the only—potent political force in the Muslim world for the foreseeable future. Some experts have even expressed surprise at the general bewilderment over Islam's political vitality. They have explained the current revival as natural and as yet another turn in the traditionally cyclical history of Islam's rising and falling fortunes.

To categorize the literature that has been produced in the last few years is a difficult task and entails the risk of oversimplification. Nevertheless, three broad categories of recent studies on Islam can be identified: (1) studies that have focused on specific aspects of Islam and Islamic thought and institutions, including such issues as Islamic economics, the relationship of Islam to politics, and Islam and development; (2) studies that could be characterized as introductions to Islam to the nonspecialist; and (3) studies that have tried to identify and analyze the underlying causes of the current revivalist wave and to develop a theoretical framework that could explain it.

Most of these works have been solid, scholarly endeavors that have enriched the pool of knowledge on Islam. Yet many others have suffered from certain flaws, some of which have also, in the past, plagued Western scholarship on Islam. The most serious of these flaws has been the excessive degree to which some authors have tried to explain the revivalist phenomenon in terms of particular characteristics of Islam, rather than by analyzing it within the context of the social, economic, and political evolution of Muslim societies.

As Dr. Norma Salem has written in the introduction to her essay on the revivalist movement in Tunisia (chapter 10), the underlying theme of many of these studies is that the revivalist movement is happening because this is the way "Muslims" behave. Of course, this is not to deny that certain specific characteristics of Islam—particularly the fusion of religion and politics that is greater than in Christian societies—and the fact that Islam is the most important component of the majority of Muslims' self-identity, both individually and collectively, have contributed to its recent political vitality. Nor is it to suggest that these aspects should be underestimated. Instead, it is necessary to remind observers that while these characteristics have always existed, Islam has not always been an overly active political force. For example, for at least the past hundred years, secular ideologies and forces have dominated the political life of the Muslim world. Moreover, both historically and in recent times, other religions that do not share Islam's political characteristics have become politicized.

To view the revivalist movement solely in terms of Islam also runs the risk of presenting it as a predominantly religious phenomenon. Yet the evidence shows that beneath the religious symbolism of the movement lie secular social, economic, political, and cultural concerns. For example, Professor Amira El-Azhary Sonbol, in her contribution on the role of Islam in Egypt (chapter 2), explains that the return to the Islamic dress code in Egypt is partly caused by the fact that it makes economic sense and hides social and economic disparities and does not derive simply from a sense of Islamic modesty. In this sense, Islamic dress resembles the uniforms that the Chinese adopted after their socialist revolution to emphasize the egalitarian and nonmaterialist nature of their new society.

Similarly, the quotation from a Moroccan preacher cited by Professor Henry Munson, Jr., in his contribution on the revivalist movement in Morocco (chapter 9), is instructive. This preacher defines the *Sharicа* (Islamic law) as "the struggle against poverty, injustice and ignorance. . . ."

Yet it must be noted that the use of Islam to express specific social, economic, or political grievances and to alter unfavorable conditions has not been limited to economically underprivileged classes. That is clearly illustrated by Professor Raymond A. Hinnebusch in chapter 3, dealing with the revivalist movement in Syria. Quite the contrary, people of all economic and social backgrounds who have in one way or another felt aggrieved have used Islam as a medium of opposition and an instrument to redress their grievances.

In the context of West African Muslim countries, Professor Sulayman S. Nyang, in chapter 13, demonstrates how demands for a greater role for Islam in West Africa have essentially been made by individuals who have been educated in Arab universities and who have felt isolated within a system dominated by Western-educated elites who speak French or English. In sum, as Professor Mohammad Arkoun points out in his contribution on Algeria (chapter 11), the Muslim revivalists are acting from the same social, economic, and political concerns that motivate secular groups, although the revivalists express their views and objectives through religious symbolism.

Of course, there is no lack of moral or religious motivations within the movement. But it is important to stress that the political vitality of the revivalist movement and its militant edge owes more to social, economic, and political factors.

An overemphasis on Islam's particular characteristics as the principal, if not the only, impetus behind the revivalist wave could also jeopardize future relations between the Western and Islamic worlds. This danger derives from the fact that the tendency to explain the revivalist phenomenon in this way has led to the advancement of such sweeping theories as the inevitable and inherent animosity of Islam toward the West and the congenital propensity of Muslims to violence. If such theories were to gain credence, the only road ahead for Western-Muslim relations would be that of conflict until the elimination of either the Muslim forces or the Western presence in the Muslim world.

To be sure, there are some points of incompatibility between the Muslim revivalists' aspirations and Western interests. But these conflicts are caused less by inherent animosities than by the legacies of Western colonialism in the Islamic world; by more recent actions of certain Western countries and their regional allies, including support for authoritarian and unpopular regimes; by the problem of the Arab-Israeli conflict and what the Muslims perceive to be the West's unfair approach to this issue; and by the fact that the conflict reflects a general desire for greater political, economic, and cultural autonomy and self-sufficiency—a desire, incidentally, that is not limited to the Muslim revivalists. Quite the contrary, once stripped of its Islamic symbolism, the Muslim revivalists' discourse regarding the Islamic world's relations with the West closely resembles that of the anticolonial nationalist and other Third World radical movements of the 1950s, 1960s, and early 1970s. In other words, it is not Islam as religion or even as political ideology that is the source of tension between the West and the Muslim revivalists. Viewed in this perspective, Western-Muslim conflict becomes far more amenable to resolution through compromise and give-and-take.

Another tendency in some of the scholarship on Islamic revivalism, particularly in those works that have tried to develop broad theoretical frameworks, has been to overemphasize historical analogies between the current revivalist wave and the previous Islamic reform movements. For example, those scholars who have applied crisis theory to explain the current wave of revivalism have concluded that revivalist movements have, in general, appeared at times when, because of major military defeats, foreign incursion, or a general sense of decline, Muslim societies have felt threatened and thus have experienced a sense of crisis.

There certainly is a lot of truth in this view. In fact, seeing crisis as a stimulus to revivalism has been a significant contribution to efforts to explain the current revivalist phenomenon. Nevertheless, the history of many Muslim countries during the past two centuries shows that the crisis theory, although important, is an inadequate explanation, or at least that past revivalist movements were overpowered by other reform or protest movements. For example, during the nineteenth and early twentieth centuries the Islamic world's state of decline and dependency was at an all-time high, and yet nationalist modernizing and largely secularizing forces gained more influence. Admittedly, during the same period there also was an Islamic reformist or revivalist movement as best illustrated by the activities of Sayad Jamal-ad-Din al-Afghani. But ultimately the modernizing trend prevailed. Moreover, historical evidence shows that a sense of crisis and decline is not the only spur to revivalist movements. In fact, most scholars agree that the initial victories by Egypt and Syria in the 1973 Arab-Israeli war, along with the oil-related increase in Arab-Muslim influence that revived the Muslims' pride and self-esteem and raised their hopes for the future, also greatly contributed to the current revivalist wave.

Nevertheless, currently a general feeling of decline and stagnation and a continued state of dependency among the Muslims is greatly contributing to the revivalist wave. But the real reason why today the Muslims are resorting to Islam to change these conditions is not—as many would suggest—because this is the way the Muslims always react. Rather, it is because, as the majority of the Muslims see it, the paradigm of modernization and the political elites associated with it have failed to avert the Islamic world's decline and end its state of political and economic dependency.

The crisis theory also implies a sense of virtual inevitability about the periodic recurrence of revivalist movements. As a result, the theory pays inadequate attention to specific actions and policies of Muslim governments that have contributed greatly to the current revivalist wave, and especially to its widespread appeal and militant edge.

For example, most scholars writing about Islamic revivalism have rightly noted disillusionment with secular foreign-inspired ideologies as a major cause for the vitality of Islam and particularly its militant brand. But not enough attention has been paid to the fact that none of these secular ideologies had been given a fair chance. For more than a century, ideals of liberal democracy have inspired the Muslim world's intellectual elites and have generated political movements aimed at creating more representative forms of government. But these efforts were largely frustrated for a variety of reasons related to the internal dynamics of Muslim societies and to external factors, at times including foreign intervention.

Admittedly, if more representative forms of government had been tried, Islam would likely have had even more influence in determining the shape of these countries' social and political institutions. Thus many of the changes of the past sixty years—especially those related to social and cultural aspects of Muslim life—might not have taken place. But it can also be argued that if the more representative forms of governance had been adopted by the Islamic countries, any changes or reforms would have been based on a broader consensus and thus would have been more in line with the traditional values and way of life of Muslim societies than many of those changes or reforms that were carried out. Thus they would have enjoyed more legitimacy and been more lasting. But the representative system was not given a fair trial. Consequently, many of the changes or reforms carried out by leaders that development experts call "modernizing dictators" are either being reversed (as in Iran) or are being challenged.

Moreover, the nature of the modernization process and the authoritarian way in which it was carried out in the Islamic world has contributed to a widespread sense of malaise—a condition which has greatly contributed to the revivalist surge. Most damaging has been the tendency in all developing societies, including Muslim countries, to emphasize material modernization and to ignore the nurturing of new social, political, and cultural attitudes and the building of new and broadly based institutions capable of dealing with the demands of modernity.

Thus, while material modernity has tended to disintegrate old sociopolitical institutions and patterns of relationships, it has not replaced them with new ones capable of harnessing and channeling newly unleashed social and political forces, or of responding to new needs. The result for the majority of people has been a growing feeling of psychological, social, and political alienation and disorientation. These feelings in turn have propelled them to seek some sense of stability and continuity by reverting to their traditional way of life. In the context of Islamic countries, that has meant a return to Islam, which constitutes such a fundamental part of the Muslim societies' traditional culture, way of life, and sociopolitical institutions.

Moreover, the process of modernization has generally been carried out in an unbalanced and unfair manner, with the economic and social benefits of modernization distributed unevenly among the Muslim populations. In addition, many Islamic leaders have used the paradigm of modernization to justify and legitimize their arbitrary rule. Thus those who have remained deprived of the fruits of modernization, those who have seen their lives disrupted by it while having been denied a say in determining its nature and pace, have resorted to traditional values, including Islam, to assert their rights and to demand their vindication.

For more than fifty years, Muslim governments have also actively eliminated alternative media for articulating social, economic, and political concerns, frequently using Islam as their main instrument. As a result, Islam has absorbed the political language and many other aspects of lay ideologies and political theories such as socialism and neocolonialism and has been transformed into almost the only vehicle for articulating societal concerns and the only medium of opposition. The impact of lay ideologies has been particularly strong on the Muslim revivalists' world view—their perceptions of the current international system and the Islamic countries' place within it. Indeed, the revivalists' views in this regard echo many of the traditional political theories current in the Third World in the past three decades. The search for freedom from both the East and the West, for indigenous solutions to indigenous problems, for an end to the state of dependency, and for economic, cultural, and political self-sufficiency is not an invention of Muslim revivalists, although it is now expressed through Islamic terminology and symbolism. Indeed, the political appeal of the militant brand of revivalism for younger Muslims is that it has incorporated many aspects of traditional Third World radicalism. These themes are still appealing because after decades of independence and development, the underlying conditions of Muslim countries still remain unchanged. Meanwhile, the arbitrary nature of rulership and the failure of the ruling elites to create an adequate sociopolitical institutional framework has created an ideological and institutional vacuum that the revivalists have attempted to fill with Islam.

Another tendency in many studies on the Islamic revivalist movement has been to see it as largely monolithic. Admittedly, some scholars have made distinctions between so-called traditional Islam and revolutionary Islam, or between what James Bill has called "establishment Islam" and "populist Islam." Largely missing, however, has been a greater differentiation among elements within the militant revivalist movement, plus a focus on the way that the revivalist movement has been manifested in different countries, reflecting the realities of each one. There has not been much systematic comparative work on this subject.

For reasons elaborated earlier, most regrettable has been the tendency of many scholars to put too much emphasis on the particular characteristics of Islam in explaining the revivalist wave, rather than to place it within the context of the Muslim world's social, economic, and political evolution. Thus the wave is viewed as essentially a religious phenomenon, shaped and colored by Muslim idiosyncrasies, rather than as an essentially social, economic, and political movement reflecting the internal conditions of Muslim societies where traditional systems have all but disintegrated without new and more or less broadly based sociopolitical systems having emerged.

Equally regrettable has been the failure to give adequate attention to the impact of specific policies and actions of Muslim governments and foreign powers in the generation of the revivalist movement, including the systematic use of Islam to combat political forces viewed as radical by Muslim countries. For example, while many now focus on the Iranian or Libyan activities to promote a militant brand of revivalism, it is largely forgotten that during the 1950s, the 1960s, and even the early 1970s, Islam was used as a conservative force by Iran, Saudi Arabia, and other countries to check the influence of certain radical ideologies—including Arab variants of socialism—and other forces demanding greater political participation and more representative forms of government.

This volume is, therefore, a modest attempt to fill some of these gaps in traditional scholarship, and an effort to place the Islamic revivalist movement in its proper social, economic, and political context. In addition, because the movement has generated strong fears in the West, an effort is being made to assess the potential for the movement to gain political power in Islamic countries and its implications for Western interests. Therefore, the primary purposes of this volume are—through a comparative study of revivalist movements in a wide selection of Islamic countries—to identify and assess the causes of the emergence and strength of the movement; its nature; the different ideological tendencies within the movement; the number, types, and political strength of various militant groups; the linkages and transnational connections among different parts of the revivalist movement; and the potential for the revivalist movement's success in gaining political power. Also, by examining the record of the Islamic Republic of Iran, an effort has been made to shed some light on the practical consequences of possible revivalist success, both for the internal development of Muslim societies and for their international relations.

The greatest part of the volume is based on the work of a study group organized by the Middle East Program of the Center for Strategic and International Studies which met at quarterly intervals from September 1985 through March 1986. In conducting the activities of the group, no attempt was made to impose a specific theoretical framework or any rigid guidelines on the discussions. Nor were contributors asked to approach the subject matter in any particular way. The basic methodology was comparative and empirical: to look into the revivalist movement in individual countries, to examine the factors behind it, and only then to try drawing some general conclusions.

These conclusions, it is hoped, will focus attention on the extremely complex and multidimensional nature of the movement and thus encourage more detailed research into specific aspects of the movement which in turn could help develop a theory to adequately explain the revivalist phenomenon. It is also hoped that these conclusions will help to put the movement in its proper social, economic, and political context, to ease the most exaggerated fears aroused by the movement, and to help in the development of sensible and realistic Western responses.

# Part I

# I

# ISLAMIC REVIVAL
## CATALYSTS, CATEGORIES,
## AND CONSEQUENCES

### R. Hrair Dekmejian

The revival of the Islamic ethos is one of the most pervasive and deep-rooted phenomena affecting the Muslim world today. Evidence of a return to Islamic life-styles and to the fundamental precepts of the faith can be seen in virtually all Muslim societies, affecting culture, social relations, economic affairs, and political life. Only after its revolutionary intrusion into the realm of politics and international affairs did the world take notice of the Islamic wave. Beginning with the Iranian revolution in 1979, a succession of dramatic events made the term *Islamic fundamentalism* a part of the West's political, scholarly, and journalistic vocabulary. The direct threat to Western interests posed by the militant or revolutionary brand of Islam was instrumental in attracting global attention. After belatedly perceiving some of the destabilizing implications of militant Islam, the Western world has now become obsessed with the subject. Yet this preoccupation has not produced objective prognostication or effective policy.

The revival of the Islamic zeitgeist had long preceded its violent manifestations in Iran and the Arab countries, although with rare exceptions it had gone unrecognized.[1] Indeed, Western specialists on Islam were conceptually and temperamentally ill-equipped to detect and prognosticate the revivalist profluence. Armed with a plethora of materialist and other theories of social causality ranging from liberalism to neo-Marxism and structural functionalism, the Western social scientist was unprepared to consider the potency of religion as a revolutionary force. This conceptual myopia had also blinded the majority of American Middle East specialists who incessantly taught that "Islam is a way of life, not simply a religion," while anticipating its "inevitable" depoliticization and encapsulation in an increasingly secularized context, in keeping with the pattern followed by Western societies. Even more serious was the perceptual impotence of Arab and Muslim intellectuals, many of whom were shocked and surprised by the emerging revivalist phenomenon in their own societies. Perhaps their training in Western and Marxist social science had been too rigorous.

This essay analyzes the contemporary revivalist movement in Islam in terms of its historical antecedents, its sociopolitical catalysts, and various guises. It demonstrates that the present revival is a consequence of the multifaceted crises facing Islamic society. Two taxonomies of Islamic groups and societies are presented in terms of their ideological orientation and types of leadership. The final section is devoted to the types of state responses to Islamic militancy and the potential threat of militant Islam to constituted authority.

## Varieties and Vocabulary of Islamic Revivalism

The revival of Islam has taken several forms. At the most general level, it represents a heightening of Islamic consciousness among the masses. This type of popular Islam is represented by the spread of benevolent societies and brotherhoods of Sufis (those who practice Sufism, a mystical interpretation of Islam) and the conspicuous observance of Islamic practices. Despite its pervasiveness and its social and spiritual effervescence, this fundamentalism is usually characterized by political passivity, except when there is an instigation from the government or an external hostile source. However, within this generally amorphous revivalist milieu, there are islands of religious activism consisting of militant Islamic groups and societies. These groups display a heightened Islamic political consciousness that is opposed to the state and its ruling elements and institutions. In the incubational environment of crisis, these militant groups have evolved in the context of a symbiotic relationship with the larger revivalist milieu that accords them the opportunity to proselytize, recruit new members, and hide when confronted with the security forces. Because of this symbiotic relationship, the contemporary revivalist movement should be regarded as a dynamic continuum between passivist spiritualism and militancy.

Specifically, these gradations of revivalist activity are reflected in the Arabic vocabulary used to describe revivalist individuals and groups. Often the proponents of Islamic revivalism refer to themselves as *Islamiyyin*—Islamists—or *asliyyin*—the original or authentic ones. Also used are the terms *mu'min* (pl., *mu'minin*) and *mutadayyin* (pl., *mutadayyinin*)—the pious or devout—in sharp contrast to *muta'sib* (pl., *muta'sibin*)—zealot or fanatic. The word *muta'sib* is often used by nonrevivalists to describe the Islamic militants who are predisposed to the use of violence. A related label is *mutatarrif* (pl., *mutatarrifin*) meaning radical or extremist. The term *mutadayyin* is given two distinct meanings: as a general reference to characterize the faithful Muslim and as a specific appellation used by the revivalists about themselves, as distinct from other Muslims. The terms *fundamentalist, revivalist,* and *Islamist* are often used interchangeably in the scholarly literature, although *fundamentalism* has assumed a new connotation in the West, meaning radicalism.

Also instructive are the specific constructs used in Islamic terminology to describe the revivalist phenomenon. Proponents and sympathizers frequently use the expressions *al-ba'th al-Islami* (Islamic renaissance), *al-sahwa al-*

*Islamiyya* (Islamic awakening), *ihya' ad-din* (religious revival), and *al-usuliyya al-Islamiyya* (Islamic fundamentalism). The most appropriate term is *al-usuliyya al-Islamiyya* since it connotes a search for the fundamentals of the faith, the foundations of the Islamic community and polity (*umma*), and the bases of legitimate authority (*shar'iyyat al-hukm*). Such a formulation emphasizes the political dimension of the Islamic movement. In terms of general usage in Islam, the concept of *tajdid* refers to the periodic renewal of the faith, while *islah* means restoration or reform.[2]

## Cycles of Crisis and Resurgence in History

The causal relationship between social crisis and religious resurgence has had substantial validity in diverse cultural settings. Islamic revivalism is no exception to this historical pattern. The recurrent waves of resurgence during periods of acute crisis have been a persistent pattern since the early years of Islam. Throughout its fourteen centuries, Islam has shown a unique capacity to renew and reassert itself against competing ideologies and social forces through its revivalist mode, an inbuilt, self-regenerating social mechanism that is triggered when the moral integrity or physical existence of the umma is under threat. This cyclical dynamic of crisis and resurgence is discernible in various historical epochs (figure 1).[3]

The conceptualization of the incidence of Islamic revivalism as a response to crisis raises an important theoretical question: What types of social crisis trigger a revivalist response? The usual explanation advanced by Western and Marxist theorists is one that rests on economic determinism: religious revival is seen as mainly the consequence of economic crisis.[4] Despite their considerable theoretical power, materialistic conceptualizations appear to provide partial explanations for the complex phenomenon of Islamic revival. In examining major historical cases of Islamic crisis and revival, one is confronted with a considerable diversity of causes (table 1).[5]

The crisis conditions in the milieux of Caliph ʿUmar ibn ʿAbd al-ʿAziz and Ahmad ibn Hanbal were primarily social and spiritual, although in Ibn Hanbal's case state repression also played a critical role. The situations faced by Ibn Hazm and Ibn Taymiyya, however, centered on internal dissension, moral decline, and the threat of extinction, which overshadowed the socioeconomic factors. Ibn ʿAbd al-Wahhab's Muwahidin warriors and reformers fought against Ottoman power as well as religious innovations and superstitions. The Sanusiyya began as a tribal Sufi movement that became radicalized in response to Italian imperialism. The Mahdiyya represented a revolutionary response to Anglo-Egyptian-Turkish rule, tribal conflicts, moral laxity, and economic distress. The Salafiyya was a reformist movement—a response to European imperial rule and cultural-economic penetration. Finally, in the case of Hasan al-Banna's Muslim Brotherhood, the catalysts of crisis included the persistence of British

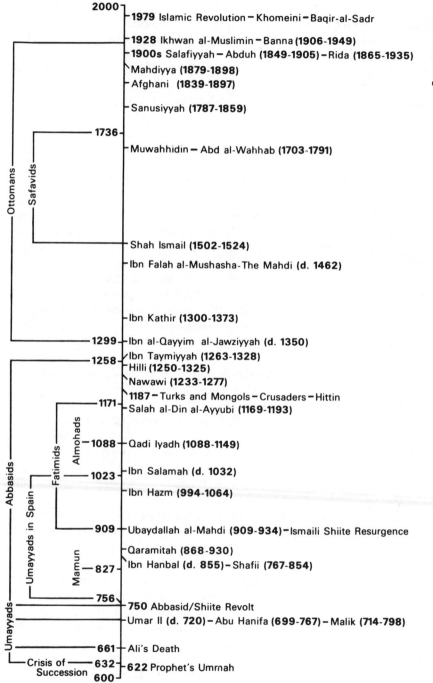

Figure 1. Stages of social crisis and Islamist response. From R. Hrair Dekmejian, *Islam in Revolution*, p. 10.

TABLE 1.
**Causes of Islamist Resurgence**

| Leader/Movement | Cause |
| --- | --- |
| ᶜUmar II (d. 720) | Umayyad's moral degeneration |
| Ibn Hanbal (d. 855) | ᶜAbbasid imposition of Muʾtazila doctrine/state repression |
| Ibn Hazm (d. 1064) | Umayyad decline and defeat in Spain |
| Ibn Taymiyya (d. 1328) | ᶜAbbasid demise/Tatar conquest/moral and economic crisis |
| Ibn ᶜAbd al-Wahhab (d. 1791) | Ottoman decline/religious-moral crisis |
| Sanusiyya (1880s) | Religious-tribal crisis/Italian conquest |
| Mahdiyya (1880s) | Religious-tribal conflict/economic crisis/Anglo-Egyptian-Ottoman rule |
| Salafiyya (1890s) | European military, cultural and economic imperialism |
| Muslim Brotherhood (1930s) | Social-economic-political crisis and British imperial presence |

hegemony, mounting socioeconomic problems, and the powerful cultural and ideological influences radiating from the West.[6]

## Crisis and Revival in Modern Islamic Societies

In view of the great social, political, cultural, and economic diversity of the Islamic world, substantial differences exist in the local conditions of the various Muslim countries. Yet the existence of significant cross-national similarities between the crisis conditions prevailing in different Muslim countries permits generalization about macro-level crisis attributes that seem valid for the larger Islamic environment. These conditions include identity conflict, legitimacy crisis, political conflict, class conflict, culture crisis, and military impotence, which act as the catalysts of Islamic revivalist responses.[7]

The validity of these crisis factors is reinforced by the self-view and world view of many Muslims, particularly the revivalists themselves. The latter's view of the Islamic condition is one of gloom and doom marked by internal degeneration, secularization, socioeconomic injustice, political repression, and military defeat. To a significant degree, these perceptions are the product of the objective conditions existing throughout the Islamic world. In the Sunni context, the breakup of the Ottoman Empire and the abolition of the Caliphate in 1924 by Turkish nationalists under Kemal Ataturk meant the ending of any pretense of Islamic unity and power. One major consequence of Islamic decline was the crisis of individual and collective identity among the Muslims. The task of finding substitute frameworks of identity was to prove difficult since Islam is an all-encompassing social system that includes religion (*din*), state (*dawla*), and law (*shariᶜa*).

In the Middle East, three main indigenous nationalisms arose as substitute identities—Turkish, Iranian, and Arab/Egyptian. They provided the underpinnings for linguistically based states. Thus, the liberal Turkish nationalism of Ottomanist reformers led by Ahmet Reza gave way first to the pan-Turanism of the Young Turks inspired by Ziya Gölkalp and then to Ataturk's secular Turkish nationalism, which is presently under challenge by Islamic revivalists. In Iran, an indigenous Persian nationalism evolved into a pan-Iranian ideology under Reza Shah based on the pre-Islamic Aryan past, only to be destroyed by the 1979 revolution and the establishment of an Islamic state. In the Arab sphere, Egyptian and Arab nationalism evolved separately until the 1950s, when Naser presided over their convergence in the framework of pan-Arabism. After the June 1967 defeat and Naser's death, the edifice of pan-Arabism began to crumble. The fallback of many Arabs from pan-Arabism was to Islam in its revivalist expression.[8]

Throughout this dialectic of shifting identities, the Islamic countries experimented with a plethora of socioeconomic systems ranging from socialism to capitalism and corporatism under a variety of regimes—monarchies, single-party oligarchies, military autocracies, and constitutional democracies. Despite periods of limited success, these countries' problems have remained unresolved. Ambitious developmental efforts have failed to produce large-scale economic betterment. There have been gross disparities of income distribution in the Muslim countries (table 2).

Indications are that during the past decade these disparities have substantially increased. For example, in less than a decade, the percentage of Moroccans in absolute poverty has risen from 28 to 45.[9] A similar trend has been observed in Egypt. In these situations, feelings of relative deprivation have generated political instability as the prospects of upward mobility have diminished. Economically, the Muslim countries' dependence on the industrialized countries has deepened.

Lack of socioeconomic justice combined with official corruption and failure of political elites to mold strong identities through socialization has produced a crisis of legitimacy, where the moral bases of authority are in question. The legitimacy crisis is further deepened by the frequent use of coercion against opposition elements and the continued military weakness of the Muslim states against the West, Israel, the Soviet Union, and other antagonists. The continuing Arab military inferiority with respect to Israel has had a debilitating impact on the Muslim psyche. These conditions are exacerbated by oil-wealth-generated consumerism and a crisis of culture resulting from the penetration of Muslim society by imported values and modern life-styles.

The foregoing conditions of crisis constitute the incubational milieu that shapes the personalities, life-styles, and world view of revivalist Muslims. At

TABLE 2.
**Income Distribution in Islamic Countries, Mid-1970s**

| | Income distribution (%) | | | |
|---|---|---|---|---|
| | Richest 5% of households | Poorest 20% of households | Poorest 40% of households | % Population in absolute poverty* |
| Bangladesh | 16.7 | 7.9 | 20.0 | 23.0 |
| Pakistan | 17.3 | 8.4 | 16.5 | 18.0 |
| Indonesia | 33.7 | 6.6 | 16.1 | 61.0 |
| Egypt | 21.0 | 5.2 | 13.9 | 9.0 |
| Sudan | 20.9 | 5.1 | 14.5 | 40.0 |
| Nigeria | — | — | 13.0 | 43.0 |
| Morocco | 20.0 | 4.0 | 11.3 | 28.0 |
| Tunisia | — | — | 11.1 | 14.0 |
| Turkey | 28.0 | 3.5 | 9.1 | 19.0 |
| Iraq | 35.1 | 2.1 | — | — |
| Iran | 29.7 | 4.0 | 11.5 | 10.0 |
| Malaysia | 28.3 | 3.5 | 11.1 | 10.0 |

*Using official exchange rates.
*Source:* World Bank, *World Economic and Social Indicators,* July 1978; M. S. Ahluwalia, N. G. Carter, and H. B. Chenery, *Growth and Poverty in Developing Countries,* World Bank, September 1978; and G. Sheehan and M. Hopkins, *Basic Needs Performance: An Analysis of Some International Data,* ILO, January 1978.

the general level, most revivalists possess a strong sense of commitment to Islam and to the observance of its basic obligations. Within this larger revivalist collectivity of popular Islam are the militant groups, consisting of radicals who are acutely alienated from the social and political order, which they seek to destroy as prelude to the establishment of an Islamic polity. These militants often follow a rigid discipline and an austere life-style and express a readiness to sacrifice themselves for their ideals.

## Coincidence and Culmination of Dialectics

A question that begs for an answer concerns the timing of the present revivalist surge. Why did revivalism appear during the seventh decade of the twentieth century? Moreover, what peculiarity of the crisis of the contemporary period produced a reaction of such great magnitude focused on revivalist Islam?

Several attributes of the present crisis set it apart from earlier periods of crisis. Its most distinctive features are (1) pervasiveness—the crisis condition is not limited to certain countries, but is pervasive throughout the Islamic world;

(2) comprehensiveness—the crisis situation is multifaceted, at once social, economic, political, cultural, psychological, and spiritual; and (3) cumulativeness—the crisis situation is cumulative, representing the culmination of unsuccessful efforts in nation-building, socioeconomic development, and military prowess. Indeed, the 1970s marked the end of an era of optimism for Islamic countries, an era in which they sought to achieve modernity by the emulation of Western and socialist models or a mix of their variants. The West's powerful technological and cultural impact had generated aspirations, hopes, and reluctant admiration for its economic and military achievements. By the 1970s these hopes had been dashed as the socioeconomic viability and moral integrity of Western civilization came under attack. Thus, the 1970s became the repository of failed dialectical processes—ideological, developmental, and political—which came together to create a situation of hopelessness and pessimism among Muslims, from which there appeared to be no exit. Hence the return to Islam as the only remaining haven of identity and authenticity. Still another distinctive feature is (4) xenophobism. A sense of xenophobia pervades Muslim society, the feeling that Islam itself is facing a mortal threat. In the opinion of revivalist intellectuals, the very integrity of the Islamic culture and way of life is threatened by non-Islamic forces of secularism and modernity, encouraged by Muslim governments.

The crisis of the 1970s coincided with the end of Islam's fourteenth century. Traditionally, the culmination of a century is marked by popular feelings of expectancy for the arrival of a renewer of the faith and the Islamic community. The 1970s were no exception to this historical pattern, except that the popular sense of expectancy was fueled by the existing milieu of crisis.

### The Islamic Alternative: Ideologies and Movements

The protracted crisis of Muslim society has brought to the fore the Islamic alternative. The mass revival of Islam has been accompanied by a withering attack from revivalist writers and preachers calling for radical change along Islamic lines. The foremost ideologues of contemporary Islamic revivalism include Hasan al-Banna, Abu al-ʿAla Mawdudi, Sayyid Qutb, Ruhullah Khumaini, Muhammad Baqer as-Sadr, ʿAbd as-Salam Farag, Saʿid Hawwa, and Juhaiman al-Utaibi. The points of view expressed by these writers are quite diverse, yet they are in substantial agreement on certain main tenets, which can be taken to represent the general ideological framework of contemporary Islamic revivalism:[10]

1. *Din wa Dawla*. Islam is a total system of existence, universally applicable to all times and places. The separation of religion (*din*) and state (*dawla*) is inconceivable. Rulership (*hukm*) is inherent in Islam; the Qur'an gives the law, and the state enforces the law.

2. *Qur'an wa Sunna*. The foundations of Islam are the Qur'an and the Sunna—the Traditions of the Prophet Muhammad and of his pious companions. The Muslims are enjoined to return to the early roots of Islam and the puritanical

practices of the Prophet's umma in the quest for authenticity and renewal. Unless the Muslims revert to the "correct path" of their pious ancestors, there will be no salvation. While Sunni revivalists revere the four Rightly Guided Caliphs, the Shi꜀a venerate ꜀Ali, Fatima, and their descendants.

3. *Puritanism and Social Justice.* The family is the cornerstone of society, where men are placed in a position of leadership and responsibility while women are the source of love and kindness. The mixing of the sexes should be controlled and women decently dressed to maintain dignity and avoid temptation. Western cultural values and mores are vehemently rejected as being alien to Islam. To this end, the mass media are enjoined to propagate Islamic values and practices instead of disseminating foreign cultural influences. The return to the correct path also requires the establishment of socioeconomic justice. All property belongs to society and ultimately to God; man only uses wealth earned through his labor. Islam recognizes the right to private property but limits it in accordance with the general welfare of the community. Wealth accumulated through monopoly, usury, and dishonesty is prohibited. The practice of *zakat* (a type of Islamic tax) coupled with state policy will promote social justice and ameliorate class antagonisms. In promoting economic development, Islamic societies should avoid falling into situations of dependency on the advanced industrial countries.

4. *Allah's Sovereignty and Rule under the Shari꜀a.* The ultimate aim of the Muslims should be the establishment of God's sovereignty on earth. It can only be accomplished by constituting an Islamic order—*nizam al-Islami*—where Allah's law (*Shari꜀a*) is supreme. The establishment of an Islamic community will guarantee the liberation of man from others and from his own desires. Thus, only through Islam can there be salvation for humanity.

5. *Jihad: The Sixth Pillar.* The good Muslim is enjoined to go beyond observing the Five Pillars or obligations of Islam and to commit himself to a life of action in building the ideal community under the Shari꜀a. To establish such a community, it is necessary to destroy the existing *jahiliyya*—the pre-Islamic society of ignorance and impiety—and to dispossess worldly rulers of their authority by waging *jihad* (holy war). The resort to jihad should not be "defensive"; it should aim at conquering all obstacles placed in the way of Islam's propagation throughout the world, including states, social systems, and alien traditions against which the *mujahidin* (holy warriors) will employ a "comprehensive" jihad, including violence. Since the obligation of jihad could involve martyrdom, Muslims should be ready to sacrifice themselves, for victory can only come with the mastery of "the art of death." Since the onset of the Islamic order in Iran, Iranian revivalists under Khumaini have shed the passivist tradition in Shiism, which eschews the waging of jihad until the appearance of the *Mahdi* (Messiah); hence the convergence of Shi꜀a and Sunni doctrines of jihad.

The foregoing five categories contain the basic elements of revivalist ideology on which there has been broad agreement among virtually all radical revivalists of the Islamic world. Beyond these basics, however, significant areas of diversity are discernible in the creeds and programs of the various revivalist societies and movements. These differences spring from these groups' varying interpretations of the Qur'an, the Prophet's Sunna, and early Islamic history. Other factors shaping ideological content include the nature of the crisis situation, peculiarities in social conditions, and the personal imprint of a leader on his society or movement. Four categories of revivalist ideologies may be identified (table 3).

## Gradualist-Adaptationist

This category subsumes a large proportion of Sunni revivalist societies now active in the Islamic world, including the Muslim Brotherhood and its many affiliates. Despite their activist orientation, these groups have sought to operate in large measure within the confines of legality as defined by governments. Cognizant of the dangers inherent in revolutionary confrontations with the authorities, these movements pursue policies of gradualism to heighten religious consciousness among the masses, while pushing for the implementation of the Shariʿa by the state. In their quest for the eventual establishment of an Islamic order, these groups show some flexibility and a readiness to adapt their ideologies and programs to modern conditions.

## Revolutionary Shiʿa

There are several variants of Shiʿa revolutionary thought, the most important of which is the one in the Islamic Republic of Iran. In sharp contrast to the

TABLE 3.
**Taxonomy of Ideologies of Islamist Societies**

| | |
|---|---|
| Gradualist-adaptationist | Muslim Brotherhood (Egypt, Iraq, Gulf States, Sudan, Jordan, North Africa) |
| | Jamaʿat al-Islami (Pakistan) |
| Revolutionary Shiʿa | Islamic Republican Party (Iran) |
| | Hizb ad-Daʿwa (Iraq) |
| | Hizbullah (Lebanon) |
| | Jihad al-Islami (Lebanon) |
| Revolutionary Sunni | Al-Jihad (Egypt) |
| | Islamic Liberation Organization (Egypt) |
| | Muslim Brotherhood (Syria) |
| | Jamaʿa Abu Dharr (Syria) |
| | Hizb al-Tahrir (Jordan, Syria) |
| Messianic-primitivist | Al-Ikhwan (Saudi Arabia) |
| | Takfir wal-Hijra (Egypt) |
| | Mahdiyya (Sudan) |
| | Jamaʿat al-Muslimin lil-Takfir (Egypt) |

political ideologies of Ali Shari'ati and the Mujahidin-e-khalq, the official doctrine of the Islamic Republic is based on Ayatullah Khumaini's concept of *wilayat al-faqih*—the guardianship of the jurisconsult. Other adherents of the Khumainist variant of Shi°a ideology include the Hizb ad-Da°wa al-Islamiyya of Iraq and its affiliates in the Gulf States, and the Hizbullah, Jihad al-Islami, and Islamic AMAL of South Lebanon.

## Revolutionary Sunni

The roots of contemporary Sunni revivalist ideologies and movements are found in the writings of several important activist theorists, particularly Ibn Hanbal (d. 855), Ibn Hazm (d. 1064), Nawawi (d. 1277), Taymiyya (d. 1328), Ibn al-Qayyim (d. 1350), Ibn Kathir (d. 1373), and Ibn °Abd al-Wahhab (d. 1792). These imams are frequently cited by present-day Sunni revolutionary ideologues because of their commitment to the renewal of the umma by a return to Islamic roots; advocacy of militancy and jihad in defense of Islam; combining of revivalist ideology with political and social activism in their personal lives; and readiness to challenge religious and political authority and willingness to suffer for their religious convictions.[11]

Contemporary Sunni revivalism was also influenced by the Sanusiyya, Mahdiyya, and Salafiyya movements of the nineteenth century.[12] More enduring was the role of Hasan al-Banna, who founded the Muslim Brotherhood. After al-Banna's assassination in 1949, the Brotherhood was suppressed by Naser's revolutionary regime in 1954–55 and again in 1965. The outcome was a split in the Brotherhood between the militants led by Sayyid Qutb and the followers of Hasan al-Hudaibi, who forswore political activism in favor of religious proselytization. Under the influence of Indian thinker Abu al-°Ala Mawdudi and his disciple Abu al-Hasan Nadwi, Qutb reformulated Ibn Taymiyya's militant strain of Sunni political thought as an ideology of protest and revolution. Since Qutb's execution in 1965, his writings have become the ideological foundation of the Sunni revivalists. The Arab world's militant Islamic societies have drawn their inspiration directly from Qutb, whose writings have received diverse interpretations. These militant revivalist societies include the Muslim Brotherhood of Syria and its militant offshoots, the Islamic Liberation Organization of Egypt and Jordan, the Jihad Organization and Takfir wal-Hijra of Egypt, and similar groups in Egypt, North Africa, Lebanon, Israel, Saudi Arabia, the West Bank, and the Gulf.

## Messianic-Primitivist

The most puritanical type of revivalist ideology is that of the messianic movements which have appeared periodically in Islamic history. In recent centuries, the mahdist phenomenon has been more common among the Sunni than among the Shi°a; the Shi°a Musha°sha°in of the fifteenth century was an exception.[13] Recent mahdist movements include al-Ansar (Sudan), Takfir wal-Hijra (Egypt),

Jamaᶜat al-Muslimin lil-Takfir (Egypt), and al-Ikhwan (Saudi Arabia). The ideologies of mahdist movements are characterized by a fierce sense of puritanism and primitivism—a quest to emulate strictly the Prophet's example and the life-styles of the first Islamic community. Thus, mahdist leaders want to recreate the Prophet's umma and oppose innovation or efforts to adapt to modern conditions.

## Leadership of Islamic Movements: A Typology

The leadership of Islamic revivalist societies and movements and their evolution appear to follow certain patterns similar to other revivalist and revolutionary movements throughout history. At their inception, Islamic revivalist societies are founded and led by charismatic types who preach a radical salvationist message to small groups of young disciples, often in clandestine settings. As the group enlarges and becomes a movement, it is led by bureaucratic-type leaders who preside over a diminution of ideological fervor and a strengthening of organizational mechanisms.

Beyond the general charismatic-bureaucratic dichotomy, the Islamic historical experience and the contemporary revivalist movements are characterized by varieties of leadership, which may be classified under four categories: mahdist, marjᶜait mujaddidist, and collegial (table 4).

### Mahdist

Islam, like Judaism and Christianity, possesses a millenarian tradition centered on a messianic promise. In Sunni Islam, the concept of mahdiship is not as clearly defined as in Judaism, Christianity, and Shiᶜism. While most branches of Shiᶜism still await the Mahdi's manifestation, the messianic call has been repeatedly sounded throughout Sunni history, down to the present time. In the Sunni belief system, the mahdist notion is embedded in about fifty traditions (*ahadith*) in an unbroken chain of authority (*mutawatir*). Ibn Khaldun stated that the Expected Messiah, al-Mahdi al-Muntazar, will issue from the Prophet's family at the "end of time," along with Jesus, to defeat the enemies of Islam.[14] Significantly, the messianic promise has continued to have contemporary expression among many Islamic revivalists. According to Mawdudi, the expected mahdi will possess special intellectual and spiritual gifts to carry out his revolutionary mission in establishing "the Caliphate after the pattern of Prophethood." Recent claimants to mahdiship have included Shukri Mustafa of Takfir wal-Hijra, Taha al-Samawi of Jamaᶜat al-Muslimin lil-Takfir, and Muhammad al-Qahtani of al-Ikhwan, the group that briefly captured the Grand Mosque of Makka in November 1979. Because of its claim to divine sanction and primitivist appeal, the mahdist type of leadership has not enjoyed a widespread following in the contemporary period.

TABLE 4.
**Taxonomy of Leadership in Islamic Fundamentalist Movements**

| Type | Leader | Movement/Society | Country |
|------|--------|------------------|---------|
| Mahdist | Ibn Tumart | Muwahidin | North Africa |
| | Muhammad Ahmad | Mahdiyya | Sudan |
| | Muhammad al-Qahtani | Al-Ikhwan | Saudi Arabia |
| | Shukri Mustafa | Takfir wal-Hijra | Egypt |
| | Taha al-Samawi | Jamaʿat al-Muslimin lil-Takfir | Egypt |
| | Ibn Falah al-Mushaʿshaʿ | Mushaʿshaʿin | Ahwaz |
| Marjʿaist | Ayatullah Khumaini | Islamic Republic | Iran |
| | Baqer as-Sadr | Hizb ad-Daʿwa | Iraq, Gulf |
| | H. Fadlullah | Hizbullah | Lebanon |
| Mujaddidist | Hasan al-Banna | Muslim Brotherhood | Egypt |
| | Mawdudi | Jamaʿat al-Islami | India, Pakistan |
| | Ibn Taymiyya | Hanbalism | Syria |
| | Muhammad ʿAbduh | Salafiyya | Egypt |
| Collegial | ʿUmar ʿAbd al-Rahman ʿAbd as-Salam Farag Hasan al-Zumur | Al-Jihad | Egypt |
| | Ghannushi and Muru | Ittijah al-Islami | Tunisia |
| | ʿUmar Amiri Ismaʿil al-Shati | Jamʿiyyat al-Islah al-Ijtimaʿi | Kuwait |
| | Saʿid Hawwa Adnan Saʿad ad-Din Muhammad al-Bayanuni | Muslim Brotherhood | Syria |

## Marjaist

This type of leadership involves the assumption of a dominant political-legal role by the Shiʿa clerical establishment, the *marjiʿiyya*. Thus, the highest religious authorities or *marjʿa* are conceived as the carriers of the divine testimony and succession, both received from the early prophets, Muhammad and the Imams. Consequently, all legitimacy is to reside in the marjiʿiyya—the collective religio-juristical stewardship of high-ranking ʿulama (Muslim religious leaders, experts in Islamic law; sing. ʿalim), who will function as the guardians of the umma during the twelfth Imam's occultation. The highest marjʿa must possess the qualities of righteousness, sincerity, leadership, and the ability to exercise independent judgment. While not infallible like the Prophet and the

Imams, the highest marj$^c$a must strive for a high degree of righteousness to qualify as the deputy general representative of the Hidden Imam.[15]

The doctrine of clerical supremacy was propounded by Ayatullahs Baqer as-Sadr of Iraq and Khumaini of Iran and, despite vigorous opposition, was integrated into the constitutional framework of the Islamic Republic in December 1979 as the guardianship of the jurisconsult.[16] The principle of clerical leadership is also upheld by the Shi$^c$a Hizb ad-Da$^c$wa al-Islamiyya of Iraq and its affiliates in the Gulf States and Lebanon.

## Mujaddidist

The notion of *mujaddid*, restorer or renewer of the faith, is embedded in the Traditions, specifically in a hadith revealed by the Prophet's companion Abu Hurayra.[17] This type of leadership is usually associated with the occurrence of revivalist movements in Sunni Islam. The mujaddid is to appear every century to regenerate the Islamic spirit (*tajdid*) and to defend the Traditions (*Sunna*) against innovation, worldly scepticism, impiety, and rigid conformity in legal interpretation (*taqlid*). Unlike the mahdis and prophets, the mujaddid does not claim divine appointment. His social and spiritual leadership role is recognized by his followers often posthumously as the result of his activities. Ibn Taymiyya, the great exponent of Hanbalism; Ibn $^c$Abd al-Wahhab, founder of al-Muwahidin; Muhammad $^c$Abduh of Salafiyya; and Hasan al-Banna, founder of the Muslim Brotherhood, are all considered mujaddidin.

## Collegial

In contrast to Islamic societies led by one dominant individual, some contemporary revivalist movements and groups possess a collective leadership. This type of leadership has been observed in several Egyptian fundamentalist groups, particularly the Jihad Organization, which assassinated President Sadat; the Islamic Liberation Organization, which unsuccessfully attacked the Technical Military Academy in 1974, and the Muslim Brotherhoods of Egypt, Syria, and the Maghrib countries. In these societies, the functions of leadership are divided among several individuals, one of whom usually becomes chief theoretician while others take charge of administrative, political, and social affairs.

## Islamic Revivalism vs. the State: A Prognosis

Revivalist Islam, since the mid-1970s, has defined the parameters of public discourse, social morality, and political activity in a large number of Islamic countries. The potency of the revivalist movement reflects the depth and pervasiveness of the crisis facing the Islamic countries and the inability of the rulers to respond effectively to the Islamic challenge. The future course of the ongoing confrontation between the militant Islamic movements and the state is likely to be determined by three factors: government policies, external stimuli, and initiatives of revivalist groups.[18]

### State Policies: Incremental Reform, Co-optation, and Repression

If the proposition that revivalism is a product of crisis is true, then the adoption of comprehensive social, political, and economic reforms should be given priority by the ruling elites. Many of the Islamic governments, however, have been unable or unwilling to initiate policy changes that are comprehensive enough to stem the tide of Islamic unrest. The usual policy response has consisted of incremental reforms, co-optative measures, and repression, including periodic campaigns against government corruption and bureaucratic ineffi-ciency; co-optation of Islamic symbols, legal precepts, and practices; and the use of the clerical establishment to bestow religious legitimacy on various gov-ernmental policies and to counter the militants' propaganda. On the whole, these policies to appease and co-opt have met partial success. In the absence of institutional means of expressing dissent, the militant groups have periodi-cally engaged in various forms of revolutionary violence against the state and its leadership. So far, however, despite the Islamic militants' success in creating mass unrest in many countries, the Iranian revolution remains their only major triumph.

### External Stimuli

To a significant degree, the future course of the Islamist movement and the magnitude of its challenge to the authorities are likely to depend on external events and developments. The victory of the Islamic cause in Iran acted as a spur to the proponents of political revivalism throughout the Muslim world. Clearly, the installation of an Islamic regime in any major Arab country is bound to have a detrimental impact on the stability of neighboring countries. Similarly, any external stimulus in the form of military defeats or diplomatic reverses may weaken the ruling elites and provoke Islamist militancy. The possible catalysts that may trigger mass fundamentalist fervor include Arab defeats by Israel, U.S. intervention on behalf of a faltering regime, and Soviet military action against a Muslim state.

### Initiatives of Islamist Groups

The future of the Islamic revivalist movement will also depend on the quality of its political and intellectual leadership. Since the suppression of the militant societies in the mid-1970s, the movement has lacked effective ideological and tactical guidance. Leading figures of various radical groups have been killed, including Salah Siriyya (ILO), Shukri Mustafa (Takfir wal-Hijra), Juhaiman al-Utaibi (Ikhwan), Musa as-Sadr (AMAL), ᶜAbd as-Salam Farag (Jihad), Baqer as-Sadr (Daᶜwa), and Marwan Hadid (Muslim Brotherhood); many others are in jail. It may be several years before new leaders emerge to organize and inspire the next phase of confrontation with the authorities. Meanwhile, the Egyptian Muslim Brotherhood and its affiliates in the Sudan, the Maghrib, Jordan, and the Gulf have adopted a policy of peaceful gradualism to Islamize society and the state through sustained political and social pressure. The success or failure of this incrementalist policy of Islamization and the general evolution of the revivalist current will depend, to some degree, on three tasks: (1) the development of a broad and flexible program that can have the widest possible appeal to major segments of the population, (2) the strengthening of transnational links between the revivalist societies, and (3) the emergence of capable leaders and cadres.

At this juncture, the Islamist movement continues to pursue narrowly defined policies that have generated apprehension among secularists, minorities, and many mainstream Muslims. Nor have the fundamentalist groups shown the capacity to project a sense of unity, although there has been increasing evidence of close cross-national ties between some Islamist societies. Usually these ties are ideological, although in certain cases some Islamist groups also maintain organizational, military, and economic relations with one another. Today's fundamentalism, however, is still a polycentric movement, consisting of country-centered groups and societies working for the establishment of Islamic polities in their respective national settings. Despite the persistence of state repression, the militant societies and their larger fundamentalist milieu will continue to pose a threat to those in power as long as crisis conditions persist and there are no alternative means of protest and political action to change the status quo.

# NOTES

1. See Bernard Lewis, "The Return of Islam," *Commentary*, Vol. 61, No. 1 (January 1976), pp. 39–49.

2. On the vocabulary of Islamist ideology, see Hasan Hanafi, "Al-Haraka al-Islamiyya al-Mu'asira" (The contemporary Islamic movement), *Al-Watan*, Nov. 20, 1982. Also useful is the French term *intégrisme*. For details, see R. Hrair Dekmejian, *Islam in Revolution: Fundamentalism in the Arab World* (Syracuse, N.Y.: Syracuse University Press, 1985), pp. 4–5.

3. Dekmejian, *Islam in Revolution*, pp. 10–11.

4. The linkage between socioeconomic crisis and religious revival is discussed by Dale W. Wimberly, "Socioeconomic Deprivation and Religious Salience: A Cognitive Behavioral Approach," *The Sociological Quarterly*, Vol. 25, No. 2 (Spring 1984) pp. 223–224.

5. See R. Hrair Dekmejian, "Fundamentalist Islam: Theories, Typologies, and Trends," *Middle East Review*, No. 4 (Summer 1985), pp. 28–33.

6. Ibid., p. 29.

7. For a detailed discussion of the crisis milieu, see Dekmejian, *Islam in Revolution*, pp. 25–32.

8. Ibid., pp. 27–29.

9. Ibid., pp. 30–31.

10. Ibid., pp. 44–46.

11. Ibid., pp. 41–42.

12. The Sanusiyya was a tribal Sufi movement that arose in North Africa in the late eighteenth century. The Mahdiyya represented a messianic revolutionary movement led by Muhammad Ahmad, who defeated the Anglo-Egyptian forces and established an Islamic state in the Sudan (1879–98). The Salafiyya was an intellectual reform movement led by Muhammad ᶜAbduh (d. 1905) and Rashid Rida (d. 1935).

13. A Shiᶜa messianic movement was led by Ibn Falah al-Mushaᶜshaᶜ (d. 1462), who proclaimed his mahdiship among the Arab tribes of Ahwaz.

14. P.M. Holt, *The Mahdist State in the Sudan 1881–1898* (Oxford: Clarendon Press, 1958), p. 22. For an excellent collection of *ahadith* on Mahdism, see John Alden Williams, ed., *Themes of Islamic Civilization*, (Berkeley: University of California Press, 1971), pp. 191–251.

15. Al-Sayyid Muhamad Baqer as-Sadr, *Khilafat al-Insan wa Shahadat al-Anbiya* (Successorship of man and testimony of prophets) (Qum, 1979), pp. 21–22, 35–36, 55.

16. Ayatullah al-Khumaini, *Al-Hukuma al-Islamiyya* (Islamic government) (Beirut, 1979).

17. S. Abu al-ᶜAla Mawdudi, *A Short History of the Revolutionary Movement in Islam* (Lahore: Islamic Publications, 1963), p. 33.

18. See Dekmejian, *Islam in Revolution*, pp. 161–168.

# Part II

# Islamic Revivalism in the Arab East

# II

# EGYPT

## Amira El-Azhary Sonbol

Religions fulfill many social and psychological needs. They offer continuity of existence beyond death and enable individuals to transcend their arduous earthly existence and attain, even if only momentarily, spiritual satisfaction. Socially, religions reinforce group norms and contribute to the establishment of moral sanctions for individual conduct. They also provide common goals and values, which in turn give a sense of stability and solidarity to human societies and contribute to their security and equilibrium. Thus, it is only logical that a people who find themselves unable to deal with problems that threaten their society, culture, and spiritual and psychological well-being should turn to religion for answers and solutions. Indeed, in societies in which secular systems offer no escape from daily frustrations caused by cultural and political alienation, identity crisis, and economic deprivation, religion has proven a refuge offering social and psychological support.

Islam, because of its all-encompassing nature, also provides alternative political, ideological, and economic structures. The Islamic religion enters into virtually every aspect of Muslims' individual and collective lives. It is the basis of social norms and moral codes according to which Muslim societies function. The predominance of a modernizing trend, which has been an outstanding feature of Islamic societies since the nineteenth century, has diverted attention from the fact that at heart, beneath the guise of liberalism or Westernism, a Muslim is basically that, a Muslim. As a child, he or she is taught the moral code of Islam; what is *halal* (allowed) and what is *haram* (forbidden) is explained in religious terms. In fact, awareness of law in an Islamic community is based on the family's or the community's inherited understanding of Islamic codes of honor. Modern man-made law is a matter left to the government and its courts and is not very well understood by the population at large.

Muslims in Egypt, all of whom are Sunnis, are taught the three corners of their faith: belief in *Tawhid*, the unity of God and his power and direction over all the world and those inhabiting it; *Nubuwwa*, this direction being sent in the form of law through the medium of a prophet who is the bearer of the news and the laws of God; and *Mi'ad*, the judgment day when those who have followed the God-sent rules will be rewarded in heaven and those who have refused to follow the right path will be punished in hell. The message is clear and simple, and the moral code in Islamic society is based on it. Thus, to a Sunni Muslim, following the dictates of Islam is the normal way, the way leading to heaven. The difficulty arises in an interpretation of what is halal and what is haram, which accounts for the fact that Islam, like other religions, has evolved and changed in answer to the needs and conditions of the times. Today, Egyptian society faces a number of problems that in many ways are similar to those faced by other Islamic countries. These problems have led to a search for a renewal of self-identity and to an Islamic revivalism by which it is hoped societal ills and anxieties can be cured.

This chapter aims to analyze the revivalist movement engulfing Egypt today in this context. It has three goals: (1) To present an explanation of the revivalist phenomenon. Social and economic issues will play a central role in this explanation, for even though revivalism is expressed in political acts and terms, it basically stems from deep social and economic problems. The political ambitions and actions of certain militant groups should not be allowed to obscure this fact. (2) To show how today's militant groups are related to one another and what kinds of relationship they maintain with more established groups, such as the Ikhwan-al-Muslimin (Muslim Brotherhood). (3) To assess the militants' current role and their prospects for success in changing Egypt's present political, legal, economic, and social systems.

## The Shape of the Movement

The phenomenon of Islamic revivalism in Egypt appears in two forms: the "popular" revivalism in the society at large, a society that is faced with insurmountable problems and is looking for answers in the only direction it can, within its own traditions; and the militant revivalism in various Islamic organizations, whose tactics may differ but whose aims are to set up an "Islamic state" ruled by the dictates of the Shari̇ʿa (Allah's law).

### "Popular" Revivalism

By nature, "traditional" society is nonmaterialist, making do with what is available, concentrating on the physical and mental welfare of family members, and saving for the future, perhaps to enlarge a family business or to send a child to school. In modern society, by contrast, social mobility has become synonymous with material goods, mostly imported from abroad. Thus anti-materialism—and anti-Westernism, since it is generally associated with the former—simply become a part of the ideology of those who have no hope of sharing in the fruits of this materialism. Meanwhile, Islam provides another kind of satisfaction and that is where the majority turns. To dress in "Islamic" garb, for instance, advances a new type of beauty, one based on simplicity and equality, rather than upon standards of physical beauty or material wealth. Such clothes are locally made and simply fashioned of affordable Egyptian fabrics, which is welcome in view of the meager resources of families with numerous children.

According to the principles of Islamic economics, the society is supposed to take care of its poor, its widows, and its orphans. The system of inheritance, family support, and *zakat* (a type of Islamic tax) are meant to do just that, as well as to ensure the nonconcentration of wealth in a few hands. Yet, with the growth of poverty during the last two decades, it has become impossible for Egyptian families to fulfill their obligations toward their poorer relatives. Such matters must be emphasized in understanding the phenomenon of Islamic revivalism. It is the treatment of such matters in Islamic law that makes it attractive to the Egyptians. The militant groups may be concerned with *Hakimiyya* (dominion, rule) or *shura* (council, consultation), but the individual who will ultimately support the passing of the Shari'a as the only law is mainly concerned with day-to-day problems.

The revivalists, then, look to Islam as a means of providing social and economic welfare.

Culturally, fathers have seen their sons and daughters influenced by what they consider to be immoral Western behavior and believe them to be neglecting their traditional duties. Thus now, as in the 1930s, there is an outcry against cinema, theater, magazines, books, clubs, and all associations that popularize modern concepts such as individualism and the lack of concern with family problems and wishes of parents and older brothers. Young people in schools have fallen under the influence of drugs. They smoke and spend money on other frivolities that the family can ill afford. This approach of the family is certainly tied to financial ability, and the movement toward revivalism has a lot to do with the antimaterialism of a society that cannot bear the burden of such expenses.[1]

Exacerbating the situation is the outstanding characteristic of contemporary life in Egypt, namely its overcrowdedness. The fact is that overcrowdedness leads to a constant struggle for mere survival and a continuous inability to cope with rising expenses in a country of limited resources that is expected to support an estimated 1.5 million additional people each year.[2] The increase in population has been accompanied by another phenomenon: urbanization. The movement of people from rural to urban centers has continued at increasing rates since the nineteenth century and has reached phenomenal proportions during the past two decades. This has been caused by growing population pressures in the countryside, the introduction of land-ownership in the nineteenth century, and the accompanying alienation of landless peasants from their villages. In addition, the attraction of the city and the search for better job opportunities have contributed to this urban drift. In fact, current conditions are not much different from those that led to the creation of the Muslim Brotherhood during the 1920s and 1930s, when Egypt was experiencing similar growing pains. In the second half of the nineteenth century, alienation of peasants from the land had caused a great influx into the cities. The growth of capitalist penetration and domestic economic domination by a foreign and national elite only worsened the condition of these newcomers. The economic gap so often pointed to today was already apparent by the end of the nineteenth century. This gap divided rich Westernized Egyptians from the "traditional" sectors of society, both urban and rural. During the rule of Naser this gap proved controllable through the implementation of socialist laws, but under Sadat's open-door policy the economic gap widened, thus generating a reaction similar to that which led to the creation of the Muslim Brotherhood.

The newcomers from rural areas bring with them more than a strong allegiance to Islamic principles and piety. They also bring distrust toward the authorities. In fact, there has been a growing villagization of the cities. Historically, the experience of rural centers with authority has been one of violence and extraction of their labor. The continued suspicion is that the same thing goes on today. Power is to be obeyed, not trusted, to be rebelled against when its regulations and tyranny become excessive, and to be attacked when it appears too weak. Whether it be Naser or Sadat, the peasants see no difference between a nationalist regime and what they previously experienced under feudalism. In summary, the real reasons for the popularity of the revivalists' call for instituting the Shariᶜa as the country's only source of law need to be looked for in the social, economic,. and political conditions of Egypt, namely overcrowdedness; the growing gap between rich and poor; the lack of an efficient government capable of providing essential services such as health care, electricity, water, and telephone; the breakdown of family structure and support systems without new structures to replace them; and a persistent lack of trust of the government.

## Militant Revivalism

This trend does not involve the large majority of the people. Unlike the Muslim Brotherhood, whose known membership in the 1940s was over one million, today's militant groups give no evidence of having wide support. But their low numbers should not be seen as the only factor limiting their potential to gain influence. The demonstrated violence of a few of them does not appeal to the Egyptians, but it is greatly feared. Still, if the militants could mount a serious bid for power, the people would probably join them, either out of fear for their lives or fear of being declared apostates.

A phenomenon worth investigating is why most of the militants are of the younger generation, graduates of universities, particularly the scientific branches, and younger members of the armed forces. The militants' leaders are often former members of older Muslim organizations, such as the Muslim Brotherhood. The answer may be found in the stress put on education as the best channel for upward social mobility. Under Naser, education had become the goal of every family and of every young, ambitious man or woman. The competitiveness for the high school certificate and all the psychological agonies accompanying it are but one example of expectations of families vying for the best college, and hence the potential for the best job. The state, through the socialist laws enacted by Naser, has become the main employer of graduates. Indeed, the educational system was designed to fulfill state needs. The scientific schools received the best high school graduates, while the schools of arts received the poorer ones. In fact, the demand was higher among students for such degrees as engineering and medicine because of the better pay.[3]

High school students who manage to get top grades enter the scientific schools with great ambitions and hopes. They expect to grow and excel in school, to leave their mark; and in the future, they are told, they will make a difference in their country and the world at large. Actually, they find themselves in over-crowded lecture halls, with no place to sit, with labs deficient in materials and instruments and examinations that are agonizing and on which they feel they are unfairly graded. Once the students graduate, they may be commissioned, after waiting nearly a year or more, to some obscure spot where their presence makes little difference. The ambitious among them cannot be content with such conditions. They become restless and often turn militant.

During Naser's rule, military academies provided a way up the social ladder. Social mobility was highest in the army and a young man could hope to move into a more affluent class by becoming a career officer. Since 1967, however, this is no longer the case. Promotions and social climbing in the army are no longer what they were under Naser, whose legitimacy as a charismatic ruler was partly based on an army that was kept satisfied. Today, social mobility is all but stagnant in an army with no prospects of fighting a war. It must be remembered that a war like the one against Yemen resulted in the enrichment of members of the armed forces; they sought assignment there to get triple pay and more. Today, members of the armed forces see a changed force, one that does not give an outlet to their ambitions as it once did. Such individuals are angry at their stagnation and they see peace with Israel as one cause.

Many students are uprooted from their homes to attend universities in the city. There they live with relatives or in campus housing. Life is difficult without family support. Conformity becomes a must, for students, particularly girls, do not want to be caught breaking the ingrained code of honor. The least they could suffer is being forced to discontinue their educations and that cannot be risked. Thus, wearing clothes that are familiar as well as "chaste" becomes an excellent solution. In Cairo and Alexandria, where the gap between rich and poor students is only too obvious, such clothes become an economic necessity, covering both the poverty and the pride of the students coming from poorer or rural areas.

Being away from what is familiar, while at the same time being alienated from the new society in which they have been planted, causes the students to search for the kind of associations that would make them comfortable. Because of the lack of concern of universities for extracurricular activities, the only available student associations are Islamic. Students join, find company, famil-iarity, and answers. It does not make them militants, but it does make them supporters of those running for elections who may be militants. Thus, students associate with and vote for those whom they can identify with and who observe the same code of honor as they do. This is not because they want to change the government or the state structure, but if that were to happen, they would probably support such a change.

Egyptian students have traditionally been involved in political protest, as illustrated by the violent demonstrations that took place following the 1967 war. When Sadat became president, the Naserite elements, those who belonged to the Arab Socialist Union, dominated most of the student unions. Sadat, in his struggle for power against the ʿAli Sabri clique, had to provide an alternative for these Leftist or Naserite groups and he found the answer in encouraging religious groups on university campuses. Through both direct and indirect means, the Muslim student associations on campuses were provided with financial, administrative, and organizational aid. More important, they were given government protection. These groups soon came to dominate the political and social life of the university campuses without any opposition, even after they became violent. Thus, the Muslim associations' influence on campuses increased as a result of Sadat's policies aimed at consolidating his power and eliminating opposition.[4]

There is another reason why young people meet up with militants and easily fall under their influence: the lack of healthy recreational facilities. The only places open to young men are the mosques, particularly the privately run mosques, which do not restrict what is said or done and allow free discussions. Some even provide services, such as schooling for children and health clinics, that are too expensive in the private sector.

Moreover, joining a militant group is perhaps the only route open to young men in Egypt through which to voice their grievances and to influence political decisions. The electoral system is supposedly democratic, but it is very difficult for the poor to win seats in the Majlis Al-Shʿab (National Assembly). Religious parties are not legalized, a predicament that forced the Muslim Brotherhood to enter into a short-lived alliance with the Wafd Party in 1984 and with al-Ahrar Party in 1987.[5] The last-minute changes introduced by the Mohy ad-Din government, which based 1985 elections on party lists and the requirement that a party should win at least 8 percent of the seats before it can be represented in the parliament, illustrates the government's panic and arbitrariness when it comes to the question of losing power. Needless to say, these actions of the ruling National Democratic Party (NDP) did not encourage people to trust the government or the system. In fact, voter apathy regarding what the government declared to be the first real democratic election Egypt had seen in years reflected this continued lack of trust.[6] Meanwhile, other parties were not viable alternatives to the NDP. The president had aligned himself with the NDP, which had no clear ideology, and in which there was no room for newcomers. The Wafd had a large base of support, but who could forget that the Siraj ad-Din was part of the pre-Naser feudal elite? The Tajamʿu Party had nothing new to offer. Socialism had not worked under Naser, and no matter how much its leader, Khalid Mohy ad-Din, denied it, the party was anti-religious and, therefore, unacceptable. The 1987 elections, while attempting to rectify the abuses of the previous election, continued the same policy of party lists and resulted in the return of the NDP as the most powerful party.

The political system itself, as set up by the September 1971 constitution and the amendments introduced to it in May 1980, is not clearly understood; it is full of contradictions, and thus confusing. It defines Egypt as a "democratic, socialist State based on the alliance of the working forces of the people." Then article 2 states that "Islam is the religion of the state and . . . Islamic juris-prudence is the principal source of legislation." Article 4 continues: "The eco-nomic foundation of the Arab Republic of Egypt is a socialist democratic system based on sufficiency and justice in a manner preventing exploitation, conducive to liquidation of income differences, protecting legitimate earnings, and guar-anteeing the equity of the distribution of public duties and responsibilities." These words were obviously meant to satisfy many social groups, from liberals who demanded democracy to socialists who demanded an upkeep of socialist laws introduced by Naser to groups who insisted on the Shari$^c$a as the basis of the state's law. Put together, they create an unworkable, and hardly under-standable, system.[7]

Thus, the young militant is an individual who has had his ambitions frustrated; he has gone to school hoping to better his conditions, and it has not worked. He sees all the makings of opulence around him and cannot share in it. His government will not allow him to participate in the political process. His am-bitions had been blown out of proportion by the promises of the Naserite regime with the ideas of socialism and social equality for all. He had become educated and had taken a job as he was told to do, but had found no equality. Under Sadat, he was told of freedom and democracy, but in fact the laws seemed to suit only a few. And the Mubarak government, which found its hands shackled with the problems it inherited from previous administrations, seemed incapable of presenting new solutions to them.

## The Evolution of Revivalism

The militants' wish for an Islamic state in which the laws will be based on the Shari$^c$a may be fulfilled after all. The activities of various militant groups, however unintegrated they may appear to be, seem to work together in such a way as to push the country closer to a fundamentalist life-style and social system. Meanwhile, the government's reliance on the $^c$ulama, particularly the Azhari shaikhs, for legitimization of its rule has tended to reinforce the militants' ideals.

A look at the history of the Ikhwan—the Muslim Brotherhood, which is the mother organization from which all other groups have sprung—will illustrate this. Soon after the Brotherhood was founded by Hasan al-Banna, its members seem to have been internally divided. A majority led by al-Banna, the supreme guide, favored a gradualist approach, delaying any confrontation with the state until the group's membership and strength would ensure its success. A minority, by contrast, believed in immediate radical action against the existing government. Thus, when Prime Minister Nuqrashi was assassinated by the Brotherhood in 1948—an action undertaken by the radical wing of the organization—al-Banna declared his innocence and horror.

Under Judge Hasan al-Hudaibi, who became the Brotherhood's supreme guide in 1952, the same situation persisted. Hudaibi opted for the spread of *da'wa* (call) and shunned violence. Yet, in 1952 massive riots and arson broke out in Cairo against Western installations, movies, and theaters and Jewish schools. Even though it was never proven conclusively, the hand of the Brotherhood was clear in these actions. The year 1952 also saw the revolution that brought the Naserite nationalist regime to power. A short period of friendship between Naser and the Ikhwan was followed by an attempt on Naser's life by the Brotherhood in 1954. Once more, the supreme guide was proven to have had nothing to do with this action.

Under the leadership of al-Sayyid Qutb, the Ikhwan, now underground and harassed by the Naserite regime, opted in favor of immediate action, and its militant elements became more prominent, although Qutb himself was essentially a philosopher who shunned violence. Following Qutb's unsuccessful plot against Naser in 1965 and his subsequent martyrdom, a number of splinter groups appeared in the ranks of the Ikhwan. These groups represented mostly the Brotherhood's militant wing and believed in a more radical approach to the question of seizure of power. And although their basic ideologies were similar to those of the Ikhwan, they leaned toward extremism in their interpretations.[8]

'Umar al-Tilimsani, the late leader of the Ikhwan, using the pages of *Al-Ahram* to answer a member of the Ikhwan who had denounced him for espousing gradualism rather than immediate action, defended his approach as the logical one. He argued that only through gradual change can the community accept Islam as the basis of its economic, social, legal, and political structure.

For the foreseeable future, the Ikhwan will remain divided on the best way to turn Egypt into an Islamic state. These divisions became clear during the 1987 parliamentary elections. One group of the Ikhwan led by Saif al-Islam al-Banna decided in favor of active participation in the elections and entered into a coalition with the two other parties. Another group, led by Supreme Guide Hamid Abul-Nasr, seemed to be blessing the former's participation in the elections but at the same time maintained its traditional position that there can be no participation in the political process before Islamization is completed. A third group refused to have anything to do with the elections. Yet a fourth group decided to join the elections as independents or as members of the NDP. The rationale of this group was that only the parliament can institute the Shari'a as the law of the land. Thus, it is important for Islamicists to have adequate representation and influence in the National Assembly. In sum, the Ikhwan does not present one front, at least as far as its methodology is concerned. The ultimate goal, the creation of an Islamic state, is, however, common to all groups.

If it is assumed that the militant wing has broken off completely from the Ikhwan, then the following question arises: Is there no connection today between the mother organization and its various offspring, and among the offspring themselves? The answer to this question is not clear. Several of the leaders of militant groups involved in violent activities against the state have proved to be former members of the Ikhwan. Thus, the leader of the Takfir wal-Hijra, Shukri Mustafa, had been an active member of the Ikhwan and had spent time in prison after Qutb's plan failed against Naser in 1965. Moreover, when the Jihad organization undertook the assassination of President Sadat, its religious and legal leader had access to members of the armed forces, who assisted with the assassination. These officers did not belong to the Jihad cell with which Islambolli (Sadat's assassin) was affiliated and may not have been members of the Jihad at all. For weapons, the Jihad's leader turned to members of the Takfir, who gave him whatever weapons were needed.[9]

Officers of the police stationed in Asyut, who testified at the Jihad trials, were convinced that the Asyut incident had wider significance. They also indicated that the Jihad alone could not have organized it. In fact, the testimony of Jihad members at the trial made clear that they had expected—indeed were told—that the uprising would include the rest of the country, even though the Jihad itself was primarily active in Upper Egypt. It is logical, therefore, to assume that there is direct or indirect cooperation between various organizations, or at least among their leadership, which in turn is closely associated with the Brotherhood, or a wing of the Brotherhood. The latter's leadership may or may not be aware of this. After all, al-Banna did not approve of the assassination of Nuqrashi or of Judge al-Khizindar by the more radical Nizam al-Khas, any more than al-Hudaibi had anything to do with the attempt on Naser's life. Irrespective of the links between the militants and the Ikhwan, the fact remains that the extremists' actions make the Ikhwan appear more reasonable and moderate. Thus the activities of the militants are helping to legitimize the Ikhwan. Still, this may be coincidental rather than the result of a broader strategy and an active cooperation between the two.

Most important, the ideas of the Takfir, the Jihad, and the Brotherhood, particularly under Qutb, are all compatible, and all groups share similar goals and basic ideology, notwithstanding the differences in their appearance or tactics. Thus, similarities are found among them in regard to the hard-line interpretations of such key concepts as halal and haram, interpretations that lack the flexibility of the traditionalists. They describe "those in power" as being the religious leaders of the "true" Islamic community, those who have learned the Qur'an by heart and have read and understood the Hadith. Piety and humility would also be required of the leaders. As for special abilities, such as diplomacy or political flair, they are neither required nor desirable since they lead away from Islamic, and toward secular, ways.

Most telling is the idea of *jihad* (holy war) and the questions of when and against whom to undertake it. According to Sunni tradition, jihad is a defensive mechanism against enemies of the Islamic *umma* (community). To revivalists, jihad becomes a way of spreading and enforcing "true faith," and is to be waged both externally against non-Muslims and internally against apostates. The book *Farida al-Gha'iba* (Forgotten duty) by ʿAbd as-Salam Farag is a most uncompromising document representing the spirit and logic of the Jihad group. Its writer forgets the forgiving nature of Islam, the Sunni belief that there is no coercion in faith, and insists on taking active measures to institute what is considered right Islamic action on a society by force. Thus we find that the militants' leaders pick and choose among the writings of the ʿ*ulama* (religious teachers and leaders), the Hadith, and the Qur'an for proof supporting their actions. Referring to *Al-Farida al-Gha'iba*, al-Tayyib al-Najjar, rector of the Azhar, explained that various verses repeated by militants in support of their actions had actually been interpreted incorrectly and outside of their true historical contexts.[10]

The militants see the form that jihad is to take in the Prophet's "Order what is equitable and forbid the reprehensible," which is interpreted as a duty on all Muslims. Thus a person becomes a sinner if he sees the wrong and does not take action against it. Cooperation with the unjust, whether they are individuals, the community as a whole, or the government and its institutions, leads to hell-fire on the Day of Judgment. To these revivalists the great sins, which are traditionally seen as being tantamount to apostasy, become all-encompassing, while the minor offenses, lesser sins which include a large array of offenses by Sunnis, are interpreted as being insignificant actions such as missing ablutions or praying at the wrong time. Furthermore, they believe that by persisting in one particular sin, the Muslim loses the credit he accumulates from other good deeds that he performs, i.e., one sin could lead to apostasy, which is not the Sunni point of view.

These interpretations are far from traditional; in fact, they can be traced to non-Sunni origin. Generally speaking, the more puritanical groups advocate a strict observance of this Prophetic demand. In Wahhabi Saudi Arabia and Shiʿa Iran the state takes it upon itself to force the Muslims not to act in certain ways, forbidding drinking or public eating during Ramadan, for example. But in Sunni states, other than Wahhabi, "Order what is equitable" has traditionally meant to guide and point the right path to people in general and sinners in particular. No force was to be used, however; each person was left to commit his own sins, and the Day of Judgment would differentiate between those who were God-fearing and those who were not. The militant groups follow the hardline interpretations similar to Wahhabism or Shiism. Thus the latter's concept of justice, which makes an observer of a sin an accomplice to it if he does not strive to stop it, appears among the militants. Does this point to a Wahhabi or Shiʿa connection? Possibly. It is no secret that the militants have received financial aid from Saudi Arabia, but mostly from Egyptians working there, as well as various Saudi religious organizations. As for Iran, during the trials of the Islamic Jihad following the events at Asyut, Iran was pointed to by militants as one of the escape routes open to them, and contacts between the Jihad and Iranian officials were admitted to.

## The Government

Interestingly, government actions have also helped intensify the militants' overall impact and their success. This has been so because every act of militancy by an Islamic group has brought about an overreaction by the government. The government, truly worried that the militants' actions could lead to a civil war in which large numbers of Egyptians, particularly non-Muslims, could lose their lives, has acted harshly toward the militants. Yet at the same time it has actively sought the support of "official" Islam in order to gain legitimacy. As a result, the voices calling for Egypt's Islamization have become stronger. The Egyptian constitution already refers to Islamic law as the main source for the law of the state.

Other instances of government action against religious extremism that have only helped the process forward include removing all religious signs from motor cars so as to end the competitive antagonism between Muslims and Copts, and preventing demonstrations such as that planned by Shaikh Hafiz Salama to protest the takeover of al-Nur Mosque by the ministry of religious endowments.[11] This last action was part of a government plan to put all private mosques under government control to stop their use as meeting places and breeding grounds for militant groups.[12] Such acts, however, are at best temporary solutions and may prove dangerous in the long run since they would eliminate the last public outlet for religious discussions. The effort to take over al-Nur Mosque of ᶜAbasiyya by Muslim activists is demonstrative of the people's anger and the possible reaction against such arbitrary decisions. Furthermore, hundreds of rooms in private homes all over Egypt are being converted into small areas for prayer in preference to government mosques. In these "sanctuaries" young people can meet, pray, and discuss religious matters.

It seems that government officials, who at one time (1985) were optimistic that they could turn matters around, have given up and are reverting to strongman tactics. Before the very latest militancy demonstrated by the Islamicists, there seems to have been an awareness that a debate was needed on the subject of the application of the Shariᶜa as the only source of law in Egypt. A great deal was written on the subject, and many forums were held whose proceedings were either publicly broadcast or published in newspapers. The government went to great lengths to correct people's misunderstandings in regard to Islamic ideals and the divergence of the militants' views from traditional interpretations of the Qur'an and the Hadith. The results, however, appeared quite meager and, if anything, seemed to push the country closer to a crisis of wider significance. The voices supporting the Shariᶜa were not only those of extremists, whom the conservative Egyptian people shunned, but those of respectable and well-known figures, intellectuals, and religious persons who demanded that the Shariᶜa be instituted. Officials, believing that a debate only helped promote revivalist views, decided to clamp down and reduce such exchanges.

The debate regarding the Shariᶜa seemed to be concentrated on a discussion of whether Egypt's current laws are compatible with the Shariᶜa or not. However, there is no real dispute about whether the Shariᶜa, or what form of it, should be instituted. The government seemed to push the discussion toward enforcing the idea that the active law in Egypt is in fact no different from the Shariᶜa. A case in point was the forum held by *Al-Ahram* in August 1985, to which some of the most illustrious names in religious and intellectual fields were invited. Its declared intention was to discuss the Shariᶜa and its implementation. The discussion seemed to be constantly moving in the direction of showing that the laws of the state as they stood, the state structure, and the position and powers of the president were in accordance with the Shariᶜa and in no need of any real change. In fact, the participants became aware of this direction, became apologetic and defensive about it, and declared that this was not their intention.[13]

This seems to be a normal approach for the government—trying to hide from reality until it is too late. Officials never interfered with militant groups, notwithstanding the crimes they were committing, until after the murder of President Sadat and the subsequent attack on police headquarters in Asyut. When that happened, the government overreacted, using all the instruments available to it—press, radio, and television—to pass on a message of what "true" Islam is. Television and radio now broadcast religious programs amounting to an average of twenty-two hours a day for the radio and 20.5 percent of the television programs. They spoke with determination about enforcing an "official" interpretation of Islam without a single instance of true debate with another point of view.[14]

A phenomenon worthy of investigation involves Shaikh al-Mitwali al-Shaᵓrawi, who has had a television program running for the past fifteen years during which he talks, surrounded by listeners. The viewers sit in total acceptance of what the shaikh has to say, and the way he presents his ideas is such that any opposition is equated to either immorality or apostasy. What the shaikh has to say is not very different from what the militants say, and, more seriously, it advocates the same type of logic that the militants use. He gives very literal, simplistic interpretations, replacing the classical Arabic with colloquial. He speaks out against the use of reason or of logic, undermining, in so doing, the validity of jurisprudence. His interpretations are puritanical and reminiscent of Wahhabism.[15] Yet the government has made him into an authority, a spokesman for the "official" point of view, not realizing how such a program further enforces the thoughts of the militants.

What the debates have most lacked has been an effort to interpret what form the Shariᶜa should take. Only a limited discussion of this matter has taken place, mainly among those who were concerned about the impact of its application on minorities and on individual freedoms. Among the ᶜulama and the intellectuals, the concern has centered chiefly on who would be the final arbiter in matters of law. The ᶜulama naturally have pointed to themselves as "those in power," while the intellectuals, disputing this right, have indicated that in each specific area the interpretation should rest with the specialists. Thus, there is no clear definition of the Shariᶜa and what form it would take if the government were to implement it.

On the other hand, militant cells are advocating a puritanical form, Wahhabi or Shiᶜa in style, by which the Qur'an and the Hadith would be the only valid sources of law. Only the religious leaders of the community would be allowed to interpret the laws given in these two sources in the most literal fashion, to suit today's problems. Yet traditional Sunni interpretation of the Shariᶜa has allowed for the incorporation of changes and local customs into the legal code. If this method of interpretation is admitted, then a bridge could be made between the demands of Islamization and those of the modernists. This would be an important step forward, and even though there would need to be an overhaul of the legal system, particularly pertaining to legal punishment, correct implementation of Shariᶜa in accordance with Egyptian traditions could be possible with minimal negative effect on the personal lives of individuals.[16]

But for this to be possible, it is vital for the government to open widely the subject of the Shariᶜa, to explain to the people the various forms it can take, i.e., which is Shiᶜa, which is Wahhabi, Kharijite, etc. Because religious education has deteriorated and has been limited to teaching children enough of the Qur'an to perform rituals, most people in the country are not really aware that there are such differences. They would have to be informed before this matter is discussed in the Majlis al-Shᶜab. Important terms such as "those in power" would have to be debated and discussed. As it is, the government has put this whole debate in the hands of the ᶜulama and others who would stand to gain in case the type of Shariᶜa being demanded by the revivalists is the one which is accepted. In fact, we see them already interpreting "those in power" as being the ᶜulama.[17] Traditionally, the religious classes have not been friends of the government. The fact that they have been forced to become its spokesmen and civil servants, and therefore subservient to it, does not mean that they would not be willing to take on a position of predominance in an Islamic state. If the different issues are not brought out in public and are not explained in simple terms so that the general public can understand, then the militants will continue to be successful in presenting their own point of view to the people on a personal and individual level and in winning them over, since that is the only point of view the people will be exposed to.[18]

Therefore, the debate must be made to include all groups on all levels, including the militants, who need to present their views and have these views, which are mostly rhetorical and dogmatic in nature, disputed by various authorities as well as by members of the public.[19] The government seems to be the only institution not aware of the fact that if Islamic revivalism is still alive and well and could ultimately cause a dramatic change in the very structure of the state and the society, it is because the system of government, the bureaucracy, and the constitution itself are simply not doing the job for which they were intended.

The present government, weighed down by enormous economic problems that have been accumulating over decades, is doing its best to face one crisis after the other. With its energies thus directed, it is unable to deal with the deeper problems and find solutions for them. As long as this continues, the revivalist movements will go on and will probably become stronger. Even if the militants fail to gain control of the government by violence, which is most likely, they may succeed in imposing their brand of Islam on the society.

What is needed to prevent this from happening is to have an honest and open debate about what kind of government and what kind of society the Egyptians really want, and then to allow their wishes to become reality. Halfway measures are leading the country to the brink of disaster. A half-etatist, half-capitalistic structure that also claims to fulfill the needs of a socialist equitable state simply cannot work in Egypt. A complete program of reform is required, no matter what or whom it costs.

# NOTES

1. The sale and use of narcotics reached critical proportions in Egypt, particularly since it involved smuggling and payment in badly needed foreign currencies. Extreme measures were being taken to stop an epidemic that had hit more than one million Egyptians, according to official sources. The actual figures were probably much higher. The government was taking all measures possible to stop this trade, which was said to be worth more than three billion pounds a year. *Al-Siyasi*, Nov. 10, 1985, p. 2. The Majlis al-Shʿab discussed a law by which the penalty for selling narcotics would be the death sentence. *October*, Nov. 17, 1985, p. 26. At the same time, religious authorities were undertaking a campaign to explain how the use of narcotics was forbidden by the Qurʾan the same as drinking alcohol, and were in fact using strict interpretations of the Qurʾan and the Hadith to justify the use of the death penalty in such an offense. *Al-Ahram*, Dec. 2, 1985, p. 13; Oct. 25, 1985, p. 13.

2. Paradoxically, even though a second salary was a must for most urbanites, because of overcrowded offices and competition between males and females in the work force great pressure was being put on women to stay home and concentrate on raising their children. The religious authorities, who were once supportive of the education of women and their entry into the labor market, began interpreting women's work as an escape from their true responsibilities at home. *Al-Liwaʾ al-Islami*, Nov. 21, 1985, p. 20. Another problem for women in Egypt was lack of security. A recent case, in which a young girl was raped by three men, brought an outcry for the institution of the Shariʿa in judging the case. It was applied, and the three were executed. Various interviews with women have shown that this lack of personal security has contributed to the uneasiness and problems of women. *Akhir Saʿa*, Mar. 27, 1985, p. 30.

3. The same system continues today. Since its deficiencies have made themselves clear, the government has been trying to introduce changes that could result in badly needed reforms. *Al-Ahram*, International Edition, Aug. 8, 1985, p. 1. See also *Akhir Saʿa*, Sept. 4, 1985, pp. 21–23.

4. Testimony given by members of the Asyut police force at the Jihad trials made

it obvious that high-level authorities had given the police specific orders not to interfere with the Islamic organizations no matter what action they took on or off the University of Asyut campus. These orders were followed even after members of Islamic organizations beat up students, harassed people on the roads for not wearing Islamic garb, destroyed campus walls that had controlled their movements, and attacked and robbed stores belonging to a Coptic jeweler.

5. The Ikhwan (Muslim Brotherhood) have declared that they have no interest at this time in creating their own political party. They do not wish to enter into the political arena until they have gained a following big enough and until the society itself has opted for the Islamic way of life promoted by the Ikhwan. For a review of the program of the Ikhwan, see "Bayan Min al-Tanzim al-ᶜAlamai lil-Ikhwan al-Muslimin," *Al-Iman* (Rabat), No. *112*, Safar *1981*. See also the interview with al-Tilimsani in the *Al-Ahram*, Dec. 3, 1985, p. 14.

6. It is doubtful whether the Umma Party under the leadership of Ahmad al-Sabahi will fill the existing political vacuum. For a good discussion of the 1984 elections, see *Arabia*, July 1984, p. 23.

7. The Arab Republic of Egypt, Ministry of Information, *The Political System in Egypt* (Cairo, 1984), p. 4.

8. The Ikhwan are referred to in newspaper articles as a separate party even though they are not legally constituted as one. See ᶜAbd al-Rahman al-Sharqawi, "Tadhkira Li-Man Yansa," *Al-Ahram*, International Edition, July 27, 1985, p. 13.

9. For a good review of the ideas of the Takfir wal-Hijra, see H. Hassan, M. Ali, and A. Kamil Ahmad, *Muwagahat al-Fikr al-Mutatarif fi-l'Islam*, 2d ed. (Cairo, 1984).

10. *Al-Ahram*, Dec. 31, 1982.

11. The Egyptian courts gave Shaikh Salama the right to hold a popular conference that the government had previously forbade him to hold using the emergency laws that it was then functioning under as an excuse.

12. See *Al-Ahram* issues published in August 1985.

13. Ibid., esp. International Edition, Aug. 9, 1985, p. 3. The Mubarak government has shown an active interest in affairs of the Islamic world. Thus it has undertaken various projects that have magnified Egypt's international role as a Muslim state. Such activities have included President Mubarak's sponsorship of two international conferences. One, the first of its kind, was directed toward the study of the medical and scientific knowledge presented in the Qur'an and was attended by doctors, scientists, intellectuals, and religious leaders from twenty-eight countries, in October 1985. One month later the second conference met, to discuss *Nubuwwa* and *Sira* and their role in today's world. *Akhir Saᶜa*, Oct. 2, 1985, p. 75; *Al-Ahram*, Nov. 6 and Oct. 1, 1985.

14. *Al-Ahali*, July 31, 1985, p. 3, talks of the minister of information's answer to those attacking his role in propagating extremist ideals, by pointing out, inadvertently, the fact that the government was either unaware or without true realization of what religious extremism really meant until it was too late. Interestingly enough, during that interview the minister declared that "there is no religious extremism in Egypt today. . . . " Will hiding from the facts get rid of them?

15. Shaikh al-Sha'rawi is a highly respected and beloved preacher who believes in the cause of Islam and the spreading of the Islamic daᶜwa. He is widely published in book form and in periodicals; he can be heard on radio as well as watched on television. *Al-Liwa' al-Islami* included four pages of his interpretations of the Qur'an. His articles deal with diverse issues; the Aug. 10, 1985, article was about Orientalists and their stand against Islam, while the Nov. 21, 1985, issue dealt with death and why Moslems should not grieve for their lost ones. An interesting point about Shaikh al-Sha'rawi, according to notes by commentators, is his constant attacks on various Islamic governments for their un-Islamic actions. The only government that he has never criticized is that of Saudi Arabia. *Al-Ahali*, July 31, 1985, p. 30.

16. *Al-Ahram*, International Edition, Aug. 15, 1985, p. 7, contains an excellent dis-

cussion by Jamal ed-Din Mahmud, vice-president of al-Naqd courts, in which he points to laws used today as being the work of many generations brought in answer to questions posed over the centuries since the time of the Prophet, all of which cannot simply be discarded today because of the call of a few groups and the support of a population that is not exactly aware of what it is demanding.

17. *Al-Ahram*, International Edition, Aug. 9, 1985, p. 3, and Aug. 16, 1985, p. 3. See also *Al-Nur*, Nov. 20, 1985, p. 1.

18. Fuad Zakariyya, "Daʿwa Ila Hiwwar," *Al-Ahram*, International Edition, July 29, 1985, p. 7.

19. So far, the discussions occurring between the ʿulama and the militants have taken place in jail, where the Jihad prisoners are kept. The idea is to correct their wrong interpretation of what is true Islam. See *Al-Ahram*, Dec. 12, 1985.

# III

# SYRIA

## Raymond A. Hinnebusch

Syria's Islamic movement has been distinctively shaped by its current character as a reaction against the Baʿth state. While in much of the Middle East Islamic revivalism expresses nativist populist rebellion against upper-class regimes linked to the West, in Syria it is linked to the privileged classes and opposes a regime originating in lower-middle strata and in the front line of struggle with Israel. Significantly, it is only recently as the initial populist character of the regime has eroded that the Islamic opposition achieved popular breadth. The roots of Syria's Islamic movement and of its opposition to the Baʿth must be sought in four basic factors, each of which explains the receptivity of somewhat different segments of the population to its message.

### The Islamic Movement and the Baʿth Party: Roots of Conflict

The original and most enduring core of the Islamic movement grew out of nativist reaction by the most traditional and religiously pious segments of the society, notably the ʿulama, against the threat posed to their way of life, at least since the fall of the Ottoman empire, by the decline of Islam, Westernization, and—a symbol of both—the rise of the Westernized secular state. Under the Baʿth, a more rigorously secular state than its predecessors, Islamic revivalism continues to express the aspirations of pious Muslims for a reunion of political power and Islamic morality. To conciliate pious Muslim opinion, the regime has tried to establish the Muslim credentials of its Alawite leaders and the personal Islamic piety of President Hafiz al-Assad, but otherwise its public discourse and policy has made few of the concessions to Islamic law and morality of states like Egypt and Sudan.[1]

The Islamic opposition also expresses the reaction of the urban establishment and its mass following in the traditional city against a rural-based regime that has damaged its economic interests. Historically, the Syrian city and village were virtually distinct "worlds": the city, residence of ruler, landlord, and merchant, held power and wealth; the village was a political vacuum, economically exploited by the urban elite. Islam itself was chiefly an urban institution. In the 1960s, however, Ba'thism became a vehicle of rural revolt against the city. The Ba'th largely recruited from the peasants and rural townsmen with a potent mixture of nationalism and populism. As the army became a major channel of upward mobility for rural youth, the Ba'th developed a strong following in it. In 1963 when Ba'thi officers seized power, the party had a heavily rural social cast. In consolidating its rule, the Ba'th replaced urbanites in the army and bureaucracy with rural partisans, turning the main institutions of the state into rural strongholds ruling over the city. It pursued land reform and socialist policies challenging the hold of the urban establishment over the economy and the village. The historic ties of the ᶜulama (religious teachers and leaders; sing., ᶜalim) to the urban merchant community made it natural that Islam, interpreted to exclude socialism, would become a vehicle of protest against this assault on urban interests. The cleavage between the Ba'th and political Islam continues to express the split between the city establishment and the village, Sunni as well as non-Sunni.

The Islamic opposition also expresses Sunni resentment of the disproportionate role played by members of the minority communities, particularly Alawites, in the Ba'th leadership. Syria, a "mosaic" society, is made up of a majority Sunni Muslim community (75.0 percent), historically dominant, and several minority communities: Christians (9.0 percent) and several heterodox Islamic minority sects—the Alawites (11.5 percent), the Druze (3 percent), and the Ismailis (1.5 percent), chiefly rural and, particularly the Alawites, traditionally deprived. The minorities, finding in the Ba'th's secular nationalism an identity that integrated them on an equal basis into the political community, were disproportionately drawn to it. Since the time of the French, who deliberately recruited from minorities, the army had been a channel of social mobility for these same deprived groups. Thus, when the Ba'th took power the minorities were already entrenched in the two institutions, the army and the party, which would rule Syria. The Ba'thization of the army, which often amounted to replacing urban Sunnis with the clients of leading minority Ba'th officers and intra-Ba'th conflicts in which Sunnis lost out to Alawites, further enhanced minority ascendancy.[2] This turnabout, in which the Sunni establishment was subordinated to a minority-dominated state, generated an enduring hostility for which Islamic fundamentalism, denying the legitimacy of rule by other than orthodox Muslims, was a congenial ideological vehicle. As long as Alawites in the regime acted in the name of Arab nationalism and social reform, opposition to their dominance remained concentrated in the Sunni establishment. But as they increasingly abused and used their power to favor their own sect, resentment of sectarian "minority" rule deepened among the wider Sunni population, becoming a powerful force fueling Islamic religious opposition.

Finally, in the late seventies, socioeconomic troubles and the faltering national legitimacy of the regime favored the spread of political Islam to wider sectors of the population who embraced it, not chiefly for religious, economic, or sectarian reasons, but as a vehicle of protest or as the only viable alternative to the regime. Social mobilization and dislocation deepened. Massive urbanization and educational expansion, exceeding the absorptive capacity of the modern sector of the economy, both raised and frustrated expectations and widened the pool of potential recruits to an ideological opposition movement. The economic opening and the oil boom subjected Syria to exceptional economic instability, fueling inflation and threatening the livelihood of broad middle and lower urban strata, while others, notably the Damascene bourgeoisie and a corrupt officialdom, enriched themselves. The Ba°th elite, visibly embourgeoised and corrupted, seemed to lose its commitment to egalitarian social change. Its murderous rivalry with other Arab nationalist forces—notably Iraq and the Palestine Liberation Organization—seemed to put its particular interests above the Arab national cause. The very limited scope for political participation in a relentlessly authoritarian regime gave little outlet to legitimate dissent. That the growing political opposition this generated took an Islamic form was natural. Both liberalism and Marxism lacked credibility beyond limited middle-class circles. The populist variant of Arab nationalism that had long dominated Syria was seriously weakened by the 1967 defeat and the inter-Arab fragmentation of the seventies. To the degree that it had been preempted and institutionalized in the regime itself, it was tarnished by the disillusionment with the Ba°th and deprived of utility as an ideology of protest. Thus, there was a certain ideological vacuum in Syria. If the state and imported ideologies had failed, Syrians could turn back to the indigenous and familiar, to an Islam deeply rooted in custom and sentiment, and with a moral content relevant to individual lives. Finally, the rise in the wealth and prestige of "Islamic" regimes such as Saudi Arabia and the spectacular success of Iran's Islamic revolution gave political Islam a credibility it hitherto lacked.

### The Islamic Movement: Leadership, Ideology, Organization

The Islamic movement in Syria embraces a diversity of forces. The Muslim Brotherhood (Ikhwan) has provided the most organized leadership and comprehensive program but other elements more on the peripheries of the political struggle—the °ulama, traditional notables, smaller Islamic associations—have contributed leaders and ideas on a more sporadic basis.

### The °Ulama

The °ulama have long been a political force in Syria, pressing Islamic demands on government and contributing to the Islamic politicization of the population. Traditionally, they have resisted the secularization of the state, demanding that Islam be designated the state religion, that the head of state be a Muslim, and that the *Shari°a* (Allah's law) be the basis of legislation. Under the secular minority-led Ba°th, their political activism has grown. The °ulama led protests against radical secularizing tendencies in the regime in the sixties and Shari°a court judges fought to introduce Islamic provisions into the 1973 constitution. Recruited from urban merchant and notable families or, in the case of a lesser *imam* (religious prayer leader) or *khatib* (religious orator), combining their religious functions with petty trade and artisanship,[3] many ᶜulama have also pressed religion into the defense of private enterprise and property, attacking Baᶜth socialism as an alien import, Marxist (hence atheistic), and contrary to Islam. While a few ᶜulama have been co-opted by the regime and many are not usually politically active, others have been allied with or have even led militant political groups. Islamic-inspired disturbances have often started with antiregime sermons in the mosques, then spilled over into protests in nearby streets, and the call to rise has often been proclaimed from the minaret. Shaikh Muhammad ᶜAbdul Hamid led Islamic militants in Hama and was killed in the 1982 uprising. In Aleppo, Shaikh Muhammad Abu al-Nasr al-Bayanuni founded the militant Abu Dharr society. Shaikh Habannakah, president of the ᶜulama association in the 1960s, led antiregime forces in Damascus from the traditional Maydan quarter; despite the sometimes violent demonstrations he headed, his influence made him virtually immune to arrest. The League of ᶜUlama long had ties with the Ikhwan and the students of the Shariᶜa faculty were a main recuitment pool for it. The Ikhwan has tried to mobilize the ᶜulama as a group against the regime; Ikhwan leader Saᶜid Hawwa, himself an ᶜalim, brought many ᶜulama into the fight against the 1973 constitution and the Ikhwan sought to enlist them in its *jihad* (holy war) in the late seventies; reproachful reminders to them of their duty to join the "lonely" Ikhwan struggle against the regime indicate their success was mixed, but as violence escalated and regime reprisals became more indiscriminate, many inactive ᶜulama were driven into Ikhwan arms.[4]

## The Notables

More on the peripheries of the Islamic coalition were the notables—rich land-lords and merchants—who lost wealth and power to the regime. They supplied money, engaged in conspiracies, and quietly nurtured antiregime sentiment; some of their educated sons became activists. Typical of them was Maᶜruf al-Dawalibi, a pro-Ikhwan religious shaikh and an Aleppine politician in the ranks of the upper-class Shᶜab Party in the 1950s. He was a staunch foe of the middle-class army officers who were challenging notable rule in that decade and pre-sided, as prime minister in the "separatist" regime, over reversals of the United Arab Republic land reform and nationalizations. He fled Syria after the Baᶜth took power and engineered several conspiracies against it with Saudi help. In the mid-seventies he was back in Syria as part of the conservative opposition.

## The Ikhwan al-Muslimin

The main leadership of the Islamic movement has been provided by overtly political organizations. Many such groups have formed and reformed over the years but the Muslim Brotherhood is the most durable, the largest, and the most politically significant of them. The seeds of the Ikhwan were carried to Syria by Shari͏ᶜa students returning from Egypt where they had contact with the parent organization. A first proto-Ikhwan group was founded in Aleppo, then spread to other provinces. Mustafa al-Sibaᶜi, Muhammad Mubarak, and Salah ash-Shash gathered these groups, along with members of older Muslim welfare and education associations that had sprung up opposing Westernization, into the Ikhwan al-Muslimin in 1946. Al-Sibaᶜi became the acknowledged leader—*al-Muraqib al-Am* (general supervisor)—of the organization, which he made a force in Syrian politics. He was born in Homs of an ᶜalim family, studied at al-Azhar, where he was a follower of Hasan al-Banna, and, on his return to Syria, was jailed by the French for anti-imperialist agitation. He then taught at the Syrian University and became dean of the faculty of Shariᶜa, a strategic position for recruiting disciples.

The Ikhwan under al-Sibaᶜi did not develop an elaborate disciplined organization as in Egypt but operated in more traditional fashion through the personal links of leader to disciples and to like-minded ᶜulama in the mosques and local Islamic associations. It favored peaceful proselytization in schools and mosques and, through its newspaper, *Al-Manar*, took part in elections. Al-Sibaᶜi fought secularizing tendencies and confronted secular politicians and Christian churchmen over the role of Islam in the 1950 constitution. Although the Ikhwan opposed secular nationalists and the left, it also expressed the nationalist and reformist sentiments of its lower-middle-class following. Al-Sibaᶜi denounced feudalism and the elite for its Westernization and alienation from the people. He was also strongly anti-imperialist, rejecting foreign economic concessions and Western security pacts as ploys to maintain spheres of influence and divert attention from Israel. Although he advocated closer ties with the East to check Western influence, he regarded the Soviets as imperialist, and insisted on neutralism. He denounced the 1948 truce with Israel and called for armed struggle and an oil embargo to liberate Palestine. He advocated an Islamic third way that was neither capitalist—rejected for allowing a small group to dominate the economy—or communist—which abolished private property and individual initiative. This order would rest on social justice and mutual social responsibility arising out of religious belief and moral activism. Private property would be legitimized within limits if treated as a trust from God and the community to be used for the common good. The rich would pay *zakat* (tax) to support a welfare state for the poor, excessively large private estates would be distributed to the peasants, and free education would be provided to all. An independent national economy adapting modern technology to Islamic ends would transform Syria from its decadent dependent state.[5] In reality, al-Sibaᶜi accepted capitalism but sought to limit its inegalitarian and materialist consequences by religious law and morality.

ᶜIsam al-Attar, a teacher, replaced the ailing al-Sibaᶜi as Ikhwan leader in 1957. Though al-Attar was a dynamic speaker, he left a lesser imprint on political Islam than the founder, for the Ikhwan was repressed under the UAR and al-Attar was exiled by the Baᶜth and forced to lead the Ikhwan through his lieu-

tenants, notably Muwaffaq Dabul, a professor at Damascus University, Adnan
Saᶜid in Ladhaqia, and Amin Yakin of Aleppo, the deputy supervisor who devoted full time to the organization and often quarreled with al-Attar. Al-Attar's
reliance on personal Damascene followers to the neglect of countrywide organization led to the decline of organized activism and of links between leadership and provinces. Nor did he have al-Sibaᶜi's good relations with the ᶜulama,
since he condemned both Sufism and the traditional schools. Despite the
repression of the Ikhwan under Baᶜth rule, al-Attar rejected demands for violent
opposition from younger members on grounds it would bring retribution. Thus,
the Ikhwan remained fairly quiescent under his leadership; indeed, it supported
Hafiz al-Assad in his quarrel with Salah Jedid, hoping for accommodation with
a less radical Baᶜth. In the late 1970s al-Attar rejected all Arab monarchies and
republics alike as repressive and reactionary but refrained from calling for violent resistance. But although he retained the loyalty of parts of the Ikhwan in
Damascus, overall leadership had passed out of his hands by then.[6]

In the sixties, a new militant leader, Marwan Hadid, arose on the fringes of
the Ikhwan in Hama. Hadid was an agronomist from a prosperous cotton-
growing family. He was convinced, by his association with al-Sayyid Qutb in
Egypt, that there could be no compromise with repressive "anti-Islamic" systems like the Baᶜth and that only armed struggle could bring them down; he
actually trained in guerrilla warfare. Al-Attar rejected this strategy, and Hadid
never joined the Ikhwan leadership; he ignored organization and preparation,
his open provocation of the regime was seen as dangerous, and his following
remained small. But he was apparently a charismatic leader and his message
and example found receptivity among younger Ikhwan leaders who would eventually replace al-Attar and steer the movement into armed rebellion. Hadid
led opposition to the Baᶜth in Hama, then broadened his activities during the
1973 disturbances and went underground to form a militant fighting faction,
al-Taliᶜa al-Muqatilah—linked to a similarly named group founded in Aleppo
by Husni Abu and Adnan ᶜUqla. (Attempts to form similar groups in Damascus
were smashed by the regime.) In the mid-seventies, Hadid led a campaign of
assassinations against the ruling elite, declaring that "the regime will disappear
only when armed groups . . . kill its members." In 1976 he was caught and he
died in prison, but his followers in Hama carried on under ᶜAbd as-Sattar al-
Zaim, a dentist from a merchant family who was killed in 1979.[7]

In 1969 a leadership crisis began inside the Ikhwan when al-Attar was challenged by prominent northern leaders, including Amin Yakin and Shaikh ᶜAbd
al-Fattah Abu Ghuddah of Aleppo, Saᶜid Hawwa and Adnan Saᶜad ad-Din of
Hama, and Adnan Saᶜid of Ladhaqia. Influenced by Hadid, they wished to
prepare for jihad against the regime. For a while, the Ikhwan split into three
groups: al-Attar's in Damascus, which was supported by Dair ez-Zor; the group
in Aleppo and Ladhaqia, which elected Shaikh Abu Ghuddah, a Shariᶜa teacher
from an ᶜalim family, as a rival general supervisor; and the Hama branch, which
remained neutral, often collaborating with but distinct from Hadid's followers.

A new militant leadership triumphed in the early seventies, though the Damascus group remained loyal to al-Attar. Adnan Sa°ad ad-Din, a middle-class educator and writer, was made general supervisor in 1975. Sa°id Hawwa, a Shari°a graduate from a middle-class family who spent years in prison for his role in the 1973 disturbances, became "chief ideologue" of the movement. °Ali Sadr ad-Din Bayanuni, an Aleppine lawyer from an °ulama family, was deputy supervisor. Husni Abu, a teacher from an Aleppine business family and son-in-law of a prominent °alim, headed the military branch in Aleppo from the clashes of 1973 into the late seventies. He was succeeded by Adnan °Uqla, a baker's son who became an engineer, served in the army, had close links with Marwan Hadid, and directed the massacre at the Aleppo artillery academy and the 1982 uprising in Hama.

In the mid-seventies, Hadid's followers remained on a separate tangent responsible for the assassinations that had not yet been officially endorsed by the national organization. He was occasionally joined by individual Ikhwan, especially from the Hama branch; this forced the hand of the national leadership, which set up military cells of its own to absorb these individual initiatives. When in 1977 the leadership endorsed jihad, Hadid's followers were largely absorbed into the Ikhwan under °Uqla, although factional divisions persisted.

The individual personalistic leadership and decentralized organization hitherto dominant was by now at least partly superseded by a collective leadership presiding over a formal organization with bureaucratic offices, chains of command, and representative bodies. The general supervisor and his deputy were elected from a *majlis al-shura* (consultative council) composed of representatives of the provincial branches and presided over an executive bureau with specialized sections for training, finance, publicity, and so forth. The military branches were divided into three-man cells. The scale and durability of the rebellion the Ikhwan mounted in 1980 and 1982 indicated a substantial advance in organizational capabilities.

As the struggle with the regime escalated, further steps were taken in the consolidation of a unified leadership. In 1980 the Islamic Front in Syria was formed, joining independent militant groups—including the Jama°at Abu Dharr and the Islamic Liberation Party, parts of the League of °Ulama, and other groups hitherto less politicized—with the Ikhwan organization under the leadership of Shaikh al-Bayanuni.[8] In 1982, however, Adnan °Uqla split off from the mainstream movement to form a more militant faction. He objected to the alliance Sa°ad ad-Din was forming with Iraq, a secular regime fighting the world's only Islamic republic, and to U.S. contacts, which, he charged, demonstrated complacency toward imperialism. °Uqla has since headed most of the fighters on the ground.[9]

To broaden its base and define the goals for which it was fighting, the front issued a manifesto and program.[10] It begins with a call to jihad against the regime—a sectarian dictatorship led by unbelievers—which, incapable of reform, must be destroyed. The core of the manifesto is an attack on what is seen as the essence of the regime: Alawite and military rule. The Alawites' Islamic credentials are denied. They are accused of collaboration with French imperialism, warned that a minority cannot indefinitely rule the majority, and urged to rid themselves of the Assad brothers before it is too late. The experience of the Ikhwan under military rule is reflected in a strong antimilitary sentiment. The military—from Husni Zaim, who settled with Israel, to the Ba‘th officers, who abandoned the Golan, and President al-Assad, who serves both U.S. and Soviet interests—have been tools of foreigners. The Alawite-dominated army is an instrument of internal repression controlling the peoples' lives, a burden on society, and, riddled with intrigue and corruption and purged of competent officers, incapable of fighting Zionism.

The Islamic movement seeks to replace this regime with a true Islamic state in which Islamic morality and law is restored in every branch of social life. Key to this is the moral regeneration of the citizen through a return to the way of the Prophet. The vices that infect society—corruption, gambling, extravagance, alcohol, prostitution, nightclubs—must be eradicated. The family and woman's role in nurturing it must be protected. Modern technology is not rejected, but only by incorporating it into an Islamic value system can the ills of materialism that plague the developed world be avoided.

In place of a single party regime of partisan favoritism and corruption, the program advocates a relatively liberal political system. When the regime falls, the Islamic front will form a provisional government and a constituent assembly will be elected to write a constitution. Government by shura would be institutionalized in a strong elected parliament dominated neither by clergymen nor by politicians.[11] An independent judiciary of Shari‘a jurists would nullify all executive action and legislation contrary to Islamic law. Freedom of expression and the press and party competition are guaranteed, except for parties against Islam or linked to foreign powers—e.g., communists. Since the majority of Syrians are Muslim, Syria must be an Islamic state, but the rights of religious minorities will be protected, and all will be treated equally before the law, thus eliminating partisan and sectarian favoritism. Citizens will be protected against the current torture, repression, and imprisonment without trial; freeing the judiciary from political pressures and appointments is crucial to this. The liberal features of this proposal have probably been stressed to broaden support against the Ba‘th; indeed, some Islamic militants, such as Adnan ‘Uqla's followers, have declared to the contrary that men have no right to govern themselves and must be ruled by the order of God through a pious caliph.[12]

The proposed economic order reflects a mixture of antistatist free enterprise and Islamic populism. Capitalism has exploited the workers but socialism, depriving workers of all rights to strike, is an even harsher tyranny. The Ba‘th system mixes the worst of the West—rampant materialism—and the East— an unproductive state sector that destroys incentives and is corrupted to enrich a small political clique. An Islamic economy will encourage private enterprise, investment, and fair profit, while avoiding excessive concentration of wealth and class conflict. Except for natural resources, public utilities, and strategic industries, private enterprise, according to Sa‘id Hawwa,[13] will be the basis of the economy "as prescribed by the Qur'an." The program avoids calling for abolition of the huge public sector, advocating only the purging of corruption and giving its workers shares in their firms. But private investment in industry must be protected from nationalizations and, while workers in this sector will be protected by a labor code, they must also cease to malinger and must work for their wages. The state should not encroach on the trade sector, which is properly private and should be allowed to freely import and export. The bloated bureaucracy must be cut and people encouraged to work in the private sector. The implementation of land reform is criticized for reducing productivity, but the issue of ownership size is avoided except to advocate giving uncultivated public lands to whoever cultivates them—most likely entrepreneurs. State farms and cooperatives have failed and should be abandoned; peasants should be liberated from the state marketing system, which pays them low prices, and be given title to land received in the reform. The procapitalist, antistatist bias of most of this program is unmistakable. However, class gaps are to be narrowed through payment of zakat by the rich to support charitable endowments for the poor, aged, students, etc., and through a state guarantee of the basic needs— food, clothing, shelter—for all citizens.

An Islamic foreign policy would be neutralist, "rejectionist," pan-Arab and pan-Islamic. Unlike the Baᶜth, which has surrendered the country to the USSR, an Islamic government would regard the latter, for its occupation of Afghanistan (a crime blessed by the al-Assad regime), as an enemy equally with the West for its support of Israel; to free Syria from dependence on the Soviet Union, a domestic armaments industry is needed. There can be no compromise over Palestine, which must be liberated by jihad, but the road to Jerusalem lies through Damascus, for the regime diverts the people from the struggle with Israel and tries to crush the Palestinian resistance. One key to independence and liberation is Islamic unity, which could make the Muslims a world power and rally them behind the Palestinian and Afghan causes. But since the Islamic movement opposes all established regimes, a wave of pan-Islamic revolution must first sweep these away. The Ikhwan initially saw the Iranian revolution as leading this wave, but its alliance with al-Assad disillusioned them. Indeed, in 1982 the mainstream Ikhwan struck an alliance with Iraq, which, it claimed, was different in composition (Sunni) and orientation from the Syrian Baᶜth. Increasingly, except for ᶜUqla's faction, Iran is regarded as a sectarian Shiᶜa regime.

As a strategy to rally a broad antiregime front, this program has strengths and weaknesses. Its economic provisions, which reflect the interests of the movement's core constituency, the private sector peripheralized by the state-run economy and frozen out of its patronage networks, appeal to both the great bourgeois families and small *suq* traders. A state with both a central role for the Shariᶜa and the ᶜulama and liberal political freedoms seeks to reconcile the desires of pious Muslims with the need for alliance with the secular opposition. Its anti-Zionism is congruent with mass sentiment but its anti-Sovietism risks Syria's ability to confront Israel. Its antimilitary and antibureaucratic biases may alienate these powerful sectors. Its mass appeal seems problematic: rejecting everything Ba{c}thist, it has little of Siba{c}i's antiaristocratic populism; and apart from scattered references to Islamic morality, there is little distinctively Islamic about it and much transparently expressive of the interests of the bourgeoisie.

## The Social Base of Political Islam

An Islamic mobilization of society depends on the numbers and social composition of movement activists. The {c}ulama are one potential such cadre, but their numbers are limited. In 1970 there were about 2,800 {c}ulama in Syria, relatively concentrated in the urban areas. Only 1,173 were available for some 5,000 villages, few of them educated, politically conscious, or with leadership status outside matters of ritual. By contrast, the Ba{c}th has cells in most villages.[14] The Syrian {c}ulama lack the numbers, unity, and organization of the Iranian mullahs and hence enjoy no comparable capacity to mobilize Islamic opposition. The numbers of lay militants have varied widely over time and area. In Aleppo they numbered about 500 to 700 in 1975 and 5,000 to 7,000 in 1978; before the heavy losses suffered at Hama, there may have been 30,000 nationwide.[15] This rapid growth suggests there is a significant pool of passive sympathizers who can be mobilized in times of confrontation and who, given the risks, must be highly motivated. Historically, activists have been drawn from families of merchants, {c}ulama, and petty employees, frequently recruited in mosque study circles. The schoolchildren of such families provided the main manpower for street demonstrations in the seventies. At an earlier time these youths would have carried on their fathers' occupations, but as education became the key to success and they went to university, a growing proportion of activists has come to be drawn from this educated middle stratum. Moreover, as the Ikhwan came to express opposition to Ba{c}th reforms, sons of higher-class families who suffered under the Ba{c}th, often "independent" professionals, joined its ranks. Reflective of these changes, of 1,384 activists in the late seventies, 27.7 percent were students, 7.0 percent teachers, and 13.3 percent professionals (79 engineers, 57 doctors, 25 lawyers, and 10 pharmacists).[16]

Broader societal receptivity to political Islam has varied widely over time. Historically, in Syria it never took on the dimensions of comparable movements in Turkey, Egypt, and Iran. Syria's modern political awakening, led by Westernized notables, including many Christians, and originally directed against Muslim Turkey, took the form of secular Arab nationalism. As political consciousness spread downward, Islamic activism appeared, but it was contained by the clientage networks of the secular notable parties, such as the Watani and Sha{c}b, and by the rise of middle-class parties, such as the Ba{c}th, Syrian nationalists, Arab socialists, and communists, which, counting many members of minority groups in their ranks, were also secularist. Indicative of the limited appeal of the Ikhwan to the emerging salaried middle class was its weakness in the army, where politicized officers became Syrian nationalists, Ba{c}thists, Naserites, but—unlike Egypt—rarely Muslim Brothers.

Nonetheless, the Ikhwan carved out a durable place in the political arena centered on the traditional urban neighborhoods. In the elections of the 1940s and 1950s, it was able to elect a handful of deputies from the popular quarters of Damascus. Later, when Naserism was sweeping the area with powerful appeal to the urban masses, the Ikhwan was on the ideological defensive; yet it still got 47 percent of the vote in a 1957 contest with a pro-Naser Baᶜthist in Damascus. Despite being banned under the UAR, it won an unprecedented ten seats in 1961, including seven from outside Damascus, indicating a broadening of its geographic base. But Naserism remained a powerful rival for the loyalty of the urban masses and, in the 1962 uprisings against the "separatist" regime, Naserist and Ikhwan mobs of indistinguishable urban lower-class composition fought in the streets.[17] With the decline of the notable parties under Baᶜth rule and of Naserism after Naser, the Ikhwan outlasted its major rivals for the support of the urban masses. The only remaining credible alternative to the Baᶜth, the Ikhwan tended to inherit the parts of its rivals' mass bases not co-opted by the regime.

Under the Baᶜth, the social bases of political Islam have widened but remain socially and regionally unevenly distributed. As before, its core support is concentrated in the traditional urban quarters among merchants, artisans, ᶜulama, and the laboring elements under their influence. Rich notable families whose clientage ties reach deep into these quarters have also gravitated to the Islamic coalition. This milieu is most sensitive to the minority and secular nature of the Baᶜth, for the ᶜulama and the mosque are concentrated in these quarters rather than in the modern parts of the cities or in the villages. This part of Syrian society has also paid the heaviest costs of Baᶜth policies. Land reform and the substitution of state agrarian credit and marketing networks for the old landlord-merchant ones has deprived the landlords and merchants of influence and wealth in the villages. Nationalization of industries, which in a few cases touched artisan workshops, was seen as an attack on business and property as a whole. The partial takeover of foreign and wholesale trade, restrictions on imports, and a growing state retail network deprived big merchants of lucrative sources of wealth and, because their distribution networks reached down to thousands of petty merchants, hurt or threatened many others. Government price fixing and market regulation alienated merchants of all sizes.[18] President al-Assad's economic liberalization did reopen opportunities in foreign trade and small manufacturing, but business must still deal with inefficient government trading and banking bodies run by unsympathetic officials or pay off corrupt ones, must compete with the government for scarce foreign exchange, and remains insecure in the face of new state interventions in fields previously private (e.g., retailing of fruits and vegetables, insecticides, and tractor spare parts).

In the late seventies, however, there was a clear geographic differentiation in the receptivity of urban Syria to Islamic opposition: while the northern cities, notably Hama and Aleppo, were hotbeds of unrest, Damascus remained quiescent. Hamawis and Aleppines may be more conservative and volatile than the calculating peaceable Damascenes, but Damascus was a center of antiregime agitation in the sixties. Under al-Assad, however, Damascus was favored at the expense of the northern cities. Al-Assad co-opted into party and government ranks middle- and even upper-class Damascenes—such as Prime Minister ᶜAbd al-Rauf Kasm. The centralization of power under the Baᶜth disadvantaged Aleppo, which was a powerful political bloc the equal of Damascus in the pre-Baᶜth regime. Closer to the center of power, personal connection, and corrupt influence, the Damascene bourgeoisie found ways to get around government regulations and enrich itself on cuts of the disproportionate share of public monies expended in or from the capital. The Damascene bourgeoisie may have been playing a double game, subsidizing the Ikhwan but, in return for concessions from the regime, ensuring that Damascus was quiet.[19] This was perhaps the better part of wisdom because Damascus is no longer the preserve of the traditional bourgeoisie. The ubiquitous presence of the huge government apparatus and massive migration from the rural areas, much of it youths making claims on the spoils of the revolution, have shifted the balance of power there. By contrast, traditional Hama suffered under Baᶜth rule. The city resented the favor shown the surrounding villages it used to dominate. The new factories around Hama largely recruited workers from rural areas. Land reform and state credit eased the dependence of peasants on Hamawi landlords and money-lenders. Small inner-city textile industries may have suffered from competition of large state factories, minimum wage laws, increases in prices paid cotton farmers, and the priority given state firms by state cotton marketing agencies. The great families—the Kialanis, Barazis, ᶜAzms—that used to run Hama found the presence of Baᶜth provincial officials in the heart of their once exclusive preserve galling.[20]

Support, if chiefly in the form of passive sympathy, clearly broadened beyond this traditional urban core in the late seventies when the educated urban Sunni middle class generally became more receptive to political Islam. This class had high aspirations, but as a result of the rapid expansion of education, it faced growing competition for scholarships and good jobs from villagers and felt discriminated against by a minority/rural-dominated regime. Blatant favoritism for Alawites sharpened these grievances. Nevertheless, the Sunni middle class has not gone over to the Islamic opposition en masse and remains politically divided. Urban high school students played a role in Ikhwan street protests, but the Baᶜth also has a massive organization in the schools that mobilized counter-demonstrations and it has had no trouble recruiting even pious Sunnis.[21] The university campus has not been swept by Islam as in Egypt; the Baᶜth has a presence there and opposition is likely to take a leftist form. The dislike of upper-middle-class professionals for authoritarian, sectarian, and socialist rule led them into tactical alliances with the Ikhwan, including professional strikes against police repression of the Ikhwan in 1979 and 1980; but they have not been particularly receptive to Islamic ideology, although as the sons of the traditional urban quarter join them they become more so. There is some sympathy for the Ikhwan in teacher and white-collar ranks, but their dependence on state employment, the strength of the secular center and left among them, and the antistatist ideology of the Ikhwan deters active pro-Ikhwan opposition. The organized industrial working class and the peasantry remain little receptive to the Ikhwan. While it always had a modest following in the trade union movement, the secular left, including the Ba°th, dominates the unions and in the sixties was even able to mobilize workers against Islamic opposition to socialism. Nor has the Ikhwan much penetrated the countryside, except in a few larger villages near the city. Rural recruitment was of low priority for the Ikhwan's urban-centered activists, and the presence of the landlord parties and later the Ba°th in the villages was an obstacle to it.[22] Thus even today, the correlation between the Ikhwan-Ba°th and the urban-rural split largely persists.

Although Syria's Islamic opposition is no exogenous creation, it has received revenue, sanctuary, and political support from Ikhwan branches elsewhere and from external forces hostile to the Ba°th. It has close ties to the strong Ikhwan branch in Jordan, where its top leaders established headquarters and training camps after fleeing Syria. Syrian efforts to make Jordan deny this sanctuary escalated into a major crisis between the states, with Syria massing troops on the border and sending agents into Jordan to seize Ikhwan leaders. Iraq provided sanctuary, arms, money, and major encouragement, including broadcast facilities during the Hama uprising. The Lebanese Kata'ib, the Turkish National Salvation Party, and °Arafat's PLO gave arms or training. Egypt's government, allied with its Ikhwan, carried on a propaganda campaign trying to turn Sunnis against the "Alawite gangs" in the regime. Saudi Arabia was a major source of Islamic funding in the sixties. Allied with Syria under al-Assad, it may have financed the Ikhwan to show the trouble it could make when he pursued policies it disliked; Saudi private sources also provided funds. The local Ikhwan branch got Kuwait's subsidy to the Syrian government cut off in protest at Hama. This wide range of support for antiregime activity, making the regime feel besieged from all sides, was a measure of its isolation in the late 1970s. The state to which the Ikhwan looked for inspiration and from which it expected the strongest support, Islamic Iran, is one place it did not get them. Iran, aligned with al-Assad, shocked the Ikhwan by denouncing it as "gangs carrying out the Camp David conspiracy against Syria."

## Regime and Opposition: The Dynamics of Conflict

The Ba°th has survived six major urban revolts in which Islamic leaders played a leading role, through varied combinations of repression, concession, and its own support mobilization. In the early sixties, when the regime, having just come to power, lacked an organized base outside the army, the Ikhwan led protests against the Ba°th's monopoly of power, which had cut short its own rising prospects, and against the socialist policies the regime was unveiling. A 1964 uprising included attacks on government buildings, and street barricades, denunciations of the "godless and socialist" Ba°th in Hama, and merchant strikes in Damascus and other cities against controls on foreign trade. The regime used artillery against Ikhwan-held mosques in Hama but, isolated, sought to mollify the opposition with a constitution enshrining Islam as a source of legislation and the right of private property. A year later, however, the regime, strengthened by the widened support base it was winning through agrarian reform and mass political organization, struck at the economic power of the bourgeoisie with sweeping nationalizations. This time, the support of the left, peasants, and armed workers and the confiscation of struck shops enabled it to isolate and suppress opposition. Intense hostility, however, persisted between regime and suq, especially after the Baʿth's 1966 leftward turn; in 1967, ʿulama-led protests expressed the alarm of conservative Muslim opinion at radical secularist tendencies in the party.[23] It was its rural base—peasant soldiers, partisans, and syndicalists—that enabled the regime to contain this opposition.

Weakened by the 1967 war defeat, Baʿth leftists were deposed by Hafiz al-Assad, who sought reconciliation with the opposition in the name of national unity against Israel. Al-Assad muted secularism, cultivated the ʿulama, and liberalized state control of the market, revitalizing the private sector. But a new round of protests against his 1973 constitution showed the limits of détente with the opposition. These protests were partly over its failure to make Islam the state religion and partly over the consecration of the Baʿth as the leading party, dashing hopes that Al-Assad would end single-party rule. Violence rocked Hama, and merchant- and ʿulama-led protests swept other cities. Al-Assad conceded a change naming Islam the religion of the president and asserted his own Muslim credentials, but it took major repression to end the revolt.[24]

By the mid-seventies the regime had crystallized into a formidable state. Power was concentrated in a dominant president, Hafiz al-Assad, whose mix of astuteness, conciliation, and ruthlessness earned him the respect of many Syrians, endowing the regime with a measure of personal legitimacy. His power rested partly on a network of Alawite kinsmen at the strategic levers of the security-military apparatus who, having a strong stake in the regime, were prepared to fight for it. But al-Assad also built alliances with key Sunni officers and politicians and replenished the top elite with new contingents of Damascene Sunnis. Both of these factions forged clientage ties with parts of the Sunni bourgeoisie. The second-tier elite continued to be a civil-military coalition drawn from all sects and regions, including the Baʿth's critical rural base and incorporating a broader coalition of interests.[25] This elite presided over a massive institutional apparatus.

The steady expansion in the firepower and size of the military under al-Assad makes violent opposition to the regime costly, if not futile, so long as the military remains loyal. The Baʿthization of the army, several Alawite-recruited praetorian guards and intelligence agencies charged with the defense of the regime, Alawite command of "coup-making units," the growing professionalization of the officer corps, its stake in avoiding political purges damaging to the integrity of the armed forces and its privileged position in society, the difficulty of mounting a successful coup in an ever larger army—all work in favor of the regime.

Sectarian animosities do run deep in the army and there have been defections, such as the massacre of Alawite cadets by a Sunni officer and instances in 1980 and 1982 of faltering military discipline when action was ordered against the civilian populace of Sunni cities; nevertheless, during the massive use of military force against Hama in 1982, the army remained loyal.

The state bureaucracy, vastly expanded under the Baʿth, is a second network of control on which a major segment of the population is dependent for employment or for essential services. The many villagers for whom the Baʿth opened up opportunities in the state and public sector have a special stake in the regime. The Baʿth party and its "mass organizations" are a political machine with a sizable corps of cadres that penetrates the countryside, providing local channels of power and patronage, and constitutes strong points in the cities; besides some 150,000 party members, the mass organizations enroll thousands of students, teachers, peasants, and workers amounting to about a third of the population. Although the party itself has been infected by sectarian rivalries, it remains a web cutting across sectarian cleavages, penetrating the Sunni as well as minority communities and incorporating a significant mass base. As ideological commitment in the party has eroded, turning it into a patronage network, its mobilizational capacity has declined. Yet, it has provided armed detachments supportive of the security forces in less accessible corners of society and has mobilized progovernment demonstrations to deny the opposition psychological domination of the streets.

Finally, the regime won legitimacy from the apparent advances of its nation-building project: petrodollars and state investment fueled economic expansion and modernization providing employment and basic goods even while resources were diverted to making Syria a military power able in 1973 and thereafter to confront Israel in defense of the Arab cause. In short, the regime was a formidable institutional obstacle to political Islam, enjoying some legitimacy in which a much wider coalition of social forces than a handful of Alawite generals had some stake.[26]

Nevertheless, a climate in which a new Islamic challenge to the regime was favorably received by many Syrians emerged after 1975. Though enriched by widened economic liberalization, the bourgeoisie was still hostile and the professional classes chafed under the heavy-handed security police. Growing inflation, inequality, and corruption and sectarianism in the regime eroded its traditional middle- and lower-class support as well. The Lebanon intervention in 1976 against Palestinians and Muslims in defense of Christian rightists greatly damaged regime legitimacy among its own supporters and Sunni opinion generally. Amid growing malaise, the Ikhwan launched a campaign of antigovernment sabotage and assassinations, seeking to demoralize the regime, expose its vulnerability, and establish the Ikhwan as a credible alternative. Scores of army and security officers, officials, and regime notables were killed, culminating in a massacre of over fifty military cadets, mostly Alawites. To check the erosion of its base, the regime raised public salaries, launched halfhearted anticorruption campaigns, and promised political freedoms to the middle class, but eschewed the major reforms that might have undercut widening sympathy for the Ikhwan.

In 1980, sensing the regime's isolation, the Ikhwan staged a major offensive in Syria's northern cities—virtual urban guerrilla warfare, which, together with massive demonstrations and ᶜulama, merchant, and professional strikes, removed whole quarters from regime control and threatened to balloon into a general uprising. Troops restored order, the regime mobilized its mass organizations "in defense of the revolution," decreeing wage increases and a new land reform, purged the professional associations, and sought in massive neighborhood searches to smash the Ikhwan network. As sabotage and assassinations, including an attempt on the president's life, continued, the security forces met terror with counterterror: prisoners were killed, opponents were assassinated or summarily executed, and assaults on Ikhwan hideouts deteriorated into indiscriminate reprisals as the regime showed the lengths to which it would go and the cost it could exact to preserve itself. But urban unrest only heightened until the showdown at Hama in 1982. There the Ikhwan concentrated its cadres for a stand against government search operations. The ᶜulama called on the city to rise, party officials were executed, and Hama was declared liberated. The regime used massive force against the city—artillery, helicopter gunships, commandos—killing thousands and destroying whole quarters, yet took three weeks to recapture it. In spite of an Ikhwan call for a general rising, the rest of Syria remained quiet and the army held firm. The Ikhwan was decimated and its sympathizers demoralized.[27]

But the return of calm to Syria's cities hardly signifies acceptance of Baᶜth rule. Political Islam is deeply rooted in the suq and the families that carry on its age-old mercantile traditions and in the pervasive religious sensibility nurtured by the ᶜulama—interests too durable, sentiments too diffuse to be eradicated by coercion alone. Nor, having failed to create a viable "socialist" alternative to the capitalist milieu that nourishes these interests or to establish political institutions capable of absorbing broad participatory demands, can the regime win the unchallenged legitimacy needed to deprive Islamic counter-elites of their mass support. But, conversely, the Baᶜth, rooted in the villages and dominating the largest and best-organized institutions in society—army, party, and state—has also proved remarkably durable. The opposition can prevail only by mobilizing a far wider coalition than it has so far been able to build—indeed, one that would pit most of the Sunni majority, including those in the regime's camp, against the numerically inferior Alawites who dominate it. But that means breaking the cross-sectarian elite coalition around al-Assad, destroying party solidarity and military discipline, and unraveling the regime's organized mass base. That seems beyond the present ability of the Islamic movement.

Where political Islam has been most successful, it has fused religious zeal with nationalist revolt against a foreign or foreign-dependent regime (as in pre-1952 Egypt, in Algeria, and in Iran), but the Baᶜth has enough of a nationalist character to largely deprive Syrian Islam of this weapon. Indeed, the Ikhwan's attacks on Syria, the last Arab regime standing against Israel, calls in question the Ikhwan's own nationalism. The Islamic leadership and its program also seem to lack sufficiently broad appeal and credibility to gain wider backing. Unlike political Islam in Iran, it can take little nurture from a rejection of modernity, for in Syria modernization, nationalized and nativized, has advanced devoid of blatant Westernization. The secular left, organized workers, government employees, and the peasantry are likely to be wary of any return of power to merchants and landlords at the expense of the state. The secular middle class and the minorities (who are about a fourth of the population) cannot favor the widened role for the clergy and religious law in public life which an Islamic victory would bring; liberal modernist Islam compatible with the secular state remains dominant among educated Syrians. Thus, the most likely prognosis is indefinite stalemate. Whether the opposition remains quiescent depends to a great extent on the regime's performance. The economic crises the regime is sure to encounter along the uncertain road of modernization may create conditions for renewed activism. Nationalist confrontations, unless they result in total disaster, tend to regenerate the regime's legitimacy, and more of them appear inevitable.[28]

# NOTES

1. R. Stephan Humphreys, "Islam and Political Values in Saudi Arabia, Egypt and Syria," *The Middle East Journal*, Vol. 33 (Winter 1979), pp. 13–15.

2. Nikolas Van Dam, *The Struggle for Power in Syria: Sectarianism, Regionalism and Tribalism in Politics, 1961–1978* (New York: St. Martin's Press, 1979), pp. 15–49.

3. Hanna Batatu, "Syria's Muslim Brethren," *MERIP Reports*, Vol. 12, No. 9 (November-December 1982), p. 14.

4. Umar F. Abd-Allah, *The Islamic Struggle in Syria* (Berkeley, Calif.: Mizan Press, 1983), pp. 116–118.

5. Ibid., pp. 91–99.

6. Ibid., pp. 101–103.

7. Ibid., pp. 103–106.

8. Ibid., pp. 107–128; *Al-Ikhwan al-Muslimin*, Vol. 3 (Al-Maktab al-Ihdad, 1985), pp. 37–48; R. Hrair Dekmejian, *Islam in Revolution* (Syracuse, N.Y.: Syracuse University Press, 1985), pp. 119–123.

9. Judith Perera, "The Shifting Fortunes of Syria's Muslim Brothers," *The Middle East* (May 1983), pp. 25–28.

10. These documents are reproduced in Abd-Allah, pp. 201–267.

11. Interview with Saʿid Hawwa, *Die Welt*, Dec. 23, 1980, p. 5.

12. Perera, p. 28.

13. Hawwa in *Die Welt*, Dec. 23, 1980, p. 5.

14. Batatu, p. 14.

15. Dekmejian, pp. 118–119.

16. Batatu, p. 20.

17. Raymond A. Hinnebusch, "The Islamic Movement in Syria: Sectarian Conflict and Urban Rebellion in an Authoritarian-Populist Regime," in Ali E. Hillal Dessouki,

ed., *Islamic Resurgence in the Arab World* (New York: Praeger, 1982), pp. 153–154; Batatu, p. 18.

18. Hinnebusch, pp. 155–156.

19. Batatu, p. 16.

20. Fred H. Lawson, "Social Basis of the Hama Revolt," *MERIP Reports*, Vol. 12, No. 9 (November-December 1982), pp. 24–27.

21. Raymond A. Hinnebusch, "Political Recruitment and Socialization in Syria: The Case of the Revolutionary Youth Federation," *International Journal of Middle East Studies*, Vol. 11 (1980), pp. 151–153.

22. Abd-Allah, pp. 91–92.

23. Itamar Rabinovitch, *Syria under the Baᶜth, 1963–1966* (New York: Halstead Press, 1972), pp. 109–145; Tabitha Petran, *Syria* (London: Ernest Benn, 1972), pp. 175–179, 197–198; A.L. Tibawi, *A Modern History of Syria* (London: Macmillan, 1969), pp. 415–420.

24. John Donahue, "La nouvelle constitution syrienne et ses detracteurs," *Travaux et jours* (April-June 1973); A.H. Kelidar, "Religion and State in Syria," *Asian Affairs*, Vol. 61, Part I (February 1974), pp. 16–22.

25. Alisdair Drysdale, "The Syrian Political Elite, 1966–1976: A Spatial and Social Analysis," *Middle Eastern Studies*, Vol. 17, No. 1 (January 1981), pp. 3–30; Van Dam, pp. 126–129.

26. Raymond A. Hinnebusch, "Syria under the Baᶜth: State Formation in a Fragmented Society," *Arab Studies Quarterly*, Vol. 4, No. 3 (Summer 1982), pp. 177–199.

27. Alisdair Drysdale, "The Asad Regime and Its Troubles," *MERIP Reports* Vol. 12, No. 9 (November-December 1982), pp. 3–11; Itamar Rabinovitch, "The Islamic Wave," *The Washington Quarterly*, Vol. 2, No. 4 (Autumn 1979), pp. 139–143.

28. See Michael Hudson, "The Islamic Factor in Syrian and Iraqi Politics," in James P. Piscatori, ed., *Islam in the Political Process* (Cambridge: Cambridge University Press, 1983), pp. 73–95, for an insightful argument on the strengths and weaknesses of political Islam in Syria.

# IV

# LEBANON

## Robin Wright

The Islamic revivalist movement in Lebanon has been both intertwined with and separate from the trend throughout the Middle East. Frustration with the failure of foreign ideologies and value systems is the single most important factor behind all revivalist movements. By the early 1970s, disillusionment had set in throughout the region, as political, economic, and social aspirations were not fulfilled by social and political systems adopted from the East or the West.

By rejecting foreign models, the Muslims, however, were not rejecting "modernization" per se, but rather the way it was carried out and the Westernization that was usually synonymous with it. Thus, the movements were prompted by both cultural and political factors. They were a reaction to the Muslims' growing frustrations and reflected their search for indigenous social and political models and solutions to their problems. Since Islam views religion and politics as inseparable, it often offered the most obvious and familiar answers.

Three specific events also contributed to the revivalist movements, both Sunni and Shi'a, in Lebanon and elsewhere: the 1973 Arab-Israeli war, during which—in contrast with the 1967 war—the Arabs fought more in the name of Islam than of pan-Arabism and won; the 1973 oil boycott and the ensuing price rise, which contributed to the Muslims' sense of power and pride by forcing the rest of the world to take the bloc of Islamic countries more seriously; and the 1979 Iranian revolution, which demonstrated that Islam could be a successful idiom of opposition, capable of "overpowering" the vast arsenal of a conventional army. Contrary to popular Western thinking, the Iranian revolution was not the original spark for the revivalist movements throughout the region but the climax of the first stage of an already deeply rooted movement.

### Revivalist Movement in Lebanon

The revivalist movements are far from united. In fact, as Thomas Lippman has correctly suggested, "There is no single worldwide Islamic resurgence, but there has been a series of coincidental upheavals in which Islam is the common expression of political dissent."[1] That applies particularly to Lebanon, where several local events and environmental factors were decisive in the Islamic revival. Although the Muslim revivalists often seemed to have common goals and tactics, different groups sprang up, often for different reasons, in four areas: the capital city of Beirut, Tripoli in the north, the eastern Beqa' Valley, and the south.

The Lebanese civil war, which began in 1975 and has continued for more than a decade, has been partly religious because it has accentuated religious cleavages in an already highly sectarian society. The underlying causes of the Lebanese civil war are still argued by all sides of the conflict. Violent incidents involving Palestinians were sparks that ignited the long-bubbling tension. Lebanon's sectarian-based power structure, however, made increasingly irrelevant by demographic changes, was at least a major cause of conflict.

By 1975, the Lebanese Muslims had come to see the national pact of 1943—an unwritten agreement among political leaders from each major religious group that determined the positions of power in government, the military, the judiciary, the civil service, and intelligence branches in favor of the Maronite Christians—as obsolete in light of the country's new demographic balance.

At independence, the Maronites had constituted the largest of Lebanon's seventeen recognized sects, followed by the Sunni Muslims, the Shiʿas, and the Druze. Lebanon's power structure based on the 1943 pact reflected this demographic balance.

But by 1975 the Muslims had clearly gained numerical majority, and thus they wanted a restructuring of Lebanon's political institutions that would improve their economic and political position. They were also challenging the Maronites' argument that, as the last Christian stronghold in the Middle East, the Christians needed, even deserved, special guarantees to assure they would not be overwhelmed or persecuted by the Muslim majority, as had happened in other Arab states.

Whatever the merits of these arguments, the civil war deepened the Christian-Muslim animosity and led many Lebanese to identify more with their religious groupings than with their state. Thus, nationalism as a focus of identity and loyalty was increasingly replaced by religion. The power of the Muslim clergy also increased, partly because the Muslims' traditional leaders were incapable of either finding or agreeing to solutions to the community's problems.

The issue of "identity" was pivotal throughout the war. As the historic crossroads between East and West, Lebanon had traditionally incorporated the cultures of both. But underneath the veneer of stability, many Christians tended to look at Lebanon as the easternmost point of Western civilization, while Muslims tended to perceive the nation as the western outpost of Eastern culture. In many ways the conflict was in part an attempt to finally define Lebanon's cultural and political allegiance: whether it was to be aligned with Europe or the Arab world.

During thirty years of Christian domination spanning the time between independence and the start of the civil war, Lebanon had increasingly emphasized Western culture. Outwardly, Beirut looked more like a European than a Middle Eastern city. Yet, the Lebanese Muslims found Western culture aggressive and often felt threatened, offended, and angered as they saw their traditional culture being overwhelmed by Westernization. Thus, as their numbers grew, many Muslims demanded cultural recognition as well as more political and economic power.

But both the Christian minority and Western interests in Lebanon failed to recognize this trend or to show respect for the country's rich Islamic traditions. This failure caused a backlash that peaked during the intense eighteen-month U.S. political and military involvement in Lebanon in the aftermath of the 1982 Israeli invasion.

Additional flashpoints for Muslim wrath were the 1978 and 1982 Israeli invasions, both designed to eliminate the perceived threat from Palestinian guns aimed at Israel's northern Galilee. But in both incursions, Lebanese Muslims also fought and died. The often tenuous alliance between Israel and the Maronite-dominated Phalange Party and the Lebanese Forces militia made the Jewish state and the Christian factions the common enemies of Islam in Lebanon and further reinforced the Muslims' anger and their sense of religious identity. The combination of these forces and factors thus created a fertile ground for the spread of revivalist sentiments throughout Lebanon.

## The Sunni Revival

As in the rest of the Middle East, Muslim revivalist groups have traditionally been divided in Lebanon, first along sectarian lines and second, in terms of moderates and militants.

Among the mainstream Sunnis, the Islamic movement emerged partly because of the perception, particularly among lower-class Sunnis, that traditional Sunni political leaders had failed to protect Muslim interests during a decade of conflict. But, as is true in other areas that have experienced a religious resurgence, the main Sunni faction also gained prominence because of the charisma and organization of a single leader. Shaikh Saᶜid Shᶜaban almost single-handedly built the Islamic Unification Movement (IUF), or Tawhid, in Lebanon's northern port city of Tripoli. It became a major faction in the aftermath of the 1982 Israeli invasion and in the absence of a central governing authority.[2]

Shᶜaban and his followers sought to establish an Islamic republic in Lebanon, with the *Shariᶜa* (Allah's law) as its base. During a visit to Beirut in 1984, when he met with other Sunni and Shiᶜa religious figures, he said, "I can see no other solution to the Lebanese crisis than the takeover of Lebanese politics, administration and bureaucracy by Muslims. If the Muslims rule, they will be fair. But if the others rule, they will strangle other sects."[3] And he claimed that it would be easier to create an Islamic republic in Lebanon than in any other Middle East nation.

In 1983, Tawhid announced it would not adhere to the dictates of a non-

Muslim regime or to Syrian influence in the north. The movement gradually formed a state within a state in Tripoli, carrying out trials and public executions of offenders of both civil and Islamic law and fighting pro-Syrian militias. The extent of its influence was evident in May 1985 when Tripoli hairdressers were forced to close down under IUF pressure; four salons had been bombed in a ten-day period because men were styling women's hair. Only after agreement was reached on segregating staff according to clientele were the shops allowed to reopen.

Shᶜaban, often referred to as "the Prince," adopted the same anti-Western attitude as many of the better known Shiᶜa factions. He often warned of impending attacks against U.S. targets in Lebanon and elsewhere. "No one can stand against the Islamic tide," he said in early 1985. "It has begun to knock at the White House door, which reinforces itself with concrete obstacles for fear of Islamic attacks." But there has been little proof that Tawhid has played a major role in any of the anti-Western incidents in Lebanon.

Followers of the shaikh were, however, thought to be behind the abduction of four Soviet diplomats in Beirut in September 1985. The Islamic Liberation Organization, a hitherto unknown group, issued a communique with photographs of the Russians, who had never before been subjected to the kind of reprisals Western envoys had regularly incurred at the hands of Islamic extremists since 1983. They demanded "a halt to the advance on Tripoli and retreat of the heretic forces away from the heroic city. These forces and Syria bear full responsibility for the lives of these men. For we shall execute them all and strike hard." The Islamic Liberation Organization was reportedly indirectly related to Tawhid. Within twenty-four hours of the abductions, one Russian was killed and his body dumped near a Beirut sports stadium.

The kidnappings were provoked by a confrontation in Tripoli. Syrian troops and pro-Syrian militias, including Lebanese communists, had attacked Tripoli in an attempt to wrest control of the city from Tawhid, which had resisted Syrian efforts to resolve both Lebanese national strife and local tension. Syrian reports had labeled Tawhid "narrow-minded" religious zealots and "troublemakers," an indication of Syria's difficulty in dealing with the independent-minded revivalists. The Sunni militants' communique noted that all the attackers' weapons, including T-52 tanks, were of Soviet manufacture, and they demanded that Moscow use its alliance with Syria to pressure it to end the fighting and withdraw its forces.

Yet, despite the abduction of the Russians in Beirut, Shaikh Shᶜaban's appeal through early 1987 was largely limited to Tripoli, with only minor support in the two other Sunni centers, Beirut and Sidon. Many Sunnis were concerned about the shaikh's ties with Tehran, where he was received on visits as a hero. He liked to point out in interviews that the Tawhid movement existed before the 1979 Iranian revolution. But he conceded its dominant influence. "I hope the Iranian revolution will bring the rule of God to all nations, as its leaders promised," he said in 1984.[4]

As a strong advocate of Islamic unity, he also maintained contact with various

Lebanese Shiᶜa clerics and militant leaders. As he noted in 1983, "We refuse to have sects and factions among Muslims. That is why we would like the Iranian revolution to be a non-Shiᶜa revolution. We want it to be an Islamic revolution only. When the revolution proclaims in Iran that it is Qur'anic, Islamic revolution, we should not antagonize it. But if it calls for a Shiᶜa revolution, we shall say: 'Keep within your territory.' "⁵

Relations between the Sunni and Shiᶜa revivalist movements were not closer at least in part because of Shᶜaban's ties to Palestinians and his militia's help and backing of Palestine Liberation Organization (PLO) Chief Yasir ᶜArafat when he made his stand against dissident guerrillas and Syrian forces in Tripoli in 1983. But Shᶜaban also occasionally criticized ᶜArafat's policies and instead advocated fighting Israel under an Islamic banner. "The Palestinian crisis cannot be solved without a unified Islamic position and an army that adopts *jihad* [holy war]. An Islamic society must be prepared to take over incentives in the whole region, and I think that will happen in the near future," the shaikh predicted.⁶

While an alliance between Sunni and Shiᶜa militants would have a major impact on Lebanon's future, it would probably not last long due to rival interpretations of Islamic rule.

## The Shiᶜa Revival

The Shiᶜa have traditionally been underrated in Lebanon. Trod on politically and socially by the mainstream Sunnis and Maronite Christians, the Shiᶜa had been minor players in Lebanese politics after independence. Historically, the leading Shiᶜa politicians were members of a few elite families who displayed little interest in the mass of poor Shiᶜa and, indeed, were among the biggest exploiters of their fellow Shiᶜa through monopolies on farm lands and businesses.

The three Shiᶜa strongholds in Lebanon—in the south, around Bᶜalbak in the eastern Beqa' Valley, and the southern suburbs of West Beirut—have been the poorest regions of the country. Their incomes and their standards of living, education, and social services have generally been the lowest. Sunnis, Maronites, and other sects had openly discriminated against the Shiᶜa. Resentment and bitterness had been increasing for decades among the Shiᶜa—as had their numbers. From the third largest sect in 1943, the Shiᶜa had grown to become, by 1985, by far the largest. And they too wanted recognition of their strength even if this meant undertaking suicide operations to win attention and to avenge perceived injustices.

After the Cairo Agreement of 1969, which allowed the PLO to establish bases in Lebanon, the Shiᶜa also became victims of the Palestinians. The PLO mobilized many of the southerners by providing military training and arms to fight the Israelis. But the alliance quickly soured as guerrillas usurped Shiᶜa lands and as increasing numbers of Shiᶜa died for the Palestinian cause. By the late 1970s, the Shiᶜa often clashed with PLO forces in the south.

Shiᶜa history is also more conducive to Islamic revival because of its emphasis on fighting oppression—by other Muslims or outside influences—through martyrdom. One of the three most revered figures in Shi<sup>c</sup>a Islam is Husain, grandson of the Prophet Muhammad and son of the fourth Muslim Caliph, <sup>c</sup>Ali. (Shi<sup>c</sup>at <sup>c</sup>Ali, as Shi<sup>c</sup>ism was originally known, means "follower of <sup>c</sup>Ali.")

Shortly after the founding of Islam in the seventh century, Husain set out with a small band of followers to defend the right of his family line to lead the growing Islamic empire controlled by the then new Umayyad dynasty, which had thousands of troops. Husain knew he faced almost certain defeat and death, but he deemed it more honorable to die for belief than to live with injustice. With the massacre of his group of seventy-two followers at Karbala, now an Iraqi city, Husain became a symbol of man's struggle against tyranny. His death is reenacted each year by the Shi<sup>c</sup>a community, much as Jesus' crucifixion is commemorated by Christians at Easter. The duty of the Shi<sup>c</sup>a today is to carry on Husain's struggle by resisting or actively challenging oppressors, to the point of losing their lives.[7]

Thus, given the Shi<sup>c</sup>a history and the specific conditions of the Lebanese Shi<sup>c</sup>a, religious revival was both more widespread and more significant among them. Yet despite their common background, the Lebanese Shi<sup>c</sup>a have reacted in different forms to their oppression and frustration.

The largest Shi<sup>c</sup>a group in Lebanon is Amal, whose acronym forms the Arabic word for hope. Amal, the Lebanese Defense Battalions, was launched in the late 1960s as the "Movement of the Disinherited" by Imam Musa as-Sadr, the charismatic cleric who was born and raised in Iran but was of Lebanese descent. That marked a crucial turning point in the emergence of the Shi<sup>c</sup>a crusade because, for the first time, Lebanon's Shi<sup>c</sup>a community was being mobilized. As-Sadr, the son of an ayatullah and born in the Iranian theological center of Qom, was also trying to wrest leadership from the traditional Shi<sup>c</sup>a landlords and representatives in government. In the past, the only groups that had demonstrated serious interest in mobilizing the Shi<sup>c</sup>a were Lebanon's two fledgling communist parties.

In the mid-1970s, as-Sadr took the movement one step further by issuing a call to arms. In a famous speech in B<sup>c</sup>albak he declared, "We do not want sentiments, but action. We are tired of words, feelings, speeches. . . . We want our full rights completely."[8] In the second speech he was bolder: "What does the government expect? What does it expect except rage and revolution? Arms are man's beauty."[9]

The imam, who was invited to Lebanon in the late 1950s by the Shi<sup>c</sup>a community to replace a religious chief who had died, was the first modern Shi<sup>c</sup>a leader to advocate using religion as an idiom of opposition in Lebanon. "This revolution did not die in the sands of Karbala, it flowed into the life stream of the Islamic world and passed from generation to generation, even to our day," he said, adding:

> It is a deposit placed in our hands so that we may profit from it, that we draw out from it as from a source of new reform, a new position, a new movement, a new revolution to repel the darkness, to stop tyranny, and to pulverize evil.

Brothers, line up in the row of your choice: that of tyranny or that of Husain.
I am certain that you will not choose anything but the row of revolution and
martyrdom for the realization of justice and the destruction of tyranny."[10]

Despite his militant words, as-Sadr did not call for an Islamic republic but
rather for equality within a multiconfessional Lebanese state. By the standards
of Shi°a militancy in Lebanon a decade later, he was a moderate.

As-Sadr disappeared in Libya on the last leg of a tour of the Arab world in
1978 when he was seeking political and financial support for the Lebanese
Shi°a. Many Lebanese claim he was imprisoned or killed by the government
of Colonel Mu°ammar al-Qadhafi, charges that have been repeatedly denied
in Libya.

After as-Sadr, Nabih Berri eventually took over Amal. He added a more
serious political tone to a movement that had been predominantly social and
military. Berri, like as-Sadr, hoped that a peaceful formula could be found to
address the grievances of the Shi°a community and to promote sectarian coexistence through reforms in Lebanon's political system.

## The 1982 Israeli Invasion and U.S. Intervention

Israel's June–August 1982 invasion and subsequent three-year occupation
served as the flashpoint for the second major turning point in Lebanon's Islamic
revival. This sparked a radicalization and a growing schism among the Shi°a,
who took the heaviest casualties and the worst property devastation when the
Israelis rolled through southern Lebanon.

U.S. intervention during this period also triggered further growth of Islamic
militancy. The revival, which until this time had not demonstrated the kind of
anti-Western attitudes that were a hallmark in Iran, became hostile to the West,
most notably the U.S., only in part because of Washington's ties with Israel.
Separate American "offenses" against Lebanese Muslims were at least equal in
terms of impact.

Amal witnessed a major rift as well as the birth of several rivals during this
period; Berri's moderation and his secular orientation began to cost him control
of Amal. The first challenge came from Husain Musawi, one of Berri's chief
lieutenants, who broke away in a dispute over Berri's reluctance to fight Israel
and because of the Amal chief's willingness to go along with U.S. mediation
efforts. Musawi and his followers moved from Beirut to B°albak, where he
formed Islamic Amal, one of the main extremist factions.

The break was to underline a key development in the Shi°a movement: the
divergence of views among the generations. Berri symbolized the first generation, the older Shi°a who remembered the days of coexistence between
Christians and Muslims, leftists and rightists. Their identity was Lebanese first,
then Shi°a. Berri wanted to restore confessional equilibrium. But the younger

generation, which had grown up during the civil war and knew nothing but bloodshed and bitter sectarian rivalry, was far more militant.

As a former prime minister lamented in an interview at the time, "Yes, all Lebanese now want justice. The problem is, for them, justice now means revenge." Many young Shiᶜas wanted justice—or revenge—in the name of their slain brothers or aunts or cousins before they were prepared to consider or accept genuine national reconciliation.

Because of the polarization, Berri at least twice almost lost control of Amal. Coincidental outbreaks of fighting, which diverted attention from internal political problems, helped him retain his leverage. But an increasing number of young Shiᶜa developed dual loyalties, to Amal and to Hizbullah, the extremist Party of God. Indeed, many Amal members—"members" is used in the loosest sense—began to openly consider themselves "hizbullahi," and they said they wanted Lebanon ultimately to have an Islamic government.

The divergence of views on goals and tactics within Amal was most evident during the three-year Israeli occupation of south Lebanon, when Amal branches were largely cut off from headquarters in Beirut. While many, maybe even most, of the southern Lebanese Shiᶜa originally welcomed the Israelis because the invasion "liberated" them from Palestinian domination, the Shiᶜa grew to resent, then rebel against, the long-term Israeli presence and the Israeli attempts to convert them into surrogate agents.

The subsequent confrontations—which first peaked during an Israeli raid on ᶜAshura ceremonies in Nabatiya in 1983 and grew almost weekly as the Shiᶜa launched major attacks and the Israelis employed an "iron fist" policy—served to further polarize the southern Shiᶜa over the next two years. Islam became the chief idiom of opposition, and martyrdom in the name of the independence and dignity of the faith became an honor. The religious slogans normally reserved for the annual ᶜAshura celebrations honoring Husain's martyrdom thirteen centuries ago were put up permanently in the southern towns and villages.[11]

Although Amal still had massive support in 1985 among the southerners, the atmosphere was ripe for exploitation by Hizbullah and other extremist groups. Hizbullah's increasing visibility occasionally led to clashes between the two Shiᶜa factions in the south and in Beirut.

In part to combat the attraction of the militants, Amal groups in three southern regions issued orders in mid-1985 banning alcohol, mixed bathing, and pornographic videos, and said the public day of rest would be switched from Sunday to Friday, the Muslim sabbath. Pamphlets explained that the orders had been issued "on the basis of Islamic duty" to protect the faithful from "falling into the trap of greed, atheism, frivolity and immoralities that run counter to Islamic law and tradition." The orders were subsequently repealed by Berri, but many in the south continued to obey them, either by personal choice or out of fear of future pressure from the Party of God.

Berri was also coming under increasing personal pressure, especially among the young, who frequently and rather cynically pointed out that the Amal leader's first wife and children lived in the U.S. and that Berri had a green card that could eventually qualify him for U.S. citizenship.

The change in Berri's public statements reflected that pressure. Shortly after he took over Amal, he said: "We support the Islamic revolution in Iran, but not on sectarian grounds. And we do not want an Islamic revolution in Lebanon. Our special relations with the Iranian revolution are based more on principle than on sectarian compatibility."[12] And in interviews in 1981, he and his chief aides tried to stress that Amal was a secular movement and not totally Shi ͨa.

In 1983, however, he took a different line: "We look to the Iranian revolution in my opinion as the third great revolution in history. First there was the French, then the Russian, and now the Islamic revolution, which is changing many things in the world. It has renewed the way for Muhammad."[13]

Intervention by the U.S. in 1983 and 1984 served to further challenge the moderates' credibility and to further provoke the militants' wrath. The Reagan administration's orchestration of a pact in May 1983 between Israel and Lebanon to end the Israeli occupation of the south was perceived by the Muslims as helping the Israelis and the Christians. Following that, in September 1983, U.S. warships opened fire on Muslim militias during the Chouf war between Maronite and Druze militias, although the Marine contingent of the multi-national force was not under fire and American lives were not in danger. The U.S. involvement—the first time American troops had gone on the offensive since Vietnam—was in response to an appeal from Lebanon's Maronite-dominated government. Thus the Lebanese Muslims' suspicion of the West, particularly the United States, increased, as did the militants' fervor, acquiring strong anti-Western dimensions. Then, thirty-four days after the warships fired, 241 U.S. Marines died when a Shi ͨa suicide driver drove his bomb-laden truck into the battalion headquarters.

All these events coincided with the growth of Hizbullah, which by 1983 was the most important Shi ͨa group to watch in Lebanon. The name comes from a Qur'anic verse that promises victory for the faithful who join Hizbullah, "the party of God." It first emerged as a major force in the Beqa' valley during the 1982 Israeli invasion. The Iranian Revolutionary Guards, militant local Shi ͨa clerics, and a handful of secondary leaders who had defected from other or-ganizations mobilized thousands of Shi ͨas in the B ͨalbak area. They showed movies and gave lectures at local mosques. They conducted "ideological semi-nars" at schools. And the "Voice of the Iranian Revolution" radio station broad-cast several hours daily of sermons, songs, and interviews.

The Party of God was originally limited to the eastern Beqa', but just over a year later—by August 1983—it had begun establishing a presence in the maze of shanty towns in Beirut's southern suburbs.

After the takeover of West Beirut in February 1984 by Shi ͨa forces—mainly Amal, but also Hizbullah and other smaller organizations—Hizbullah began openly advertising its presence. Several key positions along the Green Line dividing Christian-dominated East Beirut and predominantly Muslim West

Beirut were claimed by Hizbullah gunmen, who at critical moments were particularly active in maintaining tension. Three Party of God offices were set up;
ambulances with Hizbullah's name in big red letters often sped through the
streets; and during ᶜAshura celebrations in October 1984, Hizbullah-sponsored
rallies and speeches drew thousands.

Hizbullah was not organized in any Western sense. It had no official structure
or membership list. It had been strengthened by absorbing many of the other
smaller movements, such as the Lebanese branch of al-Dᶜawa (The Call), Islamic
Amal, and the Husain Suicide Squad. It also reportedly spawned its own cells,
such as the Organization of the Oppressed of the Earth and the Revolutionary
Justice Organization. In effect, it became an umbrella, much as the PLO once
was for eight diverse factions. But the Party of God's following in each area
depended largely on the appeal of individual religious leaders. In Beirut alone,
the activities in the Basta neighborhood differed from the branch in Hay Madhi;
the large number of groups and cells within Hizbullah often acted independently.

Hizbullah was clearly pro-Iranian. Its symbol—painted on walls, fences, and
posters on virtually every major street in West Beirut—was modeled on the
crest of the Iranian Revolutionary Guards; its slogans denouncing both East
and West were virtually identical to the rhetoric in Tehran; members openly
admitted that they had regular contacts with the Iranian Embassy in Damascus.

And its manifesto, issued in February 1985, declared:

> We, the sons of Hizbullah's nation, whose vanguard God has given victory in
> Iran and which has established the nucleus of the world's central Islamic state,
> abide by the orders of a single wise and just command currently embodied in
> the supreme Ayatullah Khumaini. . . . We have opted for religion, freedom and
> dignity over humiliation and constant submission to America and its allies and
> to Zionism and their [Christian] Phalangist allies. We have risen to liberate our
> country, to drive the imperialists and the invaders out of it and to take our fate
> in our own hands."[14]

Hizbullah openly supported the wave of anti-Western attacks beginning in
1983. After the bombing of the U.S. Embassy annex in 1984, the Hay Mahdi
leader said in an interview that he had no idea who specifically had carried out
the attack but that they were "good Muslims who were carrying out the work
of God." The early evidence indicated that Islamic Jihad's callers considered
themselves followers of Hizbullah; since there was no membership list, a "member" of the Party of God was self-designated.

Individual leaders, however, have often been more important than groups
in mobilizing the Shiᶜa, and the most interesting figure in Lebanon in the mid-
1980s was Shaikh Muhammad Husain Fadlallah. His position was often compared by many Shiᶜa to that of Ayatullah Khumaini in 1978, the year before
the Iranian revolution. "He has a mass following but no official organization,"
said an Iraqi Shiᶜa with high-level connections in Tehran.

Various intelligence groups have claimed that Fadlallah at least blessed, and maybe even selected, the two suicide bombers who drove their trucks into the U.S. and French multinational force buildings in October 1983. He has also been suspected as being the head of Hizbullah. However, the evidence indicated quite the contrary. Indeed, Fadlallah often acted to pacify angry tempers in the Shi‹a community. He is clearly a widely respected man with an enormous following drawn from all Shi‹a factions in Lebanon as well as from among Shi‹as elsewhere, notably in Kuwait and Bahrain. His scholary work, particularly a book on Islam and the logic of force, was required reading for young militants.

On several occasions, Fadlallah tried to explain the rationale for violent acts. In an interview in 1984, he said:

Although there are some people who have reservations about these [violent] methods, and I am perhaps one of them, they do not view them as negative. Instead, they see these methods as correct and representing the free will of people who cannot be stopped by any hurdles or obstacles. In the view of Muslims, for instance, this method is considered as a means of confronting America, France and Israel, which, through pressures, are trying to destroy the country and engender a mood of despair."[15]

In early 1985 he added:

We do not support or encourage attacks against purely American cultural institutions or against American individuals doing normal business in the world. But in the meantime, we feel that when America pressures the Islamic world and Muslims, especially through Israel, it is very natural that the war being waged by those opposed to the policy of the American administration take the form of attacks on strictly political U.S. interests. This is very natural. It is a battle between America and all groups which feel that America is usurping their freedom and independence, and exerting pressure on them.[16]

And he said of violence:

I believe that in all cases violence is like a surgical operation that the doctor should only resort to after he has exhausted all other methods. Every person needs to defend himself. If a man needs to use violent ways, he must use it.[17]

Fadlallah has had close encounters with violence, including a series of assassination attempts since 1981. One attempt in 1985 was attributed to a group that had ties to a Lebanese counterterrorism unit being trained by the CIA. The day after the bombing, the funeral procession, led by Fadlallah, passed by the gutted buildings. On the charred shells were massive signs: "Made in the USA." That event elevated the tension between the West and the Lebanese Shi‹a yet another notch, further polarized the young, and made the extremism of Hizbullah more appealing than the moderation of Amal.

Fadlallah has ties to Iran, which he visits at least twice a year. But this relationship, just like Iran's influence in Lebanon, has often been overrated.


## Iran's Role

Iran clearly played a major role in helping promote militant revivalism in Lebanon. The Shi'a communities in the two states have a centuries-old relationship, due to familial and clerical connections as well as business ties. A sense of "allegiance" was in part responsible for the dispatch of a Revolutionary Guards contingent from Iran to Lebanon within a week of the Israeli invasion. The paramilitary forces were clearly a catalyst to such fledgling movements as Musawi's Islamic Amal and the Hizbullah faction in the eastern Beqa' Valley, providing financial support and weapons. Iranian diplomats based in Beirut and Damascus, as well as clerics sent from Tehran, also played crucial support roles.

And dozens of Lebanese Shi'a were invited to various bases in Iran for military training, largely by the Revolutionary Guards. Iran's influence was evident during the Reagan administration's "arms for hostages" swap, when Tehran convinced Islamic Jihad to release three American captives in 1985 and 1986.

But it would be a mistake to say Iran totally controlled the various cells, which had their own agendas. Iran's involvement in Lebanon was mainly to inspire and to promote, or aid and abet, the trend. As Shaikh Fadlallah explained:

> The success of the Islamic revolution in Iran was like a force that exploded deep into the political reality of [Muslim] people, because it proved by practical means that Islam can overthrow a tyrannical regime even if this regime relies for its strength on the great powers, above all America. Islam has proved that it can serve as a new equation to compete and try to replace the other two big equations: capitalism and communism. Muslims all over the world felt that Islam is not only a religion or a relationship between the people and God, but also represents an integrated system for thinking politics and life in general.[18]

Indeed, Iran's Revolutionary Guards were missionaries more than fighters in Lebanon. There is no record of any Iranian unit taking up arms against the Israelis, who had bases less than twenty-five miles away, during the latter's three-year occupation. And Iranians did not drive the trucks into the American embassies or Marine headquarters in 1983–84, or kidnap nine American citizens between 1983 and 1985, or hijack TWA flight 847 in the summer of 1985. The Iranian presence and aid may have facilitated some, maybe even all, of these incidents. But a strong case can be made that the attacks would have happened even without the proximity and support of the Iranians. Islamic militancy, particularly among the Shi'a, had already been firmly rooted in Lebanese soil.

## Conclusion

Islamic revivalism is likely to continue to be a major influence in Lebanon in the near future for both internal and regional reasons. Internally, the political and military developments over the past decade have led to a more pervasive entrenchment of militant Islam in Lebanon than anywhere else in the Arab world. And regionally, the Levant is the site of the second major achievement of contemporary militant Islam in the Middle East.

The major Lebanese militias, including Berri's Amal, signed a Syrian-orchestrated agreement at the end of 1985 to end the decade of civil strife. But there were immediate indications that eventual implementation of the accord would be difficult, if not impossible, for a variety of reasons.

First, the militant groups such as Hizbullah and Tawhid were excluded from the pact. Second, the Israelis retained a residual presence inside Lebanon's southern border, which served as a constant irritant and source of provocation for militants. And third, the Phalange Party of President Amin Jemayel balked at the agreement—which would eventually require that the Maronites give up unspecified powers in order to even the political balance—even though its former military wing, the Lebanese Forces, had been a party to the accord. That served to further infuriate militants and to indicate that the Maronites were not interested in a realistic compromise.

The subsequent escalation in sectarian fighting, accompanied by several rounds of car bombings on both sides of the Green Line that divided the capital, led Syria to once again dispatch troops to Beirut. But Syrian attempts to control or pacify militant Muslim elements, both in the Syrian-controlled Beqa' Valley and in Beirut, were only occasionally successful because of the independent spirit of the movements. The growing power of Lebanon's second generation, among whom the Islamic revival had the greatest appeal and who were the most antagonistic toward traditional or secular leadership, did not bode well for eventual restoration of stability.

Regionally, the first major achievement of militant Islam had been the 1979 Iranian revolution. The second was the campaign by Shiᶜa fundamentalists in southern Lebanon against the Israeli occupation, which, after the Israeli Defense Force (IDF) lost more than 640 troops, led in 1985 to a decision by the government of Prime Minister Shimon Peres to withdraw unilaterally. For the first time Israel voluntarily left occupied territory under pressure from an Arab foe—without a pact on border security or the withdrawal of other foreign troops.

Both moderate and militant Lebanese Shiᶜa generally perceived the pullback as a triumph of Islam. While the Islamic revival had begun to be challenged or to wane in some other parts of the region—partly because of disillusionment with the excesses of the Iranian revolution—the revival received new impetus in Lebanon as a result of the IDF move. The Israelis, however, maintained an estimated one thousand troops along a narrow strip inside the Lebanese border, serving alongside the South Lebanese Army, a Christian-led militia. This provided an ongoing target and rallying point for militants. In early 1986, Katyusha rockets fired from southern Lebanon once again began to fall on the Galilee.

As a result of the Israeli presence and the Phalange Party's resistance to a political settlement, Islamic militancy in Lebanon is likely to have growing appeal for the foreseeable future.

# NOTES

Most of the research on the Islamic revival in Lebanon is based on personal coverage in the Middle East, which I did on a visiting basis from 1973 through 1981, after which I moved to Beirut. See also Robin Wright, *Sacred Rage: The Wrath of Militant Islam* (New York: Simon and Schuster, 1985).

1. Quoted in Edward Mortimer, *Faith and Power: The Politics of Islam* (New York: Vintage Books, 1982), pp. 286–289.
2. Tawhid was the largest and the most influential Sunni movement in Lebanon, but Tripoli also hosted other movements, such as Jundallah and ʿIbad ar-Rahman (Slaves of the Merciful). Their relationship with Tawhid constantly shifted. On some occasions or on some issues the smaller groups came under Tawhid's umbrella; at other moments they acted alone, reflecting the ephemeral and fluid nature of revivalist politics in Lebanon at this stage. Although most active Sunni fundamentalist groups were based in the north, Sidon also had Jamaʿat al-Islami, or Islamic societies, which by 1987 had become one of the three most significant political forces in the port city south of Beirut. This movement grew out of the local mosques but did not gain wider support until after the 1982 Israeli invasion. Several smaller cells were also attached to various mosques or clerics.
3. Maʾan Barazi, "Shʿaban Seeks Islamic Lebanon as He Meets Top Religious Leaders," *Daily Star* (Beirut), Nov. 14, 1984.
4. Ibid.
5. Ihsan Hijazi and Tewfic Mishlawi, eds., "Concern over Growth of Fundamentalist Movements," *The Middle East Reporter*, June 18, 1983, pp. 15–17.
6. Barazi.
7. Mortimer, pp. 188–189.
8. Quoted in Augustus Richard Norton, *Harakat Amal and the Political Mobilization of the Shiʿa of Lebanon* (Austin: University of Texas Press, 1987).
9. Norton.
10. Thomas Sicking and Shereen Khairallah, "The Shiʿa Awakening in Lebanon: A Search for Radical Change in a Traditional Way," in *Vision and Revision in Arab Society*, CEMAM Reports, 1974, Vol. 2, as quoted in Norton.
11. Personal tours through southern Lebanon, 1982–84. See chap. 8, *Sacred Rage*.
12. Lydia George, "Inside the Amal Movement," *Monday Morning Magazine* (Beirut), 1982.
13. David Ottaway, *Washington Post*, Dec. 12, 1983.
14. "Hizbullah Manifesto," read publicly after the first phase of the Israeli withdrawal from Lebanon, on Feb. 16, 1985.
15. *Daily Star* (Beirut), Aug. 18, 1984.
16. Ibid., Jan. 19, 1985.
17. *Monday Morning Magazine* (Beirut), Oct. 15, 1984.
18. Quoted in Hussein Dakroub, "A Moslem Backlash," *Daily Star* (Beirut), Nov. 7, 1985.

# V

# IRAQ

## Chibli Mallat

In 1960, writing about the theological colleges of Najaf, Fadil Jamali observed that the Shi$^c$a holy city "faces the same problems which face the Shi$^c$ah world as a whole. Is the Shi$^c$ah world going to have its religious leaders become modern and responsible? Or is religious life going to remain aloof from public needs, public conditions, and public thinking?"[1] For better or for worse, religious life did not remain aloof. In less than twenty years, the theory and practice of the Shi$^c$a $^c$ulama of Najaf have changed the course of political life throughout the Middle East.

Recent Iranian history has introduced in the area the paragon of a victorious and durable revolution. The specter of a similar revolution has also loomed large over Iraq. In exile in Tehran, the Supreme Assembly of the Islamic Revolution in Iraq (SAIRI) is ready to take over. The SAIRI—its present characteristics, its shortcomings, and its endeavors—and the development of other groups of Iraq's Islamic opposition will be analyzed in part III of this chapter. The SAIRI's ideology, derived from the writings of Muhammad Baqer as-Sadr, along with the evolution of as-Sadr's thought and his struggle against the Iraqi authorities, will be described in part II. These discussions will be preceded by an overview of Iraq's socioreligious setting and its relevance to the rise of Islamic revivalism.

## I. The Legacy of the Iraqi Socioreligious Setting

In retrospect, the 1958 revolution in Iraq seems to have stopped, and even reversed, the process of Shi$^c$a integration in the Iraqi state.

Under the monarchy (1921–58), the sectarian frictions remained below the surface, but Shi$^c$a participation increased steadily. Occasionally an event would rekindle tensions with the ruling Sunnis, as when Shi$^c$a resentment was voiced after the publication of books perceived to be humiliating to the community.[2] But the antagonisms would soon subside, and the process of integration would resume.

Except for the 1958 revolution, the integration of the Shiᶜas might have been successfully completed. Despite their inadequate political representation, their educational and material conditions had greatly improved. For example, "[I]n 1947, only half as many Arab Shiᶜas as Sunnis were in secondary schools; by 1958, that ratio had been improved to three to five."[3] This resulted partly from conscious efforts by the government and the king to balance the state, but the Shiᶜas themselves also seized the tendered opportunities to advance their position.[4] Thus, in the tribal revolt of 1935, "one of the demands of the Shiᶜi ulama was that the law school teach Shiᶜi law."[5]

Economically as well, by the time of the 1958 revolution, Shiᶜa landowners and merchants were at par with their Sunni counterparts.[6] Integration was also reflected politically. In 1947, for the first time, a Shiᶜa, Salih Jabr, was asked to form a new cabinet. And from 1947 to 1958, four of Iraq's eight prime ministers were Shiᶜa.

Despite these gains, the Shiᶜas on the whole continued to suffer more hardships than the Sunnis, for they still constituted the "poorest of the poor."[7] In terms of Iraq's Islamic movement, this bitter poverty explains in part why Islam's revolutionary discourse would become so concerned with economic and social justice, particularly since the misery of the Shiᶜa masses was also the lot of their religious leaders in Najaf and Karbala.[8] It is thus no wonder that the language of militant Islam is so attentive to the plight of the *mustadᶜafin*, the downtrodden. Echoing these griefs is a statement of Ayatullah Ruhullah Khumaini, who lived in Najaf from 1965 to 1978:

> How can we stay silent and idle today, when we see that a band of traitors and usurpers, the agents of foreign powers, have appropriated the wealth and the fruits of labor of hundreds of millions of Muslims. . . ? It is the duty of Islamic scholars and all Muslims to put an end to this system of oppression, and for the sake of the well-being of hundreds of millions of human beings, to overthrow the oppressive governments and form an Islamic government.[9]

The Shiᶜas also remained underrepresented in the army. Since the monarchy, Shiᶜas had been excluded from the officers' corps. A survey of the occupational background of political leaders between 1920 and 1958 shows that, in contrast to ten Kurds and twenty-five Arab Sunnis whose first occupation was in the military, there figured not a single Shiᶜa. But this was tempered by the relatively minor role of the army under the monarchy.[10] By contrast, the role of the military since the revolution has been of prime importance. The composition of the Supreme Committee of the Free Officers who masterminded the 1958 coup foreshadows the tendency that was to prevail in the army: only two officers out of fifteen were Shiᶜas. After the Baᶜth came to power, the army's role remained important, although decreased, and the Shiᶜas continued to be absent from the higher military ranks.

The Shiᶜa underrepresentation in the upper military was destined to become a serious liability for the Muslim militants. The scant sympathy of the army toward the ʿulama has assured the military's cohesion behind the Baʿathist government throughout the war with Iran. Even the rank-and-file soldiers have proved mostly unreceptive to the ʿulama's calls for desertion. Whereas military leadership has been traditionally closed to the Shiʿas, the marginal impact of Najaf and Karbala's leaders on the simple soldiers had more to do with the fact that the draft was not compulsory for religious students. Besides nationalist considerations, this lack of channels to army soldiers created a lasting gap between a sensitive center of power and the religious leaders.[11]

The poor representation of the Shiʿas in the upper military circles, in turn, reflected their estrangement from political power in general, a situation that has steadily worsened since the Baʿthist takeover in 1968.

## The "Sunnization" of Decision-Making

Several causes, some of which, but not all, were fortuitous, explain Shiʿa political underrepresentation under the Baʿth.

One cause relates to the internal history of the party. Internecine bickering, the defeat of ʿAli Saleh as-Saʿdi's faction, and the defection of Fu'ad ar-Rikabi (who was assassinated in 1971) deprived the apparatus of prominent Shiʿa Baʿthis. The dominance of Sunni constituency ensued, and was compounded by the importance of the Sunni-dominated officers' corps. Also, discriminatory treatment of the Shiʿas by the police at the time of the Baʿth underground period generated large-scale disaffection. "Out of the total of the 53 members of the top command that led the [Baʿth] party from November 1963 to 1970, 84.9 percent were Sunni Arabs, 5.7 percent Shiʿi Arabs, and 7.5 percent Kurds, whereas for the period 1952–November 1963, the comparable figures were 38.5; 53.8; and 7.7 percent."[12]

With the Baʿth in power, "Sunnization" intensified. From 1968 to 1977, of the fifteen members of the pivotal Revolutionary Command Council, not one was Shiʿa. The basis of Iraq's power circles had become increasingly narrow with the elevation to the highest positions of people from the village of Takrit, the hometown of both Ahmad Hasan al-Bakr and Saddam Husain.[13]

## II. The ʿUlama and the Rise of the Revivalist Movement

### Communism and the Urgency of Intervention

Since the revolution of 1920, which was ruthlessly suppressed by the British, and the short flare-ups in 1922 and in 1924, the ʿulama, who were the leaders of these revolts, had become cautious. After 1925, they rarely intervened in politics.

The revolution of 1958 brought to the holy cities of Iraq a new atmosphere, which was both challenging and threatening. Before the revolution, the traditional power of the Shiʿa ʿulama had already been put in jeopardy by their inability to respond adequately to the necessities of the intellectual and political scene, even though such an important religious personality as Muhammad Husain Kashif al-Ghata' had played a mediating role in deflating communitarian crises and, on several occasions, had expressed publicly his political ideas.[14] In particular, the Iraqi Communist Party's audience had grown significantly in the 1950s, and the Shi<sup>c</sup>a <sup>c</sup>ulama had become conspicuously worried by the impact of Marxist ideas on their followers.[15]

The concern was understandable. The <sup>c</sup>ulama's moral prestige had waned even in the Shi<sup>c</sup>a cities. The Communist Party was further strengthened after the fall of the monarchy, and in 1959, its following expanded significantly. The rise of the party was so alarming to the religious circles that the supreme Shi<sup>c</sup>a <sup>c</sup>ulama issued *fatwas* (religious edicts or legal opinions) condemning "adherence to the Communist party or lending it support . . . [as] one of the greatest sins."[16]

By issuing the anticommunist fatwas, the <sup>c</sup>ulama broke a silence maintained since the 1920s.[17] But the fatwas were not enough. To combat communism effectively, they needed an alternative ideology, a comprehensive and convincing system that would stand up to Marxism. This task was undertaken by Muhammad Baqer as-Sadr.

### As-Sadr and the Formation of an Islamic System

In terms of the development of as-Sadr's political and economic thought, three periods can be distinguished. In the first period, which coincided with the fall of the monarchy, as-Sadr wrote *Fadak fit-Tarikh* (Fadak in history),[18] *Iqtisaduna* (Our economy),[19] and *Falsafatuna* (Our philosophy).[20] Social concerns are particularly significant in *Falsafatuna* and *Iqtisaduna*, which both date from the immediate aftermath of the revolution, as they were designed to offer an Islamic alternative to the "powerful communist tide."[21] In these works, a system is constructed on the basis of traditional Islamic law and philosophy to solve the "social problem."[22] The gist of the economic model pivots on this urgency:

> When Islam said to the people, forsake injustice and establish equity, it offered concurrently the explication of injustice and equity, and put forth the equitable way for distribution, exchange, and production, as opposed to the unjust way. For instance, Islam mentioned that appropriation of land by force, without reviving it (*Ihya'*), is injustice; that land property (*Ikhtisas*), on the basis of labor and Ihya' is equity; that the gain for capital of a share in the wealth produced is unjust, if based on interest, and just, if based on profit (*Ribh*).[23]

As-Sadr further insists:

> It is true that Islam urges the rich to help their poor brothers and neighbors, but it was not content with the mere urging of the rich and their moral education. It imposed on the State to secure the needy, and to grant them a respectable life.[24]

*Iqtisaduna* introduced a theory which, due to minute details drawn from the jurists of classical Islam, represented a qualitative change in the literature emanating from Najaf. It consists of three parts: (1) In a lengthy critique of Marxism, as-Sadr displays an uncommon familiarity with Marxist literature at the time. (2) As-Sadr then summarily dismisses the capitalist world view, with the usual arguments of the hollowness of the concept of liberty, the domination of the rich over the mechanisms of power, and the alienation of individuals in a society ruled by a materialist marketplace.[25] (3) Finally, as-Sadr discusses the Islamic alternative. He does not pretend to offer a scientific analysis of Islamic economics. For him, the economic system of Islam is not a science but only one aspect of a multifaceted social whole, encompassing matters of education, public policy principles, and so forth. It is a *madhhab*, a doctrine, articulated on a goal. This goal is set by Islamic rules with a specific view of *halal* and *haram*, the permissible and the forbidden. To discover these rules, one should turn not only to the principles laid down in the Qur'an and in the traditions of the Prophet but also to the system of the law as expounded by Islam's great jurists. For these legal rules are the "irradiations of the doctrine onto the outside world, i.e., the doctrine's superstructures."[26]

As-Sadr proceeds to develop a number of concepts central to the Islamic economic system: land ownership, labor, raw materials, risk, usufruct, production and distribution, etc. In this appraisal, despite the criticism of Marxism, he drew on a traditional Marxist terminology, emphasizing the necessity to put an end to a system of exploitation and to implement a social balance that disfavors "the rich." Throughout his career, this concern permeated as-Sadr's writings, but its intensity fluctuated with the changing environment.

In the second period of his literary life, from the late sixties to the midseventies, as-Sadr wrote two major works, *Al-bank al-la Rabawi fil Islam* (The nonusurious bank in Islam)[27] and *Al-Usus al Mantiqiyya lil-Istiqra'* (The logical bases of induction),[28] which are characterized by the absence of the "social question." In both instances, the specificity of the subject matter explains the lack of concern for the poor. But also, the general mood in the area had been altered considerably by the flow of riches after the oil boom.

The third period of as-Sadr's intellectual life corresponds to the advent of the Iranian revolution. The social concern became urgent once again. But unlike the clashes in Iran, those between the ʿulama and the Iraqi state were not chiefly grounded on governmental corruption, unequal distribution of wealth, or the diplomatic attitude toward Israel and the United States. The Sunnization of the governing elite had become the main issue.

## The Response to State "Sunnization"

The way the ʿulama responded to the Sunnization of the Iraqi state illustrates the quandary in which they found themselves. Obviously, they could not demand that the Shiʿa majority rule the country. Such an appeal would have privileged Shiʿism over Islam and threatened Iraq's integrity.

At the same time, the Sunnization was too blatant to be ignored. The result was the orientation of the Islamic discourse in a direction that would indirectly—and perhaps unconsciously—solve the dilemma to the advantage of the Shi‘a ‘ulama. But the whole process was subtle and incremental.

A survey of the literature emanating from Najaf in the period 1960–80, particularly as-Sadr's works, shows how the legal interpreters oscillated between Islamic universalism, i.e., the appeal to an Islamic constituency that transcended communitarian divisions, and Shi‘a particularism, which targeted their traditional religious audience.

In as-Sadr's first and second periods, universalism dominated. *Iqtisaduna,* *Falsafatuna, Al-Bank,* and *Al-Usus*—all the major works—testify to a conscious effort not to limit the audience to the Shi‘as. But after the late sixties, as the Sunnization of the Iraqi state increased, a Shi‘a set of references permeated as-Sadr's discourse.

As-Sadr's concern for universalism did not vanish altogether. So long as the issue of the legitimacy of the contemporary ruler was not directly addressed, the tug-of-war in Najaf between particularism and universalism remained relatively subsumed. But when the politicization of the ‘ulama found repercussions in the streets, first in Iraq, then in Iran, the whole tradition of Shi‘a suffering came to the fore. In Iran, with an absolute Shi‘a majority, this was not a central problem. But in Iraq, it hampered the potential identification of the Sunnis with the ‘ulama's appeal.

As-Sadr perceived the danger. But, although his last known message called for the rise of the whole Iraqi population, "Sunnis and Shi‘is, Arabs and Kurds," to "defend the Islamic flag, whatever its sectarian color,"[29] both the development of the discourse throughout the decade and the nature of the movement that took to the streets remained at odds with the universalism of the last appeal.

From 1969 on, Shi‘a disturbances became recurrent. That year, Mahdi, the son of the important cleric Muhsin al-Hakim, was arrested for alleged contacts with the U.S. Central Intelligence Agency, and Islamic institutions and religious publications were curbed. Demonstrations were held in Najaf, in which slogans were chanted about al-Hakim's leadership and Najaf's preeminence,[30] and upon the death of Muhsin al-Hakim a year later, a large crowd assembled at the funeral. Thereafter, and through the seventies, the tension between the government and the Iraqi Shi‘as continued to mount.

## The Making of a Confrontation

The events and the political language soon acquired a strong Shi‘a flavor. Riots rocked the celebration of ‘Ashura in 1974 and 1977. The occasion, as well as the political slogans shouted during these demonstrations—which elicited a violent reaction by the government—revealed not only dismay at Ba‘thi rule, but also the Shi‘a character of the grievances: "Saddam, remove your hand, this people doesn't want you," and "Saddam, tell Bakr that the souvenir of Husain [the martyred imam of Karbala] cannot be obliterated."[31]

In as-Sadr's writings of this period, Shi<sup>c</sup>a particularism emerged in full force:

> Hence Shi<sup>c</sup>ism (*at-Tashayy<sup>c</sup>u*) cannot be divided, for it would otherwise lose its significance as a proposal to protect after the Prophet the future of the Call, which needs *both* the spiritual *marja<sup>c</sup>iyya* and the social leadership of the Islamic practice.[32]

This appeal to the leadership of the marja<sup>c</sup>iyya was the logical consequence of the growth of two tendencies that had developed in Najaf over twenty years: a significant number of <sup>c</sup>ulama had come to claim a political role for Islam, and the narrowing communitarian base of the government had elicited a particularist reaction in the form of an appeal to the rulership by the Shi<sup>c</sup>a <sup>c</sup>ulama, referred to by as-Sadr as the "marja<sup>c</sup>iyya."[33] By 1978, the cycle of turmoil and repression had brought Iraq to the brink of civil war. The victory of the Islamic revolution in Iran operated then as a major catalyst.

In June 1979, as-Sadr is reported to have expressed his intention to lead a procession to Tehran to salute Khumaini.[34] To prevent as-Sadr from leaving Najaf, the Iraqi authorities placed him under house arrest. But the cycle of violence soon intensified. On April 1, 1980, Tariq <sup>c</sup>Aziz, a high-ranking Ba<sup>c</sup>thist soon to become foreign minister, was wounded in an attempt on his life. On April 5, a bomb was hurled at the commemoration of the April 1 victims. On April 8, as-Sadr and his sister were executed.

### III. The Islamic Opposition in Iraq since the War

#### The Question of the Da<sup>c</sup>wa

Because the Iraqi Revolutionary Command Council issued on April 9, 1980, the day following as-Sadr's execution, a decree sentencing members of the Da<sup>c</sup>wa Party (Hizb ad-Da<sup>c</sup>wa al-Islamiyya, the Party of the Islamic Call) to retroactive death penalties,[35] a question has arisen concerning a possible connection between the militant <sup>c</sup>ulama and the Da<sup>c</sup>wa.

Some accounts ascribed the foundation of the Da<sup>c</sup>wa in the late 1950s to as-Sadr[36] and even to the high marj<sup>c</sup>a Muhsin al-Hakim.[37] Also, the reports of Amnesty International mention the Da<sup>c</sup>wa several times. For instance, according to Amnesty's special inquiries in Iraq, among persons arrested between 1979 and 1982 "whose legal position and whereabouts" were "still not known," eleven were said to be communists and one a member of the Da<sup>c</sup>wa. And in a list of sixteen persons who died under torture while in custody, seven were reported to belong to the Da<sup>c</sup>wa.[38]

According to Muhammad Baqer al-Hakim—the present head of the Supreme Assembly of the Islamic Revolution in Iraq—as tensions mounted in 1979, as-Sadr considered forming a leadership to replace him in the event of a worst-case scenario. Al-Hakim himself and three other <sup>c</sup>ulama were to constitute this leadership. But there seems to have been no connection between this leadership and the so-called Daʿwa. The leadership ʿulama, remarked al-Hakim, "did not have at the time any organizational tie to a group or a movement."[39] Indeed, contrary to the prevailing view, the Islamic opposition developed largely outside the frame of "political parties" such as the Daʿwa, which, if it ever was important, rapidly dwindled into insignificance. In reality, the ʿulama leadership had other means to channel its dissent.

### The Structure of the Shiʿa Tradition

In theory, there are in the Shiʿa world two categories of persons: the *mujtahid*, who exercises *ijtihad* (legal ruling) and the *muqallid*. To become a mujtahid, one ought to be proficient in all the fields of *fiqh* (law), or at least in one of these fields. The muqallid is the layman, who is devoid of such a knowledge, and who must therefore practice *taqlid*; he or she is bound to follow the mujtahid's decree.

The rules on religious allegiance (taqlid) and the way it functions in the Shiʿa world shed an important light on the relations between the militant *ʿulama* and the "rank-and-file" activists, and indicate how the process of hierarchization occurs outside the formal system of a political party. Hence the relevance of the questions addressed by the police to the demonstrators arrested in 1977, who were not asked whether they belonged to the Daʿwa but whom they followed (*Man tuqallid*, literally, Whom do you practice taqlid with?), and what their relation to as-Sadr was.[40]

But the phenomenon of taqlid and the hierarchization that ensues have long existed. The question is how they were grafted onto the revivalist movement.

Theoretically, since taqlid is compulsory, the whole Shiʿa population should have been enlisted in the movement, as long as the great mujtahids were in agreement over a specific policy. But the ʿulama had long been divided, particularly over the issue of their interventionism—or neutralism—in politics.

In Iraq, since the early 1960s, a sharp debate had taken root in Najaf. As-Sadr had started to contribute articles to *Al-Adwa'*, an Islamic journal published in the aftermath of the 1958 revolution. Muhammad Husain Fadlallah, the important Lebanese ʿalim, who lived then in Najaf, reminisces that as-Sadr

> wrote the editorials of the journal under the headline "Our message" [*Risalatuna*] until the fifth issue. He then stopped writing because of the harsh pressures that some of the powerful centers of the *hauza ʿilmiyya* [the circle of ʿulama] exerted to move him away from the direction which was imposing itself on the Muslim scene, as an organized political Islamic method.[41]

Indeed, "a bitter struggle between conservatives and reformists was taking place inside the hauza."[42] Whereas the "conservatives" were refusing to carry out any antigovernmental activity, the "reformists," represented by as-Sadr, were trying to channel activism through the established hauza.

As-Sadr lost that round, and the nonpolitical branch of the ʿulama imposed the traditional reserve. But the militant faction was increasingly strengthened by the Sunnization-Takritization of the Iraqi government. When the Iranian ᶜulama triumphed in Tehran, their militant counterparts in Iraq came to the fore.

Nonetheless, the split in Najaf remained and was complicated by the emergence of a third faction. The ᶜulama who live in Tehrani exile are the direct heirs of as-Sadr. The ᶜulama who follow Abul-Qasem al-Khu'i, the old ᶜalim who has always refused to intervene in politics, were caught up by events. Although they initially disagreed with as-Sadr and Khumaini, they could not acquiesce to the execution of their fellow ᶜulama, and Khu'i is reported to have been under house arrest since 1980. The third faction of the clergy has taken sides with the Baᶜth. Most prominent in the group is ᶜAli Kashif al-Ghata, who is the scion of an important family of Najafi ᶜulama.

Though surprising, the position of ᶜAli and the other pro-Baᶜth ᶜulama is to some extent understandable. When, in the organizational efforts of 1978–79, as-Sadr used the channels offered to him by the clerical structure and sent dozens of emissaries to represent him in all the cities of Shiᶜa Iraq, these envoys created heavy resentment among the local ᶜulama, whose position they abruptly undermined. The situation was sharply aggravated by a fatwa forbidding laymen from praying behind an imam who had not received official clearance from Najaf.[43] No doubt ᶜAli and several others were among the aggrieved and thus were ready to be enlisted by the Baᶜth.

## Repression and Kowtowing

By 1979, controlling Najaf at any cost had become the first priority of the government. But the Baᶜth was careful to avoid irremediably alienating the Shiᶜas.

More money was devoted to the adornment of the shrines and to the Shiᶜa ᶜulama who were ready to support the government;[44] the hitherto ignored Shiᶜa occasions were acknowledged and celebrated;[45] emphasis was put in everyday language on religious formulae; political leaders claimed to identify with Shiᶜa figures;[46] and Shiᶜism, and, more generally, Islam, were heeded as an important component of Iraqi history and culture. Measures were also taken to expand the communitarian basis of the government. Several Shiᶜas were co-opted into the Regional Command, in which, for the first time in 1982, Shiᶜas formed a majority.[47] In 1980, a National Assembly was elected and was reported to include over 40 percent Shiᶜas.[48] There were new elections in 1984; in both assemblies, the speakers chosen to preside were Shiᶜas close to Saddam Husain.[49]

Meanwhile, the war against the militant ᶜulama proceeded unabated. The number of victims is unknown, but according to one source in the opposition, five thousand people were killed in the repression.[50] In 1983, 130 members of the Hakim family were arrested, and six persons, including three of Muhammad Baqer al-Hakim's brothers, were executed.[51]

A comprehensive array of laws was passed to keep Najaf and Karbala in line. The mujtahids, like their nonpolitical Sunni counterparts, were put on the payroll of the government.[52] In 1981, an edict "gave the Ministry of Endowments and Religious Affairs the authority to promulgate laws and regulations governing places of worship, appointment of clergy, religious literature, and participation in religious councils and meetings."[53]

The Iraqi Nationality Law was given strict application and was coupled with measures designed to encourage the departure of undesired elements perceived to have an Iranian connection. This policy resulted in the exile of several thousand Iraqis as well as Persian residents of Iraq, who formed an important, and highly politicized, community in Tehran.

## The Iraqi Exiles in Tehran

How numerous are these Iraqi exiles? Figures vary, ranging between a few tens of thousands to several hundred thousand.[54] One analyst estimates the number of Iraqis in Iran at 350,000.[55] In 1985, among the conditions set by the Iranian authorities to stop the war was the repatriation of 200,000 Iraqi exiles.[56] Whatever the exact figure, the Iraqis of Tehran staff a considerable number of social, political, and military organizations and represent a major element in the regional equation.

The striking characteristic of the groups in Tehran that constitute the Islamic opposition of Iraq is their diversity and apparent fissipariousness, despite their common ideological outlook and essential goals—to bring down Saddam Husain and the Ba'th and to establish an Iraqi Islamic republic closely linked to Tehran.[57]

These groups organize and participate in political meetings, common prayers, social and cultural gatherings, military training, educational sessions, etc. But their diversity also betrays a lack of unity and coordination.

Around Muhammad Baqer al-Hakim and Mahmud al-Hashimi, who are respectively its head and its spokesman, the Supreme Assembly of the Islamic Revolution in Iraq is by far the most important organization. It receives the official backing of the Iranian authorities. Khumaini himself regularly meets with al-Hashimi and al-Hakim.[58] The SAIRI's military offshoot, "the mobilization forces," is active on the front and is entrusted with control of "liberated" Iraqi territory, such as the area of Hajj Omran, seen as the nucleus of the future Islamic republic. The SAIRI also sponsors a number of associations and groups, such as the Institution of the Martyr as-Sadr, the Center for Contemporary Islamic Studies, and several feminist organizations linked to the memory of as-Sadr's sister.

Ideological, social, and cultural activities find expression in a flurry of newspapers and journals. Among the newspapers, the most important are *al-Jihad*, published since 1980; *Liwa' as-Sadr* (The Battalion of as-Sadr); *Ash-Shahid* (The Martyr); *Rah-e Inqilab* (The Way of the Revolution), published in Persian; and *Kayhan al-ʿArabi*. These newspapers come out once or twice a week. Periodicals are varied, with some sophisticated articles on a wide range of subjects. The best known are *Dirasat wa Buhuth* (Studies and Investigations), *Al-Adwa'* (Lights),[59] *Sorush*, and *At-Tawhid*, the last two also published in English and Persian.

Less important than the group of al-Hashimi and al-Hakim but perhaps more efficient on the internal scene is the Organization of Islamic Action, which claimed, in 1985, the responsibility for most of the sabotage actions against Iraqi institutions inside and outside Iraq. *Al-ᶜAmal al-Islami* (Islamic Action) is the organ of this group, which is headed by Hadi and Muhammad Taqi al-Mudarrisi, brothers who were already active in Karbala in the early seventies.[60] The Mudarrisis do not enjoy the same support given the SAIRI by the Iranian leaders, and the disunity between the two groups stems from a number of differences: the Karbala'i origins of the Mudarrisis, their somewhat rash language and action, and perhaps most importantly, the fact that they do not belong to the Shiᶜa clerical hierarchy. This last trait is also indicative of a significant problem faced by the SAIRI.

## The ᶜUlama and the Leadership of the Opposition

After the death of as-Sadr, a problem of succession arose.[61] At first, a group called the Council of Ulama for the Islamic Revolution in Iraq claimed to fill the gap but did not receive Khumaini's recognition. When he refused to receive them, their legitimacy was terminated. Then the Islamic Revolutionary Army for the Liberation of Iraq was constituted, but the problem of the political leadership remained unsolved. A third organizational attempt, the Group of the Fighting ᶜUlama in Iraq, also failed. However, the guidelines of this group formed a blueprint later adopted by the SAIRI. Meanwhile, a fourth short-lived group, the Bureau of the Islamic Revolution in Iraq, was constituted. This bureau comprised two sections: (1) executive units, devoted to military activities, and (2) an advisory committee, which would act as the political body. But there was disagreement over the membership in the committee. Should the members be solely ᶜulama, or should the committee be also open to nonclerical personalities? After protracted negotiations in Ahwaz, the former formula was adopted, and the SAIRI was born. It was officially announced by al-Hakim on November 17, 1982.

That, despite the urgency of the situation, the Iraqi groups were so slow at forming a common front indicates the depth of their dissensions. The major stumbling block, besides the absence of a charismatic figure, derives from the exclusive clerical nature of the Islamic movement's leadership and the ensuing challenge emanating from the personalities who did not belong to the early Najaf circles. As spelled out by al-Hakim,

There were two formulas. The first was that the group of ᶜulama itself constitute the advisory council [to head the political branch]. . . . The second was that the advisory council be formed by Muslim personalities *without regard to whether they were* ᶜ*ulama.*[62]

The original declaration of intent of the SAIRI echoes this quandary but solves it to the advantage of the ᶜulama: the council is said to represent all the Iraqis, "Sunnis and Shiᶜas, Arabs, Kurds and Turkmen," so that "they govern themselves." It "works with all the forces determined . . . to overthrow Saddam and institute the rule of Islam."[63] Behind the appeal to all the Islamic forces, however, the leadership of the ᶜulama was asserted. Paragraph 6 states: "The line of the ᶜulama is the main line which governs the action of the council, in which the presence of the ᶜulama manifests a real existence from the numerical point of view, and in terms of their influence."[64]

## Conclusion

If refraining from organizing through a traditional party was initially useful to the Islamic opposition because it prevented police infiltration, the lack of a structured organization soon became a serious impediment to the ᶜulama's fight. When as-Sadr was killed, the momentum that his charisma had generated was rapidly lost.

The absence of as-Sadr was detrimental both in terms of organizational capacities and in terms of the nature of the ideological future of the Islamic movements. As-Sadr's activities spanned a period of over twenty years, and his writings propelled his leadership onto the Iraqi scene. But at present, neither al-Hakim nor al-Hashimi is strong enough to claim unquestionably his succession. Nothing in their published works comes close to *Iqtisaduna* and *Falsafatuna* or even to the pamphlets of as-Sadr's last years. This lack of charisma and of established scholarship has negatively affected their leadership in the SAIRI and partly explains the reluctance of several groups in the Islamic opposition to fall in line, despite the personal support that Ayatullah Khumaini, the erstwhile guest of al-Hakim's father, bestows on the SAIRI.

But more important, in the long run, than the organizational deficiencies resulting from a shaky leadership is the particularist bent that events have taken after as-Sadr's death. Because of as-Sadr's innovative talents and notwithstanding the Shiᶜa character of some of his writings, his sensitivities would have allowed him to transcend the sectarian pitfalls of Iraqi politics and perhaps even the Arab-Kurdish divisions. The present leadership is incapable of such dynamism, whatever its open claims to the contrary. The SAIRI's calls for the unity of all Iraqis against the government are rightly met with disbelief. For in practice, nothing shows the ability of the SAIRI to offer a program for both Sunnis and Shiᶜas, let alone a platform that caters to the ethnic problems.

The Islamic opposition of Iraq dislikes being perceived as exclusively Shiᶜa. But it has shown little inclination to slough its particularism. In the history of modern Iraq, there have been signs, although coy and sparse, of religious opposition that emanated from some Sunni sectors. In the fifties and the sixties, a small group of Muslim Brothers (Ikhwan) was present on the Iraqi scene. They left little trace because they were discredited by the failure of their fellows in Egypt and Syria, and they seem to have been tainted all along by suspicions of foreign attachments. Much more significant than the Ikhwan was the assassination by the Baᶜth, in the early seventies, of Shaikh ᶜAbd al-ᶜAziz al-Badri, a Sunni religious figure of Baghdad. This case remained isolated, and there is no sign of any broader Sunni revivalist movement in modern Iraq. Nonetheless, the SAIRI leadership could have capitalized on the symbol of al-Badri by trying to co-opt some Sunnis into the visible leadership of their organization.

More significantly, the absence on the Iraqi scene of a Sunni movement was rooted in geographic-political constraints related to Iraq's position in the area. The problems that would have faced such a movement are almost insurmountable. Because of the scale of internal repression, a purely internal structure cannot be established. A safe base in a country territorially contiguous to Iraq is therefore indispensable. But not a single neighboring country is amenable to hosting such a movement. The governments of Jordan, Saudi Arabia, and Kuwait have sided more or less openly with Saddam Husain. Any opposition to him from their soil is ruled out. Turkish and Syrian territories are also sealed to revivalist movements. In the case of Turkey, the official ideology is at odds with political Islam, and in Syria, despite the hatred of the Syrian Baᶜth for its southern sister-party, the government has enough problems with its own Sunni revivalist movements to keep it from wanting to open the door to such Iraqi activists.

There remains Iran. Partly because of the SAIRI shortcomings and mainly because the war has closed the border to guerrilla-style incursions, a Sunni movement has not emerged in Tehran. The Shiᶜa character of the Tehran-based Islamic movement is accentuated by the narrowness of the SAIRI program.

Despite attempts to present an Islamic image that transcended Shiᶜism, the weight of the traditional structure of the marjaᶜiyya and the vicious circle of an increasingly Sunni government and an increasingly Shiᶜa opposition have resulted in the Shiᶜa ᶜulama calling for the establishment of an Islamic state whose leadership they claimed exclusively for themselves. In the process, the Sunnis of Iraq were alienated because they never had a clerical structure that was independent from the state. But the effect was the same for any group that did not care for the institutionalized rule of the Shiᶜa religious leaders.

The fragmentation of the opposition was partly due to the difficulty of agreeing on the institutional system for Iraq if Saddam Husain were to fall. But the main reason could be that the Iraqi ᶜulama themselves did not care to broaden their base, in the hope that an Iranian victory would bring them to power without the burden of a debt to eventual partners. So far, in view of the fact that the Iraqi Islamic opposition does not seem to have been militarily efficient, either on the front or inside Iraq, the narrow-based policy of as-Sadr's successors appears to be a dangerous gambit, for it implies a total reliance on the strategic superiority of the Iranian army.

## NOTES

The author wishes to express gratitude and appreciation to Professor Richard Dekmejian and Dr. Cecilia Storr for their help, and to the School of Law at the University
of California at Berkeley for its hospitality during the preparation of this chapter.

1. Fadil Jamali, "The Theological Colleges of Najaf," *The Muslim World*, Vol. 50
(January 1960), p. 22.

2. In 1927, Zakaria Nsuly published a book on the Umayyads, which was deemed
derogatory to ᶜAli Ibn Abi-Taleb, the first imam of the Shiᶜas. In 1933, *Al-Uruba fil-
Mizan* (Arabism on balance), written by ᶜAbd ar-Razzaq al-Hisan, who was believed to
have been encouraged by government circles, suggested that the Shiᶜas were more loyal
to Persia than to Iraq. In both cases, tension mounted rapidly but was quickly deflected
by symbolic governmental measures. See V.V., "Demostrazioni di studenti e crisi min-
isteriale," *Oriente Moderno*, Vol. 7 (1927), pp. 88–89, and C. Nallino, "Recentissime
pubblicazioni di polemica politico-religiosa musulmana nell' Iraq," in *Raccolta di Scritti
Editi e Inediti*, Vol. 3 (Rome: Istituto per l'Oriente, 1941), pp. 214–220.

3. Phebe Marr, *The Modern History of Iraq* (Boulder, Colo.: Westview Press, 1985),
p. 145.

4. See the episode related in Sate' al-Husri, *Mudhakkirati fil-'Iraq (1921–1927)* (My
memoirs in Iraq), Vol. 1 (Beirut: Taliᶜa, 1967), p. 408.

5. Donald Reid, *Lawyers and Politics in the Arab World 1880–1960* (Chicago: Bib-
liotheca Islamica, 1981), p. 334.

6. See Hanna Batatu, *The Old Social Classes and the Revolutionary Movements of
Iraq* (Princeton, N.J.: Princeton University Press, 1978), pp. 271–273 (on merchants),
pp. 58–62 (on landowners).

7. Ibid., p. 49.

8. For the meager allowances of the ᶜulama, see Jamali, "Colleges," p. 17. For a
description of Najaf, see also ᶜAbdallah an-Nafisi, *Dawr ash-Shiᶜa fi Tatawwur al-ᶜIraq
al-Hadith* (The role of the Shiᶜas in the development of modern Iraq) (Beirut: An-Nahar,
1973), pp. 47–52.

9. English translation of Khumaini's 1970 conferences in Najaf on Islamic government, in Hamid Algar, ed., *Islam and Revolution* (Berkeley, Calif.: Mizan Press, 1981),
pp. 50–51.

10. According to the survey, the military constituted only a fifth of the prominent
politicians under the monarchy. Marr, *History*, p. 144.

11. The Iraqi Islamic opposition has put the number of desertions at 120,000, while
the government denies any such occurrences. *Foreign Report* (London), May 30, 1985;
*Arabia* (London), August 1985. See also *South*, April 1984. In any case, massive desertion
has so far not occurred.

12. Batatu, *Old Social Classes*, p. 1078.

13. Ibid., pp. 1078–1079, 1086–1093.

14. See Husian Kashif al-Ghata,', *Al-Muthul al-ᶜUlya fil-Islam la fi Bhamdun* (The
supreme values [are] in Islam, not in Bhamdun) (Tehran: The Organization for Islamic
Information, 1983). Originally published in 1954.

15. For an expression of the ᶜulama's dismay, see *Muhawarat al-Imam al-Muslih
Kashif al-Ghata' ash-Shaykh Muhammad al-Husayn ma'a as-Safirayn al-Baritani wal-
Amriki* (Conversations between the reformist imam Shaikh Muhammad Husain Kashif
al-Ghata' and the British and American ambassadors), 4th ed. (Najaf: Haydariyya, 1954),
p. 21.

16. *Al-Fayha'*, mouthpiece of the Islamic party, Apr. 23, 1960, quoted in Batatu, *Old
Social Classes*, p. 954. See also Bernard Vernier, *L'Irak d'aujourd'hui* (Paris: Armand
Colin, 1963), pp. 334–335.

17. They were by the same token opening the way to a bitter rivalry with the com-

munists. The two groups were never able to overcome the chasm, even when they were both pitted, as happened twenty years later, against the Ba°th.

18. *Fadak* was printed the first time in 1955 in Najaf (Muhammad Kazem al-Kubti Press). As-Sadr was then twenty-five.

19. *Iqtisaduna*, new ed. (Beirut: Ta'aruf, 1398/1977). The first edition, in two volumes, was published in the early sixties.

20. *Falsafatuna*, 10th ed. (Beirut: Ta'aruf, 1400/1980). *Falsafatuna* was first published around 1959.

21. Yahya Muhammad, "Nazarat Falsafiyya fi fikr ash-Shahid as-Sadr" (Philosophical glances into the thought of martyr as-Sadr), in *Dirasat wa Buhuth* (Tehran), Vol. 2, No. 6 (1983), p. 173.

22. *Falsafatuna*, pp. 11–53.

23. Muhammad Baqer as-Sadr, *Al-Madrasa al-Islamiyya* (The Islamic school) (Beirut: Zahra', 1973), p. 192. The two texts which constitute the *Madrasa* were written soon after as-Sadr completed *Iqtisaduna*.

24. Ibid., p. 193.

25. As-Sadr, *Iqtisaduna*, pp. 15–212 (on Marxism); pp. 213–254 (on capitalism).

26. *Iqtisaduna*, p. 348.

27. *Al-Bank al-la Rabawi fil-Islam*, 8th ed. (Beirut: Ta'aruf, 1983). Originally published ca. 1969.

28. *Al-Usus al-Mantiqiyya lil-Istiqra'* (Beirut: Ta'aruf, 1972).

29. "Baqir al-Sadr's Last Message on the Unity of the Ummah," in *Issues in the Islamic Movement 1980–1981*, K. Siddiqui, ed. (London: Open Press, 1981), p. 57.

30. "*As-Sayyed Muhsin Qa'iduna, wan-Najaf 'Asimatuna*" (As-Sayyed Muhsin is our leader, and Najaf our capital), quoted in Ahmad al-Kateb, *Tajribat ath-Thawra al-Islamiyya fil-Iraq mundhu 1920 hatta 1980* (The experience of the Islamic revolution in Iraq from 1920 to 1980) (Tehran: Al-Qabas al-Islami, 1981), p. 186.

31. Kateb, *Tajribat*, pp. 233–234. Eight persons were sentenced to death and executed in 1974 and five in 1977. The 1977 rebellions seem to have been particularly violent. See Hanna Batatu, "Iraq's Underground Shi°a Movements: Characteristics, Causes and Prospects," *The Middle East Journal*, Vol. 35, No. 4 (Autumn 1981), p. 588. For the echoes inside the Ba°th and the stiffening of its Sunni character, see Ofra Bengio, "Shi°is and Politics in Ba°thi Iraq," *Middle Eastern Studies* (January 1985).

32. Muhammad Baqer as-Sadr, *Bahth hawlal-Wilaya* (Study on the vice-regency) (Beirut: Ta'aruf, 1397/1977), p. 90 (emphasis added). See also his *Bahth hawlal-Mahdi* (Study on the Mahdi [the awaited Twelfth Imam of the Ithna'ashari Shi°as]), which was published as a separate booklet in Beirut in 1977, and in which a Shi°a political context is also evident.

33. The *marja°iyya* is the clerical structure of the Shi°a world. It consists, in order of decreasing importance, of the *Maraj°i* (plural of *marj°a*, literally, reference), who are also the Ayatullahs (the Arabic word is *Ayat Allah*, literally Sign of God), followed by the *Hujjat al-Islam* (Proofs of Islam), then by the *Thiqat Allah* (Trusts of God). The term *Ayat Allah al-°Uzma* (Supreme Ayatullah) is somewhat redundant. The supremacy of one marj°a can be recognized to this marj°a by his peers, but the exact process is not really defined, particularly in times of trouble.

34. Marr, *History*, p. 237.

35. See the Arabic text of the decree in the appendix to *Dima' al-°ulama fi Tariq al-Jihad* (The blood of the °ulama on the way of struggle) (Tehran: Wala', 1984), hereinafter cited as *Dima'*. I am grateful to Professor Hamid Algar for this reference.

36. "Al-Imam ash-Shahid as-Sayyed Muhammad Baqer as-Sadr" (The martyred Imam Sayyed Muhammad Baqer as-Sadr), in *Tariq al-Haqq* (London), Vol. 2, No. 12 (February 1982), p. 4: "[Sadr] contributed with a group of our great °ulama in constituting the Party of the Islamic Call."

37. On the role of Muhsin al-Hakim, see R. Hrair Dekmejian, *Islam in Revolution* (Syracuse, N.Y.: Syracuse University Press, 1985), p. 218, n.4.

38. But in Amnesty's terminology, a militant Shiᶜa could have been classified, out of ignorance or convenience, as a "member of the Daᶜwa." For the list, see *Report and Recommendations of an Amnesty International Mission to the Government of the Republic of Iraq, 22–28 January 1983, including the government's response and Amnesty International comments*, London, 1983.

39. Musa at-Tamimi, "Qiyadat al-Marjaᶜiyya lith-Thawra al-Islamiyya fil-ᶜIraq" (The marjaᶜiyya's leadership of the Islamic revolution in Iraq), in *Dima'*, p. 99. Hereinafter Tamimi.

40. Ghaleb Hasan Abu-ᶜAmmar, "Ash-Shahid as-Sadr Ra'ed ath-Thawra al-Islamiyya fil-ᶜIraq (Martyr as-Sadr, leader of the Islamic revolution in Iraq) (Tehran: Ministry of Islamic Guidance, 1981), p. 57.

41. Muhammad Husain Fadlallah, "Adwa' 'alal-Adwa' " (Lights on al-Adwa'), *Al-Adwa'* (Tehran), Vol. 2, No. 5 (February 1984), pp. 173–174.

42. Ibid., p. 173.

43. See Tamimi for organizational efforts of as-Sadr, p. 80.

44. A. Dawisha, "Invoking the Spirit of Arabism: Islam in the Foreign Policy of Saddam's Iraq," in Adeed Dawisha, ed., *Islam in Foreign Policy* (Cambridge: Cambridge University Press, 1983), p. 125, notes that between 1974 and 1981, $80 million was spent on the holy places. In 1982 only, $24 million was given to Najaf, and another $24 million to Karbala.

45. The warning of King Faisal was finally heeded. In a famous memorandum of 1933, he had written that "taxes and death are for the Shiᶜas and government positions for the Sunnis. For what belongs to the Shiᶜa? Not even his religious days are observed." Text of the memorandum in ᶜAbd ar-Razzaq al-Hasani, *Tarikh al-Wizarat al Iraqiyya* (History of the Iraqi governments) (Sidon: 'Irfan, 1953), Vol. 3, pp. 288–291.

46. E.g., Saddam Husain in a speech for the anniversary of the Iraqi army, *Ath-Thaqafa* (Baghdad), February–March 1982, p. 35: "O symbol of rectitude, ᶜAli, O symbol of justice, ᶜUmar, and O our grandfather, man of struggle (*jihad*) and principles, al-Husain."

47. Marr, *History*, p. 283.

48. A. Baram, "The June 1980 Elections to the National Assembly in Iraq: An Experiment in Controlled Democracy," *Orient*, Vol. 22, No. 3 (1981), pp. 391–412.

49. First Naim Haddad, then Sa'dun Hammadi.

50. ᶜAbd al-Karim al-Husaini al-Qazwini, "Harb al-Jami'a al-islamiyya fin-Najaf al-Ashraf" (The war of the Islamic university in holy Najaf), *Dirasat wa Buhuth*, Vol. 3, No. 6 (1983), p. 146. The author of as-Sadr's biography puts the number at ten thousand. Abu-ᶜAmmar, *Shahid*, p. 63.

51. See Julie Flint, "Iraq: Struggle to Death," *Middle East International*, July 22, 1983. For a list of ᶜulama eliminated, see "What Is Happening in Iraq?" sponsored by the Islamic Committee for Human Rights in Iraq, *New York Times*, Aug. 17, 1985.

52. U.S. State Department, *Country Reports on Human Rights Practices for 1982* (Washington, D.C., 1983), p. 1152.

53. U.S. State Department, *Country Reports on Human Rights Practices for 1984* (Washington, D.C., 1985), p. 1253.

54. An Iraqi exile in Paris told me in January 1986 that more than one million Iraqis lived outside the country. According to a report cited in *Middle East Economic Digest* (*MEED*), Aug. 10–16, 1985, p. 30, there are two million refugees in Iran, a quarter of whom are Iraqis.

55. R. K. Ramazani, "Iran's Islamic Revolution and the Persian Gulf," *Current History*, Vol. 84, No. 48 (January 1985), p. 7.

56. Foreign Broadcast Information Service (FBIS), *Daily Report: Middle East and Africa* (Washington, D.C.), Mar. 28, 1985.

57. In an Islamic opposition newspaper, more than twenty groups were mentioned, including the SAIRI; the Party of ad-Daᶜwa al-Islamiyya in Iraq; the Movement (Haraka) of the Iraqi Mujahidin; the Group (Jamaᶜat) of the ᶜUlama Mujahidin; the Organization of the Islamic Revolution in the Arab Peninsula; the Group (Rabita) of the Muslim Woman in Iraq; the Envoys of the Najafi Husainiyya in Tehran; the Envoys of the Karbala'i Husainiyya in Tehran; and the Rabita of the Muslim Mujahidat (fem. of mujahidin) in Iraq. *Al-ᶜAmal al Islami* (Tehran), May 19, 1985.

58. For al-Hashimi's meeting with Khumaini, see *Liwa' as-Sadr* (Tehran), May 8, 1985. For al-Hakim's meeting with Khumaini, *Liwa' as-Sadr*, June 12, 1985.

59. Named after the journal published in Najaf in the 1960s.

60. They have published several fiery and superficial pamphlets and booklets. E.g., Hadi al-Mudarrisi, *Hal Nahnu Husayniyyun, aw Kayfa Tusbihu Rafiqan lil-Husain* (Are we Husainis, or how to become a friend of Husain") (Beirut: Imam Rida, 1981); Muhammad Taqi al-Mudarrisi, *Al-Fikr al-Islami, Usuluhu wa Manahijuhu* (Islamic thought, principles and methods), 2d ed. (The Organization of Islamic Action in Iraq, 1981).

61. This paragraph is based mainly on Tamimi's article.

62. *Liwa' as-Sadr*, Apr. 18, 1984, pp. 4–5 (emphasis added).

63. *Muntalaqat wa Ahdaf* (Bases and goals), issued by the SAIRI. Quoted in Tamimi, p. 107.

64. Ibid. The awkwardness in the formulation appears in the Arabic text, and is a further indication of the problems that a sole ᶜulama leadership entails, even for its benefactors.

# VI

# THE WEST BANK AND THE GAZA STRIP

## Emile F. Sahliyeh

In the late 1970s an Islamic political movement, particularly strong among the youth, began to emerge in the West Bank and the Gaza Strip. Its followers believe that Islam, unlike the pan-Arabist and Palestinian nationalist approaches, offers a broad focus for the struggle that is capable of mobilizing the support of the Muslim world. They argue that Islam, if tried, would provide solutions to the problems that confront the Palestinians and the Arabs.

This paper will examine the factors that have led to the rise of the Islamic movement in the West Bank and the Gaza Strip. It will seek answers to the following questions: What are the manifestations of the Islamic movement in the occupied territories? How does it propose to resolve the Palestinian question? What are the attitudes of the followers of the Islamic movement toward the Palestine Liberation Organization, Israel, and the West? How do they view the relationship with the pro-PLO forces in the West Bank and the Gaza Strip? Are the followers of the Islamic movement in the occupied territories united in their political thinking? And finally, what are the future prospects for Islam as a political force in the West Bank and Gaza?

### The Rise of the Islamic Movement

The presence of an Islamic political trend in the West Bank and the Gaza Strip was discernible by the late 1970s. Nor was this the first time that an Islamic movement had emerged in Palestine in modern times. Some of the uprisings between the two world wars protesting British practices and Jewish immigration to Palestine were Islamic in nature but they also had political, economic, and social dimensions. In the 1930s an Islamic uprising was led by Shaikh Iz id-Din al-Qassam of northern Palestine, with followers drawn mostly from rural areas. The aim of al-Qassam's movement was to reawaken the Muslim masses and to lead them in a *jihad*, or holy war, against Great Britain and

Jewish immigration. The movement did not achieve these goals as it came to an end shortly after al-Qassam's death.

In the mid-1940s the Muslim Brotherhood in Egypt sent some of its followers to Palestine to preach its ideas and establish branches of the movement. By the end of 1946, several branches were set up in numerous towns in Palestine, including Jerusalem, Nablus, Tulkarem, Haifa, and Jaffa. In 1949 another branch was established in Hebron and, by the mid-1950s, branches were found in West Bank towns. During the 1948 Arab-Israeli war, the Muslim Brotherhood in Egypt dispatched some volunteers to serve alongside the Arab salvation armies to prevent the establishment of a Jewish state.[1]

In an attempt to avoid any provocation of the Jordanian regime, the Muslim Brotherhood refrained from establishing itself as a political party. In early 1953, the Brotherhood applied to Jordan's Ministry of the Interior to be licensed as an association. The movement's support of the regime and its noninvolvement in political activities were behind the King Husain government's sanctioning of the Brotherhood. As a sign of acceptance of the regime's legitimacy, the leaders of the Brotherhood movement contested the various parliamentary elections in the 1950s and the 1960s.

A new Islamic party, al-Tahrir (Liberation), was launched in 1951 by a Palestinian religious jurist, Ahmad Taqi ad-Din al-Nabhani.[2] The party's program of *inqilabiya*, or the use of military force to overthrow the existing political, economic, and social order, compelled the Jordanian government to declare the party illegal during its rule over the West Bank between 1950 and 1967. Al-Nabhani's request toward the end of 1952 to form a political party was rejected on the grounds that the party's platform contradicted the Jordanian constitution on two main accounts: first, the platform called for the election of a ruler; and second, it asserted that religion rather than nationalism was the foundation for society. As a result, the party had to operate in a clandestine manner. Like the Muslim Brotherhood, the Liberation Party drew support from towns in northern and southern areas of the West Bank.

Between 1948 and 1967 the Islamic political movement was very weak, as the Islamic movement, particularly the Muslim Brotherhood, was suppressed by Naser in Egypt and the Ba‘th Party in Syria. In addition, the political climate in the Arab world in the 1950s and mid-1960s was not conducive to a pan-Islamic movement but was characterized by hostility to the West, anticolonialist sentiments, an assertion of national independence, and the achievement of social justice and economic modernization. During this period the notions of pan-Arabism, socialism, and a commitment to the Palestinian question and the liberation of all of Palestine were the foremost elements of political legitimacy for the Arab regimes. The hostility of both President Naser of Egypt and the Ba‘th Party in Syria (the two rival champions for pan-Arab leadership) to the Muslim Brotherhood discredited the movement in the eyes of the Arab masses. The Muslim Brotherhood's support of the Jordanian monarch further discredited it among West Bank Palestinians.

The 1967 war, which marked the beginning of the demise of the pan-Arabist approach to the Palestinian question, provided the breeding ground for the reemergence of an Islamic movement in the 1970s. The delay in the rise of the Islamic trend in the occupied territories may be attributed to the fact that the political vacuum left after the defeat of the Arab armies was filled by the emergence of the Palestinian resistance movement. The Palestinian commando groups looked to themselves as the true instruments of the liberation of Palestine. This was accompanied by the accelerated growth of Palestinian national consciousness outside the occupied territories and the advent of the PLO as the sole legitimate representative of the Palestinian people. The strength of Palestinian nationalism and the widespread backing of its proponents kept the Islamic movement dormant within the occupied territories. Neither the Muslim Brotherhood nor the Liberation Party enjoyed a large mass following.

By the late 1970s and early 1980s the situation had begun to change. A number of both local and regional conditions encouraged the rise of an Islamic trend, particularly among the youth. First, Arab, Palestinian, and international initiatives to end the Israeli occupation of the West Bank and the Gaza Strip did not bear fruit. Bitter divisions in the Arab world and the split within the ranks of the PLO following the Lebanon war increased the frustration of the Palestinians. Some came to believe that both Arab and Palestinian nationalism, as well as Western, Soviet, and other international approaches to the Palestinian question, were inappropriate to accomplish the task. In their opinion only Islam, and an interpretation of the Arab-Israeli dispute from an Islamic perspective, could provide a solution to the Palestinian question.

Second, the Islamic revolution in Iran in 1979 and the assassination of Egyptian President Anwar Sadat by an Islamic group provided impetus and momentum for the growth of the Islamic trend in the occupied territories. The success of the resistance of the Islamic militia in southern Lebanon against the Israeli army further reinforced the conviction of many Palestinians that Islam is capable of ending Israel's military occupation.

Third, the Islamic movement in the West Bank and the Gaza Strip was also a response to the rise of the Likud Party in Israel with its religious arguments to justify permanent control of the West Bank and the Gaza Strip. Prime Minister Begin and other Likud leaders considered these territories an integral part of the biblical land of Israel and asserted that the Jews had an inalienable right to settle anywhere within it. Such an ideological justification for the control of the territories instigated an Islamic counterreaction among Palestinians. Frequent attacks by Jewish extremists on Islamic holy shrines in Jerusalem and Hebron reinforced these sentiments.

Israel's war against the PLO in 1982 and the accompanying bombardment of Palestinian and Lebanese civilian centers, coupled with American support of Israel's war objectives and the massacres at the Palestinian refugee camps of Sabra and Shatilla, constitute a fourth condition that further fueled Islamic feelings among the Palestinians in the occupied territories. The war was perceived as a joint Judeo-Christian conspiracy against Islam.[3]

Fifth, political developments within the West Bank and the Gaza Strip contributed further to the growth of an Islamic political trend. The Islamic movement emerged as a counterreaction to the increasing influence of the West Bank communists and other Marxist groups. In the late 1970s the local communists were in control of the main youth movements, trade unions, and other mass organizations. In their bid for power, pro-Fatah forces initially aligned themselves with the followers of Islam to defeat the communists and other Marxist groups in the student council elections between 1979 and 1981 at both Bir Zeit and al-Najah universities. Despite the fact that this alliance was tactical in nature, it gave the Islamic trend political credibility and legitimacy.

Moreover, it is possible that the rising Islamic movement in the occupied territories was supported and encouraged by either Israel or Jordan. While there is no tangible evidence to sustain this proposition, the rise of an Islamic movement serves the interests of both states by checking the growing influence of the PLO in the West Bank and the Gaza Strip. In contrast to the restrictive measures that the Israeli government has exercised toward pro-PLO groups, it has been quite tolerant of the rise of the Islamic youth movement and its activities. The growth of an Islamic movement, hostile to the PLO's secular orientation and opposed to the formation of an independent Palestinian state, can hardly be said not to serve Israel's interests and complement its policy of striking against all facets of Palestinian nationalism.

Like Israel, Jordan also has a stake in weakening the influence of the PLO in the occupied territories through the spread of an Islamic trend. By the middle to late 1970s the power base of the pro-Jordanian politicians in the West Bank had eroded. The various associations, institutions, and other mass organizations had become dominated by the pro-PLO groups and the communists. In an attempt to redress this situation, the Jordanian government may have extended political and financial backing to the Islamic activists. It should be pointed out that over the years Jordan has been publicly financing the Department for Islamic Religious Endowments in Jerusalem, which is in charge of the various mosques, properties, and imams (Islamic clergy) in the West Bank and the Gaza Strip, as well as subsidizing existing Islamic colleges. Beginning in the late 1970s, the government has been tolerant of the activities of the Muslim Brotherhood movement in Jordan, and in the 1984 partial parliamentary election, two seats were won by Muslim Brothers. In addition to Jordan's financial support of Islamic institutions, Saudi Arabia has been financing some of the Islamic institutions within the occupied territories, such as the Islamic Center in the Gaza Strip, which houses a number of nurseries and Islamic schools.

And finally, growing literacy among the West Bank-Gaza Strip Palestinians, the availability of Islamic literature, both books and magazines; the establishment of Islamic religious schools and colleges in Jerusalem, Gaza, and Hebron after 1978, and the availability of Islamic bookstores have contributed to the rise of the Islamic political movement in the occupied territories.

## The Manifestations of the Islamic Movement

The Islamic movement has become visible in several guises. It can be observed at three integrated levels within the occupied territories: the individual level, the level of social and educational institutions and associations, and the level of political groupings.

The role of the individual in spreading the Islamic movement has so far been very marginal, confined mainly to the initiatives of students in the religious schools. It is common to find students of the Islamic religious colleges visiting neighboring villages or preaching during Friday prayers of the return to Islam and the glories of the first Islamic state. There has also been an increase in the number of women donning traditional Islamic attire and men wearing beards.

Although the spread of Islam appeared to be more promising among the educational and social institutions by the late seventies than it was at the level of individual initiative, Islamic cultural reawakening through such institutions is of recent origin and is not widespread. A number of nurseries and Islamic elementary and high schools were established at about the same time, and Muslim associations for young men and women in Jerusalem and an Islamic center in Gaza were set up. Of significance was the establishment in 1978 of three *Shariᶜa* colleges teaching Islamic jurisprudence in Jerusalem, Hebron, and Gaza. The three colleges annually produce many educated young Muslims who are replacing the more traditional imams in conducting prayers in the various mosques in the West Bank and the Gaza Strip. The late 1970s also witnessed the formation of *zakat*, or charity, committees in several towns and villages to distribute money for the needy. The growing influence of Islam has also been visible in the increasing availability of religious books and magazines in recently opened Islamic bookstores in several towns, and in eight magazines regularly or occasionally published by various Islamic student blocs or institutions. These are in addition to a large number of Islamic magazines and books that are published elsewhere but are available in the occupied territories.

On the local political scene, followers of the Islamic movement have been attempting to organize themselves and formulate their positions concerning the primary issues and problems that confront the Palestinian people. In their political endeavors the advocates of the Islamic movement have not been original; such endeavors have been an extension of the already existing Islamic trends in the region. In most cases political attitudes correspond with positions expressed by external Islamic groups. Indeed, the various Islamic groups in the occupied territories consider themselves to be an integral part of the larger regionwide Islamic movement.

Politically, the Islamic forces in the occupied territories do not seem to be well developed or well organized. Followers of the Islamic movement do not enjoy an open political apparatus to coordinate Islamic activities and mobilize mass followings. Their most effective political activities have been within the student movement, where they controlled eight of the ten student councils of

the various universities and junior colleges in the West Bank and the Gaza
Strip between 1979 and 1981. The exceptions were Bir Zeit University, where
they represented 30 to 40 percent of the student body, and Bethlehem University, where their presence was limited by the mainly Christian composition
of the school.

## Muslim Groups: Differing Views

Broadly speaking, the Islamic youth movement in the occupied territories
consists of five subgroupings: the Muslim Brotherhood, al-Tahrir Party, the
pro-Khumaini group, the pro-Fatah (mainstream PLO) Muslim group, and al-
Daᶜwa wal-Tabligh. The mission of this latter group has been religious and
educational rather than political. Its activities are limited to spreading Islamic
reawakening and cultural identity rather than being preoccupied with political
activities and achieving political power.

The first group, the Muslim Brotherhood, is convinced that the reform of
the individual is a prerequisite for the transformation of society as a whole.
They further believe that the emancipation of the individual from corruption,
fear, ignorance, and materialism will lead to social reform. Their aim has been
to reconstruct Islamic society and to create an Islamic state. In their opinion,
such an Islamic reawakening can be brought about through peaceful change
and by discouraging the individual from the use of violence or revolutionary
means. The formation of a super-Islamic state would usher in the beginning of
a wave of new Islamic conquests. In addition, the Muslim Brotherhood movement has advocated ending Muslim dependency—of an economic, cultural,
social, or political nature—upon either the Western or the socialist countries.[4]

In contrast to the views of the Muslim Brotherhood, al-Tahrir Party believes
that the restoration of a proper Islamic way of life can only be achieved through
an intellectual and political revolution and the dismantling of old ideas and
corrupt regimes. Such a transformation in society would not be through peaceful
change and the reform of the individual but rather through a military coup by
enlisting the *nusra* (assistance) of the officer corps. According to the founder
of the party, Shaikh Taqi ad-Din al-Nabhani, the aim of taking over the state
militarily would be to rejuvenate Islamic life, culture, and civilization. In his
"Risalat al-Taqatul al-Hizbi," al-Nabhani urged a return to Orthodox Islam and
underlined the need to reconstitute the Islamic state. Most of the support for
al-Tahrir has come from university students in the Jerusalem, Hebron, and
Gaza areas. The party also continues to receive backing among the older and
more experienced members of society. Nevertheless, its influence in the Islamic
political movement in the West Bank and the Gaza Strip remains marginal.

The third faction consists of supporters of the Islamic revolution in Iran. The
followers of this group have expressed great skepticism about the goals and
techniques of the Muslim Brotherhood movement. They underestimate the
differences between Sunni and Shiᶜa Muslims to the extent of suggesting that

the caliphate be bestowed upon Khumaini. They consider the Islamic revolution in Iran as a hope for the Muslim world, symbolizing the first Islamic victory against the West in modern times. Although this faction is not strong in numbers, the militancy of pro-Khumaini groups, their hostility toward Israel, the West, and Arab regimes, and their belief in the efficacy of revolutionary techniques are likely to increase their attraction to the youth.

The fourth faction consists of practicing Muslims who support Fatah. As with the other Islamic political factions, it is difficult to assess accurately the influence of this group. Most of the group's membership is drawn from the traditional Islamic leadership in the occupied territories and professional communities. Its appeal to the youth is very limited.

The pro-Fatah faction argues that the PLO's reluctance to define precisely its attitudes toward the Islamic movement has been due to the organization's being in a phase of national liberation. They believe that in the future the PLO will adopt Islam. In the ongoing struggle for power within the occupied territories between the nationalists and the leftist forces on the one hand and the Muslim Brotherhood on the other, members of this faction have traditionally supported al-Fatah. Their alliance with al-Fatah, however, has weakened their political influence in the Islamic movement at large.

On the whole the Islamic movement has traditionally been concentrated in towns in the northern and southern parts of the West Bank and among the refugees. It has also found appeal among various segments of the population, including landowners, merchants, shopkeepers, and workers. Unlike the movement of the 1950s and 1960s, the recent Islamic movement has been popular among the intelligentsia, including university students and faculty. Many of its advocates are well educated and upwardly mobile; they seek to improve the quality of their lives and move away from "Western moral corruption."

Followers of the Islamic trend have maintained their own clubhouses in some of the major towns in the West Bank and the Gaza Strip, including the Young Men's Muslim Association in Jerusalem and the Islamic Center in Gaza. Advocates of the Islamic trend sponsor lectures and form study groups in mosques to disseminate Islamic values. They also celebrate Islamic holy days and circulate their magazines and books and distribute leaflets and statements expressing their political stands on a wide range of issues. Finally, the mosques have been used frequently as rallying sites for the followers of the Islamic movement to protest Jewish attacks on Muslim holy shrines.

## The Political Positions of the Islamic Movement

The political positions of the Islamic movement in the occupied territories have been shaped in part by those of external groups and in part by unfolding political developments in the West Bank and the Gaza Strip.

To the members of the Islamic movement, both Arab and Palestinian nationalism have failed to resolve the Palestinian question. Nor is this surprising, since the concept of nationalism is alien to the Arab and Islamic cultural tradition; it was borrowed from the West by a small group of mostly Christian intellectuals. The Arab Muslim masses, it is contended, did not contribute to the development of the idea of nationalism; nor did they participate in the rebellion against the Ottoman Empire, but remained committed to the preservation of Islamic unity under the banner of the Ottoman Empire.[5] The members of the Islamic Movement also view secular nationalism as divisive and attribute the Muslim world's divisions to the pervasiveness of nationalism.

Thus, to them the prevailing secularist ideas of the Palestinian and Arab nationalists are unsuited to cope with the religious nature of the struggle with Israel. While Arab nationalism has confined the conflict with the Jewish state to the Arabs, Palestinian nationalism has narrowed it down to the Palestinian people. Likewise, Marxism-Leninism conceives the struggle from a class perspective, limiting it to the working force of the Palestinians, Arabs, and Israelis against the capitalist class in these three societies.

Given nationalism's geographic limitations, the basis of attachment and commitment to the Palestinian question should be neither territorial nor national. In the opinion of members of the Islamic Movement, the Palestinian question should first and foremost be a religious one. Failure to make it an integral part of the larger Islamic movement would be not only tantamount to treason, but would also exclude millions of Muslims from the dispute with Israel. In contrast to nationalism, Islam offers a broader focus and is better equipped to liberate Palestine, as it did during the Crusades. The Muslim revivalists, therefore, demand that secular ideas be replaced by Islamic ideas.[6]

The fact that Israel under the Likud cast its claims to Palestine in religious and ideological arguments provides another significant reason for conducting the struggle with Israel on religious grounds. According to revivalists, Israel's establishment in 1948 symbolized the triumph of evil over justice. They see Israel as an integral part of the "Western offensive" against the domain of Islam to advance Western interests in the region, preserve pro-Western moderate Arab regimes, perpetuate inter-Arab divisions, erode Islamic cultural identity, and estrange the Muslims from their religion. To them, Israel serves as the nucleus for the larger Jewish dream of creating a great state between the Euphrates and the Nile.[7]

From an Islamic perspective, the Arab-Israeli conflict allows no room for compromise. The Muslim revivalists are adamant about not recognizing Israel or dealing with it even with the PLO's authorization. They consider themselves at war with any country or organization that would recognize or accept a territorial compromise with Israel. The confrontation with Israel, it is believed, should be total and comprehensive and fought with all available means. Above all, Islam's unity must be reestablished, since it was the decline of Islam and the collapse of the Ottoman Empire that allowed for the creation of Israel.

These extremist arguments have not yet been translated into tangible policies and actions against the Jewish state. On the contrary, the revivalists have so far avoided confrontation with the Israeli military authorities and have concentrated on disseminating their views and broadening their power base.

## The Islamic Trend and the PLO

The proponents of the Islamic movement in the occupied territories lament the exclusion of Islam from the politics and foreign policy orientation of the PLO. By this exclusion the PLO's leaders leave out millions of Muslims from participating in the jihad to liberate Palestine.[8] The casting of the Palestinian question as essentially an Islamic issue and the call for the replacement of Palestinian nationalism by Islamic ideology sharply conflicted with the PLO's secular orientation and its focus on Palestinian nationalism. Nor is this surprising, since the PLO leadership has no authoritative status in the context of Islam and derives none of its legitimacy from religious authority.

The Muslim revivalists differ with the PLO over its tactics and goals. The Islamic movement has been critical of the PLO's search for a diplomatic solution to the Palestinian question. It has considered the PLO's propensity for a political settlement "a liquidation of the Palestinian question" and a departure from military struggle. The Islamic advocates have also stated that they would oppose the initiation of any dialogue between the Israelis and the Palestinians. The PLO's endorsement of the Arab peace plan of Fez, its initiation of a dialogue with Jordan, and the favorable comments by some of its leaders to the Reagan Initiative drew a negative reaction from the Islamic activists in the West Bank and the Gaza Strip.

The nature of the state to be established in Palestine has been another source of conflict. The Islamic groups have expressed their opposition to the PLO's strategic goal of establishing a secular democratic state in Palestine and its narrower goal of forming a nationalist independent state in the West Bank and the Gaza Strip. While insisting on the elimination of any Israeli presence in Palestine, the followers of the Muslim revivalists have unequivocally demanded an Islamic state that would be governed by Islamic traditions, with the duties and obligations of its citizens, whether Muslim or non-Muslim, determined by Islamic law. Muslim revivalists have stated their resolve to bring about such an Islamic state even if this meant waging a jihad against the PLO.

The revivalist leaders have repeatedly asserted that they harbor no hostile feelings toward the PLO and do not offer themselves as an alternative to it. Yet there is no doubt that the Islamic movement wants to become the true and the only inspiration for the Palestinians. Nevertheless, the PLO's still widespread political legitimacy among the Palestinians, and its history of armed struggle against Israel since the mid-1960s, contrast starkly with the military inaction of the Islamic activists during the same period. Furthermore, the PLO's role in reawakening the Palestinian national consciousness has undermined the revivalists' chances of representing the Palestinian interests. In view of the divergence of the political and ideological orientations of the PLO and the Islamic activists, the Islamic groups in the occupied territories prefer not to address themselves directly to the thorny question of recognizing the PLO as the sole legitimate representative of Palestinian national interests. They have avoided an outright rejection of the PLO, while at the same time abstaining from recognizing its absolute mandate. Such an ambivalent position is intentional. A clear denunciation of the organization would diminish the chances of widening their base of popular support and of disseminating their ideas in the Palestinian community.

The proponents of the Islamic trend have rejected PLO demands that they explicitly express their recognition of the organization. They complain that among all the various PLO factions and other Palestinian groups, the Islamic movement alone has been singled out by this requirement to renew its pledge of allegiance to the PLO. They contend that the 1974 Arab Rabat summit resolution, which designated the PLO as the exclusive mouthpiece of the Palestinians, was endorsed merely in order to constrain Jordan's ambitions to recover the occupied territories and not to extract recognition from the Palestinians themselves. They argue that repeated demands to renew their allegiance to the PLO are not only unacceptable but also undemocratic, reflecting the PLO's intolerance of differing views within the Palestinian community. Finally, these repeated demands for explicit pledges of loyalty betray weakness and political incompetence.

In the past, the PLO's engagement in armed struggle and military operations against Israel had given it the political legitimacy it needed. But as its leadership began to depart from the military option, doubts and questions about the representational character of the PLO surfaced.

In view of the above arguments, the revivalists in the occupied territories granted only a qualified mandate to the PLO. Support of the organization has been made contingent upon the continuation of the jihad against Israel and a commitment to the liberation of all of Palestine. Should the PLO, however, accept a political settlement or agree to make territorial concessions in favor of Israel, its qualified mandate would be revoked.

Thus, it is the secular orientation of the PLO, but most particularly the presence of Marxist-Leninist elements within its ranks, that has been strongly resented by the Islamic groups. The hostility of Islam to Marxist doctrine is unwavering and unequivocal.

The PLO's political legitimacy and the popularity of mainstream Fatah is perhaps one of the main reasons accounting for the reluctance of the Islamic movement to sever all ties to the PLO. The Fatah/Muslim relationship has thus vacillated over the years between cooperation and quarrel. At the time of its inception, leading al-Fatah figures, including ᶜArafat himself, displayed an Islamic orientation. The influence of Islam, however, began to retreat as secular nationalism came to be the official ideology of al-Fatah. Followers of the Islamic movement have repeatedly contended that al-Fatah's leaders have resisted all attempts by the Islamic movement to incorporate Islam into the organization's

political program.[9] The result of this situation has been that the majority of the
Islamic groups have maintained their independence from the PLO, while ac-
knowledging that al-Fatah is different from the PLO's more leftist factions. Al-
Fatah's acceptable image is the reason why occasional temporary alliances with
Islamic groups (particularly the Muslim Brotherhood) have been possible from
time to time to contain the Marxist forces in the West Bank and the Gaza Strip.
Nevertheless, only a small minority of the Islamic followers prefer to work from
within al-Fatah's organization.

This limited rapprochement has often been disturbed by the insistence of
al-Fatah's leaders on excluding Islam from the PLO's doctrine. On their part,
the proponents of Islam have accused al-Fatah of directing a public campaign
against their movement and trying to arrest the growing support for it by
aligning themselves with Marxist elements in the West Bank. In particular,
they were critical of the signing by pro-Fatah groups in January 1982 of a national
unity statement condemning the Muslim Brotherhood, which brought together
all of the anti-Islamic forces within the occupied territories. Al-Fatah also joined
other nationalist forces in forming a national bloc to check the advancement of
the Islamic movement in the student council elections, labor unions, and other
institutions and professional associations.

### Future Prospects of the Islamic Movement

Despite its recent origin, the Islamic youth movement has become one of
the major political forces currently operating on the West Bank-Gaza Strip
political scene. The erosion of Palestinian national unity in the occupied territories, as a result of the divisions within the PLO in the aftermath of the
Lebanon war and the Shiᶜa success aginst Israel, are likely to enhance Islam's
appeal.

Although there is no guarantee that the Islamic route will in the future be
more successful in addressing Palestinian national grievances than pan-Arabism
or Palestinian nationalism, its future success or failure in expanding its base
will depend on both external and internal factors.

Internally, growing dissensions between ᶜArafat's supporters and detractors
over the concept of national unity would help the movement. The other internal
factor would be the ability of Islamic groups to achieve a degree of unity among
themselves. Lack of unity, plus the lack of a central leadership and a political
structure, made different groups go their separate ways.

The movement also needs a well-defined program, and a political strategy
and plan of action. Continued Islamic military inactivity will certainly undermine the movement's political credibility, and will give credence to the PLO's
claim that the movement has been sustained by the Israeli government. Finally,
despite the conservative nature of Palestinian society, the ubiquity of Palestinian nationalism among the majority of the Palestinians irrespective of their
ideological orientation will continue to provide an impediment to a complete

takeover by the Islamic movement of institutions in the occupied territories. Urban political groups in the West Bank and the Gaza Strip remain by and large secular in their orientation. Moreover, the fact that Palestinian society contains both Muslims and Christians may further limit any gains.

Externally, the stalling of Iran's revolution has adversely affected the movement. But the triumph of Lebanon's Shi⁽as has renewed Islam's prestige and appeal.

The inconclusive nature of the various diplomatic efforts to resolve the Palestinian question may convince more Palestinians that secular approaches are incapable of fulfilling Palestinian national aspirations. Israel's tolerance of the movement will also be crucial. Israel's acquiescence is likely to continue so long as the Islamic movement continues to oppose the PLO's secular orientation, Palestinian nationalism, and the formation of a Palestinian state specifically in the West Bank and the Gaza Strip. While the uncompromising attitudes of the Islamic movement toward Israel and its insistence on the formation of an Islamic state in all of Palestine seem to be very threatening to Israel, they remain essentially long-range aspirations. From an Israeli perspective, these Islamic goals do not constitute an immediate threat to its essential motive of permanently retaining the West Bank and the Gaza Strip.

But if the movement were to grow more militant, as is indicated by the growing influence of the pro-Khumaini group, Israel's attitude will no doubt change.

Jordan's role is also important. As noted earlier, Jordan may have an interest in the further growth of the Islamic movement in the West Bank and the Gaza Strip, as Islamic political gains are likely to come at the expense of the PLO, Jordan's long-time rival for control of the occupied territories. The interests of Jordan and the Islamic movement, however, are in an uneasy balance, since the latter seeks to form an Islamic state and traditionally has been opposed to Jordan's pro-Western orientation, secularism, and interest in political accommodation with Israel.

The PLO's ability to overcome its divisions would undermine the revivalists' chances, while its continued disunity would help them.

# NOTES

1. Amnon Cohen, *Political Parties in the West Bank under the Hashemite Regime, 1949–1967* (Ithaca, N.Y.: Cornell University Press, 1980), pp. 144–148.

2. Sadiq Amin, *Al-Da⁽wa al-Islamiyya Farida Shar⁽ia Wadarura Bashariya* (1978), p. 78.

3. Such views were expressed by a number of magazines published by the various groups of the Islamic movement in the West Bank, including *Al-Noor al-Ilahi*, *Al-Tali⁽a al-Islamiyya*, *Al-Sahwah*, *Al-Muntalaq*, and *Al-Nida'*.

4. Fat'hi Yakan, *Mushkilat al-Da⁽wa wal-Da⁽iya* (Mu'assasat al-Risala, 1978), pp.

228–230. See also Saʿid Hawwa, *Al-Madkhal ila al-Daʿwa al-Islamiyya* (1979), pp. 92, 130–40; and Muhammad ʿAli al-Dandawi, *Kubra al-Harakat al-Islamiyya fi al-Aʾser al-Hadith* (Cairo, 1978), pp. 134–148.

5. *Al-Noor al-Ilahi*, October 19, 1982; and July 27, 1982.

6. Al-Dandawi, pp. 20–28, 50–51.

7. "Mustaqbal Qadiyat Filistin wal-dawr al-Murtaja lil-Haraka al-Islamiyya," *Al-Nida'*, No. 6, pp. 48–53, by the Islamic University in Gaza. Similar comments are found in *Al-Nida'*, No. 2, pp. 25–30.

8. ʿAbdu Allah Naser, "Al-Islam wal-Qadiya al-Filstiniya" (Al-Manar, 1982), pp. 61–65.

9. "Munadamat al-Tahrir wal-itijah al-Islami," *Al-Mujtama' al-Islami*, April 1981, pp. 40–44. See also "Al-Islam wal-qadiya al-Filstiniya," *Al-Taliʿa al-Islamiyya*, January 1983, pp. 41–46.

# Part III

## Islamic Revivalism in the Gulf

# VII

# SAUDI ARABIA

## William Ochsenwald

Religion is the basis of Saudi Arabia's society, politics, and national identity.[1] Together with the royal house of Sa°ud and oil wealth, religion molds Saudi values, ideology, and the political system. The Kingdom of Saudi Arabia is itself a two-centuries-old Islamic revivalist and fundamentalist state, faced since 1973 with new abundance and new religiously inspired change in its regional environment.

From Saudi Arabia's historical perspective, revolutionary changes in Iran and the possibility of their repetition in other Muslim states are developments whose importance for the Arabian Peninsula is yet to be determined. More important than revolutionary Islam of the Iranian type is the prospect of gradual secularization encouraged by the Saudi political leadership as part of its drive for economic and social development.

Although religion is a crucial factor in Saudi Arabia, it is not completely independent of other forces. As the other major variables in Saudi Arabia change, to some degree Islam's importance and role will also change. If, for instance, oil revenues keep declining, this will affect conditions in Saudi society and government, and thus often those of the °ulama (religious leaders), the pious believers, those who seek to change the influence of religion in public life, and the morals and practices of the whole country. This could make elite co-opting of dissident °ulama more difficult. Or it might lead the ruling dynasty to rely even more on the °ulama in order to enhance its legitimacy. Similarly, if oil revenues were once again to rise, religious institutions, personnel, and values would be affected. This increase in Saudi wealth might reinforce materialism but it could also lead to a renewed emphasis on religion as a way of preserving traditional values. A truly momentous change in these other factors would greatly alter most of the current positions of the °ulama in Saudi Arabia as well as those of the religious fundamentalist revolutionary opposition.

In actual practice to date, adaptation rather than revolutionary change has marked the alterations in the position of Islam in Saudi Arabia. An example of this is the °ulama's opposition to secularism, exacerbated by the gradual ending of Saudi Arabia's intellectual and physical isolation. As Saudi Arabia has come into closer contact with Western secularism and materialism and as Saudi wealth has increased, changes, albeit small, have taken place in society.

Religion and the religious establishment have helped slow the rate of social change, thus making it more acceptable to the devout. Religion's current position in society may be modified by changes in other aspects of the Saudi state and society. It will, however, in all likelihood continue to remain the basis of internal political legitimacy and social values. The importance of Islam and of Islamic symbols in public life has been intensified in the 1980s. But a victory of revolutionary religious fundamentalist revivalism in Saudi Arabia is unlikely. However, in the long run, the survival of current religious and state institutions will depend on their ability to adapt to external challenges and to domestic state-induced change.

### The Role of Islam in Saudi Arabia

Islam is indigenous and crucial to Saudi Arabia. Makka and Madina are the cities where the faith got its start. The current regime's legitimacy rests upon the Arabian religious experience associated with the religious reformer Muhammad ibn ʿAbd al-Wahhab, dominant in central Arabia since the mid-eighteenth century.

The seizure of the Grand Mosque of Makka on November 20, 1979/1 Muharram 1400 by a group of Muslim militants protesting Saudi Arabia's religious and political conditions raised the issue of Islamic revival in Islam's very birthplace. The attack on the Makkan Haram showed that the Islamic revival was an issue for all Muslim countries, irrespective of the degree of their attachment to Islam. After all, Saudi Arabia was already one of the most devout and religious Islamic nations. If the Saudi government could be accused of lacking religious fervor, then other Muslim states might be liable to more serious challenges.

The 1979 incident implied the existence of fundamental problems involving the relationship between Islam and the state in Saudi Arabia. The problems chiefly hinged on the moral consequences of sudden great wealth. As in the early days of Islam, when Madina was inundated by the spoils from the conquests that established Muslim political power in the Middle East, so once again in the second half of the twentieth century Arabia was gaining immense wealth from abroad, in this case, from oil revenues. An abstemious, austere, and pietistic society suddenly was face-to-face with the values and technology of a comparatively secular West. Saudis moved to the cities, where the wealth and material goods were concentrated, leaving behind the villages, towns, and nomadic tribes' grazing regions. The response of most Saudis, whether urban or tribal, has been to maintain that wealth and Islam, technology and traditional values, economic modernization and old social customs can be made to coexist in their society.

Saudi Arabia has played a remarkably small part in twentieth-century attempts by Muslim countries to adapt and adopt seemingly conflicting Western and Islamic values. As a result, the ᶜulama and the intellectuals in Saudi Arabia have been able to maintain a cohesiveness lacking in countries that have seen a broader participation in the adaptation of Islam to modernity. Saudi fractionalization along theological, political, and intellectual lines has been relatively less widespread than in other Middle Eastern countries.

The creation of a unified nation-state by King ᶜAbd al-ᶜAziz ibn Saᶜud in 1932 and the development of oil extraction on a large scale in the 1950s bore witness to the importance of nationalism and economic development. But in Saudi Arabia, national and economic development rested upon a tacit agreement that the political leadership would not challenge the traditional Islamic beliefs. On the contrary, the Saᶜud dynasty has claimed that Islam is the root of, and the prerequisite to, satisfactory political and economic development. Saudis have argued that an Islamic revival, quite sufficient for the present and future, already happened during the life of Muhammad ibn ᶜAbd al-Wahhab (1703–87). Islamic justice, holy war, and a political leadership that carries out the duties of Muslims are the basis of a legitimate and just political and social order, and they exist in Saudi Arabia. The ᶜulama provide the theology, administration of justice, and raison d'être of the state; in return, the state and dynasty provide the military power, financial support, and political leadership.

The Saudi religious alliance was reestablished in power by ᶜAbd al-ᶜAziz ibn Saᶜud (1879–1953), who defeated the enemies of the faith and the state. Rule subsequently passed to his sons Kings Saᶜud (1953–64), Faisal (1964–75), Khalid (1975–82), and Fahd (1982–present). The monarchs have, from the point of view of the Saudi ᶜulama, upheld morality and justice and supported and supervised the pilgrimage to Makka, although technological innovations sometimes strained relations between the ᶜulama and the king. Saudi Arabia has had no constitution, except insofar as the Qur'an serves as such. The flag of Saudi Arabia graphically and dramatically presents the role of Islam in the state: it contains the Muslim declaration of faith and the crossed swords indicative of military support for Islam. Divergent regions, tribes, and cities have been held together by a common religion and the royal family's policies.

Transfers of political power within the elite have been carried out only after obtaining the consent of the men of religion, especially the descendants of Muhammad ibn ᶜAbd al-Wahhab. That was illustrated when the ᶜulama chose Khalid as king and passed over Prince Muhammad ibn ᶜAbd al-ᶜAziz. In their public statements, Saudi rulers have attributed a prominent political role to Islam. When Khalid ascended the throne, he said, "Islamic law is and will remain our standard, our source of inspiration, and our goal."[2]

In a number of concrete ways Saudi history has shown the mutual dependence of the political elite and the ᶜulama. Usually three or four seats in the Saudi cabinet have been reserved for Muhammad ibn ᶜAbd al-Wahhab's descendants, the family of the shaikh. The Organization for the Enforcing of Good and the Forbidding of Evil has ensured the observance of Islamic morality. Conflict between government and ᶜulama has occasionally erupted over specific issues, as on such questions as slavery, the private showing of movies, and feminine education, but compromises have usually taken place. Every year the kings have vividly shown their commitment to Islam by assisting in the cleaning of the K<sup>c</sup>aba in Makka and in the rituals of the pilgrimage. They thereby have associated themselves with the holiest symbols of Islam, and have done so before an audience consisting not only of Saudis but also of Muslims from around the world.

Saudi identity is defined in the pilgrimage as well as by other religious and dynastic events. The nation-state is based on national identity, but identity is defined often in religious or dynastic rather than in ethnic or shared geographic terms. The name of the country reflects the central role of the Saudi dynasty, and the political elite has largely rejected the notions of pan-Arab nationalism as espoused by Jamal <sup>c</sup>Abd al-Naser or the Ba<sup>c</sup>th Party in favor of a loosely organized pan-Islamic cooperation. Saudi Arabia, it is true, joined the League of Arab States at its inception and has remained a member ever since, but it has opposed the political and economic merger of the Arab states. In response to Arab nationalism, the Saudis have developed close ties with Persian Gulf Arab states and with conservative non-Arab Muslim states. The World Muslim League, which was created in 1962, has been a Saudi instrument and has its headquarters in Makka. Its financing and administration are largely Saudi. Its purpose was said to be to combat the enemies of Islam who were trying to draw Muslims away from their faith and destroy their unity. The kingdom has also been among the chief backers of the several conferences held by Muslim heads of state, foreign ministers, and economic organizations. Among these, the Organization of the Islamic Conference, established in 1972, provided a permanent institution to strengthen Saudi dynastic purposes in the cold war among the Muslim states of the Middle East, as well as to emphasize the leadership of Saudi Arabia, as guardian of the holy places in Makka and Madina, for the whole Muslim world. Through such means Saudi Arabia seeks influence among neighboring states, prestige among the world's Muslims, and leadership of the bloc of Islamic countries.

The chief foreign enemies of Saudi Arabia are defined as such by their religion, or lack thereof. According to textbooks used in Saudi schools, Zionist Jewish Israel, the atheistic Soviet Union, and secular nationalism are all basically one force in opposition to Islamic Saudi Arabia. It is said to be incumbent on Saudis, therefore, to work for Muslim liberation movements, such as the Afghan *mujahidin* (holy warriors), who are fighting against Soviet troops. Saudi Arabia has no formal diplomatic relations with the Soviet Union despite the USSR's considerable presence in the Middle East. The Islamic Republic of Iran is also opposed by the Saudi state, which fears an excess of Islamic zeal combined with the antimonarchical sentiments in Tehran. Iran, in turn, has fostered Shi<sup>c</sup>a revolutionary organizations in the Gulf generally and in Saudi Arabia specifically, and has encouraged disturbances during the pilgrimage.[3]

Opposition to both the Soviet Union and Israel has led to a basic contradiction in Saudi foreign policy, for the United States has been the chief opponent of Soviet expansionism, and yet has also been the chief ally of Israel. The close military, diplomatic, and economic ties between the Saudis and the Americans, based on a convergence of interests on a global level, have so far prevailed over Saudi dislike of American pro-Israeli policies.

Saudi domestic administration has been even more heavily influenced by religion and religious values than has foreign policy. Three areas where religious values and government policy particularly intersect have been in the administration of justice, education, and the pilgrimage.

Justice has been occasionally administered directly by the kings in personal adjudication of disputes, but most cases have been decided by religious courts. Following the death of the chief religious judge, who was a member of Muhammad ibn ʿAbd al-Wahhab's family, King Faisal created a Ministry of Justice in 1970. The first minister of justice was a Jidda religious judge, who subsequently played a prominent role in the World Muslim League but who was not a member of Muhammad ibn ʿAbd al-Wahhab's family. King Khalid in 1975 named members of that family to be minister and chief judge. Commercial cases and semijudicial complaints against the government, however, have been beyond the reach of the ʿulama and are dealt with directly by royal nonclergy appointees. Islamic criminal law is credited for the low level of crime in Saudi Arabia as well as the implementation of the Islamic moral code. But indications of increased crime rates in the 1970s, especially against foreigners, do not support such claims. The eroding efficiency of Islamic justice could damage the regime, which considers itself the agent for Islamic justice.[4]

Education has been one of the main emphases in Saudi development. As a result, new colleges and educational institutions have opened and the number of students has dramatically increased. The Ministry of Education and the Ministry of Higher Education stress that the purpose of all education is to inculcate religious values. Competition between Saudi graduates from secular American universities and graduates from Saudi institutions, who have a more religious education, has increased as economic constraints have decreased the number of available government jobs. Most of the sons of prominent princes are educated primarily in secular schools, often abroad. And the number of students in specifically religious career preparation programs has remained very low. At the Islamic University of Madina in 1979–80 there were only about 380 students.[5]

In addition to upholding Islamic justice and spreading education, the Saudis are proud of their part in the Hajj pilgrimage. The pilgrimage has a strong emotional impact on most Muslims who perform it. Thus the Saudis, who host and manage it, gain in prestige and religious legitimacy as a result. Another consequence of the pilgrimage is to make Saudi Islam seem normative to many pilgrims. Internally, the pilgrimage remains the chief social, political, and religious event of the year. Islam thus is an ever-present reality for the government.

## Islamic Militant Revivalism and Saudi Arabia

While Islamic revivalists still disagree over the precise organization of a modern-day Islamic state, they do agree on certain basic principles, most of which are already implemented in Saudi Arabia. For most revivalists, law should be based on the *Shariᶜa* (Allah's law), the Muslim states should cooperate with each other, nationalism should be de-emphasized, the public role of women in society should be limited, non-Muslims should have only a small voice in government, rulers should be pious and act politically on the basis of their piety, unworthy innovations should be eliminated from the faith, and states should be successfully administered so as to be able to reach religious goals. Islam is to provide a basis for a society that will follow neither the West's materialism nor the East's atheism. Only a few of the goals sought by most revivalists— namely, an integrated, religiously dominated educational system that systematically rejects Western values; foreign policies opposed both to the Soviet Union and to the United States; and the reformulation of Islam so as to make it more pertinent to modern life—are lacking in Saudi Arabia.[6] Some revivalists also favor ᶜulama rule of the state, a situation obviously not existing in Saudi Arabia. But in the most profound sense, Islamic revivalism has been successful in Saudi Arabia for two centuries. That leaves little room for militant revolutionary revivalists. Thus, the small secret militant groups that exist in Saudi Arabia are weak and fragmented. The only exception is a small group of Saudi Shiᶜa and Sunnis that is backed by Iran.

The excesses and failures of the Islamic Republic of Iran since 1979 have been sufficient in themselves to discourage imitation; in addition, the link of Khumaini's revolution to Shiᶜa Islam has discouraged the largely Sunni majority in Saudi Arabia from emulation. If Iran should emerge triumphant from its war with Iraq, however, Saudi militant revivalists might take heart and attempt to seize power.

One incident dramatically illustrated the strengths and weaknesses of religious discontent hidden beneath the surface of Saudi stability: the seizure of the Makkan Haram in 1979. Some hundreds of armed men and their families seized the mosque, closed its gates, and broadcast a demand to the worshippers inside it that they recognize one of the rebels' leaders as the expected Mahdi, or deliverer.

The two leaders of the rebels were Juhaiman ibn Muhammad ibn Saif al-ᶜUtaibi and his brother-in-law, Muhammad ibn ᶜAbd Allah al-Qahtani. Juhaiman, the chief organizer, had been a member of the Saudi national guard; some of his theological pamphlets had been printed in Kuwait. Muhammad, a twenty-seven-year-old former theology student at the Islamic University of Madina, was proclaimed the expected Mahdi. Apparently their followers were chiefly members of several Saudi tribes, including Najdi tribes that had been involved in the religious opposition to King ᶜAbd al-ᶜAziz in the 1920s; Saudi theological students; and some Arab immigrant workers. In addition to calling for recognition of Muhammad as the mahdi, they demanded a moral cleansing of the kingdom, denounced widespread corruption and bribery among the royal family, and opposed the presence of alcohol in the country. Since the Qur'an does not recognize the principle of monarchy, they argued, rulership should be based on devotion to Islam and election by Muslim believers, not heredity.

World reaction to the event was hostile. The leaders of most Muslim states sent messages to the Saudi government supporting it. Within Saudi Arabia, however, there were disturbances among the Shiᶜa population concentrated in the eastern oil-producing region on the occasion of the holy mourning day of ᶜAshura. These disturbances were largely a reaction to the revolutionary situation in Iran and to the seizure of the American embassy in Tehran. There was no direct connection between the Shiᶜa and the Mahdists in Makka.

The Saudi ᶜulama issued an opinion authorizing the use of force in the sacred area. Shaikh ᶜAbd al-ᶜAziz ibn Baz, chairman of the Board for Islamic Research of Riyad, condemned the attack as sedition, insurrection, atheist, and a perversion of Islam. Saudi forces gradually retook control of the Haram, captured the militants, and freed the hostages. During the bitter fighting Muhammad was killed, along with dozens of his followers. Over sixty of those captured, including Juhaiman, were subsequently executed in different cities.[7]

The immediate repercussions of the attack were minimal. By December 8 the Haram had been partially repaired. Several military and civil leaders were removed or resigned, including the director of public security. Vague promises of a constitution were repeated. Development aid to areas where Shiᶜas lived was increased, and stricter measures were undertaken to enforce the segregation of men and women and to encourage the performance of prayer. The most important lessons of the events were the government's surprising lack of prior information and its unwillingness to act earlier. The regime was unwilling to make any major changes in policies or institutions as a result of the incident.

### Co-opting Revivalist Islam

The monarchy had successfully co-opted Islamic revivalists even before 1979 and, by doing so, had greatly lessened the likelihood of drastic change inspired by Islamic revolutionaries. Saudi Arabia has assisted Islamic revivalists abroad, including giving aid to insurgents in such places as Eritrea; has sponsored Islamic organizations; and has donated money to build mosques, print Qur'ans, encourage proselytization, and so forth.[8]

The government has ensured a stricter application of Islamic law as favored by the revivalists. That has been crucial, since it has maintained the religious-political consensus upon which the regime's legitimacy rests.[9]

Two issues have been crucial to relations between the pious and the Saudi rulers: corruption among the royal family, an issue that involves the concept of equal justice for all regardless of rank, and the extension of political participation to a broader segment of society by means of the idea of *shura*, or consultation.

Flagrant abuses of the law, personal immorality, and diversion of public funds by some of the ruling elite are offensive to many whose respect for the ruling dynasty goes back to the relative egalitarianism of pre–oil boom days. Yet as long as royal rule has rested upon consensus among the chief factions of the House of Saud, it has been difficult to ensure equal justice under the law for the royal princes. A greater degree of royal absolutism may well emerge in response to this need.

A consultative council, it has been argued, especially abroad, would provide a channel for the expression of the views of the ᶜulama—they would probably have a certain number of seats reserved for them—as well as the new middle and upper classes of businessmen and technocrats. If this much-discussed and often-promised council should emerge, it would raise the issue of the ᶜulama's veto power over legislation or ordinances they might consider offensive to the Shariᶜa. A basic law or constitution has been drafted and has been submitted to the king, who has delayed any serious consideration of it by the royal family, but the text of the proposal is as yet not known. The basic law, which presumably embodies the concept of shura, was drafted by an eight-man committee formed in March 1980 and chaired by Prince Nayif, minister of the interior. Its draft has been examined and debated by at least some ᶜulama.

If such a council is not created, the regime in its present form is unlikely to last very far into the future.[10] If the religious sensibilities of the ᶜulama are not taken into account in the structure of such a basic law and council, as on the question of ultimate sovereignty belonging to God, one of the key supporting groups behind the monarchy, the ᶜulama, will be offended, alienated, and weakened.

### The ᶜUlama and Opposition to the Regime

The Saudi ᶜulama have not been systematically and thoroughly studied, and relatively little is known about their career patterns, their intellectual and theological education, or their opinions concerning current issues. General treatments of Saudi Arabian history merely emphasize the earlier obscurantism of the ᶜulama and their rigid opposition to new scientific and technological changes as they affected society. Neither have the ᶜulama's theological training schools and the newly established theological universities been closely examined. More information is also needed on the role of foreign ᶜulama who teach in Saudi Arabia, the intellectual abilities of new recruits into the Saudi ᶜulama, their interaction with the new middle class, and their general views on basic issues, such as the congruence of monarchy and Islam or the question of egalitarianism in Islam.

Despite this lack of information, a tentative analysis of the ᶜulama may still be made. In the last few years, the students studying secular subjects abroad and returning to Saudi Arabia have met competition from an increasing number of graduates from Saudi schools. That has not been true in the ᶜulama's case, since most of them are still educated in the kingdom. Those ᶜulama who are descendants of Muhammad ibn ᶜAbd al-Wahhab have been tutored by their families and have not attended any university. Some of the younger Saudi ᶜulama, however, have been exposed to currents of thought popular among foreign ᶜulama who are now teaching in Saudi Arabia. The latter may be followers of the Muslim Brotherhood in Syria or the new Islamic Egyptian revivalists. Ironically, the Saudi regime has indirectly encouraged the spread of such ideas by sponsoring international religious conferences promoting the pilgrimage, encouraging pan-Islamic groups, and allowing foreign ᶜulama to teach in Saudi schools.

The social background of the ᶜulama is mostly urban, and many have followed their fathers' careers. The ᶜulama work in courts as judges and are appointed by the government, which also selects the members of the Dar al-Ifta (Institute for the Issuance of Religious and Legal Opinions), founded in 1953, and the Council of the Grand ᶜUlama, founded in 1971. ᶜUlama also serve as mosque functionaries, teachers and school administrators, members of public morality committees, and combinations of these occupations. Since they are paid public employees, they have become bureaucratized and subsumed within the state structure. Some, especially in the Hijaz, however, choose to remain outside government employment and support themselves by gifts and charitable endowments; these sources of income are less available for Najdis. As some of Muhammad ibn ᶜAbd al-Wahhab's Najdi descendants have chosen secular careers, their collective importance within the ᶜulama has relatively decreased.[11]

Since the 1950s more and more of the ablest young Saudis have chosen secular careers. Thus, a real decline in the efficacy of the senior ᶜulama will be felt in the 1990s, when those who made career choices in the 1960s will reach the top ranks.

The new ᶜulama will increasingly interact with members of Saudi society who have received educations substantially different from their own, especially professionals and military officers. In the past, conflict between religion and secularism in the Middle East has led to considerable social friction, and the secularly oriented new officers and professionals have generally won. The social composition of the Iranian revolutionaries of 1978–79 and the memberships of Egypt's militant revivalist groups have shown that religious fundamentalists are drawn from many different social groups. The officers and professionals themselves may be militant revivalists.

A 1980 poll of about a thousand Saudi high school and university students showed that they have preserved their religiously inspired values. The students said they evaluated persons primarily on the basis of their moral characters rather than on career achievements; they also valued the family very highly.[12] Values inculcated in Saudi youth by their textbooks are inspired by religion. Tribalism is criticized on the ground that it is contrary to Islam, while nationalism of the European type is viewed as narrow and fanatical. In Saudi textbooks,

Saudi Arabia is the center of the Islamic world, and its political and social system should be imitated by others.

Some university students in Saudi Arabia, as in other parts of the Middle East such as Egypt, have been turning to new Islamic revivalist groups. Since the Makka incident of 1979, loosely organized associations that are dedicated to puritanical reform, and are anti-American in foreign policy, have been formed in Saudi universities, particularly in the scientific faculties. While their numbers are not yet large, their clothing and habits provide visible and striking proof of dissent from the Saudi regime's educational values.[13]

The views of educated adults on revivalist Islam are largely unknown, since discussion circles, literary clubs, prayer or meditation groups, and professional networks remain unstudied.

By the nature of their professions, journalists and university intellectuals, the presumed rivals of the ʿulama for leadership in ideas and values, can publicly present their views, although radical opinions cannot be expressed without fear of governmental retribution. In the publicly available media, the journalists' and academics' views on religious topics are, mostly, similar to those of the religious and political establishment. The state's co-optation of these groups and of the ʿulama has been, so far, successful. In many cases academics have chosen dissertation and research topics that are far removed from present concerns. At the same time, some internal criticism of intellectual isolation and corruption among the ʿulama themselves as well as in the government has been permitted. In general, there has been a lack of direct relevance of much of the intellectual work to the current changing Saudi situation.[14]

The ʿulama, in conjunction with the political elite, have been flexible in adapting Islamic law and social practices to changed circumstances, particularly those arising from new technological and commercial situations.[15] An example was the flight of Prince Sultan ibn Salman on the United States space shuttle in 1985 and the accompanying theological debate over the direction of prayer down toward the earth and Makka below. The ʿulama supported the prince's participation.

The relative flexibility of the ʿulama on such questions has eased the way for gradual change and has kept the ʿulama from becoming as irrelevant as the Sunni ʿulama in some other Arab states. Nevertheless, technically trained Saudis and intellectuals often ignore the contribution of the ʿulama to society, while many ʿulama are unable to communicate effectively with Western-trained intellectuals, as pointed out by Sulaiman ʿAbd al-ʿAziz al-Sulaim, minister of commerce since 1975.[16]

The appointment of ʿulama to high posts in government has involved the ʿulama in crucial government decisions. Their involvement has raised the key issue of whether or not they have represented Saudi society before the government on questions of equal justice and corruption. This question, which was so important for Iran in the 1970s, has political implications for Saudi Arabia as well. As the ʿulama have gradually ceased to exercise their option to criticize the government, they have lost part of their function. Thus others, who have been willing to criticize corruption, have emerged to challenge the moral position of the monarchy and the ᶜulama.

Another challenge to the present Saudi system has perhaps begun to appear from within the ranks of the ᶜulama, as opinions on the theological uniqueness of Wahhabi Islam have changed among the younger ᶜulama. Increasing contacts with ᶜulama from abroad and an education that has begun to emphasize those factors that unite Muslims rather than those that divide them have gradually contributed to narrowing the gaps between Saudi and other Muslims. As the conviction that Wahhabi Islam and the Saudi dynasty are uniquely entitled to rule lessens, treatment of non-Wahhabi Muslims and particularly Shiᶜas will improve, but legitimacy of the present regime will decrease. On the other hand, the Saudi government, insofar as it battles world atheism, led by the Soviet Union, and struggles against Jewish Zionism, as seen in Israel, may recapture religious legitimacy among revivalist Muslims.

If Islamic revival means an increase in the power, prosperity, and effectiveness of the state, then certainly in the 1980s Saudi Arabia has undergone an Islamic revival. But if Islamic revival means an intensification of the role of Islam in public life, then little has happened in this area, because Saudi public life was already suffused with Islam.

Difficult problems in the adaptation of a puritanical and moralistic society to great affluence have been dealt with by Saudi ᶜulama and the regime, but not in any very new or profound fashion. The elite's failure to preserve old moral values and the spreading of corruption were among the reasons for the attack on the Makkan Haram in 1979. But militant revivalists remain a small opposition. It is difficult to see how the role of Islam in public life can be significantly strengthened in Saudi Arabia, unless an egalitarianism, similar to that of Libya or Iran, becomes predominant among revivalists and popular among groups unhappy with a contracting economy.

The Saudi alliance of religion and dynasty continues despite some secularization. The generational transfer of religious values and religiously based social and political views seems to have been achieved. Both leftist and militant revivalist oppositions are fragmented and weak. But if the economy worsens, or the influence of foreign elements grows, the strength of the Wahhabi-Saudi religious-political synthesis may be severely tested.

# NOTES

1. For an expanded treatment of the introductory material in this chapter, see William Ochsenwald, "Saudi Arabia and the Islamic Revival," *International Journal of Middle East Studies*, Vol. 13, No. 3 (August 1981), pp. 271–286.

2. Jean-Louis Soulié and Lucien Champenois, *Le Royaume d'Arabie Saoudite* (Paris: Michel, 1978), p. 229.

3. For an insightful review of the motivations behind Saudi foreign policy, see James

114 The Politics of Islamic Revivalism

Piscatori, "Islamic Values and National Interest: The Foreign Policy of Saudi Arabia," in Adeed Dawisha, ed., *Islam in Foreign Policy* (Cambridge: Cambridge University Press, 1983), pp. 33–53; Olivier Carré, "Idéologie et pouvoir en Arabie Saoudite et dans son entourage," in Paul Bonnenfant, ed., *La peninsule arabique d'aujourd'hui* (Paris: CNRS, 1982), Vol. 1, pp. 235–236.

4. Carré, "Idéologie," pp. 240–241; Ayman al-Yassini, *Religion and State in the Kingdom of Saudi Arabia* (Boulder, Colo.: Westview Press, 1985), pp. 115–117.

5. Al-Yassini, *Religion and State*, p. 112.

6. John L. Esposito, *Islam and Politics* (Syracuse, N.Y.: Syracuse University Press, 1984), pp. 152–155 and 224. For an establishment Saudi's views on Islamic reform, see Ahmad Zaki Yamani, *Islamic Law and Contemporary Issues* (Jidda: Saudi Publishing House, 1388 Hijri).

7. For the Makkan Haram incident in general, see Ochsenwald, "Saudi Arabia," pp. 271, 276–277; William Quandt, *Saudi Arabia in the 1980s: Foreign Policy, Security, and Oil* (Washington, D.C.: Brookings Institution, 1981), pp. 94–96; *Al-Madinah* (Jidda), 16 and 17 Muharram 1400; *Journal Muslim World League* 7 (January 1980), p. 10; R. Hrair Dekmejian, *Islam in Revolution* (Syracuse, N.Y.: Syracuse University Press, 1985), pp. 141–144; and Joseph Kechichian, "The Role of the Ulama in the Politics of an Islamic State: The Case of Saudi Arabia," *International Journal of Middle East Studies*, Vol. 18, No. 1 (February 1986), pp. 58–68. Alexander Bligh, "The Saudi Religious Elite (Ulama) as Participant in the Political System of the Kingdom," *International Journal of Middle East Studies*, Vol. 17, No. 1 (February 1985), pp. 47–48, argues that the ʿulama were indecisive and neutral. That does not seem to have been the case. Although clearly the royal family was supreme, the ʿulama have remained far stronger than Bligh acknowledges.

8. Piscatori, "Islamic Values," pp. 46–49; ʿAbdullah M. Sindi, "King Faisal and Pan-Islamism," in Willard A. Beling, ed., *King Faisal and the Modernization of Saudi Arabia* (Boulder, Colo.: Westview Press, 1980), pp. 184–201; Aharon Layish, "ʿUlama and Politics in Saudi Arabia," in Metin Heper and Raphael Israeli, eds., *Islam and Politics in the Modern Middle East* (London: Croom Helm, 1984), p. 40. For an exaggerated view of this process, see Daniel Pipes, *In the Path of God: Islam and Political Power* (New York: Basic Books, 1983), pp. 303–321.

9. For an earlier example of a similar religious-political synthesis in Arabia, though not under Saudi auspices, see William Ochsenwald, *Religion, Society, and the State in Arabia: The Hijaz under Ottoman Control, 1840–1908* (Columbus: Ohio State University Press, 1984), esp. pp. 220–226.

10. Esposito, *Islam and Politics*, p. 111; Mark Heller and Nadav Safran, "The New Middle Class and Regime Stability in Saudi Arabia," *Harvard Middle East Papers, Modern Series* 3 (1985), pp. 14–16. For a review of prior promises of a constitution and council, see Layish, "ʿUlama and Politics in Saudi Arabia," pp. 43–44.

11. Layish, "ʿUlama and Politics in Saudi Arabia," pp. 29–32; al-Yassini, *Religion and State*, pp. 48, 72, 79.

12. Monte Palmer et al., "The Behavioral Correlates of Rentier Economies: A Case Study of Saudi Arabia," in Robert Stookey, ed., *The Arabian Peninsula: Zone of Ferment* (Stanford, Calif.: Hoover Institution, 1984), pp. 17–36.

13. Dekmejian, *Islam in Revolution*, p. 147.

14. Ochsenwald, "Saudi Arabia and the Islamic Revival," pp. 280–284. Also see, for example, the background data given for the Saudi contributors to Khurshid Ahmad and Zafar Ishaq Ansari, eds., *Islamic Perspectives: Studies in Honour of Mawlana Sayyid Abul Ala Mawdudi* (Jidda: Saudi Publishing House, 1979). However, the contribution of Ismail Ibrahim Nawwab to that volume, "Reflections on the Roles and Educational Desiderata of the Islamist," pp. 43–55, has a great deal of pertinence to the present situation in Saudi Arabia, though it is couched in somewhat general language.

15. For an excellent discussion of the question of ʿulama flexibility, see James Pis-

catori, "Ideological Politics in Saudi Arabia," in James P. Piscatori, ed., *Islam in the* Political Process (Cambridge: Cambridge University Press, 1983), pp. 62–63; James Piscatori, "The Roles of Islam in Saudi Arabia's Political Development," in John Esposito, ed., *Islam and Development: Religion and Sociopolitical Change* (Syracuse, N.Y.: Syracuse University Press, 1980), p. 132.

16. See Sulaiman ᶜAbd al-ᶜAziz al-Sulaim, "Constitutional and Judicial Organization in the Kingdom of Saudi Arabia," Ph.D. diss., Johns Hopkins University, 1970, as cited in al-Yassini, *Religion and State*, p. 99.

# VIII

# KUWAIT AND BAHRAIN

## *Joseph Kostiner*

The current wave of Islamic revival has been characterized by two main trends. One has been the revival of early (or fundamental) Islamic concepts and ideas aimed at providing a renewed Islamic value system for what is perceived by the revivalists to be a confused and malaise-plagued society. The second trend has been radical-political, as seen in the activities of militant groups.[1] In the Gulf countries (notably in Kuwait and Bahrain, which are the focus of this paper), both these trends surfaced during the 1960s and 1970s. During this period, revivalist activities were sporadic and did not entail significant political consequences. Iran's Islamic revolution, however, drastically intensified revivalist trends in the Gulf.

The interplay of two factors in general determines the character and intensity of Islamic revivalist movements: the "political culture" or value systems prevalent in a society and the salient political and socioeconomic characteristics of a society. These include such factors as the disparities often caused by rapid modernization within a traditional society. In the Gulf region, prior to the Iranian revolution, neither the local political culture nor the existing socioeconomic conditions were conducive to the emergence of revivalist trends. The traditional political culture of the Gulf region is essentially based on values derived from early local states which in fact were "tribal confederacies." The foundations of such states were ad hoc arrangements of power-sharing between tribal groups, mainly nomads, and a dynastic ruler, based in a town. The tribes fulfilled the military functions and the ruler, aided by the urban population, fulfilled their commercial and religious needs.[2] Under these conditions, the dominant societal values were those of survival and commerce. The Gulf's coastal communities took advantage of their favorable geographic location and developed an interest in maritime commerce. As Ernest Gallner shows in his discussion of Muslim tribal societies, Islam provided the common idiom and moral code of such a society, functioning as its representative "high culture." However, Islam as such—and the °*ulama* (religious leaders) as its representatives—neither governed the political body of tribal states nor interfered with or altered these states' inherent socioeconomic structures.[3]

Even in exceptional cases, this general rule applied in reality. For example, the Wahhabi doctrine underlined society's obligation to abide by the divine law (*Shari͡a*) and the ruler's obligation to consult the ͡ulama on state affairs. In practice, however, particularly during the twentieth century, the ͡ulama's role was limited to several specific educational, judicial, and religious functions in the Wahhabi Saudi state. Also, while senior ͡ulama were occasionally consulted by the ruler, ͡Abd al-͡Aziz as-Sa͡ud (Ibn Sa͡ud), it is clear from Saudi history that the ͡ulama did not control the process of decision making. Moreover, despite the formal and outward piety of Wahhabi society, this doctrine never completely changed the deeply rooted tribal values or the commercial values of urban dwellers.[4] In fact, attempts by the Ikhwan al-Najd—the most fervent of Wahhabi tribal groups—to impose the Wahhabi doctrine by force on the tribes and towns of the Gulf area generated a revulsion among their populations against radical Islamic doctrines. They also remained highly suspicious of any title that included the word *Ikhwan* (Brethren), although in later times this title referred generally to the Egyptian Muslim Brethren rather than to the Saudi variety.[5]

The above reality also generally applies to the Gulf's Shi͡a populations. Thus, the conflicts that developed between Sunni and Shi͡a groups in Bahrain in 1923 were essentially a struggle over economic and administrative interests and ended in the establishment of a Shi͡a autonomous court system, incorporated into the state's central judicial system.[6] In sum, political and socioeconomic interests prevailed over Islamic values in forming the local ethos.

The rapid modernization which the Gulf states underwent over the past two decades (and particularly after 1973) hardly altered this basic reality. No doubt rapid modernization did have certain negative and potentially destabilizing consequences, including increased social and economic gaps, growing (and sometimes frustrated) expectations of newly educated groups, the injection of approximately three million foreign workers, and the adoption of a Westernized, luxurious life-style.[7] However, the positive effects of modernization tended to balance its negative impact. The welfare system developed by the Gulf states provided the local population with free health care, social security, and education. Infrastructural housing, communications, and transportation projects also eased physical burdens. Although oil revenues were accumulated chiefly by leading upper-class families, a major share permeated throughout the entire system, enabling other strata to improve their living conditions. In Jacqueline Ismael's words, "What this paternalistic welfare system did was to transform the indigenous population into a leisure class with a capacity for consumption of luxury foreign goods."[8] The Gulf regimes also enabled the population to gain access to their leaders through the tribal medium of open audience (*majlis* or *diwan*). Parliamentary experiments (in Bahrain, attempted in 1973 and lasting twenty months, and in Kuwait from 1963 to 1976 and from 1981 to 1986) and the relatively free press permitted in Kuwait and Bahrain served at least as limited and temporary outlets for political pressures.[9] Because of these different devices, the socioeconomic crises and the atmosphere of malaise that have spurred militant revivalism elsewhere in the Islamic world were prevented from emerging in the Gulf.

Demographic conditions in the Gulf also discouraged Islamic revival, especially its militant brand. In 1978, of 1.5 million Kuwaitis, approximately 0.8 million were immigrants; of 300,000 Bahrainis, approximately 100,000 were immigrants; and of 6.5 million Saudis, approximately 2 million were immigrants.[10] The varied ethnic origins of these immigrant groups—Palestinians, Yemenis, Egyptians, Iraqis, Asians, and Europeans, each with their distinct religious and cultural practices—and the different types of citizenship which they received prevented the cementing of cohesive émigré political communities. A broadly based body-politic that could be effectively mobilized into an Islamic revivalist movement was therefore nonexistent in the Gulf. Moreover, the political inclination of many of the immigrants (notably the Palestinians and the Egyptians) was leftist, and they were often aligned with like-minded indigenous students and workers. Indeed, encouraged by South Yemen's and Iraq's radical politics, these elements occasionally organized themselves into leftist, even revolutionary, opposition bodies such as the Popular Front for the Liberation of Bahrain, the Arab Nationalist Movement in both Kuwait and Bahrain, and various leftist bodies in Saudi Arabia. These organizations seem to have absorbed and channeled most of the activists who harbored social grievances during the sixties and seventies. Thus, leftists and Arab nationalists constituted the main opposition in Kuwait's assembly prior to its dissolution in 1976.[11]

The Gulf's indigenous Shiᶜa communities' evolution has also been affected by different social and economic factors that have tended to balance one another.[12] Irrespective of their numbers (a minority of 5 percent in Saudi Arabia, over 10 percent and in some estimates about 30 percent in Kuwait, and a majority of about 60 percent in Bahrain) the Gulf's Shiᶜas have long been subjected to physical persecution and economic discrimination by the Sunnis. Shiᶜa lands were often confiscated and their physical safety violated, particularly by fervent Wahhabi zealots. Since the 1920s, however, due both to British influences and to initiatives of the modernizing rulers Ibn Saᶜud in Saudi Arabia, Ahmad ibn as-Sabah in Kuwait, and ᶜIsa al-Khalifa in Bahrain, the Shiᶜas have enjoyed more physical protection and freedom to perform their religious-communal practices. Nevertheless, economically and politically, the Gulf's Shiᶜas still occupy the lower echelons of society. Even in Bahrain, where the Shiᶜa constitute a majority of 70 percent of the citizenry, their representatives hold only five relatively minor cabinet positions. Their representatives in Kuwait's consultative assembly numbered a handful. Nevertheless, Shiᶜa communities have also produced families of considerable wealth and high social rank. In the past three decades their middle strata were able to improve their economic conditions by taking jobs with the oil companies and in public and private business. These factors in turn helped reduce the impact of socioeconomic factors as spurs to Shiᶜa revivalism in the Gulf prior to the Iranian revolution.

Moreover, while the Shi°as maintained a communal and religious collective identity, their internal divisions were also considerable. In Bahrain, for example, the Shi°as were of local Arab origin and included veteran families from Iran (known as "Baharna") while most of Kuwait's Shi°as were relatively new immigrants from Iraq. These differences in their origins in turn discouraged the Gulf's Shi°as from engaging in militant activities on a religious-sectarian basis.

Thus, until the time of the Iranian revolution, in the Gulf states Islam constituted a component in what Ali E. Hillal Dessouki has called the "dualism" of Arab-Islamic societies. This dualism refers to the coexistence among Muslims of traditional and Islamic sentiments alongside modern and secular practices.[13] Also before the Islamic revolution, Islam was both a moderating and an integrative factor, rather than a radical-reformist and antigovernment catalyst in the Gulf. This role is evident in the course of the development of Islamic movements and their ideology in the region.

The Gulf's Sunni elements were inspired by motifs propagated by the Muslim Brethren but modified by the ethos and socioeconomic realities of the Gulf. Because Shi°a revivalist literature was printed mainly in Persian and was rarely translated into Arabic, Shi°a revivalism was hardly evident in the Gulf prior to Iran's Islamic revolution.[14]

The role and development of Sunni revivalist movements is well reflected in the words of Ismail al-Shatti, a prominent Muslim figure in Kuwait who is the leader of the Islamic Social Reform Groups (Jam°iyyat al-Islah al-Ijtima°i) and editor of *Al-Mujtama* (Society) newspaper. In a speech delivered at the University of Kuwait on March 1, 1983, al-Shatti emphasized that it was "the fight between good and evil" that activated human history, rather than economic materialism (as Marx suggested) or the dynamic of challenge and response (as Toynbee maintained). Accordingly, it was Islam's role to maintain goodness and morality. Al-Shatti thereby belittled the importance of mundane economic and modernization drives in history and, by implication, Islam's relevance to these factors. Rather, he saw Islam's role as focused on moral issues, albeit ones that could be widely applied. He illustrated this principle by showing how fervent Sunni Muslims actually played this role in Kuwait's modern history, usually by applying Islamic law and morality in government (i.e., in the crises of 1921 and 1938), rather than by promoting resurgent ideas or by acting as a radical opposition. This mode of behavior continued in the next decades. Al-Shatti further explained that Kuwait's fervent Muslims had come under the influence of the Egyptian Muslim Brethren and their leader, Hasan al-Banna, in the late 1940s; later on, some of their members were arrested following the Muslim Brethren's attempts on the life of Egypt's President Naser in 1954.

Even these events did not alter the fundamental, relatively nonmilitant nature of Kuwait's Islamic groups. The principal body, the Guidance Society (Jam°iyyat al-Irshad), led by °Abd al-°Aziz al-°Ali al-Mutawa and Yusuf al-Qinai, split into two factions: al-Mutawa led "the establishment faction" and Muhammad al-Adsani the "youth faction"; neither seemed to have developed revivalist trends. The leftist paper *Al-Tali'a*, in recounting al-Shatti's lecture, therefore opposed his claim to crown the Islamic bodies in Kuwait as "opposition" movements, because they had not acted as such.[15]

In the 1970s the activities of the Gulf's Islamic groups gradually intensified and became somewhat radicalized. This development was probably prompted by a variety of factors. First was the weakening of the leftist trend caused by the failure of Arab socialism to resolve the Arabs' political and economic problems. A second factor was the effort made by oil-rich states such as Libya and Saudi Arabia to utilize their newly acquired wealth to promote Islamic activities throughout the Muslim world.[16] Third, in the 1970s, Gulf modernization accelerated and intensified, causing hitherto unknown perils—entrenched social gaps, Westernized life-style and education, islands of corruption among the elites—thus generating a sense of disorientation and uneasiness in some quarters in the region. Fourth, during this period ideas of militant Islamic revival, as maintained by the Egyptian Takfir wal-Hijra organization, were introduced to the Gulf by Pakistanis, Egyptians, and other expatriate workers.[17]

It was for all these reasons that some Sunni Islamic bodies slowly began to promote principles of pious Islam as an alternative to the "false" idols of modernity, Westernization, and socialism. These constituted popular reactions rather than preplanned political initiatives. They were appealing to a variety of social groups, notably the students, but had little impact at the political level. Thus in 1971, two Kuwait organizations, the Social Reform Group and the Social Educational Group—both influenced by Muslim Brethren ideologies—attempted to impose separate higher education for female and male students. In November of that year members of the groups rioted at the university and preached in Kuwait's mosques to that effect. However, at that time the majority of students still openly opposed the Islamic bodies' program.[18]

Similarly, during the 1970s, groups of Saudi students became acquainted with radical revivalist ideas through meeting their counterparts from Egypt and Pakistan at the Islamic University at Madina and hearing lectures on the centrality of Islamic principles in the life of Muslim societies from Saudi Arabia's leading ᶜalim, ᶜAbd al-ᶜAziz ibn al-Baz. These students, being of humble tribal origin and harboring Ikhwan revivalist sentiments, filled the preconditions of Islamic revival. They had deep-rooted Islamic ethos and political culture and bore the sustained socioeconomic difficulties typical of poor tribal immigrants to modernized cities, where they became alienated by the immense wealth and Westernized life-style.[19] Under these circumstances, the pious and radical students and immigrants from Egypt and Pakistan became these students' social and ideological interlocutors. The phenomenon of collaboration between these groups was surprising not only in view of their distant origins, but also because, for the first time in the region's modern history, Islam was being related to as a manifesto for social protest. Moreover, although al-Baz's preachings were by no means directed against the Saudi government, these students found in his strict puritanism a platform to oppose what they perceived as a Westernized and corrupt elite.[20] This group eventually launched the attack on the Grand

Mosque in Makka on November 20, 1979. But prior to Khumaini's rise to power, these groups did not indulge in violent overt opposition. Rather, they sought to cope with modernization and change by trying to reintroduce Islamic morality and values into day-to-day practices and institutions.[21]

## The Impact of the Iranian Revolution: The Shi°a Response

The Islamic revolution in Iran had a clear impact on the Shi°a population in the Gulf and a less decisive effect on the Sunnis. There are several reasons for this development. First, Khumaini's ascent to power undoubtedly did influence the Sunni world, inasmuch as it created what Sivan calls an "appealing idiom."[22] Khumaini termed his revolution as generally Islamic rather than sectarian, presented Islam as an alternative to what had been perceived as corrupt and Westernized rule, and particularly noted its strong social message for the down-trodden (*mustad°afin*). Moreover, the Iranian revolution showed how fervent Muslims could actually use force to achieve political goals. However, while Iran's Shi°a revolution no doubt influenced Sunni Islam, the two remained deeply separated over political and theological questions. We must note in particular that the Shi°a belief in the godly prenominated line of imams as rulers of society—all descendants of the caliph Ali—was rejected by the Sunni concept of a normal human ruler being elected from the Prophet's tribe, Quraish. The concept of rule by clerics as a substitute for the divine imam is also alien to Sunni practices. Consequently, the impact of Khumaini's revolution on Sunni believers was at once strong and devoid of any substantial effects.

In addition, after the Iranian revolution, Khumaini's regime sought to move openly against regimes in the Gulf by directly approaching the Gulf's Shi°a communities, many of whose leaders were old acquaintances of the new Iranian regime. This direct link, set against the background of lasting Shi°a grievances, constituted a major catalyst of Shi°a unrest.

After 1978, Shi°a activities in the Gulf went through several stages.[23] The first wave focused on two personal agents of Khumaini, Hadi al-Mudarrisi in Bahrain (a Shi°a of Iranian origin who had been exiled by the Shah's regime) and Khumaini's brother-in-law, °Abbas Muhri, in Kuwait. Both bore the title *Hujjat al-Islam* (Proof of Islam) and through their sermons called for turning their respective states into Islamic republics. They also demanded the prohibition of alcohol and the reintroduction of religious instruction in schools. This effort met with little success. In September 1979 the entire Muhri family was expelled from Kuwait. In Bahrain, demonstrations took place on August 17 and 19, 1979; during the second (held upon the return of an associate of al-Mudarrisi, Muhammad °Ali °Akri, from Tehran), twenty-eight participants were arrested. Al-Mudarrisi was then expelled on August 31, and calm returned.[24]

This wave reflected the interests of its initiators, including Iran, rather than those of the wider local Shi°a communities. Declarations made by Ayatullahs Ruhani and Muntazeri during this period stressed Iran's historic claim to Bahrain. The two Iranian speakers also called for Islamic revolutions along the Iranian model throughout the Gulf.[25] There is evidence that both al-Mudarrisi and Muhri—old associates of Khumaini—had been appointed as his personal representatives and charged with spreading his message in the Gulf.[26] Moreover, their activities involved mainly their own relatives and other Shiᶜa mullahs. With the exception of the August 19 riot, there is no evidence to suggest that the Shiᶜa masses departed from their political inactivity. This last event, however, did catalyze a new wave of Shiᶜa activism that was more broadly based and reflected authentic Shiᶜa grievances. This effort was probably prompted by the growing influence of Khumaini's personality and of the example set by the successful Iranian revolution. Iranian propaganda also sought to accelerate this trend. Through pamphlets, tape cassettes of Khumaini's sermons, and broadcasts in Arabic by the Iranian Voice of the Islamic Revolution, the local Shiᶜa communities were roused to act against the "unlawful Gulf regimes." In addition, the attack on the Grand Mosque in Makka, though carried out by Sunni zealots, carried a strong message of Islamic and antigovernment fervor that corresponded to Iranian propaganda and further agitated the Shiᶜas. Finally, the dynamic that often ensued when local security forces disrupted Shiᶜa religious practices and occasionally arrested religious leaders—acts perceived by the Shiᶜa communities as offenses against their communal and religious practices—involved a wide and violent chain reaction of demonstrations.

Actual unrest took several forms. On November 28, 1979, Shiᶜas in the eastern Saudi Arabian province (al-Ahsa) tried to perform the Ashura processions publicly. When the Saudi National Guard attempted to stop them in Qatif, Abqiq, and Safwa, they rioted. The intervention of the National Guard resulted in seventeen deaths.[27] On February 1, 1980 (the first anniversary of Khumaini's return to Iran according to the Hijri calendar), Shiᶜas rioted in Qatif, stoned two large banks, and set fire to fifty vehicles. The National Guard intervened once more, killing four people.[28] Agitated by the Mosque event, Kuwaiti Shiᶜas turned a demonstration into an attack on the U.S. Embassy, which was withstood by security forces. Subsequently, twenty-five Shiᶜas (of Iranian origin) were sentenced to periods of imprisonment.[29] On April 24, 1980, following the execution of Iraq's Shiᶜa leader, Muhammad Baqer as-Sadr, the Shiᶜas demonstrated in Manama, Bahrain; the new chain of riots stopped only in May.[30]

Several elements illustrate the authentic and broadly based nature of these events. As developments snowballed, the number of participants in the Shiᶜa riots rose to hundreds and even thousands—equivalent to "mass" events in regional terms. Improved cooperation between clerics and masses produced a new organization, the Islamic Front for the Liberation of Bahrain (IFLB), founded in early 1979 in Tehran. Led by al-Mudarrisi, the IFLB collaborated with the Iraq-based Shiᶜa underground group ad-Daᶜwa to further Islamic revolution.[31] Moreover, for the first time Shiᶜa elements in the Gulf raised their own deep-rooted grievances, formulated in an anti-Western and anticorruption phraseology that echoed Islamic revivalist expressions. Shiᶜas in Kuwait and Saudi Arabia criticized their governments' subservience to the West, together with "governmental corruption." During the November 1979 riots in al-Ahsa, demands were raised to halt Saudi oil supplies and redistribute Saudi wealth, so that the Shi'as would get their proper share.[32] In Bahrain, too, Shi'as demanded to be treated in a way befitting their majority status. A variety of Shi'as indicated that they viewed Khumaini as their religious leader.[33]

Subsequent events, however, acquired a different character. Shi'a activities then focused mainly on large-scale sabotage and terrorist acts committed by small trained underground groups in sharp contrast to the more broadly based and politically directed wave of 1979–80. Several factors explain this change: First, the dynamics of the Iran-Iraq war presumably convinced the Iranian leaders to cease instigating popular but strategically useless mass actions. Instead, they focused on sabotage and terrorism, as means of both disrupting Iraq's supply lines in the Gulf (Kuwait being a main supplier) and deterring Gulf governments from extending massive aid to Iraq, as they had been doing since the war erupted in 1980. In the case of Bahrain, "deterrence" took the form of an attempt to topple the government. Second, the IFLB and ad-Da'wa groups realized that they must employ different tactics to counter the measures by which local governments had curbed the riots of 1979–80. These had included a combination of brutal force used against rioters, the expulsion of troublesome Shi'a leaders, and development projects that governments (notably the Saudis) bestowed upon their Shi'a communities to dissuade them from engaging in overt antigovernment activities.[34] Spokesmen for the militant Shi'a organizations now stressed direct "antigovernment actions," based on the Shi'a "sacrificing spirit," which the "fighters" should use against local governments.[35] Newspapers such as *Al-Thawra al-Islamiyya* (Islamic Revolution), which appears in London and reflects the Shi'a militants' opinions on the Saudi royal family, set out to completely discredit the family's image by depicting it as corrupt, subservient to the West, dictatorial, and deviating from the Shari'a,[36] thus legitimizing the use of force against the Saudi government.

Several events highlighted this wave. On December 13, 1981, the Bahraini authorities announced the interception of a 75-member group that had intended to topple the local government and to announce the establishment of an Islamic republic. The plot was organized by the IFLB, with al-Mudarrisi designated to rule the new regime. IFLB members allegedly trained in Iran were infiltrated into Bahrain, where they were to take over strategic points and (with the aid of Iranian forces to be landed by Hovercraft) gain control over the state.[37] Since this abortive plot, Bahrain authorities have discovered several additional attempts to subvert their government.[38]

On December 12, 1983, ad-Da'wa saboteurs infiltrated from Iraq, launched a series of explosions in Kuwait, hitting the U.S. and French embassies as well as the Shu'aiba industrial depot and additional targets, all selected because of their connection with the Western powers or their function as departure points for Kuwaiti assistance sent to Iraq.[39] The continuing Iran-Iraq war and the interception of twenty-five of the saboteurs have since triggered further actions aimed at releasing the prisoners and disrupting Kuwait's security. Thus, on

December 6, 1984, a Kuwaiti passenger plane was hijacked to Tehran as a means of pressuring Kuwaiti authorities to release the prisoners. On May 25, 1985, an attempt was made on the life of the Kuwaiti ruler, Jabir as-Sabah, who escaped with light injuries. On July 7, 1985, shots were fired at a cafe located on Kuwait's waterfront; a group called the Black Brigades, made up of several Shi$^c$a groups active in Iraq and Kuwait, instigated the attempt.[40]

As these activities indicate, Shi$^c$a actions have on occasion been well organized and quite lethal. But they have also lost the popular appeal they had during 1979. In the 1980s Shi$^c$a militancy in the Gulf acquired no broadly based infrastructure that could have been the hub of a guerrilla movement. It was rather a product of several small hit squads. Moreover, Shi$^c$a activities have become dependent on foreign (i.e., Iranian) aid, provided either directly or through a local group for training and organization. In addition, the Shi$^c$as' latest activities have been completely subject to Iran's strategic interests. Hence, despite the favorable sentiments the Shi$^c$as felt toward Iran's revolution, Shi$^c$a subversive activities in the Gulf did not enjoy popular, widespread, and active support; nor did an authentic local Shi$^c$a leadership emerge in the Gulf.

## The Sunni Response

Sunni revivalist activities in the Gulf region do not reflect any sort of clear dynamic that can be broken down into logical stages. Somewhat artificially, then, two major chronological phases of Sunni activity may be distinguished. First is the period 1979–81, during which Sunni activists searched for the proper mode of action. As mentioned earlier, the Iranian revolution seemed an impressive example for the Sunnis. Nevertheless, large-scale cooperation between the Sunni and Shi$^c$a revivalists did not occur. Apart from objective theological differences, Khumaini's bid to revolutionize the Gulf mainly via the Shi$^c$a communities discouraged such cooperation. Additional reasons—including opposition from Gulf governments; internal strife in the Iranian regime; the developing alliance between Iran and the Asad regime in Syria (identified by Sunni activists as the suppressor of the Muslim Brethren there); Iran's anti-Arab image, cultivated by the Iran-Iraq war; and Iran's tendency to compete with the Sunnis to recruit support for its position in the war among European based Muslim communities—further prevented Sunni-Shi$^c$a cooperation.[41] Having ruled out collaboration, the Sunnis remained confused by other aspects of Khumaini's ascent to power. Several essays published in the Kuwaiti Arab-Nationalist monthly Al-$^c$Arabi during 1979 and 1980 demonstrated this confusion. They argued that Islam was being misinterpreted by different sides; on the one hand, there were those (meaning the Iranians) who tried to portray Islam as an "external" religion, forcing people to study the Qur'an, wear modest clothes, change their rulers, and implement the Shari$^c$a. These activists did not care about the intrinsic meaning of Islam, and in fact encouraged divisiveness. On the other hand, the Western religions and Westernized Muslims demanded separation of religion and state and imposed liberal or socialist interpretations alien to the true Islam.[42] Sunni revivalists had therefore to sift through different interpretations in search of ways of articulating their ideas.

Interestingly, Sunni revivalists in the Gulf states hardly engaged in violent activities. Most Sunnis were probably deeply influenced by the largely quietist tradition of Islam in the Gulf region and were also deterred by the initial Shiᶜa unrest. There were, however, a few exceptions. One was the attack on the Grand Mosque in Makka on November 20, 1979; the Sunni perpetrators may have been incited by the example set by Khumaini's revolution as well as by the Shiᶜa motif of awaiting the deliverer (Mahdi), which recurred in the ideology of the Mosque capturers.[43] The peculiar social composition of this group and its deep cultural and socioeconomic frustrations, which may have made it susceptible to violence, were noted earlier. The unusually charismatic character of its leader, Juhaiman al-ᶜUtaibi, might have further elicited such a reaction.[44]

Other acts of sabotage, such as the destruction of the Kuwaiti office of Iran Air on May 26, 1980, an explosion in the Iranian embassy in Kuwait a week later, and a further explosion in the daily *Al-Ra'y al-ᶜAmm* on July 12,[45] were in fact manifestations of heightened Sunni-Shiᶜa tensions. The Iranian targets were hit by the Sunnis, the newspaper office by the Shiᶜas. Although the actual causes for these events remain unclear, it is evident that, in these instances, Sunni revivalists, inspired by Muslim Brethren ideologies, took a completely divergent and hostile route to that of the Shiᶜas. However, even this Sunni tactic was short-lived, thus further indicating that the Sunnis were still in search of a suitable vehicle of expression.

The elections for the Kuwaiti State Assembly (Majlis Al-Umma, sometimes referred to as the consultative assembly), which took place on February 23, 1980, offered a new avenue of activity for the revivalists. Of fifty members, four Shiᶜas were elected, but in comparison to the ten Shiᶜa members in the previous assembly (which had been dissolved in 1976), Shiᶜa influence appeared to be in decline. On the other hand, five Sunni revivalists were elected.

Thus, after 1980 a new phase of Sunni activism emerged: societal reform through parliamentary and related public activity. Several factors explain this inclination. First, it allowed Kuwaiti Sunni activists to adopt a variety of initiatives and gain influential positions. Second, the Sunnis were able to introduce changes without having to rely on the Shiᶜa movement, whose cooperation they shunned. Third, the political constellation in the assembly itself was very tempting for the Sunni activists. The veteran Arab nationalists and leftist deputies who had been the main opposition in previous assemblies were not reelected in 1980 (probably due to the government's manipulation of constituencies), and most elected members were of tribal descent and quite loyal to the government. The Sunni activists therefore found themselves in a situation that allowed them to act as the only effective opposition in the assembly, seeking to forward their ambitions.

The Sunni revivalists developed a combination of two interrelated activities; one was legislative, within the assembly, and was mainly pursued by the two fundamentalist (*salafiyyin*) members elected, Khalid Sultan and ʿIsa Majid al-Shahin. They favored judicial and ecumenical changes that would turn Kuwait into a puritanical society. The other members, followers of the Social Reform Groups like Salih Fadlallah and, in the 1985 elected assembly, ʿAbdullah al-Nafisi, supported this line, but focused more on changing educational and social practices as a means of introducing an Islamic life-style. Assembly activities— the initiation of laws, participation in debates, etc.—suited both of these purposes. In a number of articles al-Shatti and al-Nafisi justified their tactic. Al-Shatti explained that parliamentary work endowed the revivalists with societal credibility and that he viewed himself as a "gradualist reformer" who believed in evolutionary change through public and assembly work.[46] Al-Nafisi wrote a series of articles in *Al-Mujtama*ʿ during 1981–83, in which he tried to demonstrate that, in a struggle waged in the name of Allah, Islam favored political action, tolerated different interpretations and policies, and focused mainly on true belief, thereby rejecting heresy and abuse.[47] Al-Nafisi made it clear that truly Islamic factions could adopt different and yet legitimate lines of activity. These groups' activities were echoed in several other Gulf principalities, notably Bahrain, but Kuwait remains their hub.

The interplay of political pragmatism and persistency in reforming society has also been displayed in these groups' social inclination. Recruitment of students is the Social Reform Groups' main aim. Since 1979, it has continuously controlled Kuwait's student union.[48] Its main constituency (as reflected in the careers of al-Shatti and al-Nafisi) comprises young people of professional and academic backgrounds who became acquainted with revivalist ideas during their studies in local or Western universities. They seek to cultivate a meaningful and productive life through religion and to abandon Western-style consumer habits.[49] However, typically, they have not called for complete destruction of the present life-style, but rather to complement and reform it. These groups' activities have led the Gulf governments (within the framework of the Gulf Cooperation Council) to decide to implement the Shariʿa in their countries.[50] Kuwait's revivalists have submitted an amendment to the constitution to the effect that Shariʿa would become the only source of legislation in the state, but so far have failed to pass it.[51] In May 1984, Khalid Sultan's strong opposition defeated a proposal to renew Kuwaiti financial assistance to Syria's Arab Deterrent Force in Lebanon. The veto was a response to Syria's suppression of the Muslim Brethren and, as Sultan implied, was aimed against the heretical nature of Syria's leading (ʿAlawi) sect. In October 1985 the revivalists also engaged in a fierce debate in the assembly over their demand to dismiss the minister of education because of his (and the government's) intention to cut religious studies programs at the universities.[52]

In the 1985 elections, Sultan and Shahin lost their seats, considerably weakening the revivalists. However, the election of ʿAbd al-ʿAziz al-Mutawa and al-Nafisi, together with three other Social Reform Groups members, all quite popular among students, indicates that this group might develop into a new and forceful factor in Gulf politics.[53]

## Conclusion

Iran's Islamic revolution had a multidimensional impact on the development of Islamic revivalism in the Gulf region. On one hand, it constituted an encouraging example to all revivalist groups. On the other hand, Khumaini's revolution produced a regime whose policies and theological beliefs were rejected by the Sunni majority in the Arab world. Moreover, this revolution encountered a Gulf Arab society whose basic characteristics had created a diversified revivalist movement. The Gulf's revivalist movement was highly fragmented along ethnic and religious lines. Moreover, the Gulf's underlying characteristics did not predispose it to the emergence of a militant revivalism that could result in a revivalist revolution.

Consequently, the groups who propagated Islamic revival in the Gulf differed from one another in their theological basis, the mode of action they chose, and the degree of their intensity. In view of their socioeconomic conditions, the Gulf's Shiᶜa populations were more receptive to militant revivalism. Thus, Shiᶜa groups eventually emerged that focused on sabotage and terrorism directed against local governments. Yet, despite the favorable sentiment Khumaini enjoys among local Shiᶜas and despite the Shiᶜas' deep-rooted grievances, these groups do not enjoy broadly based support and have failed to attract the majority of the Shiᶜas. Rather, they command cadres of highly trained professional activists, committed to the ideals of Islamic revolution and subservient to Iran's strategy in the region.

The Sunnis have developed two main groups promoting revivalist ideas, one focusing on judicial-ecumenical changes, the other on social reforms. Both groups preferred to act as "established" oppositions, mostly in Kuwait's parliamentary assembly. They enjoy wide support among students and young professionals and have a potential to develop further. The dissolution of Kuwait's assembly in July 1986, however, posed a major challenge to this trend.

# NOTES

1. See J.S. Voll, "Renewal and Reform in Islamic History: Tajdid and Islah," in J.L. Esposito, ed., *Voices of Resurgent Islam* (New York: Oxford University Press, 1983), pp. 32–47; Ali E. Hillal Dessouki, "The Islamic Resurgence: Sources, Dynamics and Implications," in Dessouki, ed., *Islamic Resurgence in the Arab World* (New York: Praeger, 1982), pp. 3–34; Daniel Pipes, *In the Path of God* (New York: Basic Books, 1983); and Emmanuel Sivan, *Radical Islam* (New Haven, Conn.: Yale University Press, 1985).

2. For an analysis of examples of tribal confederacies, see T. Asad, "The Bedouin as a Military Force: Notes on Some Aspects of Power Relations between Nomads and Sedentaries in Historical Perspective," in C. Nelson, ed., *The Desert and the Sown* (Berkeley: University of California Press, 1973).

3. E. Gellner, *Muslim Society* (Cambridge: Cambridge University Press, 1977), pp. 50–56.

4. See J. Kostiner, "On Instruments and Their Designers: The Ikhwan of Najd and the Emergence of the Saudi State," *Middle Eastern Studies*, Vol. 21, No. 3 (July 1985), pp. 298–323.

5. Related by a leader of an Islamic revivalist group in Kuwait, Isma'il al-Shatti, as quoted in *Al-Tali'a* (Kuwait), Mar. 25, 1983.

6. F.I. Khuri, *Tribe and State in Bahrain* (Chicago: University of Chicago Press, 1980), pp. 68–114.

7. A good discussion of these problems is provided in Avi Plascov, *Security in the Persian Gulf III: Modernization, Political Development and Stability* (London: Gower, 1982).

8. J.S. Ismael, *Kuwait Social Change in Historical Perspective* (Syracuse, N.Y.: Syracuse University Press, 1982), p. 132.

9. See A. Hottinger, "Political Institutions in Saudi Arabia, Kuwait and Bahrain," in Sh. Chubin, ed., *Security in the Persian Gulf I: Domestic Political Factors* (London: Gower, 1981), pp. 1–18.

10. See A.G. Hill, "Migration and Development in the Gulf States," in Chubin.

11. Information about leftist bodies is provided by Plascov; see also H. Lackner, *A House Built on Sand* (London: Ithaca Press, 1978), pp. 89–109; *Financial Times (FT)* Survey, Feb. 25, 1977.

12. See J. Kostiner, "Shi'a Unrest in the Gulf," in M. Kraemer, ed., *Shi'a Resistance and Revolution* (Boulder, Colo.: Westview Press, 1987).

13. Dessouki, p. 24.

14. Sivan discusses this issue in a chapter on the impact of the Iranian revolution added to the Hebrew version of his book (see n. 1), published in Tel Aviv by Am Oved, 1986.

15. *Al-Tali'a*, Mar. 23, 1983; *Al-Watan*, Mar. 2, 1983.

16. Daniel Pipes, *In the Path of God*, promoted this thesis.

17. Sivan gives an excellent analysis of these ideologies in *Radical Islam*.

18. *Al-Tali'a*, Nov. 17, 1971, and Mar. 23, 1971; *Al-Ra'y al-'Amm (RA)*, Nov. 14–17, 1971.

19. On such social problems, see Sh. Kay, "Social Change in Modern Saudi Arabia," in R. Niblock, ed., *State Society and Economy in Saudi Arabia* (London: Croom Helm, 1982), pp. 171–185.

20. The buildup of this group was summarized by J. Buchan, "The Return of the Ikhwan 1979," in D. Holden and R. Johns, *The House of Saud* (London: Sidgwick & Jackson, 1981), pp. 511–526.

21. *Al-Yaqza*, Feb. 19, 1979.

22. Sivan (see n. 14).

23. This analysis of Shi'a events was first put forward in Kostiner, "Shi'a Unrest in the Gulf."

24. *RA*, Aug. 31 and Sept. 25, 26, 28, 1979; *Al-Nahar*, Sept. 7 and 26, 1979; *Al-Mustaqbal* (Paris), Sept. 29, 1979; *Al-Usbu' al-'Arabi (UA)*, Sept. 24, 1979; *The Middle East*, October 1979.

25. *RA*, Sept. 27, 1979; *Al-Nahar* (Beirut), Sept. 22 and 28, 1979.

26. *Al-Mustaqbal*, Sept. 15, 1979; *Al-Dustur* (Beirut), July 1985.

27. *International Herald Tribune (IHT)* and *FT*, December 4, 1979.

28. *Al-Ahram* (Cairo), Feb. 21, 1980; *FT*, Mar. 12, 1980.

29. Kuwait News Agency, Dec. 1–3, 1980, quoted by BBC Monitoring Service, Dec. 3 and 4, 1980.

30. *Al-Nahar*, May 18, 1980; *Al-Khalij* (UAE), Aug. 18, 1980.

31. *Al-Dustur*, May 6, 1985; July 1, 1985.

32. *IHT*, Dec. 4, 1979; *Christian Science Monitor*, Feb. 20, 1980; *The Middle East*, July 1980.

33. *IHT*, July 7, 1982.

34. *FT*, Apr. 24, 1982.

35. Quoted in *Al-fath al-Islami* [published by an underground Shiᶜa organization active in Iraq and the Gulf], Vol. 2, No. 2 (n. d.), pp. 15–18.

36. See, for example, *Al-Thawra al-Islamiyya*, July 1984.

37. *Al-Anba'* (Kuwait), Dec. 20, 1981; *Al-Qabas* (Kuwait), Jan. 4, 1981; *Al-Dustur*, July 1, 1985.

38. For instance, *Al-Watan al-ᶜArabi* (Paris), Sept. 15, 1983.

39. *Al-Khalij*, Dec. 13, 19, and 22, 1983; *Al-Watan*, Jan. 25, 1984; Feb. 11, 1984.

40. *Al-Dustur*, May 6, 1985.

41. *Al-Mujtamaᶜ* (Kuwait), Mar. 25, 1986, and Apr. 8, 1986; Sivan (see n. 14).

42. *Al-ᶜArabi* (Kuwait), March, April, and June 1979 and June 1980.

43. See Buchan; see also a special issue of the Iraqi *Sawt al-Taliᶜa*, No. 22, May 1980.

44. Ibid.

45. Kuwait News Agency, July 13 and 17, quoted by BBC; July 18, 1980; *RA*, Mar. 31, 1981.

46. Al-Shatti's interview with *FT*, Feb. 11, 1985; see also James Bill, "Resurgent Islam in the Persian Gulf," *Foreign Affairs*, Vol. 63, No. 1 (Fall 1984), pp. 108–127.

47. *Al-Mujtamaᶜ*, Apr. 20 and 27, 1982; June 1, 1982; Feb. 15, 1983. See also Muhammad ᶜAbd al-Hadi's article in *Al-Mujtamaᶜ*, Dec. 20 and 27, 1983.

48. *Al-Taliᶜa*, May 22, 1985.

49. *FT*, Feb. 22, 1984; Feb. 11, 1985.

50. *Al-Watan*, Mar. 1, 1984.

51. *Al-Watan*, Jan. 4, 1983.

52. *Al-Mujtamaᶜ*, Oct. 29, 1985.

53. *Al-Dustur*, Mar. 4, 1985.

# Part IV

## Islamic Revivalism in Africa

# IX

# MOROCCO

## Henry Munson, Jr.

In this overview of the Islamic revival in Morocco during the 1970s and 1980s, I shall describe the main militant Islamic groups and individuals involved, with particular attention to their ideological orientations and their social bases of support.[1] (I use the term *militant Islamic* to refer to people actively committed to the goal of a strictly Islamic state and society, regardless of how this goal is understood.) I shall also attempt to explain the appeal of the movement.

### Jamᶜiyyat al-Shabiba al-Islamiyya

The most radical tendency among Morocco's dozens of militant Islamic groups is represented by Jamᶜiyyat al-Shabiba al-Islamiyya, the Society of Islamic Youth. This group was founded in 1972 by ᶜAbd al-Karim Muti', an inspector in the Ministry of Education and a former activist in Morocco's teachers' union and in the socialist party, l'Union Socialiste des Forces Populaires (USFP).[2] Muti' was the group's murshid ᶜam, or supreme guide, until 1975 and has remained the dominant personality in the group since then, although his leadership has been rejected by some factions.[3] He is said to have had some kind of religious experience during the course of performing the pilgrimage to Makka in the late 1960s, when he was in his thirties.[4] After this experience, he attempted to reframe his social activism in Islamic terms and became bitterly hostile to the secular left.[5] Such transformation of leftist activists into Islamic militants seems to have occurred fairly frequently in the late seventies and early eighties.[6]

A passage from an editorial entitled "Join the Fight, Revolutionary Muslim Youth," which appeared in the first issue of the review *Al-Mujahid* in 1981, illustrates al-Shabiba al-Islamiyya's radicalism (the review was published by a faction of al-Shabiba al-Islamiyya in Belgium):

> our present and our future are caught between the hammer of American imperialism and the anvil of its agents represented by the corrupt monarchical regime and those who support it. . . .

> Your review appears in these circumstances in order to be, God willing, in the vanguard of an authentic Islamic revolution in Morocco; a revolution that enlightens the horizon of this country and liberates its people to bring them back to the Islam of Muhammad and those of his people who have known how to follow him—not the Islam of the merchants of oil and the agents of the Americans.[7]

This passage demonstrates how misleading it would be to characterize groups such as al-Shabiba al-Islamiyya as "fundamentalist." The young people in this movement have more in common with the liberation theologians of Latin America than they do with the Christian fundamentalists of the United States. They tend to stress the condemnation of foreign domination and social injustice more than the need to conform to the laws of God.

Al-Shabiba al-Islamiyya has attracted most of its support from secondary school and university students, although its leaders have often been civil servants like Muti'.[8] Given that the secular Marxist left is also strongest among students, and given that al-Shabiba al-Islamiyya and the left tend to stress the same themes, albeit in different idioms, radical Muslims and radical Marxists have frequently clashed on the school and university campuses of Morocco.[9]

On December 18, 1975, two young members of al-Shabiba al-Islamiyya assassinated ʿUmar Ben Jellun, an influential leader of the USFP.[10] The two men accused Muti' of masterminding the murder.[11] Muti' fled to Saudi Arabia. He has said that while it is true that he was asked to arrange the murder, he refused to do so.[12] When several of Muti's close associates were tried and sentenced in 1980 for helping to plan the assassination, some important documents reportedly linking Muti' and several other leaders of al-Shabiba to important government officials disappeared, prompting sharp protests from Islamic militants as well as the secular left.[13]

Muti' reportedly lived in Saudi Arabia and Kuwait from 1975 through 1979.[14] Moroccan intellectuals of the secular left generally believe that the Moroccan government authorized Muti''s escape to Saudi Arabia to avoid disclosure of the government's role in Ben Jellun's murder.[15] While there is no proof that this is true, it is worth noting that the Moroccan government never requested Muti''s extradition from Saudi Arabia or Kuwait despite the close ties linking the three countries.[16] On the other hand, many scholars and journalists claim that Muti' helped the Islamic militants who seized the Masjid al-Haram of Makka in 1979 and fled Saudi Arabia shortly thereafter.[17] According to the *Quarterly Economic Review of Morocco*, Muti' escaped to Libya after the Makkan fiasco.[18]

Whatever the accuracy of these various claims concerning the mysterious Muti', it does seem that the Moroccan government initially favored the growth of al-Shabiba al-Islamiyya for the same reason Sadat initially supported the Jamaʿat al-Islamiyya in the universities of Egypt: to curb the Marxist groups that had dominated student politics in the sixties.[19] But like Sadat, Morocco's

King Hasan II eventually realized that Islamic militancy could pose a greater threat to his regime than could the secular left.

It is also worth noting that most members of al-Shabiba al-Islamiyya, like many other Islamic militants, condemn Saudi Arabia because of its monarchical political system, the corruption of its elite, and its role as a client state of the United States.[20] One would therefore expect a leader of al-Shabiba al-Islamiyya to be sympathetic to the militant Islamic opposition to the Saudi regime (as well as to the revolutionary Islamic regime in Iran). But we do not know much about Muti''s own views except that he advocates the use of violence against Muslims who have been "led astray," a position that has led some members of al-Shabiba al-Islamiyya to reject his leadership.[21]

In the years following the assassination of ʿUmar Ben Jellun in 1975, al-Shabiba al-Islamiyya split up into a number of bitterly antagonistic factions, primarily because of disputes over the policies of Muti'. This factionalism was repeatedly condemned in letters to the editor of *Al-Jamaʿa*, the principal militant Islamic review from 1979 through 1983.[22] Muhammad Tozy lists four such factions in Morocco and another in France.[23] He renders the names of three of these factions in French as La Commission revolutionnaire, L'Avant-garde estudiantine islamique, and Le Mouvement des Mujahidines.[24]

In July 1984, seventy-one members of al-Shabiba al-Islamiyya, including Muti' and nineteen others tried in absentia, received sentences ranging from four years' imprisonment to death for belonging to an outlawed association, attempting to distribute subversive tracts, publishing texts defaming King Hasan II, and plotting to overthrow the government.[25] According to their defense attorneys, most of the accused were high school students.[26] In October 1985, thirty members of the Mujahidin faction of al-Shabiba al-Islamiyya (led by ʿAbd al-ʿAziz al-Nuʿmani, who was allegedly involved in the assassination of Ben Jellun along with Muti') received sentences ranging from a year to life imprisonment on similar charges.[27]

However, although the members of al-Shabiba al-Islamiyya and similar groups would like to overthrow the government of Hasan II, they are in no position to do so. Some members of al-Shabiba participated in the protests against the presence of the Shah in 1979 and in the riots of June 1981 and January 1984, but they did not organize or control these events.[28] In the whole of Morocco, there are probably no more than a few thousand members of the various factions of al-Shabiba al-Islamiyya, most of them students.[29] Most of the dozens of other militant Islamic groups in Morocco are probably even smaller and have a similar social base of high school and university students.[30]

## ʿAbd as-Slam Yasin: Morocco's Principal Militant Islamic Theorist

If al-Shabiba al-Islamiyya represents the left wing of Morocco's militant Islamic movement, ʿAbd as-Slam Yasin, who edited the now illegal review *Al-*

*Jamaᶜa* from 1979 through 1983, represents its political center. It should be emphasized that Yasin does not appear to have ever been the leader of an organization of his own. He has tried, however—without much success—to unite the many already existing militant Islamic groups in Morocco.[31] Although criticized by some of the radicals of al-Shabiba because of his emphasis upon preaching *(ad-daᶜwa)* and education, as opposed to armed revolt, Yasin is without question the principal theorist of militant Islam in Morocco.[32]

Yasin was born about 1928, and was thus about fifty-six years old in 1984.[33] He is the son of a Berber-speaking peasant of sharifian descent (i.e., of putative patrilineal descent from the Prophet Muhammad) and claims to have grown up in "material poverty."[34] However, he studied under ᶜulama at a "religious institute" after memorizing the Qur'an, which suggests that his father was not so poor as to require his labor when he was a boy. Dissatisfied with what he calls the "mediocrity" of the education imparted at this institute, Yasin says he then sought "broader knowledge."[35]

Despite the fact that he spent over thirty years as an inspector and administrator in the Ministry of Education, Yasin does not appear to have had any formal secular education after leaving the religious institute.[36] In his book *La Revolution à l'heure de l'Islam*, published in France in 1979, Yasin speaks of himself as "self-taught" in apparent reference to his command of the French language.[37]

Like most militant Islamic theorists, Yasin goes out of his way to refer to Western theorists, e.g., Descartes, Montesquieu, Hegel, Marx, and Lenin.[38] The purpose of such references would appear to be to impress his readers with his mastery of Western thought, and of Marxist thought in particular, so as to be in a better position to wean impressionable students away from Western ideologies, and away from Marxism in particular. But the nature of Yasin's references to these theorists suggests that he is only superficially familiar with them.[39]

Yasin asserts that he was discharged by the Ministry of Education in the 1970s because of people "who do not like to see the *Islamiyyun* possess influence."[40] Like most Islamic militants in Morocco, he uses the neologism *Islami* to refer to any Muslim actively striving for a purely Islamic polity and society patterned after the polity of the Prophet Muhammad and the first four "rightly guided" caliphs.[41]

Yasin's first political act appears to have been the writing of a 114-page *risala* (epistle) addressed to King Hasan II in 1973.[42] Yasin had an unknown number of copies of this work printed, bound, and distributed before sending a copy to the king himself. In this epistle, *Al-Islam wa al-Tufan* (Islam or the Deluge), Yasin articulates some of the main themes of his later writings, notably the condemnation of imperialism, Westernization, moral decay, and social injustice.[43] However, *Al-Islam wa al-Tufan* incorporates elements of the popular Moroccan Islamic world view that are relatively absent from Yasin's later writings, and totally absent from the publications of more radical militants (e.g., those of al-Shabiba al-Islamiyya). In it, for example, Yasin stresses his patrilineal descent from the Prophet Muhammad as well as that of the king and speaks favorably of Sufi mysticism, noting that he himself had been a member of the Bushishiyya Sufi order.[44] Yasin does not mention his descent from the Prophet nor having belonged to the Bushishiyya order in the brief autobiography he presents in the second issue of *Al-Jama^c a*.[45]

It is clear from *Al-Islam wa al-Tufan* that Yasin takes pride in his sharifian descent and was not simply trying to speak in terms of the monarchical cconception of Islam in his epistle to the king, although the latter intention may well have been involved also. The reason he does not refer to this in his writings for *Al-Jama^c a* is that they were directed to vaguely radical, educated young Muslims who had a more revolutionary and egalitarian perception of Islam. But even in *Al-Jama^c a*, Yasin occasionally urges his radical young readers not to condemn all Sufi brotherhoods as obscurantist and reactionary distortions of Islam.[46] He is, in other words, generally more sensitive to the popular interpretation of Islam than are the radicals of al-Shabiba al-Islamiyya and comparable groups. He is thus able to communicate with a much greater variety of Islamic groups than are the more radical militants.

The Moroccan government responded to Yasin's epistle to the king and the publication of two of his books, *Al-Islam Ghadan* (Islam tomorrow) and *Al-Islam bayna al-Dawla wa al-Da^c wa* (Islam between the State and the Call), by having him confined to a psychiatric hospital-cum-prison for over three years (1974–77).[47]

Yasin only began to attract widespread attention in 1979 (the final year of Iran's Islamic revolution) with the publication of his Islamic review *Al-Jama^c a* (The Group). The authorities had "obstructed," to use Yasin's word, the initial publication of *Al-Jama^c a* for at least a year.[48] And the fifth and tenth issues were prohibited and confiscated in 1980 and 1983 respectively.[49] An eleventh and apparently final issue was clandestinely published in May 1983. At some point during these years, Yasin was also prohibited from preaching in mosques.[50]

*Al-Jama^c a* was the most widely read militant Islamic periodical in Morocco from 1979 through 1983. It is therefore worth mentioning that it had a circulation of only 3,000.[51] We can get some idea of the relative significance of this circulation by comparing it with the circulations of some of Morocco's principal newspapers in 1983: *Le Matin du Sahara* (which reflects the government's views), 70,000; *Al-Alam* (organ of the Istiqlal party), 50,000; and *Al-Muharrir* (organ of the USFP), 17,000.[52] Clearly, *Al-Jama^c a*'s circulation was not very impressive compared to that of these newspapers. And while the review's small circulation can be partly explained in terms of fear of the government and the lesser circulations of reviews as opposed to newspapers, it also reflects the crucial fact that only an infinitesimal minority of Moroccans has been involved in the militant Islamic movement, most of them students—as Yasin himself has conceded.[53]

In December 1983, Yasin tried to publish a daily newspaper called *Al-Subh*

(The Dawn). In this new publication, Yasin wrote an editorial entitled "The sun will soon rise in Morocco," which was interpreted by the government as a call for an Islamic revolution.[54] The paper was prohibited and Yasin was arrested.[55] About sixty of Yasin's generally young followers were arrested for protesting his arrest when he appeared before a judge in Sale on February 13, 1984, on charges of endangering public order.[56] On April 30, five of Yasin's closest associates were arrested, including the director of secondary school education in Marrakesh, a professor in that city's teacher's college, two secondary school teachers, and a businessman.[57] And Yasin was sentenced to two years' imprisonment on May 24.[58] The relatively minor protests provoked by Yasin's arrest and sentence demonstrate that, although he is Morocco's most important militant Islamic ideologist, he is in no sense the leader of a mass movement.

In the last clandestine issue of *Al-Jama$^c$a*, Yasin said that he wanted to establish an Islamic political party that would participate in the electoral process like any other party.[59] And his daughter Nadia Yasin also stressed this goal after her father's arrest.[60] This represented a radical shift in strategy since, in the July 1982 issue of *Al-Jama$^c$a*, Yasin had dismissed Moroccan elections as a farce.[61] This shift in strategy can be seen, in my opinion, as a sign of Yasin's awareness that Morocco's militant Islamic movement was in no position to seriously challenge the regime of Hasan II.

### Al-Jama$^c$a: The Major Themes

Yasin's essays in *Al-Jama$^c$a*, as well as his other writings, reflect the influence of the militant Sunni theorists Sayyid Abul A$^c$la al-Mawdudi (1903–79) of Pakistan and Hasan al-Banna (1906–49) and Sayyid Qutb (1906–66) of Egypt, all of whom he praises for their contributions to the revitalization of Islam.[62] Yasin also praises Khumaini and the Islamic revolution in Iran.[63] But, like most Islamic militants in the Sunni world, he is much less familiar with Khumaini's writings.

Referring to the *fatwa*, or legal decree, which the Moroccan government induced the Moroccan $^c$ulama to issue condemning some of Khumaini's ideas as heretical, Yasin told a French interviewer: "C'est une contribution à l'imperialisme qui dirige les États contre les forces sociales de l'Islam. . . . "[64] This "anti-imperialist" motif is among the principal themes that pervade the pages of *Al-Jama$^c$a*.

In the first paragraph of his essay "ad-Da$^c$wa ila Allah" (The Call to God), Yasin declares:

> And the Muslims of the earth are weak, defeated and unsuccessful. They suffer
> from worldly pressures and roll along on the margin of the struggle of the giants
> [the United States and the Soviet Union] while their countries are poor. And

they are under the oppressive burden and threat of exploitative desires for in their countries are resources that the feverish *jahili* economy pants after.[65]

Yasin's usage of the adjective *jahili* and the noun *al-jahiliyya* reflects the influence of Sayyid Qutb, the most famous ideologist of the Egyptian Muslim Brotherhood who was executed by the Naser regime in 1966.[66] Whereas in ordinary popular usage *al-jahiliyya* refers to the ignorant savagery that existed before Islam, Yasin, like Qutb, uses this term to refer to all societies that are not governed according to Islamic law.[67] And by referring to both the industrialized superpowers and the secular regimes of the nominally Islamic world as jahili, Islamic militants such as Qutb and Yasin are likening their cause to that of the Prophet Muhammad and the first Muslims. The militant interpretation of the traditional notion of jahiliyya is a novel one, just as many of the militant Islamic interpretations of traditional Islamic symbols are novel, but not so novel as to be unintelligible to more traditional Muslims.[68]

Yasin contends that virtually all the Islamic countries are client states of the two superpowers: the United States and the Soviet Union.[69] And he views the influence of European conceptions of democracy, capitalism, socialism, and communism as the ideological facet of the domination of the Islamic world by al-jahiliyya. Referring to the hegemony of the Europeans over the Islamic world, he laments "the emptiness of our markets of anything but their goods, the emptiness of our minds of anything but their ideas, and the emptiness of our hearts of anything but jahili incentives. . . . "[70] And he vehemently condemns Morocco's westernized intellectuals in particular for their "theoretical and practical dependence" on the jahiliyya of the capitalist West and the communist East.[71] Yasin's condemnation of the "imperialism" of both the capitalist West and the communist East and his view of Westernization as a form of cultural dependence linked to economic and political dependence are two of the most common themes in the militant Islamic literature of the twentieth century.[72]

From Yasin's point of view (and from that of most militant Islamic ideologists), the idea of a return to Islam is not only a goal sought in and of itself, but it is also a means to an end, that end being liberation from foreign domination in all its forms. Speaking of the Arab defeat in the 1967 war with Israel, Yasin declares:

> God the powerful and exalted wanted the Arabs to taste shame at the hands of their most contemptible enemies when their desire for life, any life, had greater control over their hearts and minds than the lofty principles that they disavow. . . .
> These are the logical consequences: God honored the Arabs with Islam as ᶜUmar said. And when they looked for honor in other places, they became lowly and contemptible. . . . And shall we accept failure and shame for the Arabs? No! We want them to have power, honor and success. And we want them to discover the source of their past greatness by the rebirth of their true identity.

> For the Arabs are Muslims. . . . the Arabs will never return to their greatness
> unless they open their hearts to Islamic brotherhood and cooperation, and their
> minds to the guidance of Muhammad.[73]

As I have emphasized elsewhere, this view of foreign domination, and affliction in general, as a sign of the wrath of God is a recurrent theme in the
militant Islamic literature.[74] And unlike some of the other themes in the militant
literature (e.g., the contention that there is no distinction between religion and
politics in Islam), it is also deeply embedded in popular Islam, as we can see
from the following statement by a marginally literate peddler from Tangier:

> Why did God allow the Christians to rule over the house of Islam? Why did
> God allow the Jews to take Palestine and holy Jerusalem? Why does God allow
> the Christians to live like sultans in our land while we are like slaves in their
> land? This is God's punishment. And this is God's test. Muslims have left the
> path (kharju min at-tariq) of Islam.[75]

The Muslim militant thus explains foreign domination as well as all the problems that afflict the Islamic world in a manner that makes perfectly good sense
from the point of view of the traditional Muslim. And the militant solution to
the problem—return to the path of God and he will free you from the domination of the unbeliever and all the other problems that afflict you—makes
equally good sense, given the premise that affliction is a sign of the wrath of
God. This argument is in fact a fundamental source of the appeal of militant
Islam today.

There is also the issue of "cultural authenticity." Returning to Islam is a
means of regaining one's authentic cultural identity as opposed to imitating the
culture of the West. Yasin specifically rejects this explanation of the appeal of
militant Islam, declaring: "We are not looking for authenticity."[76] But his references to "the emptiness of our minds of anything but their ideas" and "the
rebirth of [the Arabs'] true identity" suggest that Yasin is in fact looking for
cultural authenticity, among other things.[77] And this question of cultural authenticity is an extremely important one for those educated Moroccans haunted
by a sense of inferiority vis-à-vis Western culture as well as by a loss of their
authentic cultural identity.[78]

But while resentment of foreign domination and, less explicitly, the need for
cultural authenticity, do play a central role in Yasin's writings, he is also disturbed by social injustice in Morocco. In his essay "Daʿwa ila Allah," Yasin
writes that Islam "takes from the rich to give to the poor."[79] He states that "the
poor miserable people groan beneath the oppression of the oppressor class"
and "Islam is a call of love, but there is no love but by the elimination of social
distinctions in wealth and access to education, health, and security."[80]

This is, once again, not the kind of rhetoric normally associated with "fundamentalists," which is one reason it seems more reasonable to refer to people
like Yasin as "militant" rather than "fundamentalist" Muslims. It is true that

condemnation of social inequity is not as common a theme as is the condemnation of foreign domination and deviation from Islam in Yasin's writings. But it is most definitely an important aspect of Yasin's militant Islamic ideology.

There is, however, another dimension to Yasin's writings that is more strictly religious and might legitimately be called "fundamentalist." It is clear that Yasin is outraged by what he perceives as moral degradation and rejection of the laws of God in Moroccan society. He writes:

> in our country, the citizens who respect the time of prayer at work are threatened with dismissal. Now it is the apostates, the sinners and the drunks who govern the country while the real believers are prevented from practicing their religion. The management of politics and the economy is the prerogative of a class of exploiters. The precepts of God are pushed aside.[81]

We thus find Yasin condemning the Moroccan elite for its immorality as well as for its imitation of the West, its exploitation of the poor, and its willingness to perpetuate Morocco's status as a client state of foreign powers. This same multifaceted hostility toward the Moroccan elite is articulated by al-Hajj Muhammad, the peddler in *The House of Si Abd Allah* (al-Hajj Muhammad speaks of the Moroccan elite as "the Fassis" since the core of the Moroccan elite consists of prominent old families from Fez):

> Now the Fassis rule as the Christians used to. *They* have villas, cars, and servants. But those of us who toil for a mouthful of bread have gained nothing since independence.
> And the Fassis and the other rich Moroccans have forgotten their religion. They have become like Christians. Sometimes they speak French among themselves. They send their children to French schools. They marry French women. And even their Muslim wives and daughters bare their bodies like Christian whores. They wear bikinis at the beach and short skirts and low-cut blouses in the streets. . . .
> And even today the Christians still control Morocco. . . . [82]

It is likely that Yasin's radical conception of Islam and his Islamic critique of the Moroccan elite and the government could appeal to Moroccans like al-Hajj Muhammad, the marginally literate peddler. But it is also likely that this peddler has never read or heard of Yasin's writings. And the Moroccan government is determined to make sure that this remains the case.

### The Popular Preachers

A number of popular preachers also regularly preach militant Islamic themes in mosques not controlled by the government, but their numbers are not known. Some of them are less radical than Yasin or al-Shabiba. Tozy contends that in Casablanca, which had a population of two million in 1982, there are only four to six private mosques where such relatively militant preachers preach.[83] However, the sermons of some of these preachers, e.g., the Faqih al-Zamzami of Tangier, are taped and sold clandestinely, like the tapes of the preacher Shaikh Kishk in Egypt and those of Khumaini in prerevolutionary Iran.[84] And the cassette tapes of the sermons and lessons of Shaikh Kishk himself are widely sold in Morocco's largest cities as well as in France's Maghribi neighborhoods.[85]

Tozy quotes the Faqih al-Zamzami of Tangier as saying: "Islam intervenes in [all] the affairs of society from A to Z . . . the preacher must therefore speak of everything that concerns Muslims."[86] Al-Zamzami says he refuses to restrict his sermons to trivialities "so that the government will like us; that is not what God has commanded us, we are not hypocrites. . . . "[87] And al-Zamzami's son, who preaches in the old city of Casablanca, declared in a sermon given in April 1983 that the Shari⁽a (Islamic law) should be applied in all sectors of life. And he defined the Shari⁽a as "the struggle against poverty, injustice and ignorance, which are the true enemies of faith. . . . "[88]

Mohammed Selhami describes another free preacher preaching to about forty men after the evening prayer in a small mosque on the outskirts of Casablanca. This man is a carpenter in his thirties:

> For about an hour the holy man preaches and recites a *hadith* concerning human injustice. Nobody moves. The argument is entirely political. One would think oneself before a member of the opposition in parliament fulminating against the government. Only one person is spared: the king. It is not an accident. The imam [leader of prayer] explained to us later that his sovereign was a man deeply attached to Islam. "He is the descendent of Siyyidna [our Lord] Muhammad. To criticize him is to attack the family of the prophet." On the other hand, the imam is particularly hostile to certain members of the king's entourage, including some ministers "who give him bad advice."[89]

Some of the mosques where these preachers preach are important gathering places and recruitment centers for the militant Islamic movement, and are therefore closely watched by the police.[90] And some of these "free preachers" have been arrested.[91] But those still allowed to preach generally avoid openly advocating an Islamic revolution.[92]

It is hard to know how many of Morocco's relatively militant preachers are in fact committed to an Islamic revolution and how many simply want reform. But many Islamic militants in Morocco condemn Egypt's Shaikh Kishk because he writes for a government-controlled newspaper and because of the praise he has received from Saudi periodicals.[93] For these more radical militants, it is not enough to demand the implementation of Islamic law in all aspects of life. Such implementation must be combined with a social revolution and the termination of dependence upon foreign superpowers. Some of Morocco's "free preachers" are probably less committed to these "revolutionary" and "anti-imperialist" goals than are the students in al-Shabiba al-Islamiyya.

### The Bushishiyya Brotherhood and Jama^c^at al-Tabligh wa al-Da^c^wa

In his study of Islamic militancy in Morocco, Tozy refers to two Islamic groups as having affinities with the militant Islamic movement: the Bushishiyya Sufi brotherhood (to which ^c^Abd as-Slam Yasin once belonged) and the Jama^c^at al-Tabligh wa al-Da^c^wa, or Society for the Transmission (of the true Islam) and the Call (to the true Islam).[94] But both these groups claim to be, and do indeed appear to be, apolitical.[95] Although the Jama^c^at al-Tabligh wa al-Da^c^wa has been defended by Yasin, it has been condemned by more radical Islamic militants because of its emphasis on the moral transformation of the individual rather than the revolutionary transformation of society. Most militants would probably condemn the Bushishiyya order for the same reason, not to mention the antipathy of the militants to all Sufi brotherhoods in general.

### Conclusion

Morocco's militant revivalists are primarily high school and university students and secondarily civil servants (especially teachers and administrators in the Ministry of Education). But not all Moroccan students are Islamic militants, and only 5 to 10 percent of university students support an Islamic revolution.[96]

The movement has not so far attracted many of Morocco's urban poor. The peddler and the carpenter/preacher cited earlier demonstrate, however, that some of Morocco's urban poor and working class are, or could become, sympathetic to much of what the militants are saying. The shopkeepers may listen to the sermons of Shaikh Kishk and they may share some of the values of the militants, but there is no indication that they share the militants' commitment to the idea of an Islamic revolution. The Moroccan peasantry has also not been drawn to Islamic militancy, except for some high school and university students of peasant origins. Many peasants, as well as some of the other more traditional strata of Morocco, continue to revere the king as a descendant of the Prophet Muhammad and as "Commander of the Faithful." Some army officers (educated young people again) are of a militant Islamic orientation, but their numbers are not known. Nor do we know how many officers are potential Moroccan Zia ul-Haqs—i.e. advocates of internal Islamization coupled with continued dependence on the United States—as opposed to more radical militants.

Given the dire economic situation in Morocco, as reflected in the riots of June 1981 and January 1984, a successful coup by militant Islamic officers is a real possibility. But that would appear to be the only way a militant Islamic regime could replace that of Hasan II in the near future. The militant Islamic movement in Morocco seems to be impotent at the moment. Its most prominent leaders are in jail or exile. And the fervor generated by the Iranian revolution has cooled down considerably.

But the apparent present impotence of the movement should not be interpreted to mean that the movement has been permanently eliminated. People like Yasin are articulating some widespread popular grievances, and they will be around so long as these grievances exist.

# NOTES

I would like to thank Jean-François Clément, Georges Joffé, and Muhammad Tozy for helping me to obtain much of the data upon which this paper is based. My research in Morocco in 1976–77 was made possible by fellowships from the Social Science Research Council and the Fulbright-Hays Program of the Office of Education.

1. See Henry Munson, Jr., "The Social Base of Islamic Militancy in Morocco," *The Middle East Journal*, Vol. 40, No. 2 (Spring 1985), pp. 267–284, and idem, "Islamic Revivalism in Morocco and Tunisia," *The Muslim World*, Vol. 76 (July–October 1986).

2. Remy Leveau, "Islam officiel et renouveau islamique au Maroc," in Christiane Souriau, ed., *Le Maghreb musulman en 1979* (Paris: CNRS, 1983), p. 212.

3. Muhammad Tozy, *Champ et contre-champ politico-religieux au Maroc*, Thèse pour le Doctorat d'Etat en Science Politique, Faculté de Droit et de Science Politique d'Aix-Marseille, 1984, p. 348.

4. Hamid Barrada, "De Rabat à la Mecque," *Jeune Afrique*, No. 990–991 (Dec. 26, 1979, and Jan. 2, 1980), p. 38.

5. Ibid.

6. Tozy, *Champ et contre-champ*, p. 401; Bruno Etienne, "L'Islam à Marseille ou les tribulations d'un anthropologue," *Les Temps Modernes*, No. 452–454 (March–May 1984), p. 1617; *Al-Jamaᶜa*, No. 7 (November 1980–January 1981), pp. 70–75. Iranian students have told me of similar transformations of Iranian intellectuals, the best-known case being that of Jalal Al-e Ahmad. See Nikki Keddie, *Roots of Revolution: An Interpretative History of Modern Iran* (New Haven, Conn.: Yale University Press, 1981), pp. 202–205.

7. Zouhaier Dhaouadi and Amr Ibrahim, "Documents," *Peuples Méditerranéens*, No. 21 (October–December 1982), pp. 57–58.

8. Tozy, *Champ et contre-champ*, p. 346.

9. Barrada, "De Rabat à la Mecque," p. 38.

10. Ibid.

11. Ibid.

12. Ibid.

13. Ibid.; *Al-Jamaᶜa*, No. 5 (February–March 1980), pp. 108–109, and No. 6 (April–July 1980), pp. 92–94; Tozy, *Champ et contre-champ*, p. 347.

14. Mohamed Selhami, "Les frères marocains," *Jeune Afrique*, No. 990–991 (Dec. 26, 1979, and Jan. 2, 1980), p. 37; Barrada, "De Rabat à la Mecque," p. 38; Tozy, *Champ et contre-champ*, p. 347.

15. Barrada, "De Rabat à la Mecque," p. 38.

16. Tozy, *Champ et contre-champ*, p. 347.

17. Barrada, "De Rabat à la Mecque," p. 38; Leveau, "Islam officiel et renouveau islamique au Maroc," p. 212; Tozy, *Champ et contre-champ*, p. 348; Jim Paul, "Insur-

rection at Mecca," *MERIP Reports*, No. 91 (October 1980), p. 4. (Muti' is referred to as Joutti in the latter article. This is probably a typographical error.)

18. *Quarterly Economic Review of Morocco*, 1984, No. 2, p. 11.

19. Richard Parker, *North Africa: Regional Tensions and Strategic Concerns* (New York: Praeger, 1984), p. 96; Mark Tessler, "Politics in Morocco: The Monarch, the War, and the Opposition," *American Universities Field Staff Reports*, No. 47 (1981), p. 15; Hamied Ansari, "The Islamic Militants in Egyptian Politics," *International Journal of Middle East Studies*, Vol. 16, No. 1 (March 1984), p. 123; Gilles Kepel, *Le Prophète et pharaon: Les mouvements islamistes dans l'Egypte contemporaine* (Paris: Editions La Découverte, 1984), p. 130; Mohamed Heikal, *Autumn of Fury: The Assassination of Sadat* (New York: Random House, 1983), pp. 129–134.

20. Dhaouadi and Ibrahim, "Documents," pp. 57–58; *Al-Jamaᶜa*, No. 2 (June–August 1979), pp. 46–47, No. 5 (February–March 1980), pp. 13–14, No. 6 (April–July 1980), pp. 30–52; Christiane Souriau, "Quelques données comparatives sur les institutions islamiques actuelles du Maghreb," in Souriau, *Le Maghreb musulman*, p. 377.

21. Tozy, *Champ et contre-champ*, p. 351.

22. *Al-Jamaᶜa*, No. 5 (February–March 1980), pp. 105–115, and No. 6 (April–July 1980), pp. 92–94.

23. Tozy, *Champ et contre-champ*, p. 349.

24. Ibid.

25. *Le Monde*, July 20, 1984, p. 3, and Aug. 2, 1984, p. 3. The first of these articles refers to a group called al-Jihad, which is said to be a faction within the Mouvement Islamique, which is said to be led by ᶜAbd al-Karim Muti'. These are presumably among the evanescent factions of al-Shabiba al-Islamiyya, although they are not mentioned by Tozy in his discussion of the group. See Tozy, *Champ et contre-champ*, p. 349.

26. *Le Monde*, Aug. 2, 1984, p. 3.

27. *Al-Sharq al-Awsat*, Oct. 18, 1985, p. 1, Oct. 26, 1985, p. 1.

28. The presence of the Shah in February and March 1979 provoked a series of strikes in the universities, schools, and public utilities. See Leveau, "L'Islam officiel et le renouveau islamique au Maroc," p. 209. On the riots of June 1981, which were sparked by food price increases, see Mohamed Selhami, "Mourir à Casablanca," *Jeune Afrique*, No. 1070 (July 8, 1981), pp. 15–18. On the riots of January 1984, which were precipitated by an increase in the fee paid by students in order to take the *baccalaureat* exam at the end of high school as well as by increases in basic food prices, see Jim Paul, "States of Emergency: The Riots in Tunisia and Morocco," and David Seddon, "Winter of Discontent: Economic Crisis in Tunisia and Morocco," *MERIP Reports*, Vol. 14, No. 8 (October 1984), pp. 3–16; and Jean-François Clément's forthcoming paper, "Stratégies repressives et techniques du maintien de l'ordre: Les revoltes urbaines de janvier 1984 au Maroc."

29. See Munson, "The Social Base of Islamic Militancy in Morocco."

30. Ibid.

31. Bruno Etienne and Muhammad Tozy, "Le Glissement des obligations islamiques vers le phénomène associatif à Casablanca," in Souriau, *Le Maghreb musulman*, p. 254; Tozy, *Champ et contre-champ*, p. 395.

32. Tozy, *Champ et contre-champ*, p. 404.

33. *Le Monde*, Feb. 15, 1985.

34. Tozy, *Champ et contre-champ*, p. 386.

35. Ibid.

36. Ibid.

37. ᶜAbd as-Slam Yasin, *La Revolution à l'heure de l'Islam* (Marseille: Les Presses de l'Imprimerie du College, 1979), p. 2. This work is discussed by Jean-Claude Vatin in an unpublished paper entitled "Seduction and Sedition: Islamic Polemical Discourses in the Maghreb."

38. Yasin, *La Revolution*, p. 2.

39. *Al-Jama^ca*, No. 2 (June–August 1979), pp. 22, 24–25.
40. Ibid., p. 123.
41. The gallicized form of this word, *islamiste*, has become standard in the French scholarly literature on Islamic militancy.
42. Tozy, *Champ et contre-champ*, p. 381.
43. Ibid., pp. 390–393.
44. Ibid., pp. 386–387.
45. *Al-Jama^ca*, No. 2 (June–August 1979), p. 123.
46. Ibid., No. 5 (February–March 1980), pp. 118–120, and No. 7 (November 1980–.January 1981), pp. 76–77.
47. Ibid., No. 2 (June–August 1979), p. 123.
48. Ibid., No. 11 (May 1983), p. 4.
49. Ibid.
50. Ibid.; Souriau, "Quelques données comparatives," p. 377.
51. Tozy, "Champ et contre-champ," p. 394.
52. *The Middle East and North Africa 1983–84* (London: Europa Editions, 1983), p. 516.
53. *Al-Jama^ca*, No. 2 (June–August 1979), p. 43; Souriau, "Quelques données comparatives," p. 378.
54. Tozy, *Champ et contre-champ*, p. 383; *Le Monde*, Feb. 15, 1984.
55. See Clément, "Stratégies repressives," p. 38.
56. *Quarterly Economic Review of Morocco*, 1984, No. 2, p. 11.
57. *Le Monde*, May 3, 1984.
58. *Quarterly Economic Review of Morocco*, 1984, No. 3, p. 6.
59. *Al-Jama^ca*, No. 11 (May 1983), p. 94.
60. *Quarterly Economic Review of Morocco*, 1984, No. 3, p. 6.
61. *Al-Jama^ca*, No. 10 (July 1982), p. 31.
62. Ibid., No. 2 (June–August 1979), pp. 119–121, and No. 5 (February–March 1980).
63. Ibid., No. 5 (February–March 1980), pp. 6, 15–16, and No. 10 (July 1982), p. 3.
64. Souriau, "Quelques donnees comparatives," p. 378.
65. *Al-Jama^ca*, No. 2 (June–August 1979), p. 11.
66. See Yvonne Yazbeck Haddad, "The Qur'anic Justification for an Islamic Revolution: The View of Sayyid Qutb," *The Middle East Journal*, Vol. 37, No. 1 (Winter 1983), pp. 14–29.
67. Sayyid Qutb, *al-Ma^calim fi al-Tariq* (Beirut: Dar al-Qur'an al-Karim, 1978), pp. 17–18.
68. Henry Munson, Jr., *The House of Si Abd Allah: The Oral History of a Moroccan Family* (New Haven, Conn.: Yale University Press, 1984), pp. 20–21.
69. *Al-Jama^ca*, No. 2 (June–August 1979), p. 48.
70. Ibid., p. 12.
71. Ibid.
72. Hasan al-Banna, *Rasa'il al-Imam al-Shahid Hasan al-Banna* (Beirut: Dar al-Andalus, 1965), p. 221; ^cAli Shari'ati, *Fatima Is Fatima*, trans. Laleh Bakhtiar (Tehran: Shari'ati Foundation, 1983), pp. 103–104; Hamid Algar, ed., *Islam and Revolution: Writings and Declarations of Imam Khomeini* (Berkeley, Calif.: Mizan Press, 1981), p. 276.
73. *Al-Jama^ca*, No. 2 (June-August 1979), pp. 3–5.
74. Munson, *The House of Si Abd Allah*, pp. 23–24.
75. Ibid., p. 68.
76. *Al-Jama^ca*, No. 2 (June–August 1979), p. 22.
77. Ibid., pp. 12, 4.
78. Munson, *The House of Si Abd Allah*, pp. 55–56, 112–113.
79. *Al-Jama^ca*, No. 2, p. 37.

80. Ibid., p. 49.
81. *Al-Jamaᶜa*, No. 4 (December 1979-January 1980), p. 14.
82. Munson, *The House of Si Abd Allah*, pp. 21–22.
83. Tozy, *Champ et contre-champ*, p. 302; Mohamed Lahbabi, *L'Economie marocaine, Notions Essentielles, Tome 1: Les Fondements de l'économie marocaine* (Casablanca: Les Editions Maghrebines, 1977), p. 200.
84. Tozy, *Champ et contre-champ*, p. 296.
85. Ibid., p. 282; Bruno Etienne, "L'Islam à Marseille ou les tribulations d'un anthropologue," p. 1629.
86. Ibid., p. 297.
87. Ibid.
88. Ibid., p. 301.
89. Selhami, "Les frères marocains," p. 37.
90. Ibid., p. 302.
91. *Al-Jamaᶜa*, No. 5 (February–March 1980), p. 109.
92. Selhami, "Les frères marocains," p. 37.
93. Tozy, *Champ et contre-champ*, pp. 281, 283; Kepel, *Le Prophète et pharaon*, pp. 165, 169.
94. Tozy, *Le Champ et contre-champ*, pp. 268–280, 307–345.
95. Ibid., pp. 276, 334–335.
96. Munson, "The Social Base of Islamic Militancy," pp. 271–275.

# X

# TUNISIA

## *Norma Salem*

The relationship of Islam to politics has become of front-page interest since the spectacular events of the revolution in Iran in 1979. The failure of Western experts to understand, let alone to predict, the "Islamic" revolution led American policymakers astray. More fundamentally, this failure demonstrated the weakness of both the Orientalist approach and the area-studies approach to the study of the relationship between Islam and politics.

From such a critical perspective, we are confronted by two problems. On the policymaking level, there is the need to assess the extent to which Islamic revolutions similar to that in Iran are possible or imminent in other countries. But in order to be able to do so, we need to develop analytic tools beyond the Orientalist and the area-studies approaches. Consequently, this paper has two objectives: (1) to describe the Islamic movements claiming a role in politics, using Tunisia as a case study; and (2) to attempt to develop analytic tools capable of allowing us to understand and to assess these movements.

As preliminary to the development of a theoretical framework, the limitations of the traditional Orientalist and area-studies approaches will be reviewed. A historical outline of socioeconomic and political developments in Tunisia during the twentieth century will provide a background for the sociological and ideological analyses of the situation during the 1980s. Finally, the conclusion will attempt to assess the possible future scenarios despite the fact that we are still in the initial phase of trying to sort out the real meaning of the Islamic integralist movements which seem to be enveloping the Middle East and North Africa.

### Review of Orientalism and Middle East Area Studies

Even before the Iranian revolution, the Orientalist approach had been criticized. This first stream of criticism found fault with the Orientalists for using stereotypes that are traceable back to the medieval conflict among the monotheist religions and revolve around three themes: falseness, violence, and licentiousness.[1] It is truly remarkable how present-day stereotypes of Muslims, and more particularly of Arabs, may still be classified in these categories: the shifty-eyed Arab, the irrational Palestinian (or Shiʿa) terrorist, and the lustful shaikh.[2]

The second stream was even harsher, since it criticized Orientalism in terms of the "discipline's" theoretical premises. It considered that the essentialism and ahistoricism of Orientalism were disturbing,[3] as they seemed to explain— or to explain away—over 900 million people and 1,400 years of history in a neat formula: Islam consists of an eternal "essence" which explains Muslims completely. Moreover, the basic unit of study, the "Orient," as opposed to some similarly ahistorical essence, the "Occident" or the "West," was attacked.[4] The basic contention of this second stream of criticism is that Orientalism, by positing an "Orient" different by its very essence from the "Occident," leads to circular thinking. People act the way they do because they are "Orientals" and their strange behavior proves that they are essentially different. Thus, we note that the increasing role religion is playing in politics is usually considered a phenomenon specific to Islam—because Islam is what it is. Yet the Roman Catholic Church has been an important actor in the politics of Poland; the Likud, Gush Emunim, and the Kahane movement insist on a greater role for Judaism in Israeli politics; the Sikh movement in India was instrumental in the assassination of Indira Gandhi, and so on.[5]

As for the area-studies approach, there is a similar problem with the definition of the unit (or area) of study, since there is no consistent criterion that serves to define the "Middle East." The area covered by the term *Middle East* may include a few more or a few less countries, depending on the author, as there is no independent criterion—geographical, cultural, political, or otherwise— that justifies one choice over the other. Why include Iran but not Pakistan? And if Pakistan, why not Algeria? Moreover, the situation has changed drastically since World War I, when the term came to be accepted in its present meaning, so that Turkey is now a NATO ally and an associate member of the European Economic Community. Consequently, the Eurocentric military perspective that underlies the historical background of the term has lost much of its relevance. Nevertheless, the Arab countries, which claim a cultural communality and have established a common political forum, the League of Arab States, could logically form a coherent unit of study. In fact, there exist sufficient indicators to consider the Arab countries a subsystem in terms of international relations.[6]

In the second place, there is the question of the applicability of social science concepts, which were developed in the framework of European history, to the "Middle East" or to "Islam." Some scholars hold that it would be a mistake to even attempt to construct universal paradigms for the analysis of different societies. They consider that the historical experience of Third World countries is so different from historical developments in Europe and the industrialized countries that totally new categories should be created. Others consider that only Islamic categories can be used to understand and to explain Islamic phenomena.[7] Personally, I have not given up on the idea of building universal concepts applicable across cultures. But such cross-cultural concepts can become truly universal only by being broadened in the light of the historical experiences of all peoples and not simply of Europeans.

In summary, the Orientalist and area-studies approaches have not been sufficiently fruitful because they have not succeeded in overcoming the following problems: the inappropriate or ambiguous definition of the unit of study, the prevalence of stereotypes, and the lack of historical perspective and of conceptual depth. This does not mean that these approaches have nothing to contribute; on the contrary, a rigorous perspective can only lead to their rejuvenation.

## Theoretical Framework

The study of the Middle East and of Islam has not contributed much to the development of theory in social sciences.[8] This lack of theory was perhaps one of the reasons for the inability of researchers to make sense of, or even to name, the so-called Islamic "renaissance, resurgence, reawakening, renewal, regeneration, revitalization, re-emergence, resurrection, rebirth, reconstruction, reassertion, revolution, revivification, reform and revival."[9]

Other terms have also been used to qualify the phenomenon, such as *fundamentalist, militant,* or *radical* Islam, but all these terms carry connotations beyond the Arabic which may distort the image of the phenomenon even before an English-speaking audience realizes the problem. The fact that the specialists in the field do not agree on the term to be used to name the phenomenon under study is an indication of both theoretical and empirical weaknesses. To some extent, the term *Islamism* has been used to avoid the problem of intrusive connotations, as it is the closest translation of the Arabic *islami* which seems to have appeared first among Maghribi Muslims to distinguish between *muslim* and *islami,* the latter referring to those who see in Islam a political ideology.[10] The term *Islamist* is not particularly satisfying since it may prevent the observers from seeing similarities with situations where other religious traditions are being transformed into political ideologies. Perhaps *integralists* could serve as a more general term; it is derived from the French *intégristes* and refers to the ideological stance of considering "religion" and "politics" to be an "integral" unity. Moreover, this term is very close to the Islamic *tawhid* , referring to the "unity" of God within theology and to the "unity" of religion and politics within religio-political theory. The main advantage of the term is its capacity to be used cross-culturally, which would allow us to speak of Christian integralists, Jewish integralists, Sikh integralists as much as of Muslim integralists. Where we refer to people, the adjectival *Muslim* will be used and where we refer to objects or abstract concepts, the adjectival *Islamic* will be used—thus, "Muslim integralists" and "Islamic integralist movements."

Beginning with Dessouki's *Islamic Resurgence in the Arab World,* the need to elaborate a theoretical framework has been expressed and a number of attempts have been made.[11] Most of these attempts have centered on the Weberian concept of "crisis" or on the Toynbeean concept of "challenge and response."[12] The following remarks are intended to add to this evolving corpus of theoretical work and hopefully to lead us to a clearer understanding of the relationship between religion and politics within a particular area so that it could be seen as comparable to other areas.

The first step in developing our theoretical framework is to define our basic area of study. As mentioned above, there are sufficient indicators to justify a regional approach based on the Arab world, considered as a subsystem, for macro purposes. Moreover, the actual states may be considered viable micro units of study when we consider any political question with the proviso that, at present, the legitimacy of both the Arab subsystem, as a whole, and the existing Arab states, considered individually, is still weak and should not be taken for granted. The second step is to maintain a comparative perspective even if it is not made explicit so that we avoid the trap of considering the phenomena under study as locked within specific frontiers. The third step is to have a historical perspective in order to be able to comprehend change as it occurs. Finally, the comparative and the historical perspectives should allow us to use concepts cross-culturally, as long as we realize and make explicit the limits of their applicability.

It is particularly important to reexamine those ideological assumptions that are often confused with the basic definitions of fundamental concepts. For example, it is usually assumed that only in the "West," as opposed to the Islamic "East," are the two concepts of "religion" and "politics" unrelated both as theoretical concepts and as historical phenomena in terms of both ideas and institutions. Historically, this is not true either in the West or in the Islamic East—as the long struggle between church and state in Europe and the struggle over the succession of the Prophet in the Islamic East demonstrate. Whether "religion" and "politics" should or should not be related is an ideological issue beyond the basic definitions of the two concepts.

That "there is no distinction between religion and politics in Islam" is such a prevalent assumption that it is time to reexamine it critically. In the first place, the Arabic language does distinguish between the concepts of *din* (religion) and *siyasa* (politics), *dawla* (state) and *sultan* (power). The fact that many Muslim thinkers argue in favor of subjecting politics to the exigencies of religion indicates that such an ideal situation did not always exist either historically or even ideologically. As Hermassi noted:

> The task is not made any easier for the scholar when the Islamists themselves behave according to these same premises and take pleasure in assuming that their dream is itself reality. To continue conceiving of Islam as an essence which, by definition, is transhistorical, means to forbid oneself from distinguishing between Islam and Islamism and from differentiating between a religion and the process by which that religion is transformed into ideology.[13]

To my mind, one of the few new approaches to the problem of the relationship between religion and politics which might bear fruit is the study of Islam as discourse—in other words, the study of how Muslims express themselves. Although several authors have pointed out the importance of studying Islamic "ideology" and Islamic "symbols," very few have actually done so in specific terms. Such an approach, I suggest, could draw on two very rich traditions— political economy and literary criticism. The following attempt at constructing a "political economy of the symbolic" is based on the work of Pierre Bourdieu.[14]

According to Bourdieu, language—as a mode of knowledge—defines those who use it as much as the reality it represents and the same may be said of all "symbolic forms," including religion. Religion, as "collective representation" or a common set of symbols, serves as an instrument of knowledge as well as of communication or, more precisely, as a symbolic medium which structures reality and is itself structured. As a structured system acting as structuring principle, religion acts to consecrate and legitimate (or deconsecrate and de-legitimate) the world view received through experience by transforming implicit outlines of perception and action into ethics, a systematized and rationalized system of explicit norms. Religion is predisposed to assume an ideological func-tion by lending the value of absolute to what is relative and by lending (or withdrawing) legitimacy to what is arbitrary. It assumes this function inasmuch as it reinforces the material (or symbolic) forces which may be mobilized by a group. As such, religion also serves as a factor delimiting and, thus, identifying the community concerned.

This view of religion, as "collective representations" which lend meaningful integration to social reality, allows us to avoid the illusion of the absolute au-tonomy of religious discourse (the idealist view) as much as the reductionist practice of considering religious discourse as the mere "reflection" of social structure (the crude materialist view). The process of transforming sociopolitical realities into the supranatural structure of the universe and, thus, structuring the perception of social reality may be considered "symbolic labor." The process of transformation includes the phases of production, reproduction, and diffu-sion. The accumulation of this "symbolic labor" may then be considered to constitute "symbolic capital."

The social functions of religion are to provide the justification (or the rejection) of a specific social structure. The vision of the world proposed by religious movements is the product of more or less well-defined groups speaking on behalf of other specific groups, and the constitution of a religious domain is dependent upon the objective dispossession of those who are excluded (lay-persons) because they lack *religious capital* (accumulation of religious labor) and who recognize the legitimacy of their own dispossession by the mere fact of not recognizing it as such. An important point which Bourdieu insists upon is that a religious ideology can, by definition, exert a mobilizing effect only to the extent that the socioeconomic interests that sustain it are hidden both to those who produce it and to those who consume it. Nevertheless, the analysis of the internal structure of the religious message cannot ignore the sociologically built functions it fulfills for the producer groups and for the consumer groups. These social functions fulfilled by religion for a group or a class are necessarily differentiated with respect to the position occupied by each group or class both in the structure of class relations and in the division of religious labor.

The *exchange* relations established on the basis of the differing interests between the specialists and the laypeople and the *competitive* relations opposing different groups of specialists constitute the dynamic principle within the religious field. The *circulation* of the religious message necessarily implies a reinterpretation achieved consciously by the specialists or unconsciously by the process of cultural diffusion. Such reinterpretation depends upon the economic, social, and cultural distance between the producers, the merchandisers, and the consumers.

The religious capital which different religious groups can invest in the process of reinterpretation depends on the relationship between religious *demand* (i.e., the interests of groups or classes of laypersons) and religious *supply* (i.e., either "orthodox" or "heretical" services of specialists). Moreover, religious capital determines the nature, the form, and the strength of the strategies followed by such groups or classes to satisfy their religious interests as well as the division of religious labor. Consequently, it also determines the division of political labor. Bourdieu insists on the "interconvertibility" of "symbolic" interests and (material) economic interests. At the limit, wars of religion are neither violent theological quarrels nor class conflicts. They are both at the same time because the categories of religious thought make it impossible to think and to undertake class conflict as such by allowing conflict to be thought of and undertaken as religious conflict.

### Historical Background

That Islam should play a role in politics is not a new theme on the Tunisian scene. During the struggle of liberation from France, Islam provided the moral, cultural, and ideological symbols needed to formulate resistance as early as the Djellaz cemetery riots of 1911. Such nationalist figures as Thaalbi, Sfar, Khider Houssine, and Tahar Haddad called for the defense of Islamic values. Even Habib Bourguiba insisted in 1929 on the retention of the veil as a symbol of Tunisian identity.[15] But, following World War II, it was Salah Ben Youssef— a rival of Bourguiba—who wielded Islamic symbols and who allied himself with organizations based around the university mosque of the Zaytuna in Tunis. On the international level, Ben Youssef drew support from the Arab "East" and from the nonaligned Third World. In contrast, Bourguiba, at that point, emphasized the themes of progress and development and allied himself with the labor federation, the Union Générale des Travailleurs Tunisiens (UGTT). On the international level, Bourguiba drew strength from his ability to influence the French authorities. Concomitant to these alignments, Ben Youssef emphasized the Arab-Islamic identity of Tunisia while Bourguiba emphasized the specificity of the Tunisian identity, as such.[16]

Following independence, for which Bourguiba claimed credit, he set out to gradually "reform" Islamic institutions. At the beginning, consistent with his gradualism, these reforms were undertaken in consultation with Muslim religious specialists; such was, among other reforms, the Code of Personal Status (August 13, 1956), which was based on a liberal modernist interpretation of Islamic law.[17] In contrast to Kemal Ataturk, Bourguiba did not break completely with the Islamic cultural heritage of Tunisia; thus, the Code of Personal Status was prepared with the assistance of "liberal" *ulama* (religious leaders) of the Zaytuna and only a small minority resisted its promulgation. But the trend was clear toward the domination of the religious realm by the political realm as further reforms were implemented. Shari^c a courts were abolished (September 1956), and the system of *habus*, whereby property was donated for "religious" purposes (more often than not, these were social services such as hospitals, schools, and public works), was taken over by the state. In Iran, incidentally, the failure of the Shah to take over such property and the continued ability of the religious specialists to collect funds gave them an autonomous economic base from which to launch the revolution. That is not the case in any of the Arab countries, where the official religious hierarchy (serving the courts, the schools, and the mosques) is practically incorporated into the civil service and is, therefore, dependent on the state.

In other moves by Bourguiba, the Islamic educational system was incorporated into the state system and the Zaytuna was reduced to the Faculty of Theology of the University of Tunis.[18] Even the mosques became dependent on the state for their maintenance and for the salaries of the preachers. Moreover, to enter into the political realm it became necessary to be able to speak two languages (French and Arabic) and move in two cultures (European and Arab-Islamic). As a consequence of these reforms, that fraction of the political elite whose symbolic capital was based on knowledge of Arabic and of Islam and on the control of Islamic institutions was dispossessed of political power and social mobility.

Bourguiba is a populist and he knows full well that to mobilize the masses, political leaders must either themselves build up political capital (for example, Ataturk's successful war of liberation) or draw upon the symbolic capital of mass culture. Consequently, Bourguiba's reforms never went to the extent of rejecting the Islamic dimension of Tunisian identity; for example, the 1959 constitution proclaimed Islam the state religion (article 1) and required the president of the republic to be a Muslim (article 37). In fact, the Tunisian government and the Socialist Destour Party (better known by its French acronym, PSD, for Parti Socialiste Destourien) never explicitly proclaimed their secularism.[19]

During the 1960s and the early 1970s, the dominant themes in the political discourse of Tunisian political leaders were progress, modernization, and development. Actually, Bourguiba attempted to transform himself into a religious specialist by lending Islamic religious justification to these new themes. During the month of Ramadan in 1960 (February 5), he called for an end to the fast, which hinders development since it decreases production and increases consumption. But his attempt was limited by the very logic of its legitimation. He presented his view as a novel interpretation of Islamic law; Tunisia was fighting a holy war against underdevelopment and, since Islamic law allowed breaking the fast during holy war, it was therefore permissible to break the fast. Unfortunately, he failed to obtain the approval of any of the ᶜulama and Ramadan continued to be celebrated. In a way, this failure was indicative of the later failure to maintain the "socialist" economic policies of the Ben Salah government during the 1960s. The constant insistence, in Tunisian political discourse, on Bourguiba's role in the independence movement may be considered, with hindsight, as a symptom of the inability of these symbols (progress, modernization, development) to provide sufficient legitimacy by themselves.

Tunisia is considered to be among the better off countries of the Third World,[20] with a per capita income of about $1,200 per year. Moreover, Tunisia is noted for its evolutionary development and its "moderate" policies in domestic and foreign affairs, and it has enjoyed a continuity of political institutions that may be unrivaled in the Arab world. Unfortunately, Tunisia has not been able to avoid the consequences of the upheavals in the world economy as inflation spiraled in the United States beginning in 1966 and spread to the rest of the world during the 1970s. These general problems interacted with the pressures characteristic of Third World countries, particularly a burgeoning population, which, despite efforts to control it, is still growing at 2.1 percent a year; symptomatically, over two-thirds of Tunisia's almost seven million people are under twenty-five years of age.

Although the liberal economic policies of the Nouira government of the 1970s improved production, it was unable to maintain a stable distributive pattern. By 1978, 22.5 percent of the population was still living below the poverty line, sharing in only 5 percent of the national product while the top 20 percent of the population shared in 50 percent of the national product.[21] Expressed differently, national revenue increased by 205 percent during the decade between 1970 and 1980, but gross salaries increased by only 168 percent. Thus, the share of salaries in the national revenue actually decreased from 51 percent to 45 percent.[22] As a result, the salaried "middle" classes faced a blocked future and downward mobility for their children.[23] While unemployment was 14 percent among the general population in 1983, it was over 25 percent among those less than twenty-five years old.[24] Since the state is one of the most important employers, the blockage of the salaried middle classes became a problem of the state. In fact, these problems were affecting a wide spectrum of social groups and soon were expressed in dramatic fashion.

On the political level, several explosive incidents occurred—the Black Thursday riots in Tunis in January 1978, the Gafsah revolt of January 1980, and the bread riots of January 1984. In the 1978 incidents, a general strike and demonstrations led by the country's federation of trade unions, the UGTT, over degenerating economic conditions led to violent riots with many deaths and widespread arrests. At Gafsah, a phosphate-mining town in the south, the revolt expressed dissatisfaction with regional disparities. The third in the series of incidents was a direct result of measures required by the International Monetary Fund of the Tunisian government to end the subsidies on basic necessities, such as bread and cooking oil, which had been instituted following the Gafsah incident.

Each of these explosions exposed the dissatisfaction of different sectors of Tunisian society. In 1978, the unions, representing the salaried white-collar and blue-collar workers squeezed by inflation, led the demonstrations. In 1980, the Gafsah invasion by Tunisian commandoes, probably trained by Libya, exposed the regional disparities whereby the south and the center of Tunisia did not benefit as much as the littoral from the development policies of the government. The 1984 bread riots were led by students, illustrating the alienation of youth despairing of obtaining their share under the Tunisian sun and the failure of the forced PSD/UGTT alliance to achieve national consensus. The events of 1978, 1980, and 1984 illustrate the "crisis" in Tunisia with respect to two levels of problems—the economic problems of production and distribution in a situation of dependency, and the ideological problem of achieving a national consensus to tackle these problems.

The period between the appointment of the Mzali government in April 1980 and its dismissal in July 1986 is characterized by the continuation of the economic policies of the Nouira period accompanied by an attempt to build a national consensus around a basic alliance between the government/PSD and the UGTT. The UGTT, in fact, is the only organization with a spectrum of political tendencies large enough and a base wide enough[25] to enable it possibly to forge the social alliances needed to construct a national consensus. Unfortunately, the UGTT was brought into the political process not as an independent party, nor as a loyal opposition, but within a forced Patriotic Front with joint PSD-UGTT lists.

The hard-liners within the PSD and the UGTT resisted these moves and the problem was further complicated in view of the underlying struggle for the succession to the two Habibs, Bourguiba (head of the government/PSD) and Achour (head of the UGTT). By the end of 1983, it was clear that the alliance was breaking down as the government more or less encouraged the establishment of a rival confederation of trade unions, the UNTT (Union Nationale des Travailleurs Tunisiens). With the failure to build a national consensus, it was thus no surprise that "bread riots" broke out when the price subsidies on basic necessities were removed in December. The measure was quickly rescinded by Bourguiba.

In retrospect, these "riots" may be considered to be the beginning of the end of the Mzali government. During 1984 and 1985, the government continued to pressure the UGTT by linking further salary increases to increases in productivity, rather than to price increases, and by ending the automatic 1 percent salary deductions destined to finance union activities. The conflict between the government and the UGTT escalated further during the second part of 1985 as the UGTT responded by increasing the number of strikes and as the government began to arrest UGTT members and to close down a number of the federation's offices. The tensions between the UGTT and the government were echoed on the campuses and a number of university students were arrested in January 1986.

The credibility of the Mzali government was not helped any when, on October 1, 1985, Israeli jets attacked the headquarters of the Palestine Liberation Organization near Tunis, killing thirty to fifty people and wounding many more, including Tunisian civilians. The Tunisian government lost even more of its "symbolic capital" when the U.S. administration declared that the Israeli attack was "legitimate," although the following day the White House amended its position, declaring that the raid was "understandable" but could not be condoned.

At this point, Mzali attempted a further rapprochement with the Islamic integralist movement by inviting some of the leaders to meet with him.[26] But the attempt failed miserably as the Islamic integralist movement decided to support the UGTT and in February 1986, five opposition parties—the Communist Party, the Movement of Social Democrats (MDS), the Popular Unity Movement, the Progressive Socialist Movement, and the Islamic Tendency Movement (MTI)—announced the formation of a Committee of Solidarity with the UGTT and for the Defense of Democratic Freedom.

In view of this failure to build social consensus, Bourguiba began to shift course and to undermine the authority of Mzali. In January 1986, Bourguiba for some unexplained reason "banished" his own wife, Wassilah, and his son Habib, Jr., from the presidential palace, along with his long-time adviser Allala Laouiti, and replaced them with his niece Saida Sassi and Mansour Skhiri. In February, the progovernment faction of the UGTT was reported to be in control of all UGTT offices; in March, U.S. Vice-President George Bush came to Tunisia on an official visit; in April, Bourguiba replaced Mzali as interior minister but allowed him to continue as prime minister; in May, he replaced Minister of Culture Bashir Ben Slama, a friend of Mzali, with Zakaria Ben Mustapha, the mayor of Tunis; in June, he personally appointed the members of the Central Committee of the Socialist Destour Party and the party's political bureau; and in July he dismissed Prime Minister Mzali and named Finance Minister Rachid Sfar as his replacement.

It is this new administration that is supposed to sell to the Tunisian people the agreement for economic "reform" made with the World Bank and the International Monetary Fund. The IMF declined to reschedule Tunisia's debts but agreed to lend Tunisia U.S. $268 million over eighteen months. In return, the Tunisian government has committed itself to reduce its budget deficit to zero within five years, excluding debt amortization. Moreover, the IMF has asked that this be achieved "by substantial cuts in investment spending, a

gradual reduction in commodity subsidies and a revision of the taxation system."[27] In the short term, Tunisia faces a difficult task in mobilizing new capital
resources to cover its 1987 financial gap and it may have to cut investments
even further. Since the reduction in commodity subsidies is to be "gradual,"
it is possible that these measures will not be immediately apparent to the general
population and "bread riots" may be avoided. The crux of Tunisia's difficulties
lie more in the medium term and in the long term as its position of dependence
makes it vulnerable to factors beyond its control, such as being squeezed out
of the European Economic Community markets by Portugal and Spain. If the
economy fails to grow by 4 percent annually, the country faces the prospect of
further increases in unemployment and a general fall in the standard of living.[28]
It is within this framework of "crisis" that an Islamic integralist movement
developed in Tunisia.

### The Islamic Integralist Movement

Parallel to these upheavals, a coherent Islamic integralist movement developed in Tunisia at such a pace that, after the movements in Egypt and Pakistan,
it may be considered among the most articulate in the world.[29] The signal for
the reentry of Islam on the political scene came on the "night of power" in
1979 when Hind Cheibi presented herself before Bourguiba wearing a new
version of the veil.[30] In 1929, Bourguiba had defended the veil as the symbol
of Tunisian identity and of the legitimacy of the Tunisian struggle for independence. This is usually forgotten as he is mainly credited for the 1956 Tunisian
Code of Personal Status, which gives women the most liberal rights in the Arab
world. It is ironic, therefore, that fifty years after his own defense of the veil,
it should become the symbol of those questioning Bourguiba's legitimacy.

It is crucial to note that the Muslim integralists were *not* involved in the
three major political upheavals of 1978, 1980, and 1984. Their uninvolvement
in the 1984 riots is particularly interesting, since the student leaders did not
use Islamic symbols, despite the claim of the Muslim integralists that they are
particularly strong in the secondary schools. In fact, it is thought that the Islamic
integralist movements were initially encouraged by the government itself
against the leftist tendencies, viewed as incipient Marxism, of the opposition
following the demonstrations of June 1968.[31]

In their early stage, the Islamic integralist movements revolved around the
editors of several journals and a number of preachers affiliated with large urban
mosques, particularly the Zaytuna in Tunis. Interestingly enough, the most
intense activities during this first phase of the late 1970s occurred in the Sahel,
which is the home base of the Socialist Destour Party. And government reaction
was mostly conciliatory—removing signs of the more obvious abuses (from a
strictly Islamic point of view) and emphasizing its own Islamic convictions and
behavior. The revolution in Iran does not seem to have caused much worry to

the Tunisian government and it was only in December 1979 that the government banned the Islamic integralist monthly *Al-Ma$^c$rifa* for criticizing Saudi Arabia with respect to the Grand Mosque attack in Makka.

Following the Gafsah incident in January 1980, a number of Muslim integralists were arrested for demonstrating against the military aid offered by France and accepted by Tunisia.[32] It is also possible that this harsh treatment signaled new policies by the recently appointed Mzali government with a political program based on "pluralism," rather than the prevalent one-party PSD system, and a cultural program aimed at increasing the Arab-Islamic (but not integralist) content of the Tunisian educational system.

Information about the organizational aspects of the various Islamic integralist movements in Tunisia are sparse indeed and the names of the two better known groupings indicate their diffuse organizational structure—the Islamic Tendency Movement (Harakat al-Ittijah al-Islami), known as the MTI (Mouvement de tendance islamique in French), and the Islamic Progressive Movement (al-Taqaddum al-Islami), or the MPI (Mouvement du progrès islamiste in French). Not much is known about a third group, the secretive Islamic Liberation Party (Hizb al-Tahrir al-Islami), as its aim seems to have been to infiltrate the army. This is the only one of the Muslim integralist groups of Tunisia with an organizational framework that goes beyond Tunisia itself. It was founded in 1950 in Egypt by the "enigmatic" Taqi ad-Din al-Nabahani,[33] who is believed to be of Palestinian origin, and the party headquarters is believed to be in Germany. It is important to note that, in Tunisia as in other areas, a variety of Islamic integralist groups exists and that we should not fall into the trap of considering the reentry of Islam into the realm of politics as a monolithic phenomenon.

## Sociological Analysis

Who are these Muslim integralists? There are very few sociological studies of Islamic integralist movements, mainly because Muslim integralists refuse "to play the conventional role of research subjects" and they simply refuse to give out any information, suspecting all researchers to be working against them. To my knowledge, only Sa$^c$ad ad-Din Ibrahim in Egypt and Elbaki Hermassi in Tunisia are conducting such research.[34]

According to Hermassi, who does not distinguish between the various groupings but is basically dealing with the MTI, the Islamic integralist movement in Tunisia is "first and foremost a movement of the educated youth" and, consequently, schools and universities serve as its bases. The median age of his sample group was about twenty-five years, while of the founders of the movement, usually older, almost half were less than thirty years old. Over 80 percent of his sample were university students and almost 75 percent of the leadership consisted of either secondary school teachers or university students, with the remaining 25 percent being white-collar and blue-collar workers. Although living in urban centers, a large percentage of the membership was of rural origin and, surprisingly, women were active participants.[35] Though the MTI is centered in Tunis, only 29 percent of the sample were born in the capital, while 38 percent came from the coastal areas (surprisingly, since this is the base of the Socialist Destour Party), 23 percent from the center-south, and 7 percent from the north-west. Also, 21 percent of the sample were the children of low-level white-collar workers, 46 percent of urban or agricultural workers, and 29 percent belonged to families where the father either had died or was an invalid. The study concludes that these were young people who came from the poor "layers" of Tunisian society, often from destitute families. Such an interpretation might be exaggerated; if we compare these figures to the socio-economic profile of Tunisian society (with the lower 20 percent living off 5 percent of the national product), the poor "layer" of Tunisian society is not overrepresented. On the contrary, 67 percent came from families above the poverty line; they are neither the destitute nor the disinherited.[36] Perhaps more pertinent to the issue, the study finds that 48 percent have illiterate fathers, 27 percent have fathers with primary-level education, and 19 percent have fathers with a Zaytuna mosque–university education.

This outline of the social basis of the Islamic integralist movement, though perhaps not detailed enough, indicates some similarity to the Islamic integralist movement in Egypt in terms of age (under thirty) and geographical origins (urban of recent rural origin) but differed somewhat in class affiliation (in Egypt, two-thirds of the fathers were middle-level government employees, while in Tunisia almost half of the fathers were urban or rural workers) and in family background (in Tunisia, almost one-third came from families that had suffered some trauma, while in Egypt most of Ibrahim's sample came from families with no death of either parent, no divorce or separation). None of the sources indicates any particular links between the Islamic integralist movements in Tunisia and those outside Tunisia (with the possible exception of the little-known Islamic Liberation Party), other than in terms of exchange of ideas as transmitted in the printed media.

The orientation of these young people is the result of the great expansion in the educational system in Tunisia following independence, which held the promise of rapid social mobility. This mobility is now being blocked by the world economic crisis, which impinges negatively on Tunisia. It has been noted that the usual mode for social mobility, the civil service, is presently limited and, moreover, has been undermined by inflation.[37] In dependent countries of the post–World War II period, the state was the main locomotive for "modernization" and social mobility. The "crisis" may then be seen to be a result of the present inability of the state to fulfill this basic role. It would seem, therefore, that actual class affiliation is not as important for the rise of Muslim integralists as an incongruity between high aspirations and the decrease in economic and political opportunities. In other words, these are the young upwardly mobile professionals ("yuppies") of the Islamic Third World, caught in a bottleneck.

## Ideological Analysis of the Islamic Integralist Movements

According to Hermassi, Muslim integralists are voracious readers not only of religious materials but of newspapers and magazines dealing with public events. We have yet to compile a complete list of the publications of the various Islamic integralist groups and to build a comprehensive overview of this material. In the meantime, the following presentation of the ideological positions of the two most important groups, the MTI and the MPI, may be considered to be preliminary glimpses. While important differences of emphasis do exist between the two main Muslim integralist movements, it must be noted that the ideas of both movements are clearly distinguished—and deliberately so— from the discourse of official Muslim leaders as well as from the manifestations of popular Islam.[38]

During the early period of their development, the Muslim integralists elaborated their ideological positions within study groups in the mosques of Tunis and, for a time, within the Association for the Preservation of the Qur'an.[39] A few leaders such as Shaikh Mistawi proposed to achieve the group's goals by a policy of infiltration and takeover of the PSD, but this proposal was rejected. The principal mode of action chosen was to establish a distinct counterculture, puritanical and egalitarian, within those social spaces such as the schools and the university that were relatively free of PSD influence and, therefore, vulnerable to leftist orientations.

### The Islamic Tendency Movement

The MTI is led by Rashid Ghannushi and ᶜAbd al-Fattah Muru, a member of the earliest study group established in Tunis in the 1970s. These study groups were to form the backbone of the MTI.[40] The MTI first signaled its existence in September 1980 with the publication of what may be considered a manifesto, *Westernization and the Inevitable Dictatorship*.[41] Ghannushi is a secondary school teacher, and the MTI found ready adherents in the secondary schools and in the mosques, where it led study groups for adults. University campuses soon became an arena for confrontation between leftists and Muslim integralists and, according to Ghannushi, the Muslim integralists "are nowadays considered as the strongest of all movements among students."[42] We need further study on the student organizations, both in Tunisia and in other Islamic countries, in order to gauge the seriousness of such assertions and to understand why the "scientific" faculties, such as medicine and engineering, seem to be more vulnerable to penetration by Islamic integralist groups.

The MTI gained a nationwide reputation when it applied for legal recognition as a political party in preparation for the elections of 1981.[43] The MPI had applied for political recognition even earlier but then withdrew its request. It is possible that the divergence between the MTI and the MPI may have occurred at this point. The MPI may have taken the position that the Islamic

integralist movement had not completed the educational phase and was not yet
ready for political action. They may also have felt that participation in the
elections did not conform to the strategy agreed upon, which was to avoid the
social spaces defined by the PSD. In July 1981, a series of incidents in schools,
universities, and other public places occurred when Islamic integralist groups
tried to enforce the fast of Ramadan. In particular, an attack on the bar in a
Club Med center led the government to arrest seventy-six leading militants of
the MTI, including Ghannushi and Muru. At their trial, sixty-eight MTI militants were sentenced to prison terms ranging from six months to eleven years.
As a result, the MTI was barred from participating in the elections and its
leaders were imprisoned. But soon the government changed its attitude, and
in August 1984 most of the Muslim integralists were released from prison.

Without indicating that he is limiting himself to the MTI, Hermassi offers
an outline of its ideology based on his reading of *Al-Ma$^c$rifa* (the group's journal)
and *Westernization and the Inevitable Dictatorship*, written by Ghannushi, the
most prolific of MTI's leaders.[44] Between 1972 (first publication of *Al-Ma$^c$rifa*)
and 1979 (when the journal was suspended by the government), the problems
perceived by the Muslim integralists were presented in an idealist fashion
without the elaboration of a program of action. These issues may be grouped
into four types: (1) doctrinal and moral, (2) intellectual and cultural, (3) social,
and (4) political. During the last year of publication of the journal, there was
an increase in political issues.

Ghannushi's book begins by criticizing the development models pursued in
the Arab world because they are based on a superficial knowledge of the West
and because they are not rooted in the culture of the masses, in Islam. Because
these models are not rooted in the Islamic culture, political leaders have to use
force to impose them and, thus, negate the very essence of the Western model,
which is freedom. Ghannushi does not propose to establish an Islamic state.
He calls for democracy and urges that the MTI play a role in the process of
political pluralism. In summary, we find the usual criticism of the West, but
it is rather tempered since the West is still given credit as the pioneer of freedom
and of equality.

Hermassi does not ask any question about the extent to which these positions
were influenced by the historical context of their publication, in preparation
for the pluralist elections promised for 1981 by Mzali. Such a question is quite
pertinent in view of a different interpretation of MTI ideology, based on a
number of its journals: *Al-Mujtama'* (Society) and *Al-Habib* (The Beloved) as
well as *Al-Ma$^c$rifa*. The main emphasis in the earlier articles in these journals
is on criticism of the actual state of religious observance and on the call to a
"return" to "pure Islam." This return to pure Islam must be total in all the
details of daily life, whether in the public sphere or in the private sphere, from
the style of dress through educational programs to the bases of the law. It means
a withdrawal or divorce from the rest of society, which, some Muslim integralists
believe, is living a second *jahiliyya* (pre-Islamic age of ignorance and impiety).

The second aspect of the Islamic integralist ideology of the MTI is its call to activism; refusing the actual state of damnation is not enough as this must be followed by an active re-Islamization of the community. This action (*da^cwa*) is multiple and must be organized in phases. The first phase involves the construction of the intellectual aspects of the movement and corresponds to "a perfect understanding of Qur'anic principles and of their applications." The second phase is that of "collective action" and represents the entry of Islamic integralism into the political arena as the means to impose the proper Islamic mode of life. Finally, the third phase is "to plan the da^cwa in a creative development of its own knowlege and its own practice" (meaning, perhaps, to take over political power).[45] Here may lie a fundamental difference between the MTI and the Islamic Liberation Party. Where the MTI proposes a gradual process of reeducation and mobilization of the population in order to achieve political power, the ILP proposes to achieve political power (by military coup, if necessary) in order to reeducate the population to "true" Islam.

The first two steps in the MTI program presuppose a resistance against the West and against the development model copied from the West in order "to defend the Islamic personality from dissolution within the melting-pot of the West." It also presupposes a resistance against popular Islam, despite the fact that the latter is considered as the "real foundation" of the Tunisian identity. In sum, it would seem that the MTI (at least before the call for pluralist elections apparently tempted the leadership) proposed to build a society parallel to both the Westernized and the populist sectors of Tunisian society. This is to be followed by an active phase of political involvement, including cooperation with other political groups—to prepare, perhaps, for the complete takeover of political power.

The MTI ideology, broadly speaking, may be considered to be similar to that of moderate or "reformist" Islamic integralist movements in other countries, such as the Muslim Brethren in Egypt.[46] The main intellectual inspiration is Ibn Taymiyya (1263–1338) and the modern-day Abu al-^cAla Mawdudi and Sayyid Qutb. The main thrust is an adherence to the principle of God's absolute authority (i.e., withdrawing legitimacy from those actually in power) and the censure of contemporary society and government because of their failure to apply the Shari^ca (the *hakimiyya* of God and the *jahiliyya* of government and society). Only a fuller and more detailed analysis of MTI texts could determine whether Ghannushi's bid to participate in the elections of 1981 was a change of direction or a logical evolution in the positions of the MTI.[47]

## The Islamic Progressive Movement

The second current of Muslim integralists in Tunisia, the MPI, differs somewhat from the MTI. While the MTI calls for change according to a model found in the past, the MPI calls for change according to a model projected into the future. Moreover, the MPI does not hesitate to explicitly borrow Western concepts, particularly from Marxism. That is why one of its journals is titled *15/21*, referring to the future twenty-first Western century as much as to the future fifteenth Islamic century.

The MPI distinguishes between Islam, as the eternal and unchanging truth of God expressed in the Qur'an, and Islamic thought, which is "the human attempt to understand the substance of Islam at a particular stage of history."[48] Such a view is close to the basic perspective of earlier reformers in Tunisia such as Tahar Haddad, who justified his position concerning reform in the status of women using precisely this historical view. He had even gone to the extent of considering the Qur'an itself to be a product of the historical circumstances of seventh-century Arabia.[49]

One of the most important issues treated by the MPI is the meaning of Islamic government. The MPI rejects Mawdudi's view, which places legitimacy solely within the divine purview, and, in contrast, defines the popular will as the source of legitimacy. Further, the MPI believes that "Islam denies the view that the nature of political power must be religious; it differentiates between the two realms but holds that they should not be separate." Moreover, the MPI questions the existence of a model Islamic society; any Islamic society has to be actual and historical. Three characteristics would qualify a society as Islamic: (1) it forms a context in which Islamic law is elaborated and applied; (2) it is humanist in that the individual may find self-fulfillment; and (3) it is collective in the sense that the majority determines the evolution of society. The positions of the MPI, based on the theoretical basis of a society evolving in history, are oriented in a different direction from the MTI. Instead of "purifying" Islamic society and Muslims from everything alien, it calls for the reform of both society and law since both are subject to historical evolution.[50]

## Conclusion

Having presented the sociological and ideological features of the Islamic integralist movements in Tunisia, can we assess their importance for the political future of Tunisia? What role do the Islamic integralist movements play in the two crises, the socioeconomic crisis of the gap between the expectations of youth and the inability of a dependent economy to fulfill these expectations and the political crisis of the lack of national consensus to solve these problems?

In the first place, we need to note that the Islamic movements in Tunisia have failed to take over the government, have failed to establish control over the two major political institutions of the country—the PSD and the UGTT— and have failed to infiltrate the army. Their absence from the major socioeconomic upheavals of 1978, 1980, and 1984 illustrates their failure to transform these crises into some form of "Islamic revolution." In sum, they have failed to speak on behalf of social groups wider than that fraction of the salaried middle class which is being blocked in its upward mobility.

If we consider the issue in terms of the symbolic capital which various groups can invest in order to achieve and to maintain political legitimacy, we may clarify several aspects of the Islamic integralist movements in Tunisia. As mentioned above, the reforms of the 1950s destituted that fraction of the elite whose cultural and ideological capital was based on knowledge of Arabic and of Islam and on the control of Islamic institutions. Ghannushi himself states:

> I am of the generation of Zaytuna students during the early years of independence. I remember we used to feel like strangers in our own country. We had been educated as Muslims and as Arabs, while we could see the country totally moulded in the French cultural identity. For us, the doors to any further education were closed since the university was completely westernised. At that time, those wanting to continue their studies in Arabic had to go to the Middle East.[51]

His attempt to gain access to the new forms of political capital, which required a knowledge of French language and culture, ended in failure as "family circumstances" prevented him from pursuing higher studies in France. The sense of frustration is all too clear.

If the Islamic integralist movement succeeds in articulating Islamic symbolism with the social concerns of a broader spectrum of various sectors of society, either those sectors previously organized by the UGTT or the unemployed urban poor or the regionally disinherited, it might then form a viable challenge to the PSD. There are indications of a new perspective within the MTI, which is beginning to attempt precisely that. For example, Ghannushi states, with the excitement of new discovery, in a recent interview:

> The social confrontation between the rich and the poor is a Marxist formula which did not correspond to our understanding of life. Later on, we realised that Islam also has a say in that confrontation and that, as Muslims, we could not stay indifferent to it. Islam gives support to the oppressed.
>
> In our country we found that the group allied with international capitalism exploits the common people and by that, the harmony and balance in society is broken. It is true that Islam does not pretend to absolute equality in people's material status because that is just impossible, but it is also certain that in an Islamic society it is not admissible that a few people have everything while others are dying of hunger. . . .
>
> Our position then was very clear—we were on the side of the oppressed. From that point on we began to develop a consciousness and a sensibility towards social realities. The Islamists started to participate in the trade union movement's activities and nowadays represent a very powerful force in this field.[52]

An even more recent interview given by Ghannushi further elaborates the new sensitivity of the MTI with respect to broad social issues. In many ways, the interview also indicates the basic continuity of Tunisian political discourse as Ghannushi borrows the concepts of "realism" and "activism" from the PSD and the emphasis on the "time factor" or historical perspective from the MPI.[53] But this language seems to be quite new and has not yet been developed to appeal to a broad base of the disaffected, the *mustadᶜafin*. Clearly, the ideological positions of the MTI, and probably of the MPI, are shifting and only further study could allow us to grasp these changes as they occur within the framework of socioeconomic and political events.

This process of "ideologization" is not necessarily the monopoly of the Islamic integralist movements as there are other ideology-carrying social groups that are also struggling either to maintain or to attain legitimacy. In my view, there are three main producers of ideology in Tunisia: the PSD/government, the UGTT, and the Muslim integralists. None of them has succeeded in producing an ideology that represents a national consensus and none has been able to either maintain or produce an ideology that would speak to the regionally disinherited or to the urban lumpen-proletariat. Moreover, none of them has been able to forge those social alliances that have been characteristic of Tunisian politics for over two centuries. Neither the MTI nor the MPI seems to be developing the organizational bases needed to become a mass party.

In 1981, Mzali tried to forge an alliance with the UGTT and failed. In 1985, he attempted a rapprochement with the Muslim integralists and failed. It is yet to be seen whether the Muslim integralists will be able to forge an alliance with the UGTT. The establishment in February 1986 of the Committee of Solidarity with the UGTT with the participation of a broad front of opposition groups from the Communist Party to the MTI indicates the central importance of the UGTT in the development of any national consensus. Though not impossible, an alliance between the Islamic integralist movement and the UGTT is rather far-fetched. In sum, the chances for an "Islamic" revolution in Tunisia are dim.

The intervention of the army has not been considered a serious alternative because of the long history of civilian political institutions in Tunisia. One would have to go all the way back to the Ottoman period of the early eighteenth century for an example of military interference in politics, with the establishment of the Husaynid dynasty, which in itself may be considered a transformation of the military into a civilian dynasty. Nevertheless, the dismissal of Mzali and his trial in absentia is an indication that the political institutions of Tunisia, including the PSD, are being gradually emptied of all credibiity and legitimacy. As the various organizations are debilitated, the possibility of military intervention may yet arise.

# NOTES

1. Norman Daniel, *Islam and the West: The Making of an Image* (Edinburgh: Edinburgh University Press, 1958). Also see his *Islam, Europe and Empire* (Edinburgh: Edinburgh University Press, 1966); R.W. Southern, *Western Views of Islam in the Middle Ages* (Cambridge, Mass.: Harvard University Press, 1962); and J.D. Waardenburg, *L'Islam dans le miroir de l'Occident* (Paris: Mouton, 1963).

2. These stereotypes may be somewhat subtle or sophisticated in scholarly works but they are rampant in school textbooks, in the mass media, and in popular culture. See Marie McAndrew, "L'Image du monde arabe dans les manuels scolaires québecois: Dernier racisme legitime?" *The NECEF* (Near East Cultural and Educational Foundation of Canada) *Newsletter*, pp. 3–4; Edward Said, *Covering Islam: How the Media and the Experts Determine How We See the Rest of the World* (New York: Pantheon, 1981); and Jack G. Shaheen, *The TV Arab* (Bowling Green: Bowling Green State University Popular Press, 1984). There is no doubt in my mind that these stereotypes—subtle, sophisticated, or blatant—blinded the policymakers to the actual problems in Iran and, generally, in Islamic societies.

3. Anouar ⁣ᶜAbdel-Malek, "Orientalism in Crisis," *Diogenes* 44, pp. 103–140; ᶜAbdel-Latif Tibawi, "English-Speaking Orientalists: A Critique of Their Approaches to Islam and Arab Nationalism," *The Muslim World*, Vol. 53, pp. 185–204, 298–313; Abdallah Laroui, *La Crise des intellectuels arabes: Traditionalisme ou historicisme?* (Paris: Maspero, 1974).

4. See Edward Said, *Orientalism* (New York: Vintage Books, 1978).

5. Norma Salem, review of *Radical Islam: Medieval Theology and Modern Politics* by Emmanuel Sivan, *The Middle East Journal*, Vol. 39, No. 4, pp. 866–868 and Ghassane Salame, "L'Islam en politique: Les experiences arabes d'aujourd'hui," *Politique étrangère*, Vol. 47, No. 279, pp. 365–379.

6. Bahgat Korany and Ali E. Hillal Dessouki, eds., *The Foreign Policies of Arab States* (Boulder, Colo.: Westview Press, 1984), and William R. Thompson, "Delineating Regional Subsystems: Visit Networks and the Middle Eastern Case," *International Journal of Middle East Studies*, Vol. 13, No. 2 (May 1981), pp. 213–235.

7. See Elbaki Hermassi, *Etat et societe au Maghreb: Etude comparative* (Paris: Anthropos, 1974), p. 9, and Kemal H. Karpat, "The Ethnicity Problem in a Multi-ethnic Anational Islamic State: Continuity and Recasting of Ethnic Identity in the Ottoman State," in *Ethnic Groups and the State*, ed. by Paul Brass (London: Croom Helm, 1985). The latter takes this position to an extreme as he states that "social science premises and concepts do not have universal validity" and changes in Islamic areas "can be properly studied and understood only within the Islamic world's own terms of reference," pp. 96–97. Such absolute cultural relativism leads to a dead end when taken to its logical conclusion since it cannot distinguish between "etic" categories, referring to the perception of the informant, and "emic" categories, referring to the epistemological concepts developed beyond the limits of the culture involved; see my remarks in *Habib Bourguiba, Islam and the Creation of Tunisia* (London: Croom Helm, 1984), pp. 1–3. Gilles Kepel, in his fascinating book *The Prophet and Pharoah: Muslim Extremism in Contemporary Egypt*, trans. by Jon Rothschild (London: Al-Saqi Books, 1985) is fully aware of the problem, namely, that the study of Islam and of history in the Arab world presents a "challenge to Western categories of thought," p. 22. He also maintains that what is needed is "to reconstruct that [Islamic] system's grammar and lexicon, and thus also the Muslim cultural tradition from which it issued and the contemporary Third World in which it functions," pp. 23–24. He does not explain how such "reconstruction" is to be accomplished but, to my mind, we cannot avoid using cross-cultural concepts in order to forge links between the "informant" and the "observer." Kepel also agrees that a central issue concerning Islamic discourse is its ability to "legitimate or withhold legitimacy from the political regime," p. 59; cf. Salem, *Habib Bourguiba*, pp. 171–172.

8. On the poverty of theorization in Islamic and Middle Eastern studies, see Salem, *Habib Bourguiba*, p. ii. Also see Rex Brynen, "The State of the Art in Middle Eastern Studies: A Research Note of Inquiry and the American Empire," *Arab Studies Quarterly*, Vol. 8, No. 4 (Fall 1986), pp. 404–419.

9. For the list of "names," see Yvonne Y. Haddad, "Muslim Revivalist Thought in the Arab World," *The Muslim World*, Vol. 76, No. 3–4, (July-October 1986), p. 145.

10. The term *islamiste* seems to have been first used by Habib Boularès, as reported

by J. F. Clément, "Pour une compréhension des mouvements islamiques," *Esprit* (January 1980); see Olivier Roy, "Fondamentalisme, intégrisme, islamisme," *Esprit* (April 1985), pp. 1–7.

11. For examples of attempts at theoretical construction, see Ali E. Hillal Dessouki, ed., *Islamic Resurgence in the Arab World* (New York: Praeger, 1982); Jean-Claude Vatin, "Religion et politique au Maghreb: Le renversement des perspectives dans l'étude de l'Islam," in *Islam et politique au Maghreb* (Table Ronde du CRESM, Aix) (Paris: CNRS, 1981); R. Hrair Dekmejian, "The Anatomy of Islamic Revival: Legitimacy Crisis, Ethnic Conflict and the Search for Islamic Alternatives," *The Middle East Journal*, Vol. 34, No. 1 (Winter 1980), pp. 1–12, and his *Islam in Revolution: Fundamentalism in the Arab World* (Syracuse, N.Y.: Syracuse University Press, 1985).

12. Saʿad ad-Din Ibrahim, "Anatomy of Egypt's Militant Islamic Groups: Methodological Notes and Preliminary Findings," *International Journal of Middle East Studies*, Vol. 12, No. 4 (1980), pp. 423–453; Dekmejian, *Islam in Revolution*, and Elbaki Hermassi, "La société tunisienne au miroir islamiste," *Maghreb-Machrek* 103 (January–March 1984). Ibrahim situates this sense of "national crisis" on the international scene (defeat of 1967, increasing foreign presence in Egypt), while Dekmejian situates it at several levels—crisis of identity, crisis of legitimacy, misrule/coercion, class conflict, military failure, and a cultural crisis—and Hermassi speaks of a "crisis of authority."

13. My translation; the original in French (Hermassi, "Société," p. 39) is:

> Pour le savant, la tâche n'est rendue facile lorsque les islamistes eux-mêmes se comportent selon ces mêmes postulats et s'amusent à prendre leur rêve pour la réalité. Continuer à concevoir l'Islam comme essence par définition trans-historique, c'est s'interdire de distinguer entre l'islam et l'islamisme, de faire la différence entre une religion et un processus d'idéologisation de cette religion.

Whether he means to do so or not, Hermassi is here distinguishing between an implicitly "emic" category (religion, or *din*) and an "etic" category (ideologization of religion) since he assumes a cross-cultural definition of *religion* beyond its ideologization.

14. Pierre Bourdieu, "Genèse et structure du champ religieux," *Revue francaise de sociologie* 12, pp. 295–334, and *Outline of a Theory of Practice*, trans. by Richard Nice (Cambridge: Cambridge University Press, 1977), originally titled *Esquisse d'une théorie de la pratique, précédé de trois études d'ethnologie kabyle* (1972). Bourdieu is one of the rare social scientists who have contributed to the construction of social theory by using field data from the Arab world. Bourdieu's theoretical framework is presented at some length because of the possible rich applications which other researchers may find in it. The main ideas of labor expended in the process of ideologization, of symbolic capital, and of the interconvertibility of symbolic and material capital have informed the analysis in this paper, but further work is needed to work out the full implications of Bourdieu's ideas with respect to the Islamic integralist movements overall.

15. Salem, *Habib Bourguiba*, p. 133.

16. Ibid., pp. 154–158.

17. Personal interview with Ahmed Mestiri (May 1982), former minister of justice and now leader of the Mouvement des Democrates Socialistes (MDS). See Norma Salem, "Islam and the Legal Status of Women in Tunisia," in *Muslim Women*, ed. Freda Hussain (London: Croom Helm, 1980), particularly pp. 141–148.

18. The "reform" of the educational system was meant to socialize the youth of Tunisia in the new values but, perhaps, it also maintained a sense of the "alienness" of these values by insisting that the "pure sciences" should be taught in French.

19. Y. Ben Achour, "Islam perdu, islam retrouvé," in *Le Maghreb musulman en 1979* (Paris: CNRS, 1981), pp. 65–71.

20. The portrait of Tunisia in this period is based on a reading of *Maghreb-Machrek, Jeune Afrique, Annuaire de l'Afrique du Nord,* and *The Middle East Journal*.

21. Georges Joffé, "Islamic Fundamentalists Suppressed in Tunisia," *Index on Censorship*, Vol. 48, No. 82, pp. 32–33.

22. Hassine Dimassi, "Le Crise économique en Tunisie: Une crise de régulation," in *Tunisie 1984: L'Etat, l'islamisme, l'économie*, special issue of *Maghreb-Machrek* 103 (January–March 1984), pp. 57–69, and Michel Camau, "Où va la Tunisie?" in ibid., pp. 8–38.

23. Issa Ben Dhiaf, "Chronique politique, Tunisie," *Annuaire de l'Afrique du Nord* (1982), pp. 656–687.

24. Ibid. (1983), p. 869.

25. Ibid., p. 879.

26. "Tunis Raid: The Other Side of the Coin," *Arabia* (December 1985), p. 32.

27. "IMF Sets New Targets for Tunisia," *Middle East Economic Digest* (17 January 1987), p. 28.

28. Ibid., p. 29.

29. As early as 1980, the movement had established a publishing house and a bookstore, *al-Raya*, and had published over a hundred titles; see Mark A. Tessler, "Political Change and the Islamic Revival in Tunisia," *The Maghreb Review* 5 (1980), p. 12. At that time, a number of Islamic integralist journals were also published.

30. Souhayr Belhassen, "Femmes tunisiennes islamistes," *Annuaire de l'Afrique du Nord* (1979), p. 77.

31. Joffé, "Islamic Fundamentalists," pp. 32–33, and Tessler, "Political Change," p. 16. It is clear that the Sadat government in Egypt also actively encouraged the "Islamicists" in order to counter the leftist student groups on the university campuses; see Ghassane Salame, "L'Islam en politique: Les expériences arabes d'aujourd'hui" *Politique Etrangère* 47 (1982), p. 370, and Kepel, *Prophet*, p. 133.

32. Joffé, "Islamic Fundamentalists," p. 32.

33. Kepel, *Prophet*, p. 93.

34. Ibrahim, "Anatomy," and Hermassi, "Société." Kepel, *Prophet*, has some additional information on the sociological background of the Muslim integralists in Egypt.

35. Hermassi, "Société," and Susan Waltz, "Islamist Appeal in Tunisia," paper presented at the Annual Meeting of the Middle East Studies Association, New Orleans, November 1985.

36. Hermassi, "Société," p. 33. These conclusions are tentative since the categories presented by Hermassi are rather broad and do not permit finer analysis.

37. Ibid. Also see Kepel, *Prophet*.

38. Zouhaier Dhaouadi, "Islamismes et politique en Tunisie," in *Islamisme en effervecence*, special issue of *Peuples Méditerranéens* 21 (October–December 1982), p. 161.

39. Hermassi, "Société," pp. 44 and 47. Also see Tessler, "Political Change," p. 12.

40. Abdul-Habib Castenera, "Nobody's Man—But a Man of Islam, "*Arabia* (April 1985/Rajab 1405), p. 18.

41. Hermassi, "Société," p. 53.

42. Ibid., p. 19.

43. Ibid., p. 53.

44. Ibid., pp. 49 and 53.

45. Dhaouadi, "Islamismes," pp. 161 and 166.

46. Kepel, *Prophet*, p. 103.

47. For the communique of the Islamic Tendency Movement on the eve of the 1981 elections, see the French translation published in *L'Islamisme en effervescence*, special issue of *Peuples Méditerranéens* 21, pp. 576–580.

48. Dhaouadi, "Islamismes," pp. 167–168.

49. Salem, "Islam and Status," pp. 141–148.

50. For a representative article presenting MPI views, see Krichen Zyed, "Pour une nouvelle exegèse de l'Islam," in *L'Islam en effervescence*, special issue of *Peuples Méditerranéens* 21, pp. 15–21.

51. Castenera, "Nobody's Man," p. 18.

52. Ibid., p. 19. Henry Munson, Jr., "Islamic Revivalism in Morocco and Tunisia," *The Muslim World*, Vol. 76, No. 3–4 (July–October 1986), p. 212, states that as early as the middle of 1981, "Islamic militants . . . were . . . becoming increasingly conspicuous in the labor federation (probably in the white collar unions)." This statement is partly based on Issa Ben Dhiaf's "Chroniques politiques—Tunisie" in *Annuaire de l'Afrique du Nord* (1982), pp. 686–688. Unfortunately, this is a complete misreading both of the Ben Dhiaf articles and of the relations between the UGTT and the Muslim integralists. Ben Dhiaf was not referring to improved relations of the Muslim integralists with the UGTT but with the UGET (Union Géneral des Etudiants Tunisiens), which was then dominated by the PSD. In fact, it would seem that the PSD used the Muslim integralists to counter the growing influence of the left among the students. There is no evidence that Muslim integralists, of any tendency, lent their support to the UGTT at any point earlier than 1985. On the contrary, Ghannushi himself states that "We had no unionist activity because we were somehow prejudiced in such a manner that unionism was alien to us"; see Castenera, "Nobody's Man," p. 19.

53. See the three-part interview, "What We Need Is a Realistic Fundamentalism," "The Sudan Experience Shows a Way Forward for Islamists," and "Let Us Then Opt for the Leadership of the Sages," in *Arabia* (October 1986/Safar 1407), pp. 13–15, (November 1986/Rabi al-Awwal 1407), pp. 14–17, (December 1986/Rabi al-Thani), pp. 17–19. For the concepts of "realism" and "activism" in Bourguiba's political discourse, see Salem, *Habib Bourguiba*, pp. 53–54 and 143–44, respectively.

# XI

---

# ALGERIA
## *Mohammad Arkoun*

> The affirmation of the attachment to Islam
> and the insistence on the option for Socialism
> come then both from the roots of November
> Revolution, and they are not a political at-
> tempt aiming to establish a formal balance
> between Islam and Socialism.
>
> National Charter 1986

The Islamic movement in Algeria—and indeed the rest of the Muslim world—
can best be understood by analyzing the relationships between society, state,
and religion. These three concepts correspond to major Islamic political themes
since the Classical Age as expressed by three current Arabic words, *dunya*,
*dawla*, and *din*.

The use of these three Arabic concepts in order to analyze the current state
of relations among society, state, and religion has the great merit of shielding
the study from Western prejudices, as reflected in terms such as radicalism,
revivalism, and fundamentalism. These are nothing but catch-all words and a
collection of confusions using the umbrella of Islam.

Islam today is less than ever a scientifically elaborated concept. Very few
Muslims and Orientalists have thus far tried to elaborate the theoretical framework that would be needed in order for Islam to be used as a scientific concept.

For this to be possible, each Muslim society should be considered and studied
as a laboratory where Islam is experienced and where it receives specific de-
terminations. The following presentation, therefore, will analyze the Algerian
case in this theoretical perspective. The approach is pragmatic. First, it will
enumerate main events and facts concerning religious manifestations in Algeria
since its independence, because "serious" scholars prefer "facts" to mere theoretical elaborations. Nevertheless, while acknowledging the necessity to base
any attempt at explaining the current Islamic movement on concrete and in-
disputable "facts," the underlying belief in this presentation is that Muslim
intellectuals have the responsibility to do what Orientalists refuse to do. That
is to go beyond the mere effort to collect and to describe "facts," and for the

first time begin to think about, or rethink, the problems related to Dunya, Dawla, Din, not only according to classical Islamic thought, but also according to modern scientific thought. Thus, after enumerating the facts, the text will develop an engaged knowledge of Islam in Algeria and, beyond the Algerian example, of Islam as a religion and a tradition.

## Events and Facts

A well-organized Islamic movement started in Algeria in 1931 when ᶜAbdul-Hamid Ben Badis established the Algerian ᶜUlama Association. Ben Badis, like Tahar Ben Ashur in Tunisia and Allal-al-Fasi in Morocco, introduced in Algeria the spirit and the main ideas of the well-known Reformist Movement (*Salafiyya*) initiated in the nineteenth century by J. D. al-Afghani and Muhammad ᶜAbduh. Because this movement had strong nationalist dimensions, the French colonial administration prevented its expansion. In fact, the slogan used in Algeria until independence was: "Algeria is our fatherland; Arabic is our language; Islam is our religion." This slogan reflected an ideology formed by a mixture of politics, culture, and religion. This ideology was adopted by the Front for National Liberation (FLN) during the war of independence and has been enforced as a political program since independence. The Islam promoted by the ᶜulama was both urbanized and urbanizing. It was based on traditional learning and scriptural references rooted in the Maliki School, and it was receptive to some new ideas borrowed from French culture. Thus, the Islam of the ᶜulama was opposed to the so-called folk Islam represented by the Marabouts, the Sufis, and the very ancient Berber language and cultures, such as those of Kabylie, Chawiya, Mzab, Quarsenis, and the Touaregs.

After independence, all expressions of Islam in Algeria were more or less affected by the spirit and teachings of the ᶜulama movement. Constant references made to Ben Badis and his successor, al-Shaikh al-Ibrahimi, by Algerian officials is evidence of the impact the ᶜulama movement's views have had on Algerian Islam.

Indeed, after independence, young generations have shown greater impatience for the restoration and application of authentic Islam as a means to eliminate colonial influences and to redeem Algeria's original Arabic and Islamic personality. Thus, immediately after independence, an association was created with the name al-Qiyam (The Values), and it published a review called *Muslim Humanism*, in whose pages it expressed its ethical and religious program. Until 1963, Muhammad Khider, one of the historic leaders of the November Revolution, supported this association. But Boumediene, after becoming president, dissolved it (September 22, 1966) and then prohibited its reestablishment (March 17, 1970). The members of al-Qiyam adhered to a strict Islamic moral code and wanted to ensure its application in Algeria. This association also wanted to eradicate all vestiges of non-Islamic influences from Algeria. For example, the members and the association tried to destroy statues of a Roman theater in Guelma. That was an isolated incident, however.

Boumediene's conception of the state and the new Algerian society was basically modern and secular. He wanted to transform Algerian society's archaic tribal structures and beliefs into a modern economic and political organization. During his leadership, Islamic movements were well controlled by the minister of religious affairs, a practice that has since continued.

This control has been imposed through two strategies: limiting the activities of the extremist movements and preventing violent demonstrations and arresting the demonstrators. Nevertheless, violent confrontations took place between leftist and Muslim students of the Ben Aknoun Students' Residences (Algiers) on November 2, 1982, followed by other demonstrations and the distribution of pamphlets. On December 20, 1982, an underground Muslim organization was discovered with stolen firearms, and thirty people were arrested. President Chadli Bendjedid criticized these "small groups" and charged that they were inspired and paid by foreigners.

These confrontations were different from those which took place in March 1980 in Tizi-Ouzou, the regional capital of Kabylie. There, students protested because the government had prohibited a lecture on Berber culture by the well-known writer Mouloud Mammeri. Yet even though the motives of the students in Tizi-Ouzou were purely cultural, the government reacted as strongly as it had in the case of Muslim-inspired demonstrations. The government did promise to introduce Berber studies in some universities, but this commitment has yet to be honored.

From April 7 to 29, 1985, 135 members of an underground Islamic movement were tried; 70 were condemned to prison, and 65 were discharged. From September 1 to 6, 1985, fundamentalists involved in the events of Ben-Aknoun were tried; 7 were condemned, and 12 were discharged.

The government's firm stand against Islamic groups clearly shows that it has the political will to stop or limit the expansion of religious protest.

In the meantime, however, the government—under both Boumediene and Bendjedid—has encouraged the population's Islamic tendencies. Since independence, many mosques have been built in Algerian cities and even in small villages. Since August 27, 1976, Friday has replaced Sunday as the official holiday. In some cities alcoholic drinks have been banned. Religious festivals are fully observed and are declared official holidays. Religious teaching is officially provided in all schools, and religious ceremonies and lectures are broadcast on radio and television.

In addition, for the past twenty years the government has been holding an annual seminar on Islamic thought. This is done by the Ministry of Religious Affairs, with the participation of ʿulama from all over the Muslim world. The proceedings of the seminar are published and disseminated through official media. Also the review *Al-Asala*, published by the Ministry of Religious Affairs, expresses and expands the trends and themes of official Islam in contemporary Algeria.

Yet the tension and, at times, the hard struggle continue between the government and the fundamentalists. The debate over the adoption of a family code clearly illustrates this tension. This has long been delayed in Algeria because it raises fundamental difficulties in dealing with the laws related to personal status. The most controversial aspect of this body of law is that of the status of women—namely, how to deal, in a modern state, with such issues as polygamy, inheritance laws, repudiation, divorce, and women's freedom to choose their future husbands. The *Shariᶜa* (divine law) has specific rules regarding these issues, but many women in Algeria who took part in the war of liberation feel that they have earned the right to full equality with men.

During a hard and long discussion, the fundamentalist "true" Muslims stood in opposition to the "modernists." The result was the adoption of a rather conservative family code published June 9, 1986, with Algerian women once again losing the battle.

There have been other instances of tension and confrontation between Islamic and secular forces in Algeria. Yet the principal actors and opposition forces involved in these confrontations, and their basic arguments and strategies, have remained remarkably unchanged. Thus far, the dominant actor has indisputably been the state. Its control over the whole society is so strict, so comprehensive, and so efficient that sociologists, anthropologists, and even reporters are unable to identify clearly any Islamic or other movements and associations, or their leaders, that are not sanctioned by the state. In sum, Islam in Algeria has been nationalized exactly like the land and the industry.

Nevertheless, Islam as a social, psychological, and political force has not been totally mastered by the state. Rather, it is manipulated and used by the state and secular society as an increasingly difficult competitor. It is this competition which provides the richest subject of a scientific inquiry into the social and historical process of symbolization and desymbolization in a given society. Viewed in this perspective, Algerian society does not differ from other Muslim societies. Therefore, a relevant description and critical analysis of the ongoing competition between the state and Islam in Algeria would contribute to an understanding of the causes of Islamic revivalism throughout the Muslim world.

## The Thinking History of Muslim Societies

An analysis of Algerian society is best done not on the basis of classical or contemporary Islamic categories, but rather by focusing on those forces which historically have determined the shape of Algerian and other Maghrebian societies. In this context, the main questions become: What place does Islam occupy within the system of forces shaping and controlling Maghrebian societies? And at which changing levels of society does Islam operate, creating either new possibilities of emancipation or more difficulties in the process of modernization?

These questions are particularly relevant to Algeria because, during the postindependence period, secularizing and modernizing elements have been stronger there than in many other Muslim countries. In trying to answer these questions, however, one is immediately handicapped by the lack of operational concepts; the terms *secularization, modernization, religion, Islam, state, civil society*, and many others currently used by social scientists are more confusing than enlightening. Moreover, most scholars dealing with Islam and Muslim societies totally ignore the key concept of *social imaginaire*, with its philosophical, sociological, and anthropological implications.[1]

Islamic discourse,[2] past and present, has insisted on its high level of rationality: Islamic faith is in total harmony with right guided reason (raison *orthodoxe*).[3] The unconditional acceptance of this postulate, however, leads one to ignore all the psychological mechanisms through which historical and social realities are hidden and then are transformed into mental images or representations. Yet this is precisely how all ideological constructions regarding society—ancient or modern, underdeveloped or developed—are currently formed. From this point of view, therefore, there is no difference between the *social imaginaire* that produces nationalist ideology and the *social imaginaire* that produces Islamist revivalist movements. In fact, both use mental images abstracted from historical realities and systematically transformed into mythological "truths." The development of nationalist ideology in Algeria is a concrete example and a result of this process.

Any discourse—leftist, rightist, Islamic, secular, academic, popular—produced in Algerian society since independence has been either implicitly or explicitly determined by the following postulates:

1. There is a mythical division of Algeria's history. Before 1830, Algeria was a rich, strong country and displayed a distinct national personality, even in the time of Roman occupation and Turkish conquest. After 1830, French colonialism systematically destroyed this personality until it was restored by the rise of the National Liberation Movement on November 1, 1954. The Algerian war of liberation (November 1, 1954–July 5, 1962) is viewed both as a continuation of the national resistance started with Massinissa and Jugurtha against Roman occupation and as a new birth of Algerian personality. This postulate also holds that the Algerian nation existed without any discontinuity since antiquity.

2. The Algerian nation is based exclusively on Arabic language and culture and the Muslim religion. Arabs did not conquer Algeria in the seventh century; instead, they opened (*fath*) it to the divine truth taught to humankind by the Qur'an and by the Prophet's tradition. Arabic culture and Islamic teachings have been fully received by all social groups in Algeria; there is no more place for Berber language and culture, no more need to refer to it even though it is still alive in large groups like Kabylie and Chawiya, or smaller groups like Mozabites and Touaregs. Two Algerian historians, Mubarak al-Mili and Tawfiq al-Madani, have systematically developed this mythological view of Algerian history since 1830. This vision of Algerian history is still taught in schools, and it is promoted by the publication of frequent articles and books and by the holding of conferences and celebrations. The history of the revolution, as pre-

sented in the mass media, insists particularly on the archetypic components of the Algerian nation.

3. The revolution of November 1954 did not stop on the day Algeria recovered its sovereignty. It has been further developed and enriched by the socialist revolution, and it has been improved theoretically in official charters such as the constitution of 1963, the national charter of 1976, the Algiers charter of 1986, and the national charter of 1986, which have been adopted through universal popular vote.

These three postulates, with all their historical, sociological, cultural, and political implications, together operate as a general constraining paradigm for *social imaginaire* and the common political vision in Algeria. All problems are seen in terms of this ideal paradigm and are solved by it. Introducing a new idea, a critical look, and new knowledge from outside is thus immediately rejected as a betrayal of the national interest.

No political opposition to the regime, no private newspaper, no association, no access to the mass media, no free school is tolerated. All initiatives are strictly controlled through the rigorous application of the paradigm. Cultural demands, as well as religious protests demanding the application of authentic Islam, are repressed when they do not fit the paradigm.

To understand this ideological context, one must examine the evolution of the state and civil society in Algeria from 1962 to 1985.

### State and Society

Between the colonial administration and the new state that emerged in July 1962, there was a violent ideological rupture, but substantial formal and institutional continuity has survived. While any imitation of the colonial regime was totally rejected, the new state has been conceived and structured according to the well-known French Jacobin model of a centralizing state. While formal characteristics of a democratic state have been adopted, the party and its political bureau have controlled all levels of decision making.

During the first three years of independence (July 1962–June 1965), the official ideology was more influenced by Arab nationalism and socialism as represented in the Arab revolution of Jamal ᶜAbd al-Naser than by Islamic ideas. Algerian militants engaged in the war were educated in the tradition of secularized French culture, *philosophie des lumières*, rather than that of Arab and Islamic culture. Indeed, many leaders like Ait Ahmed, Krim Belkacem, Amirouche, Ferhat ᶜAbbas, Boudiaf, and Ben Khedda used the intellectual framework of utopian socialism for the elaboration of their own vision for Algeria. They were thus accused by the Arabists of being too influenced by French culture. Ben Bella was converted to the socialist revolution, but he mixed it with a romantic attachment to Arabism and to Naser's theory of the "Great Arab Nation."

This process shows how *social imaginaire* remains a leading force in Algerian society and politics. The trend that called for an "Algerian Algeria" has been eliminated by those who have imposed a triumphant ideology based on a mix of utopian socialism and a romantic definition of Arab and Muslim nation.

Boumediene came to power in June 1965 with the deep conviction that Algeria should and could be transformed from its archaic, conservative tribal structures into a modern, industrialized, and urbanized society. His vision was basically secular and Western-inspired, as illustrated by a statement he made in a speech delivered in Lahore at the Islamic summit in February 1976: "Hungry people have no need to listen to verses . . . they do not want to enter Paradise with an empty stomach . . . they need food, education, hospitals. . . . "

Actually, Boumediene wanted to challenge Naser's Arab socialism, which he judged to be too romantic compared to the positivist standards of the Algerian socialist revolution. He initiated two major socialist programs: the establishment of so-called industrializing industries under the direction of the dynamic and methodical minister Belaid Abdesslam, and the agrarian revolution. Together with the nationalization of the oil industry, these decisions had a tremendous impact on Algeria's traditional social structures and on their cultural expressions.

The evaluation of these policies is beyond the scope of this study. Suffice it to note that they generated a high degree of self-confidence in the Algerians' collective consciousness regarding their brilliant future. In the beginning, the human price to pay for this policy was not evident. Thus, the enthusiasm was great. But the disappointment was later to equal the enthusiasm and, as in Iran, was to strengthen the Islamic revivalist movement.

During the 1970s, demographic changes had already altered society, but until the death of Boumediene (December 1978), modern secular trends dominated Algerian society, thus leaving a limited role for religion.

Since 1971, there has been in Algeria a Code of Socialist Management that has aimed to abolish in firms "the frontier between politics, economy and technology." To achieve this goal, however, would require new education for workers, development of new patterns of relations to work, to the state, and to society. It is beyond the scope of this study to describe various aspects of workers' resistance—mostly by poorly trained peasants who have moved to the cities—to these new norms. It is more relevant to describe the anthropological configuration of social movements in Algeria after 1975.

The traditional bourgeoisie in Algeria had already been broken by the colonial impact; it has been eliminated by the war of independence and the socialist revolution. New classes are being formed, but regional, ethnic, and linguistic affiliations and loyalties are still important. This may explain why class struggle has been superseded by the emergence of groups of young militants who refer to a religious program (an Islamic vision), ethnocultural ideal (Kabylie, Mzab), or sexual division (women fighting for a modern family code). For the first time, nationalist ideology is criticized by these movements, but devotion to Algeria as a unified nation is unanimous. No major political crisis has affected the state since the coup of June 19, 1965. Even the succession of Boumediene did not cause an open power struggle. The official view attributes this political stability to the existence of a broad popular consensus regarding the legitimacy of the so-called "historical leaders" (those who participated in the war of liberation). However, this stability can also be explained as being the result of the weakness of social classes, the lack of mass political organizations and consciousness, and the low level of political debate among professional groups.

No doubt the maintenance of national unity is still a sacred aim shared by all citizens, despite their disappointment with many aspects of official policy. But other factors are also at work. For example, daily official references are made to the sacrifices of the martyrs of the war for independence, and such references enhance the state's legitimacy. This legitimacy is newly acquired and is based on the following factors: the historical legitimacy of the revolutionary leaders; the social legitimacy conferred upon the state by those citizens who have benefited socially and economically from the state's socialist policies; and the state's foreign policy, which has enhanced Algeria's national dignity and international prestige. By relying on these factors, the Algerian state has compensated for its lack of legal and historical legitimacy dating back to preindependence days, as has been the case in Morocco and Tunisia. Furthermore, Boumediene was a charismatic leader and used a language which satisfied the Algerians' need for national pride and for ethical values.

In sum, the success of the state in pacifying the country, developing an active economy, and developing a large middle class accounts for most of the Algerians' commitment to the continuation of the process of nation-building, even if it means strict state control on all social and political activities. This does not mean that there never was, or is not now, any discontent. Quite the contrary. And it is in this context that the role played by religion as a refuge, as a den, as a springboard for all kinds of opposition, social protest, and psychological reactions should be analyzed.

### Islam in Algeria

The Muslim world's current problems cannot be approached only through the ideal teaching of Islam; nor can they be solved on the basis of these teachings, as the Muslim militants claim. On the contrary, it is rather difficult to adequately determine religion's place and functions in a mobile and complex social context created throughout the Muslim world as a result of the process of economic and cultural modernization.

The first question to be asked is how Islam was introduced to Algeria. What is the extent of its presence in Algeria's different ethnocultural groups? What are the dominant aspects of religious expression within each group? Yet, despite the importance of these questions, this historical and sociological approach to the study of Islam in the Maghreb is even less used in current scholarship than it was during the colonial period. Quite the contrary, political scientists are eager to listen to and to interpret the official or elitist discourse. They in turn contribute to the expansion of this discourse while ignoring the opinions of ordinary people who lack access to the written media or the official mass media. In fact, there is an "objective" solidarity beween learned, official, academic scholarship and the new states that are trying to enhance their own legitimacy.

Historically, because of two factors, Algerian society has been different from the societies in Morocco and Tunisia. First, unlike Morocco and Tunisia, Algeria after the first Arab-Muslim conquest of the Maghreb did not have the experience of a centralizing Islamic state on a continuous basis. As a result, tribal structures and solidarities in Algeria enjoyed more political autonomy and did not experience the tension between a unifying Islamic state and the segmentary society[4] as strongly as did other Maghreb societies. It is for this reason that, to date, different social communities in Algeria like the Kabylie, Chawiya, Mzab, Touaregs, and Quarsenis maintain a strong and distinct cultural and even institutional identity. Second, there have been discontinuities in the diffusion of Arabic language and culture and of important aspects of Islamic thought and teachings in Algeria. Thus, Berber is still widely spoken. Ibadi law is applied in Mzab, together with pre-Islamic Berber institutions. In Kabylie, Islamic law (Shari‛a) was not fully applied until 1962. In fact, the comprehensive and systematic Arabization and Islamization of Algerian society dates only from independence.[5]

This view of Algerian history and society is not shared by Algerian nationalists. On the contrary, the official view maintains that French colonialism used Berber particularism in order to divide Algerian society and to cut it off from its "authentic" Arab and Islamic heritage. This view is "sacred" because it is one of the foundations of the state's legitimacy. Moreover, according to the official theory, the process of nation-building (Unity of the Nation) cannot succeed if any anthropological or historical approach to the study of Algerian society is permitted. Thus, the so-called colonial science is rejected, and any attempt to provide an ethnological explanation for Algeria's historical and social evolution is labeled as neocolonial thinking.

Nevertheless, some Algerian intellectuals, like Mustafa Sacheraf, have already reacted against the systematic use of nationalist ideology in order to reject or deny objective realities described by social sciences and, especially, by history. Meanwhile, the same ideological view is used by the so-called Islamic revivalists and, in fact, explains their radicalism more than does any specific Islamic principle.

As in all North Africa, Algerian Islam has a homogeneous Malekite expression (except in the Mozabite Community) with a closed reproduction (*taqlid*) of a tradition codified since medieval times by Western Muslim doctors, including Ibn Abi-Zayd al-Qayrawani (d. 386/996), al-Qadi-‛Iyad (d. 566/1169), and al-Shatibi (d. 790/1388). Two prominent North African leaders of the Salafi movement already mentioned, the Moroccan Allal al-Fasi and the Tunisian Taher ben Ashur, have called and worked for the revival of al-Shatibi's thinking in the line of "the goals of the Shari‛a." The equivalent of this trend in Algeria has been represented by Ibn Badis and the ʿUlama Association. But Algeria has depended on the two famous Islamic universities—al-Zaytuna in Tunis and al-Qarawiyyin in Fas—for intellectual sustenance, because it lacked an Islamic institution of learning of the same caliber. Thus many Algerians have been trained in Tunisia, Morocco, or Cairo. Even today, Algerians go to these institutions in order to get proper Islamic training. In addition, branches of brotherhoods (turuq), like Tijaniyya, Qadiriyya, or ʿAmmariyya, over the years have founded centers for learning called Zawiyya where a narrow scholastic "orthodox"[6] Islam was taught until the creation of the ʿUlama Association (1931). As noted earlier, this association represented an urban, nationalist, and militant Islam against the so-called popular or folk Islam taught and practiced in rural areas by religious teachers known as Marabouts. In Algeria, the Marabouts were used by the French colonial administration as mediators between the colonial rulers and the rural population, thus facilitating French rule. Consequently, they have been accused by nationalist ʿulama of being the colonial regime's collaborators.

Independence changed the expression of Islam in Algeria. As noted before, after independence Islam was "nationalized."[7] All aspects of religious life in the society are controlled by the minister of religious affairs. The ancient Marabouts and Sufi teachers have lost their authority and the imams appointed by the minister have replaced the personalities who were previously selected by the community in each village.

Theoretically, in the hierarchy between religion and the state (din and dawla), the state is supposed to be subordinate to the divine teachings of religion, with the ʿulama being the representatives of the authority which is derived from the divine law and which the ʿulama interpreted. In reality, however, in Algeria dawla as a political power dominates and manipulates din as the source of authority.

The conflict between authority and power in Islam has existed since the time of the Prophet's death. But this conflict in the context of modern history has taken a new direction and has led to radical changes in the relationship between political power and authority in Muslim societies. The first Muslim dynasty—the Umayyads who came to power in 661—reversed the hierarchy of din and dawla imposed by the Prophet in Natura. But the general mentality, the prevailing cultural and social values, the economic system of production and exchange, and the basic relation of man to his physical environment remained the same as those known in Arabia at the time of the emergence of Islam. Even during the rule of the ʿAbbasids the axes of thought, the categories of knowledge, the system of representation, rites, and collective attitudes which supported religions—revealed and others—were neither destroyed nor disqualified as they have been in recent decades under the standardizing violence of modernization.

The positive aspects of Algerian policy since independence were noted earlier. But the cultural and intellectual price paid for this policy must also be mentioned.

When Boumediene decided to create a thousand socialist villages spread all over the country, he wanted to move the peasants from their ancient misery to a "modern" life-style. But it never occurred to him that in doing so he was also destroying the "symbolic capital," the code of honor common to all Mediterranean societies, which historically had assured their cohesion, harmony, security, cultural creativity, and solidarity. This both goes far beyond Islam and is deeper than any political decision to modernize material life. Islam as a cultural expression had integrated the values and structural systems of solidarity, production, and exchange that existed in the societies before its penetration of these societies. By contrast, in a very short time, the modern state has imposed radical changes on societies that have deeply affected their semiotic and symbolic universe. The result has been the imposition on an archaic society of a material modernity cut off from its scientific process, its cultural environment, its intellectual tools, and its support system. In the Algerian context, this has been the ultimate meaning and the disastrous result of the nationalization of religion.

It is only within this context that one can understand what is really at stake in the ongoing struggle around Islam. It was noted that Islam in Algeria, as in other Muslim societies, functions as a refuge, a den, a springboard for all kinds of opposition, social protest, psychological reactions, and cultural expressions. But what does that mean exactly?

Before answering this question, the following point needs to be made. So far in the course of this chapter, no Islamic movement in Algeria that could operate openly (as other movements do in other Islamic societies) has been discussed, although many of the factors that have led to the spread of such movements elsewhere also exist in Algeria. For example, the economic development model encouraged by the state has led to a rapid secularization of Algerian society. This secularization is sufficient reason for believers to challenge the economic model, given the fact that this process is disqualifying and dislocating Islamic ethics and politics as a force in society. If this has not happened to the same extent as it has in other Muslim countries, it is because Algeria's leaders have understood this problem very clearly. Thus, they have severely controlled Islamic forces and in this way have prevented the emergence of any association or movement not initiated, inspired, or directed by the single party. Meanwhile, they have displayed a keen sensitivity to the people's religious beliefs and practices. As a result, the state itself has come to dominate the religious scene with its initiatives. It has built schools, high-level institutes for Islamic studies, and mosques. It also has held seminars on Islamic issues and has encouraged pilgrimages and the celebration of Islamic festivals and other important occasions. As a result, nothing has been left for others to claim or to fight for. This policy so far seems to have been successful. Not only has it prevented the emergence of large violent movements, but it has also permitted the process of forging national unity to continue without interruption. Even the traditional so-called Sufi brotherhoods have been more tolerated than in the first years of independence, provided, of course, that they keep out of politics and contribute to the success of official policy.

Nevertheless, certain underground Islamic groups have emerged. But state control is so efficient that it is impossible to undertake a systematic sociological study of these groups, which have been developing in Algeria since the 1970s. There is no visible opposition to the government. But this does not mean that a deep and total consensus has been achieved between the state and civil society regarding religion. On the contrary, large social groups, or emerging classes in the large cities and in some rural areas, favor a greater recognition of religious freedom by the state. Meanwhile, the liberal democratic trend is still strong in Algeria, and has many supporters among political leaders. If this trend were to become dominant in Algeria, it would lead to a radical change in present institutions and in the relationship between the state and civil society.

Too much attention has been focused on the voices that are demanding a return to an authentic Islam, and the importance of the so-called Islamic revivalist movement has been greatly stressed. Yet in Algeria, the majority of society does not speak with a strong voice. If this majority were allowed to speak, our vision of the Algerian society would change radically. This applies to other contemporary Muslim societies as well.

In light of these observations, the question posed earlier can now be answered.

### Symbols, Signs, Signals

Symbols, signs, and signals are the common tools used in all societies, languages, and cultural expressions. As structuring data, they come before what we call religion. Religion is the visible and audible part of a complex manipulation of realities expressed through symbols, signs, and signals. Currently, there is no generally accepted theory of symbols. The consideration of the status of sign in the genesis of meaning began only recently with semiotics, after F. de Saussure defined language as a system of signs.[8] Signals are currently better understood and used more frequently in daily exchanges. The discussion of different theories regarding these three concepts is beyond the scope of this study. They will be used only to explain what could be called the semantic disorder and the symbolic destruction that have resulted from the "modernization" of Muslim societies. To give a clear idea of the difference between symbol, sign, and signal, the example of the verse in the Qur'an will be used.[9]

As a proposition articulated by God to reveal something unknown and unknowable by human reason alone, each verse is a symbol. It provides infinite possibilities of meaning; it suggests thoughts and explanations on the level of ultimate, absolute existence. It is thus always open, never fixed or closed in one interpretation. At the same time, it is enriched by successive interpretations through the use of exegesis and according to changing cultural and historical requirements. The Qur'an itself gives this definition when it repeats very often: "These are symbols (*ayat*) proposed by God so that you can think about it (or through it)."

As a proposition interpreted by exegesis according to Arabic grammar and lexicology, the verse is a system of signs—in the linguistic and semiotic meaning. At this level, the symbol is fixed and closed in the linguistic-semiotic signs. But these signs are still pregnant with various meanings. Indeed, that is why many exegeses of the same verse have been and are possible.

The lowest degree of meaning is found when a verse is treated as a signal. This is what happens every day in contemporary Islamic discourse. When a scientist "demonstrates," with "modern" scientific reasoning, that all scientific discoveries are already announced in the ayat, he reduces these ayat to mere signals referring to one meaning, just as the red or green light regulating traffic refers only to one possible understanding.

Symbols, signs, and signals can emerge, be enriched, or disintegrate according to changing historical circumstances, and according to the possibilities offered by each culture. In a mythical context, however, symbols are redrawn and are enriched by the group, which is engaged in a creative historical experience. This has been the case with the prophets and, to a lesser degree, with recent secular revolutionary leaders. In our ideological context, where secular leaders become powerful manipulators of masses, symbols and signs are dislocated and are used as signals, which have to be obeyed by everybody.

This brief explanation gives an idea of what is meant by the dislocation of the "symbolic capital" accumulated by Muslim societies during many centuries. This symbolic capital was destroyed by the introduction of material modernity into Islamic societies by local elites and historical leaders. Ataturk, more than Egypt's Naser, represents the type of leader who, through a brutal ideology called secularism, broke the semiotic universe of the transitional society.

All Muslim societies went through this process during the 1960s and the 1970s. In Algeria, this process is reflected in the destruction of the rich symbolism of the Kabylie's traditional house by the new middle class, which replaced it with "French" villas and low-cost buildings. The same has been true of music, dance, dress, celebrations, literature, economic practices, and political institutions.

Under the trauma of this semantic and semiotic violence, Islam therefore becomes a refuge, a den, and a springboard. These new functions of religion also correspond to rapid social stratification. The new privileged categories (not yet homogeneous classes), those forces supporting the state and sharing its power (the army, the police, the bureaucracy monopolizing the control of the mass media, and the big nationalized firms) use Islam as a springboard to preserve their power, enhance it, or regain it after a challenge. There is a hard mimetic competition between these privileged categories and the dominated categories suffering from what can be called semantic, semiotic, and structural violence. These last categories are the masses mobilized by exhilarating speeches promising an eschatological future (perfect justice, brotherhood, independence from imperialism, total freedom, true participation, political and economic power), but regularly forgotten, marginalized, and submitted to a continuous, constraining process well described by Jalal Amin as "the modernization of poverty." For these masses who are uprooted and cut off from their semantic and semiotic universe, Islam becomes a refuge and eventually, for those who find a leader, it becomes a den from which to fight against the illegitimate state and the oppressive ruling elite.

Islam is thus shared, used, disputed, and manipulated at many levels, by all social actors with various ambitions and through different cultural tools. The game is social, political, and secular; the instruments of the game are found in Islam because it is a rich stock, an illuminated legacy of symbols, signs, and signals. That is why there is this mimetic competition for the control and exploitation of the symbolic capital, without which no group can gain, keep, or exercise power. Viewed in this perspective, the so-called Islamic revivalist movements thus become just one component of the dialectic forces operating in the sociopolitical space as a whole. They are produced by the ruling elite as far as they shape the behavior, the conceptions, and the answers of this elite. Their aims, their protesting discourse, and their concrete programs are ultimately as secular as those of their opponents or oppressors. The religious, spiritual concern is totally absent, obliterated despite the obsessive claims of such religious signals as the obligation for men to have a mustache, for women to wear a veil, and so forth. These are signals because there is no appropriate effort to insert them into a modernized Islamic theology, architecture, urbanism, law, or culture. One should speak only of a juxtaposition or a superimposition of ancient decontextualized elements in the nonmastered, borrowed space of an unthought—and still unthinkable—modernity. One can also speak of a process that uses traditionalization to cover under traditional signals the unavoidable eruption of material modernity.

The validity of these observations, in the case of Algeria, can be shown through an examination of official charters prepared and promulgated periodically by the state and the collective attitudes developed about women.

The official charters are conceived, discussed, and finally written under the supervision of some recognized intellectuals in the party. The language used in these documents is typically secular, positivist, and militant. It postulates the existence and the actual performances of right guided and guiding leaders who are perfectly aware and confident of the massive certitudes that enlighten the political, economic, social, and cultural policies agreed to by the nation and for the nation. Islam is mentioned as the religion of the state, without any intellectual attempt to solve the continuous contradiction between the Marxist strategy on one side and the theological requirements of the Qur'an as a divine revelation on the other side. This should be the task of the ᶜulama; but the prevailing cultural and political constraints contained in the national charters prevent the emergence of such a style of thinking and research. The ruling elite and the Islamic movements agree on one special point: Islam should remain a stock of symbols, signs, and signals at the disposal of the competing actors. If it is reinterpreted in a scientific perspective, it will not work easily as a refuge, a den, or a springboard. That is why critical study of the Qur'an and its exegesis, the Hadith, and the principles (usul) of the Shariᶜa is forbidden by those who have an interest in monopolizing the authority inherent in the mastery of these religious sciences. In the scientific council of the new University for Islamic Sciences operating in Constantine in Algeria and headed by the well-known Egyptian ʿalim Muhammad al-Ghazali, intellectual and spiritual issues are shifted to political concerns and control.

The prevailing attitude about the legal status of women shows more clearly the weakness of modern thought in contemporary Algeria. Women in Mediterranean culture traditionally have been the focal point of the values contained in the code of honor. Architecture, urbanism, law, and division of space into private and public parts have traditionally been directly affected by the necessity to protect women and their sexuality as the highest symbol of each family's honor. These conceptions and practices can be found in ancient Greece, southern Italy, Sicily, Andalusia, the Maghreb, and the Middle East.[10] Islam had only to confirm and make sacred an ancient preexisting order. But the current interpretation of Islam by competing actors is totally alien to these historical and anthropological realities; it is said, dogmatically, that the status of women is fixed by God in the Revelation and rightly interpreted centuries ago by the authorized doctors of law. Women, actually, are treated just like the beard and the mustache. They are no more than signals used to separate the "true believers" from the "infidels," meaning those militants seeking a new political order and those who monopolize an illegitimate power and impose it on the *umma* (community). These signals are internalized by the believers/militants as symbols related to the Revelation, which in turn illustrates the continuous ambiguity of symbols, signs, and signals in all societies. There is no way to convince a believer/militant that he is actually destroying the values for which he fights. This can only be done when *social imaginaire* is touched either by a generalized scientific education or by a violent revolution, which would develop new systems of representation.

The foregoing has made clear that our knowledge and our vocabulary about Islam and Muslim societies are still those handed down from the nineteenth century and even from the Middle Ages. Westerners, including learned Islamologists, prefer to immobilize Islam by using the substantialist, fixist, essentialist vocabulary spread and imposed by militant Muslims. They refuse to consider first of all the sociohistorical dynamism through which the nature and functions of traditional religions are transformed. To describe accurately the process of this transformation and to risk some hypothesis about the creative tensions among religion, history, and society thus remain urgent tasks.

# NOTES

1. I have explained elsewhere why and how I use the concept of *social imaginaire* to analyze the structure of the common Muslim consciousness and the kind of history produced by it. See M. Arkoun, "Leaders et imaginaire social dans le monde musulman contemporain," presented at a conference in Jyvaskyla, Finland, June 25–26, 1986.

2. On this concept, see M. Arkoun, "L'Islam dans l'histoire," *Maghreb-Machreq*, No. 102 (1984).

3. See M. Arkoun, *Critique de la raison islamique* (Paris: Maisonneuve-Larose, 1984).

4. E. Gellner used the theory of the segmentary society in *Saints of the Atlas*, and the theory was later discussed by many other authors.

5. See G. Granguillaume, *Arabisation et politique linguistique au Maghreb* (Paris: Maisonneuve-Larose, 1984).

6. The concept of orthodoxy is one of the keys to rethink the whole theology of Islam, as I showed in my *Critique de la raison islamique*.

7. *Nationalization* as used in the official discourse means actually the monopoly of the state (etatization) over all forms of social and political activity and the citizens' participation in this activity as the employees or officers of the state.

8. See E. Gilson, *Philosophie et linguistique* (Paris: Jean Vrin, 1969).

9. Other examples can be found in architectural constructions such as the minaret, the dome, the arch, and the mihrab, all well-known elements of the mosque reused as signals of a "modern" Islamic architecture. See the numerous and important publications of the Aga Khan Award for Architecture, especially the review *MIMAR*.

10. See the contribution by M. Aymard in F. Braudel, *La Méditerranée, l'espace et l'histoire* (Paris: Flamarion, 1985), pp. 205–223.

# XII

# SUDAN

*John L. Esposito*

On April 5, 1985, the government of Ja°far al-Numairi was toppled in a bloodless military coup d'etat after sixteen years of rule. From September 1983, al-Numairi had guided his own self-proclaimed Islamic revolution in the Sudan. Explaining this experience requires an analysis of Sudan's Islamic past and its political realities in the 1970s.

## Sudan's Islamic Political Heritage

Sudan's Islamic political heritage has deep roots: the Funj Islamic state, the formal Islamic policy of Muhammad °Ali during Ottoman Egyptian rule, and the Mahdist Islamic state.[1] Islam first came to Africa through the early Arab-Muslim conquests of the seventh century. As was true in much of Africa, however, the spread of Islam in the Sudan was due primarily to the activities of merchants, itinerant preachers, and, in particular, Sufi (mystic) brotherhoods or orders (*tariqas*).[2] By the sixteenth century, the Christian kingdoms of northern Sudan had been replaced by an emerging Islamic society, while the South retained its African religious traditions and was later influenced by Christian missionaries in the nineteenth and twentieth centuries.

The significance of Sufism for Sudanese politics and society cannot be over-estimated.[3] The Sudanese Islam is Sufi Islam. Sufi preachers from the Arab East and native holy men established their orders, which became the dominant social structures, thus giving Sudanese politics a sectarian nature. Religious teachers associated with Sufi orders performed most activities: some focused on the spread of Sufism through preaching and initiation into an order; others assumed a more traditional role associated with the °*ulama* by teaching and administering the *Shari°a*; and they served as advisers to tribal chiefs and intermediaries between the people and their rulers. Occasionally they criticized, warned, and admonished tribal chiefs.

Sufi orders were organized around their leaders and their descendants, "holy families," who possessed their spiritual power (*baraka*).[4] The tombs of pious ancestors served as an order's center, the headquarters for its leadership, and a sacred site for pilgrimage, for the performance of Sufi devotional rituals, and for its school.

## The Funj Sultanate (1504–1820)

Sufism flourished during the sixteenth century under the Funj sultanate, an Islamic state established in what today is northern Sudan.[5] As an Islamic state, it generally enjoyed the support of the tariqas, which were the recipients of royal patronage and land grants. By the eighteenth century, internal disintegration and an invasion by the army of Muhammad ʿAli ended the Funj sultanate and established Ottoman-Egyptian rule.

## Ottoman-Egyptian Rule (1820–1881)

ʿAli attempted to establish a more centralized government, to introduce modern Westernizing reforms—which threatened the traditional political and religious order—and to restrict the local leaders' political and military independence. The Sufi orders were divided in their response. Some, like the Samaniyya, were resistant whereas others, such as the Khatmiyya, cooperated. But dissent grew, and by the 1880s popular uprisings challenged Ottoman suzerainty. Finally, Muhammad Ahmad, the Mahdi, overthrew Egyptian rule and established an Islamic state.

## The Mahdist State (1885–1899)

Muhammad Ahmad (1848–85) was a member of the Samaniyya order. He blamed both Ottoman-Egyptian imperialism and the corruption of Sufism for Sudan's social and moral decline. Drawing on a long tradition of religious revivalism and popular eschatological belief, he declared himself the Mahdi ("the guided one"), the divinely inspired leader sent by God in the last days to establish God's rule on earth in a morally and socially just society.[6] The Mahdi called upon the people to strive toward God's path and waged a holy war (*jihad*) against the corruption of Egyptian occupation. He united his followers against fellow Muslims (the Egyptians), denouncing them as infidels who

> disobeyed the command of His messenger and His prophets . . . ruled in a manner not in accord with what God has sent. . . . altered the sharia of our master Muhammad, the messenger of God, and . . . blasphemed against the faith of God.[7]

The corruption of Sudanese society was attributed to foreign (Turko-Egyptian and local non-Islamic) influences. Thus, Ottoman-Egyptian Muslim rulers, not European colonialism, precipitated this militant Islamic revivalist movement.

The Mahdi movement, like similar revivalist movements across the Islamic world at that time, such as the Wahhabi in Arabia and the Fulani in Nigeria, believed that it was reenacting Islam's paradigmatic event, recreating the first Islamic movement and state established by the Prophet Muhammad. Mahdist victories, like the early successes of Muhammad, were viewed as validation of a divinely sanctioned and guided mission. By 1885, when the Mahdi died, the Mahdist movement had rid Sudan of Egyptian occupiers and had created an Islamic state. The Mahdist state lasted fourteen years until its defeat by an Anglo-Egyptian army in 1899. It left a legacy of religious identification, leadership, and ideology associated with the state that has continued to influence Sudanese politics. The Mahdi period has provided an important reference point for Sudan's political development because it came to be viewed as the first independent Sudanese state and it joined the idea of Sudanese nationalism with Islam in an Islamic state. Thus, Sudan's historical, political, and socioreligious experience has made Islam a force to be reckoned with by political leaders, whatever their ideological proclivities.

## Modern Sudanese Politics

The Sudan was governed by the Anglo-Egyptian Condominium from 1899 until national independence in 1956.[8] During that period the Ansar, followers of the Mahdi, and the Khatmiyya vied for political influence and later emerged as political parties. The Khatmiyya had been the historic opponents of the Mahdiyya or Ansar. They refused to acknowledge the Mahdi's religious claims, cooperated with Ottoman-Egyptian rulers, and, under the condominium, advocated a union with Egypt. Their differences were institutionalized politically during the mid-1930s when modern political parties developed in the Sudan. Among the new parties, the Ansar and the Khatmiyya were dominant. The Ashiqa party, Khatmiyya-supported and led by Isma'il al-Azhari, formed the core of what would later become the National Union Party. (By 1956 the bulk of the Khatmiyya would shift their support to the People's Democratic Party.) The Umma (Nation) Party constituted the political wing of the Ansar. Among the non-Sufi parties were the Sudanese Communist Party and the Muslim Brotherhood's Islamic Charter Front. The force of religion in politics was clearly evident. As Gabriel Warburg observed:

> Indeed, on the eve of the Sudan's independence, in the years 1953–1956, it became clear that despite the emergence of an educated elite with political aspirations, the real masters of Sudanese politics were the leaders of popular Islam, and primarily the heads of the Ansar (Sayyid ᶜAbd al-Rahman al-Mahdi), and of the Khatmiyya (Sayyid ᶜAli al-Mirghani).[9]

After independence, the Ansar and the Khatmiyya continued to struggle for power.[10] However, their comparable strength in national elections tipped the balance to an alliance and civilian rule (1956–58) under the National Union Party, led by al-Azhari. Despite secular nationalist leadership, Islam was declared the official state religion and the Shariᶜa a basic source of law. This did not allay the concerns of the Ansar and Khatmiyya, who set aside their differences and issued a demand for an Islamic republic with a parliamentary form of government and the Shariᶜa as the *main* source of law.

Civilian rule ended abruptly in 1958 with the military takeover by General Ibrahim ᶜAbbud, who dissolved the Constitutional Assembly and banned political parties. Nevertheless, the influence of religious leaders could be seen both in ᶜAbbud's attempt to gain their approval prior to the coup and in the Ansar's opposition to military government.

The ᶜAbbud military regime was overthrown by the civilian revolution of October 1964, which was supported by the Communist Party. Concerned about the growing influence of leftists in government, traditional forces reasserted themselves and dominated national elections in 1965 and 1968. The Communist Party was banned and there were calls for the drafting of an Islamic constitution. On May 23, 1969, led by the dominant factions of the Umma Party and the Khatmiyya, all political parties in the Constituent Assembly agreed that the Sudan should be a presidential republic with an Islamic constitution. Elections were scheduled for June 1969. Sadiq al-Mahdi and al-Hadi al-Mahdi, Ansar leaders, were expected to assume the positions of prime minister and president, respectively. But on May 25, 1969, a group of young army officers led by Colonel Jaᶜfar Muhammad al-Numairi seized power and thus began the May revolution.

Three important ideological forces were at work in the Sudan of 1969–70: Islam, Arab socialism, and communism. Historically, Islam had been intertwined with Sudan's political development and had thus become an integral component of Sudanese nationalism and independence, even during the post-independence drift toward secularism.

Al-Numairi's accession to rule introduced a new ideological factor in the drift toward secularism, namely state, Arab socialism.[11] The Free Officers' May revolution, like many other of the Arab world's radical socialist revolutions in the 1960s, was patterned after that of the hero of Arab socialism, Naser.

Initially, the Sudanese Communist Party (SCP) and other leftists supported the May revolution, since they feared that the Umma Party and Sadiq al-Mahdi might gain power. They soon became a costly liability to the regime. Their presence in the government, the influx of foreign Marxist advisers, and government attempts to abolish local and provincial administrations and to nationalize domestic and foreign businesses united traditional elites (tribal, commercial, and religious) against communism and its influence in the government. Sadiq al-Mahdi sharply criticized al-Numairi's exclusion of traditional political forces from the government. This led to arrests in 1969 and the bombardment of the Ansar stronghold on Aba Island in March 1970, killing thousands of Ansar, including their spiritual leader, al-Hadi al-Mahdi. The Ansar were crushed, but al-Numairi's actions prompted the formation of an opposition coalition, the National Front, which included Sharif al-Hindi and the Democratic Union Party (Khatmiyya), Sadiq al-Mahdi and the Umma (Ansar), and Hasan al-Turabi of the Islamic Charter Front (Muslim Brotherhood).

Al-Numairi's relations with the communists deteriorated in 1971 and consequently the SCP opposed the formation of the Sudan Socialist Union (SSU), its leader was exiled, and three communist members were expelled from the Revolutionary Command Council (RCC). In July 1971 the communists overthrew al-Numairi and the RCC, in order to turn the May revolution into a "true proletariat." Their success was quickly reversed when the use of the Red flag in public demonstrations identified the coup as Marxist and rallied anticommunist forces. With assistance from Qadhafi's Libya and Sadat's Egypt, al-Numairi toppled the three-day-old regime. He also purged the Communist Party, executed its leaders, reversed his pro-Soviet position, and became a close ally of the United States, Egypt, and Saudi Arabia. He inaugurated an open-door (*infitah*) economic policy to attract Western and Arab capital, dissolved the RCC, installed a permanent constitution, and had himself elected president of the republic (1971), with wide-ranging powers.

In a masterful stroke, he reunited the Sudan, signing the Addis Ababa agreement (February 23, 1972), which settled the seventeen-year civil war between northern and southern Sudan, creating a semiautonomous southern region with its own regional government.[12] Also, a vice-president from the South was named to the central government, rebel forces were integrated into the military, and it was agreed that half of the 12,000-man army stationed in the South would be southerners. In January 1973, he formed the Sudanese Socialist Union as the official party and the political arm of his regime. Al-Numairi also appealed to Islam to enhance his legitimacy and gain popular support. The media emphasized his personal piety and he often referred to Islam in his public statements. Political leaders with Sufi backgrounds, not associated with the Ansar and Khatmiyya, were given more prominent positions.[13] Finally, the 1973 constitution recognized Islamic law and custom as the "main sources of legislation."

In these policies, al-Numairi was motivated primarily by domestic events but he was also influenced by broader Islamic currents. The disastrous Arab defeat by Israel in 1967 and Naser's death in 1970 had helped to lessen the hold of Arab socialism and to generate an Islamic revivalism.

In Egypt, Anwar Sadat used Islam rather than Arab socialism to gain political legitimacy, to distance himself from Naser's shadow, and to counter the left. Arab victory in the 1973 Arab-Israeli war—which was cast in Islamic terms—and the impact of the Arab oil embargo renewed a sense of Islamic pride and identity, which was shared by most Muslim rulers. Moreover, Sudan's greater concern for Islam attracted Saudi support, which had become more important since Libya now backed al-Numairi's opposition, the National Front.

The year 1977 proved to be a turning point in Sudan's Islamization. Despite al-Numairi's success in reunifying the country and his appeal to Islam, he remained at odds with the National Front, representing the major Islamic organizations and the defunct political parties. An abortive coup d'etat in 1976, led by Sadiq al-Mahdi and the Ansar, constituted the most important challenge since that of the communists in 1971. Al-Numairi prevailed, but it became clear that the National Front remained a persistent opposition to be reckoned with;

the Front, in turn, was forced to accept al-Numairi's staying power. A series of meetings between al-Numairi and Sadiq al-Mahdi thus resulted, leading to a formal agreement in July 1977. The agreement included an eight-point program of political reforms. It dissolved the National Front, reconciled many of the traditional forces, and intensified Islam's role in Sudanese politics.

According to the agreement, traditional party leaders were allowed to engage in politics in exchange for the dissolution of the National Front.[14] A general amnesty enabled Sadiq al-Mahdi to return from exile, freed some nine hundred political prisoners, and permitted members of the Ansar, Democratic Unionist Party, and Muslim Brotherhood to compete in national elections in February 1978, where they won a significant number of seats in the National Assembly.

Al-Numairi also named Sadiq al-Mahdi, Hasan al-Turabi, Ahmad ᶜAli al-Mirghani, and other opposition members to the SSU's central committee and political bureau. A committee for the revival of Islamic law was created under the chairmanship of Hasan al-Turabi to review Sudan's legislation in terms of its conformity with Islamic law. It soon became clear, however, that the signing of the agreement did not bring national unity. Resistance from a variety of sources, sectarian, military, and southern, remained strong. The prospect of implementation of Islamic law and the creation of an Islamic state raised special concerns for southerners, who feared an erosion of their rights as non-Muslims. But the Muslim Brotherhood benefited from National Reconciliation.

The Muslim Brotherhood had been founded in 1954. Since its creation, the Brotherhood rejected Westernization and secularization and advocated the establishment of an Islamic order and the adoption of an Islamic constitution. Its members criticized Sufism's assimilation of popular non-Islamic beliefs and practices, and thus alienated many of the local Sufi leaders.

The Brotherhood acquired prominence during the mid-1960s under the leadership of Dr. Hasan al-Turabi, its secretary general. Al-Turabi had returned from France with a doctorate in international law and become dean of the Law School at Khartoum University. A charismatic leader among university students and young professionals, he tried to mobilize popular support for the eradication of communism and the introduction of an Islamic constitution. The Brothers attracted other sympathetic groups and formed a new political party, the Islamic Charter Front. At the university campuses, they organized students and contested student elections against communist student organizations. Campus politics provided a testing ground and launching pad for broader political action. The Islamic Charter Front, allied with the Ansar, Khatmiyya, and others, succeeded in having the Communist Party banned in 1965, but their hopes for an Islamic constitution were dashed when al-Numairi came to power with leftist support in 1969. Thus, they joined the National Front and cooperated in efforts to overthrow al-Numairi's communist-supported regime.

Unlike other members of the National Front, the Muslim Brotherhood accepted the fruits of National Reconciliation and became involved in the political process. One explanation is that al-Turabi accepted al-Numairi's apparent return to Islam and found his observance of Islamic rules and his advocacy of a greater role for Islam in public and private life coincided with the Brotherhood's program.

Another reason was that the Brotherhood's strategy had always been to change society through the development of a new elite who would enter and influence all sectors of education, the professions, and government. The creation of the Islamic Charter Front was an extension of this logic. As a political organization, it continued to press for change "within" the system. While the long-range goal might be the creation of an Islamic state under a suitable Muslim leader, the Brotherhood was content in the short run to establish itself as a recognized political force to be taken seriously by any government, whatever its orientation. Thus, whether al-Numairi was sincere or not, al-Turabi could view his new initiative as offering the Brotherhood an opportunity to influence policy.

From 1977 onward, the Muslim Brotherhood was closely associated with al-Numairi's regime. Al-Turabi, Sudan's attorney general, and the Muslim Brothers secured senior governmental positions and won a substantial number of seats in the new People's Assembly elected in 1980. Their strength in governmental institutions also was expanded. During the early 1980s throughout the Sudan, student government elections were dominated by Islamic issues and invariably Muslim Brotherhood candidates won. Student politics spilled into the streets as Islamically oriented students marched in support of the Brotherhood and Islamization, chanting: "Non-Western, non-Eastern, Islamic 100 percent."[15] Muslim Brothers and their sympathizers also became the key figures in a burgeoning system of Islamic banks and insurance companies.

Many military and secular nationalist leaders and non-Muslims in the South, however, were concerned that Numairi's increasing Islamization and the Brotherhood's influence would exacerbate sectarian politics. A minority within the Brotherhood also viewed al-Numairi as an opportunist and al-Turabi's accommodation as a betrayal of the Brotherhood's principles. In general, Islamic leaders remained critical of the Brotherhood's new role in government. The Ansar remained ambivalent, resisted full reconciliation, and accused al-Numairi of dragging his feet on promised reforms and of betraying the Arab cause by supporting Anwar Sadat's Camp David policy. Sharif al-Hindi remained in exile in Britain and in 1979 formed the Sudanese Democratic Front, an opposition coalition that called for free elections and a multiparty democracy. The Khatmiyya leader, Sayyid Muhammad ʿUthman al-Mirghani, who was concerned about the increased influence of the Muslim Brotherhood and the potential erosion of Sufi influence, joined with the heads of other Sufi orders and created the Islamic Revival Committee.

By the early 1980s a series of events had dashed the initial hopes, engendered by the Addis Ababa accords and National Reconciliation, for greater unity and prosperity. In little more than a decade, the Sudan had moved ideologically from a leftist to an increasingly Islamic orientation. However, the initiation and delineation of this new direction was not due primarily to traditional religious leaders, but to Ja'far al-Numairi himself. It was very much "al-Numairi's Islam" in style and content. Why?

Seemingly, personal and political factors influenced al-Numairi's turn to Islam in his life and government. His brush with death during the communist coup in 1971, illness, and the so-called midlife crisis led to his personal reconversion. He adopted a holistic approach to Islam and wrote a book, *Why the Islamic Way*, about his return to Islam in which he called for the application of Shari'a in the Sudan.[16] But some remained skeptical, as the following statement by a southern leader and former minister of culture, Bona Malwal, illustrates:

> [al-Numairi] also made Islamic history in that his "path" to Mecca, the holy headquarters of Islam in Saudi Arabia, lay, as we have seen above, through Moscow, the headquarters of international communism. It appears clear that Numayri is using Islam not from religious conviction but for reasons of political expediency.[17]

The post-reconciliation appeal to Islam offered Numairi a new way out of a deteriorating situation. It was consonant with his leadership style, had continuity with the Islamic character of Sudanese political history and social culture, and thus was potentially capable of consolidating popular support among Sudan's 70 percent Muslim population. Throughout his regime, al-Numairi had ruled through a variety of alliances: leftist, military, tribal, and religious. Yet he would use them only for as long as was necessary, shifting from one partner to another lest any become too strong in its own right.[18] His strength was in maintaining a balance between alliance building and keeping potential rivals disorganized and relatively weak. As a result, he could count on the loyalty of few. Events of the 1970s had narrowed al-Numairi's political options. The communist coup of 1971 had made him antileftist, and his brand of Arab socialism had failed. Sudan's economy had deteriorated and its national debt would reach $9 billion by 1985. In response to the World Bank and the International Monetary Fund, Sudan had lifted government subsidies on bread and sugar, causing riots in 1979 and in 1982. Periodically, the government had had stormy relations with political parties, national Islamic organizations, dissidents in the South, and the military.

Troubles in the South and within the military in the early 1980s underscored the growing political fragmentation. In 1980 al-Numairi dissolved the regional government and regional assembly in the South, and in 1981 he imposed a military regime and partitioned the South. Guerrilla warfare followed, waged by groups such as Ananya II and the Sudan Popular Liberation Army (SPLA), led by Colonel John Garang and supported by Libya and Ethiopia. The grievances against the government were both political and economic. The Muslim government of the North was viewed as dominating the South politically and exploiting its economic resources. Al-Numairi's decision to redraw geographic boundaries would have placed the South's oil deposits within the North. The building of a major refinery in the North to process oil from the South also became an explosive issue. Al-Numairi exploited the rebellion in the South to strengthen ties with the West, especially the United States. Maintaining that the SPLA guerrillas were Marxists supported by Libya and Ethiopia, he reinforced the Sudan's image as a bulwark against communism in Africa and asked for increased U.S. military aid.

Moreover, al-Numairi had a confrontation with his main source of support, the military, who were angry with his reform policies and official corruption. Al-Numairi's response was to fire his first vice-president and dismiss the commander-in-chief of the army and twenty-two of his senior officers.

Despite the above-noted criticisms and problems, al-Numairi's turn to Islam retained its potential for popular support since it resonated with popular Islamic sentiments and co-opted many of the themes of his Islamic opposition.

On September 8, 1983, al-Numairi declared the Sudan an Islamic republic, issued an official decree for the application of the Shariʿa, and named this an "Islamic revolution" with wide impact on politics, law, and society. In addition to his religious belief, political ambitions, and the Sudan's domestic conditions, regional events like the Iranian revolution (1979) and the assassination of Sadat by Muslim militants (1981), prompted al-Numairi to control or co-opt Islamic forces.

### Numairi's Islamization Program

Sudan's Islamization program was very much "al-Numairi's Islam." The government-appointed committee to revive Islamic laws (1977) and its chairman, Hasan al-Turabi, had drafted a number of bills, none of which were acted upon, since al-Numairi did not like to share power or credit. By the 1980s, he had become concerned about the Muslim Brotherhood's growing influence. Thus, he relied upon Awad al-Jid Muhammad Ahmad, a young lawyer, and Nayal Abu Garun, the son of a Sufi leader, to provide a liaison with local Sufi leaders, whom al-Numairi cultivated as an alternative to national Islamic leaders. More than twenty laws, regulations, and policies were hastily formulated, without consultation with the attorney general or the chief justice. The result was a series of ad hoc laws—poorly drafted and often written in vague, inconsistent, and contradictory language whose implications were rarely appreciated—which were issued by presidential decree. Their implementation and application were equally erratic, dependent upon al-Numairi's presidential decree and his "decisive justice courts," not the Sudan's duly established judiciary.

For contemporary Islamic revivalism, Islamic law provides the blueprint for the good society; its restoration is the sine qua non for the renewal of Islamic society. The foci of al-Numairi's Islamization program were thus law and the judiciary, enactment of Islamic laws, and the creation of decisive justice courts.

Sudan's British-based legal system was not simply replaced by the Shariʿa.

Instead, al-Numairi enacted a number of Islamic regulations and policies over the next two years that tended to replace or modify some existing laws. Sudan, like Libya, Pakistan, and Iran, reinstituted Qur'anic punishments (*hudud*, "limits" of God). This new "Islamic" penal code was followed by the Evidence Act and the Civil Transaction Code (which affected contracts, civil disputes, sales, rents, and loans), the Military Forces Act, and the Police and Prisons Act. The new Islamic orientation of law was broadly defined in the Judgment (Basic Rules) Act, which declared that Islamic law and Arabic language were to replace English law and English language. Judges were directed to look first to the Shari'a and Sunna (example of the Prophet) and to Islamic principles and precedents for guidance.

In the socioeconomic sphere, new guidelines were enacted in areas of taxation and banking. The Zakat Tax Act of 1984 replaced much of the state's taxation system with an alms tax. Zakat is an annual "poor tithe" on the accumulated wealth of a Muslim that is to be applied toward the needs of the poor. Although such a tax had been voluntary in modern times, the Sudan, like Pakistan and Iran, turned zakat into a state tax, intended to replace Sudan's income tax.

Al-Numairi also stated his intention to convert all of the Sudan's banks into interest-free institutions and this became an especially controversial issue. Many Islamic revivalists believe that Islam's traditional ban on *riba* also applies to any form of bank interest. In recent times Islamic banks have been established in many countries, offering an alternative interest-free banking system, and Sudan already had five such banks. The move to an Islamic banking system in the Sudan, as in Pakistan and Iran, was to be the first step in basing the entire economy on Islamic principles. These policies greatly disturbed Sudanese and foreign interests, including U.S.-based multinationals. The judiciary's powers were curtailed by the introduction of the decisive justice courts. Al-Numairi had been frustrated by an assertive and professional judiciary that had often acted independently in cases involving arbitrary government actions. He accused the magistrates of corruption, drunkenness, and inefficiency, and in June 1983, he fired forty-four judges. Others protested and resigned, and a three-month strike by judges paralyzed the legal system. Thousands were arrested and brought before government-appointed judges, whose decisive justice courts often functioned like military tribunals that employed Islamic punishments. In May 1984, European-style dancing was banned and a nightclub owner was sentenced to twenty-five lashes for permitting heterosexual dancing.[19] While the new courts were admittedly swift, opinions vastly differed on their independence and the quality of their justice.

Al-Numairi used Islam to direct, and thus control, Sudanese Islamic revivalism and to enhance his legitimacy by appropriating a religiopolitical status. He replaced Hasan al-Turabi with a more subservient attorney general. Sadiq al-Mahdi, the leader of the Ansar, was first placed in "protective custody" and then imprisoned. With the greater emphasis on Islam, Sadiq's direct descent from the Mahdi and his leadership of a national Islamic organization threatened al-Numairi's own attempt to enhance his legitimacy through an appeal to Islam.

Sadiq had been critical of al-Numairi's Islamization program, maintaining that the introduction of the Shariᶜa was premature. He argued that the enforcement of Islamic punishments was contingent upon the eradication of the grave Sudanese unemployment and poverty. The event that precipitated Sadiq's imprisonment was a march of the Ansar to the Mahdi's tomb, where many of the Ansar publicly pledged *baya* (an oath of allegiance) to Sadiq as the Mahdi's successor.

Al-Numairi tried to enhance his own status as an "Islamic" political leader by releasing a reported 13,000 prisoners to give them a "second chance" under Islamic law; by destroying $11 million worth of alcohol; and by forcing senior members of the government, judiciary, military, trade unions, and the SSU to perform the baya, pledge allegiance to him, and acknowledge him as a Muslim ruler. Many even expected al-Numairi to declare himself imam, the religiopolitical leader of the state, but on July 11, 1984, he was rebuffed by the People's Assembly, which postponed a vote on a series of amendments that would have ratified his Islamic laws and his religiopolitical status.

For a while, however, internal Sudanese politics helped al-Numairi's Islamization. Traditional political parties were relatively weak and the local Sufi religious establishment supportive and compliant. Al-Numairi's military style and his penchant for quick and decisive action and for public attention also influenced his method of Islamization. Thus, he found the more careful, intellectual approach of al-Turabi, with its sensitivity to problems of Islamic and Western jurisprudence, tedious and confusing.[20] His singular control of the process also resulted in a traditional style, rather than the more reformist approaches advocated by Sadiq and al-Turabi. His Islamic legislation and the decisions of his courts were, in their interpretation of Islam, conservatively based on medieval Islamic legal manuals and showed no awareness of the need for reform.

Initially, Islamization proved popular since many felt that it reduced crime and corruption. However, al-Numairi's use of Islam for personal benefit, the erratic decisions of the decisive justice courts, and the indiscriminate use of flogging undermined his image at home and abroad. Al-Turabi and the Muslim Brothers had welcomed the implementation of Islamic law, but they were uncomfortable with its formulation and implementation, although they continued to be publicly supportive. Critics of the regime saw little distinction between the Muslim Brotherhood and al-Numairi's program. The Ansar, Republican Brothers, Khatmiyya, secularists, and southern opposition leaders opposed Islamization and regarded the Brothers as the architects of al-Numairi's program. Even conservative Muslim states like Saudi Arabia became concerned as increased international media coverage of a seemingly endless number of floggings and amputations created a negative image of Islam and Islamic justice. In response, the government accused the international press of conspiring against the new Islamic direction, and in September 1984 it convened the First International Conference for the Implementation of Shariᶜa in Sudan. More than two hundred official delegates from the Islamic world and a number of observers gathered to learn about Sudan's Islamization program. In his inaugural address, al-Numairi declared: "The 25th of May Revolution is but one historical phase in the great, long-awaited Islamic Revolution."[21]

Although apparently quite successful, the conference proved a turning point in al-Numairi's relationship with the Muslim Brotherhood. For some time, government and SSU officials, who had been against Islamization, had warned al-Numairi about his alliance with the Brotherhood and its infiltration of governmental and extragovernmental institutions. The organizers of the conference on Shariʿa were the Supreme Council for Religious Affairs and the Faisal Islamic Bank, both controlled by the Brothers. As the event unfolded, it was clear that the Brothers had upstaged al-Numairi by organizing a large demonstration. Several hundred thousand persons marched before the reviewing stand. With a seemingly endless line of marchers stretched back from Khartoum across the bridge to Omdurman, al-Numairi ended the parade after several hours, claiming fatigue. But the Brotherhood proved to their colleagues in the Islamic world and to al-Numairi their effectiveness and the popularity of Islamization. Al-Numairi, however, concluded that he needed to curb this Islamic competitor. In subsequent months he limited and criticized the Brotherhood and, finally, made them his scapegoat.

In March 1984, Sudan's doctors went on strike. Omdurman was bombed by what the government claimed was a Libyan plane. As a result, Egypt and the United States hastily rushed military aid (AWACS) and al-Numairi declared martial law (April). In June, Sudan's elected People's Assembly resisted government pressures and postponed ratification of al-Numairi's constitutional amendments to establish Sudan as an Islamic Republic. In July, a new opposition coalition, the National Salvation Front, was formed by the Ansar, Khatmiyya, SCP, and others. Their program included the abolition of laws considered not truly Islamic, the guarantee of civil rights especially for non-Muslims, and retention of the Shariʿa as a source of legislation. Although John Garang, leader of the SPLA guerillas, participated in the discussions, he refused to join the coalition unless complete secularization was accepted.

Political instability was exacerbated by economic deterioration caused by famine, decreasing Arab aid, and currency devaluations. Al-Numairi responded with a series of reforms. He canceled the state of emergency (September) that had been in effect since April, discontinued floggings and amputations in the North (October), reversed his decision to divide the South, and gave assurances that Shariʿa would not be implemented there.[22] Talk of an imminent introduction of an interest-free Islamic economy also subsided and the zakat law was abolished.

Nevertheless, the political and economic situation remained unstable. The United States froze $114 million in economic aid (December) and joined with the IMF in pressing the Sudan to introduce economic reforms. The U.S. Congress and the Reagan administration communicated their concerns about the violation of human rights and threatened to withhold economic and military aid. In March 1985, Vice-President Bush led a U.S. delegation to the Sudan, promising American aid in exchange for needed economic reforms. Meanwhile, rumors circulated in Khartoum and elsewhere that Bush had reiterated Washington's concerns about Islamization. Saudi Arabia and Egypt, which were particularly concerned about the strong presence and influence of "Islamic fundamentalists" (the Muslim Brotherhood) in the Sudanese government and their potential to serve as an example to militant Islamic groups in Saudi Arabia and Egypt, also pressured al-Numairi.

Al-Numairi sought to secure and strengthen his rule by making concessions to his allies and southern opposition and by cracking down on his opposition. In January 1985, amid growing criticism of Islamization, he selected an easy target, the Republican Brothers, to symbolize his intention of silencing his critics and to rally popular Muslim support. Masking authoritarianism by Islamic orthodoxy, he arrested, tried, and executed the founder and leader of the Republican Brothers, Mahmud Muhammad Taha, for apostasy on January 18, 1985. Taha had been a nationalist fighter against the British and a strong supporter of al-Numairi. He had also been an opponent of sectarian politics and attempts to implement Islamic law. Many Muslims, including the Ansar, Muslim Brotherhood, and local Sufi leaders, regarded Taha's religious claims and his reinterpretation of Islam not as liberal reformism but as heresy. Taha's specific offense was the distribution of a pamphlet openly critical of al-Numairi's version of Islamic laws, which, the pamphlet charged, had "distorted Islam in the eyes of intelligent members of our people and in the eyes of the world, and degraded the reputation of our country."[23]

A crackdown on the Muslim Brotherhood in March 1985 signaled al-Numairi's attempt to salvage his tottering regime, answer his critics, and redirect blame for the Sudan's ills away from himself. Thus he eliminated the Muslim Brotherhood as a political force and made it a scapegoat for his regime's failures. In early March, in a statement to reassure his American allies as much as assuage the Sudanese populace, al-Numairi claimed to have thwarted a coup by the Muslim Brotherhood, which he claimed was armed by Iran. On March 10 he accused the Muslim Brotherhood of exploiting religion, and, comparing its members to the communists, he denounced them as fanatics, a diabolical group that sought to undermine national unity (in the South) and create another Iran.[24] The following day, al-Numairi dismissed the Brotherhood's members from the government and the SSU and arrested two hundred of its leaders. He also ordered a review of all judgments by his decisive justice courts prior to March 10 because of alleged misapplication of the Shariᶜa by Muslim Brotherhood judges. In succeeding weeks, the Brotherhood was denounced for everything from hoarding to international terrorism supported by Libya and Iran.[25] The move against the Brotherhood was a response to the U.S., Egypt, and Saudi Arabia as much as to his domestic critics. Indeed, it occurred immediately after the Bush visit, and the rumor circulated that U.S. aid was made conditional on suspending Islamic criminal punishments and dismissing Islamic fundamentalists, halting contacts with Libya, and accepting the economic reforms demanded by the IMF.

In late March the government, yielding to IMF and U.S. pressures, lifted subsidies on staples. That offered al-Numairi's critics a rallying point and enabled them to transcend their differences and to harness popular support. A coalition of trade unions, professional organizations, political parties, and organizations (the Umma Party led by Sadiq al-Mahdi, the National Republic Party of the Khatmiyya, the Muslim Brotherhood, and the SCP on the left) now had an issue that united them in opposition to al-Numairi. They were supported by a number of senior officials in the army and the SSU. In all, some forty-five professional unions and political parties constituted what came to be called the "spring movement." They demanded al-Numairi's resignation. Hours after al-Numairi left the Sudan on March 27 to meet President Reagan in Washington, his military and security forces were battling demonstrators in the streets. On March 27–28 popular street demonstrations and food riots broke out in Khartoum and other centers. Al-Numairi moved quickly, having thousands arrested and 854 condemned to be flogged.[26] But strikes spread and by early April the Sudan was paralyzed by a general strike. On April 4 more than 20,000 demonstrators marched through the streets of Khartoum chanting, "Down with one-man rule" and "Down with the USA." On the morning of April 5 General Abdul Rahman Siwar al-Dhahab, a senior officer, led a military coup as al-Numairi's plane was landing in Cairo for refueling on his return from Washington. The sixteen-year al-Numairi regime and his Islamic experiment were thus ended.

The transitional government consisted of two components. The military, headed by General al-Dhahab, ruled through the Transitional Military Council (TMC). And, in response to civilian pressures, a predominantly civilian cabinet was established, headed by a new prime minister, Jazuli Dafallah. Elections were promised by March 1986. There also was a flurry of political activity, with more than forty traditional political forces. The Umma Party led by Sadiq al-Mahdi and the Democratic Unionist Party (DUP) associated with the rival Khatmiyya order remained dominant. Hasan al-Turabi of the Muslim Brotherhood forged his own alliance, the Islamic National Front (INF). The outspoken critic of al-Numairi's Shariʿa experiment, Sadiq al-Mahdi, was able to emerge from prison, rally his traditional Ansar supporters, build a coalition, and project the Umma Party as centrist and pluralistic.

In April 1986, the Sudan held its first multiparty elections in eighteen years. Of the 300 constituencies, the Umma Party won 99 seats, the DUP took 63, and the INF captured a surprising 58 seats. Although al-Turabi lost his bid for a seat in the National Assembly, the INF swept 26 of the 28 seats reserved for university graduates and demonstrated its ability to win in areas other than its usual urban, professional constituency. Muhammad ʿOthman Mirghani, the Khatmiyya head of the DUP, had in January 1986 entered into an unofficial alliance with the INF and had advocated a three-party coalition, hoping to use al-Turabi and the INF as a counterweight to Sadiq al-Mahdi on such issues as Sadiq's close ties with Libya. However, when Sadiq and al-Turabi were unable to get together, the DUP joined with the Umma Party and Sadiq returned to power as prime minister. Al-Turabi and the INF constitute the major opposition party. Sadiq and the Umma Party had long been proponents of an Islamic state and an Islamic constitution. But during the election and after, they sought to reassure both domestic and external forces (non-Muslim southerners as well as disenchanted Muslims in the North and foreign allies) by distancing themselves from Sudan's so-called Shari⁽a experiment. However, like al-Dhahab, Sadiq has been reluctant or unable to simply cancel al-Numairi's Islamization program lest he appear anti-Islamic. Meanwhile, al-Turabi and the INF are pressing for Islamization, maintaining that it was al-Numairi's idiosyncratic interpretation, and not authentic Islamic law, that was at fault.

Despite overtures from both al-Dhahab and Sadiq, John Garang and the SPLA have continued the war in the South. However, despite the insurgency, many southern leaders remain active in government and politics.

The fall of al-Numairi has also brought changes in the Sudan's foreign policy. Al-Dhahab pledged to continue a pro-Western alliance; the $250 million in U.S. economic aid and $40 million in U.S. military aid are vital to the Sudan. Similar assurances were given to Saudi Arabia and Egypt. Nevertheless, both al-Dhahab and Sadiq also reestablished relations with Libya, Ethiopia, and Iran. Such actions, along with Khartoum's denunciation of the U.S. bombing of Libya in April 1986 as a "terrorist attack" and anti-American demonstrations and violence, which led to the evacuation of three hundred American personnel, have strained U.S.-Sudanese relations.

### Conclusion

Sudan's Islamic experiment under Ja⁽far al-Numairi may be viewed as an irrational aberration or it may be regarded as a logical response, given al-Numairi's personal disposition and the historical and political realities of the Sudan. Al-Numairi's return to stricter Islamic observance brought him into line with the Islamic, Mahdist tradition of the Sudan, which had combined Sufism with Islamic political activism and government. In many ways, al-Numairi attempted to enhance his legitimacy and popular support by forging his own neo-Sufi, Islamic state. He cultivated relations with local Sufi leaders and diffused the opposition from national Islamic organizations by appealing to Islam and incorporating the Muslim Brotherhood within the government. If the followers of Sadiq al-Mahdi ultimately remained aloof, other branches of the Ansar did not. Al-Numairi was willing to live with resistance from a divided South in order to mobilize the Muslim masses behind him.

Sudan's flirtation with Islamization raises two major questions similar to those raised by Islamic political revivalism in other countries.[27] The first question is whose Islam? Who is to formulate and implement a country's Islamic path? Is it to be the head of state, the military (Sudan, Libya, Pakistan), monarchs (Saudi Arabia, Morocco), the clergy (Iran)? How will traditional Islamic political concepts of consultation (*shura*) and community consensus (*ijma⁽*) inform the institutions and decision-making processes of modern Islamic states? The experience of the Muslim Brotherhood underscores the thorny and precarious position of modern Islamic organizations in this process. Working for change within the system but often in opposition to the regime often leads to government repression. However, the alternative of cooperation with the government in exchange for representation and influence can often result in losses greatly outweighing potential gains. Short-term influence in the government by the Brothers was offset by a "guilt by association." Ultimately, the Brothers were blamed for all of al-Numairi's Islamization measures and their failure. Moreover, in the post-Numairi period, the Brotherhood has had to struggle to regain its credibility and support. In contrast, Sadiq al-Mahdi's opposition and imprisonment under al-Numairi enhanced his credentials.

The second question is what Islam? What interpretation of Islam is to be implemented? Will the greater Islamization of state and society be based upon the restoration of past legal and social practice or a reinterpretation (*ijtihad*) of Islam? Whether a more traditional or reformist direction is followed will determine the nature and scope of the impact of Islamization on questions of political participation, banking and taxation, the status and role of women in society, and the rights and duties of non-Muslims in states governed by Islamic ideology and law. While the call for a return to Islam in personal and public life is viewed by Islamic activists as an answer to the ills of contemporary Muslim societies, the example of the Sudan, as well as Iran and Pakistan, has raised many questions and issues.

Islam has proven effective in rallying popular support. Its implementation, however, has often divided its advocates as much as its opponents. The establishment of more Islamically oriented modern states necessitates new, more indigenous models for political and social development. That will mean a process of redefinition and experimentation. How to prevent experimentation from becoming exploitation, by either a government or a group, remains a central issue for Islamic revivalism and a major challenge to its credibility and success.

# NOTES

1. For a general introduction to Sudanese history, see P.M. Holt and M.W. Daly, *The History of the Sudan from the Coming of Islam to the Present Day*, 3d ed. (Boulder, Colo.: Westview Press, 1979), and John Obert Voll and Sarah Potts Voll, *The Sudan: Unity and Diversity in a Multicultural Society* (Boulder, Colo.: Westview Press, 1985).

2. See Yusuf Fadl Hasan, *The Arabs and the Sudan, from the Seventh to the Sixteenth Century* (Edinburgh: Edinburgh University Press, 1969).

3. John O. Voll, *The Political Impact of Islam in the Sudan: Numayri's Islamization Program* (Washington, D.C.: State Department, 1984), pp. 20ff. I am especially indebted to John Voll for his comments and suggestions.

4. P.M. Holt, *Studies in the History of the Near East* (London: Frank Cass, 1973), chap. 7.

5. A number of Islamic states emerged after 1500. See R.S. O'Fahey and J.L. Spaulding, *Kingdoms of the Sudan* (London: Methuen, 1974), chap. 4.

6. P.M. Holt, *The Mahdist State in the Sudan, 1881–1898*, 2d ed. (Oxford: Clarendon Press, 1958).

7. As quoted in John O. Voll, "The Sudanese Mahdi: Frontier Fundamentalist," *International Journal of Middle East Studies* 10 (1979), p. 159.

8. For differing perspectives, see Muddathir Abd al-Rahim, *Imperialism and Nationalism in the Sudan* (Oxford: Clarendon Press, 1969), and Peter Woodward, *Condominium and Sudanese Nationalism* (Totawa, N.J.: Barnes and Noble, 1979).

9. Gabriel R. Warburg, "Islam in Sudanese Politics," in *Religion and Politics in the Middle East*, ed. Michael Curtis (Boulder, Colo.: Westview Press, 1981), p. 308.

10. For a political history of the post-independence period, see Peter K. Bechtold, *Politics in the Sudan: Parliamentary and Military Rule in an Emerging African Region* (New York: Praeger, 1976).

11. Peter K. Bechtold, "The Contemporary Sudan," *American-Arab Affairs*, No. 6 (Fall 1983).

12. For background on the history of the conflict, see Dunstan M. Wai, ed., *The Southern Sudan: The Problem of National Integration* (London: Frank Cass, 1973), and Robert O. Collins, *The Southern Sudan in Historical Perspective* (Tel Aviv: Shiloah Center, 1975).

13. Idris Salim El Hassan, "On Ideology: The Case of Religion in Northern Sudan," Ph.D. diss., University of Connecticut, 1980, p. 174.

14. See Mohammed Beshir Hamid, *The Politics of National Reconciliation in the Sudan: The Numayri Regime and the National Front Opposition* (Washington, D.C.: Center for Contemporary Arab Studies, Georgetown University, 1984), and John O. Voll, "Reconciliation in the Sudan," *Current History*, Vol. 80, No. 47 (December 1981).

15. *Sudanow*, Vol. 7, No. 12 (December 1982), p. 5.

16. *Al-Nahj al-Islami li madha* (Cairo: Al-Maktab al-Misri al-Hadith, 1980).

17. Bona Malwal, *The Sudan* (New York: Thornton Books, 1985).

18. Bechtold, "The Contemporary Sudan," pp. 101ff.

19. *The Arab News*, May 31, 1984.

20. Voll, *Political Impact*, pp. 101–103.

21. Quoted in "Numeiri's Version of Sharia," *Horn of Africa*, Vol. 8, No. 1, p. 38.

22. David B. Ottaway, "Muslim Law Threatens Sudan Unity," *Guardian Weekly*, Sept. 30, 1984.

23. Quoted in Judith Miller, "Sudan Publicly Hangs an Old Opposition Leader," *New York Times*, Jan. 19, 1985.

24. Foreign Broadcast Information Service (MEA), Mar. 11, 1985.

25. *The Economist*, Mar. 16, 1985, p. 54.

26. *Washington Post*, Apr. 1, 1985.

27. For more extended and comparative discussions of these issues in contemporary Islamic revivalist politics, see John L. Esposito, *Islam and Politics* (Syracuse, N.Y.: Syracuse University Press, 1984), chap. 6.

# XIII

# WEST AFRICA

## Sulayman S. Nyang

In recent years, as a result of the Islamic revolution in Iran and the political activism of other Islamic groups, the term *Islamic revivalism,* or some variant of it, has become familiar in the West. No doubt the Iranian revolution emboldened revivalist groups throughout the Muslim world.

In Africa south of the Sahara, where Islamic militancy was strong during precolonial and early colonial periods, the Muslim revivalist movement has not yet reached the same level of intensity as it has in the Middle East. There are rumblings here and there, but no major political volcano has erupted yet.

In analyzing the revivalist movement in West Africa, this study will focus on (1) the historical background of Africa's Islamic revivalism; (2) Islamic revivalism in the transitional period from precolonial times to colonial rule, with special attention to its salient characteristics, including the reasons for its limited appeal, the decline in revivalism in West Africa during this period, and the role played by colonial powers; (3) the record of relationships between the West African states and the Muslim revivalist groups; and (4) the new forms of Islamic revivalism in West Africa, with special attention to external and internal factors behind these new trends.

## Historical Background

Islamic revivalism in West Africa dates as far back as the Middle Ages. Revivalist ideas came to West Africa with the peddlers of Islam. According to Sudanese scholar Aziz Batran, two of these ideologies with the greatest revolutionary impact were Kharijism (the ideology of the Kharijists, who believed that any devout Muslim had the right to become the leader [*Khalif*] of the Islamic community) and the Shiʿa doctrine of Mahdism (belief in the coming of the Messiah). Batran claims that both ideologies "are basically religious drives towards equity and justice promised by Islam but not realized under iniquitous and oppressive governments. Indeed, they provided religious legitimization for revolutionary action."[1] In Batran's view, such revolutionary moves and idioms helped the aggrieved masses to express "their political, religious, and socioeconomic grievances and . . . goaded them into radical action aimed at the building of a better world and the attaining of a satisfying religion."[2]

Views differ on the inspirational sources of West Africa's Islamic movements. P. D. Curtin finds a common origin for West African Islamic movements in the activities and example of Nasir ad-Din (d. 1677).[3] M. A. al-Hajj thinks that the answer lies in the precedence of the jihadic movement called al-Murabitun (Almuravid) in the eleventh century.[4] Omar Jah traces the origins back to the Kharijists in North Africa in the eighth century.[5] Batran, on the other hand, suggests that the eighteenth- and nineteenth-century jihadists of West Africa probably drew inspiration from more contemporary and closer sources,[6] including the revolutionary achievements of their ancestors in Bondu, Futa Toro, and Futa Jallon. Other sources would be the peaceful reform endeavors of Shaikh al-Mukhtar al-Kunti[7] and Muhammad ibn Abdal-Karim al-Maghili,[8] the Sufi reaction to the rise of Wahhabi fundamentalism in Arabia, and the examples of Shaikh Ahmad Lobbo,[9] al-Haj ᶜUmar,[10] and Shaikh ᶜUsman dan Fodio.[11]

One of the outstanding intellectual representatives of West Africa's revivalist tradition was Shaikh al-Mukhtar al-Kunti (1729–1811). He provided the intellectual arguments and justifications for the role and activities of the *mujaddid* (renewer and reformer). Building on the earlier Islamic concept of the Mahdi and the classical Muslim notion of the mujaddid, al-Kunti argued that since an ideal religious community would last for a definite period, God in his mercy would occasionally send out men of learning and moral authority to guide the *umma* (community) along the right path until the arrival of the Mahdi himself.

Al-Kunti and his followers believed that the advent of the mujaddid was in direct response to crises caused by decadence and the absence of social justice. This crisis situation, according to him, would take place at the beginning of every century in the Islamic calendar.

The history of Islamic revivalism in West Africa is also related to the much earlier rise of the Murabitun movement of ᶜAbdullah Ibn Yasin. According to legend, Yasin was recruited by a Sanhaja Berber king, Yahya Ibn Ibrahim, who wanted to provide proper religious instruction to his people. However, ᶜAbdullah Ibn Yasin was too puritanical and uncompromising, and thus the Sanhaja people he was asked to instruct drove him out. He retreated toward the mouth of the Senegal River and there established his *ribat* (fortress-cum-seminary). Soon a large number of followers joined him and he thus developed his movement, al-Murabitun (People of the Ribat).

The goals of Yasin's movement were to (1) provide religious instruction for the Sanhaja Berbers, (2) eliminate un-Islamic practices among the Sanhaja Berbers, and (3) establish a political order that could guarantee the development of a new Islamic society and polity.[12] According to P. F. de Moraes Farias, a further goal was "to reform the traditional Berber military technique in order to bring about a re-enactment of the original ways of waging *jihad* as revealed in the Qur'an."[13]

This revivalist movement paved the way for the spread of Islam in Africa south of the Sahara. The conquest of Ghana in 1076 by the Almuravids led to the conversion of the people of this medieval kingdom, who later dispersed over a large area between the Niger and the Senegal rivers and carried Islam with them. Though Ghana regained her independence, the Almuravids set up an Islamic state in Ghana that lasted for a decade.

Despite the achievements of the Almuravids, trade (trans-Saharan) and not the sword was the major factor in the spread of Islam in West Africa. From the latter part of the eleventh century, the Soninkes became one of the most active agents of Islamization. Through their trading activities, they converted the Mande Djula, who in turn carried Islam to the forest zone. In fact, the Soninkes and the Mandinka peoples, who are ethnically cousins, have traditionally been involved in the spread of Islam. Thus, in studying the roots of contemporary Islamic revivalism, it must be borne in mind that the present advocates of Islamic fundamentalism among the Mande-speaking people are not dabbling in anything new.

In the eighteenth and nineteenth centuries, other groups of West African Muslims drawing inspiration from the earlier movements set out to reassert themselves against their pagan neighbors. These new brands of revivalists were concerned about the decadence in their midst. Living as minorities among Africans whose beliefs they considered reprehensible, the West African Muslims saw in *jihad* (holy war) a way of cleansing their societies and their neighborhoods. Their commercial interests also were constantly threatened by the activities of the non-Muslims, and jihad provided them with the best means of capturing power and protecting their interests. The Muslim leadership also believed that the creation of an Islamic state was the best way to guarantee the effective practice of the Islamic teachings and the institutionalization of the Shariᶜa.

In West Africa, the earliest identified jihads were waged in Futa Jallon and Futa Toro by Malik Sy (d. 1699) and Sulayman Bal.[14] The most effective of these jihadists was Shaikh ᶜUsman dan Fodio of Nigeria and Niger. Born in Gobir in what is now the Republic of Niger, this Muslim scholar established one of the most powerful jihadist movements in Muslim history. He wrote profusely and recruited a large following because of his scholarship and piety. As a result of his efforts, his movement conquered much of what is now northern Nigeria and Niger. What distinguished him from the earlier leaders was his willingness to do battle with the ᶜulema al-su (vile clergy). In his view, such men constituted a great abomination and their presence in the Muslim community was as destructive as that of the unbelievers. Al-Haj ᶜUmar, the Torabe leader who founded the so-called Tukulor Empire, was another Muslim leader who succeeded in establishing an Islamic state in West Africa.[15]

The jihadist movement was also served by the labors of Maba Jahu Ba of Senegambia[16] and Muhammad Lamin Drame[17] of the same region. Another leader was Samori Toure, whose jihad was to the south of the Senegambian region.[18] The most important difference between these two fundamentalists and their predecessors in Nigeria and elsewhere in West Africa was that they launched their movements at a time when the Europeans were already bent on creating spheres of influence in Africa. As a result, the Muslim fundamentalists of the nineteenth century found themselves fighting a much more formidable foe. With great reluctance, they accepted the unavoidable reality that they were fighting a losing battle. Thus many of their leaders decided to make peace with the new European conquerors.

## From Precolonial to Colonial Times

Ironically, the arrival of European powers helped advance the rapid expansion of Islam in West Africa. Admittedly, African jihadists could no longer aspire to an Islamic state through conquest. However, the peaceful expansion of Islam continued through the utilization of the facilities created by the European powers.

During this period a number of developments affected and, indeed, shaped the character of revivalist movements in West Africa, with significant implications for later revivalist movements. The most important of these developments was the redirection of trade, which resulted in the shift of trade routes from the Sahara to the coastal areas and the loss of Muslim power due to the political and military dominance of the Europeans. Throughout West and Central Africa, Muslims found themselves hemmed in by long-standing African rivals and European intrusions that preceded the implantation of Western colonial values propagated by the missionary schools and secular colonial regimes. Because of this new social and political order, the African who converted to Christianity found himself adopting the conqueror's language as his own. This association of the language of the conqueror with the message of Christ was destined to affect the Muslim attitude toward Western languages. Indeed, the late adoption of Western skills and knowledge in Muslim Africa was largely occasioned by suspicion and fear of the missionary. Since English and French were the tools of instruction employed by their Christian rivals, Muslim leaders soon associated Westernization with de-Islamization.[19] That explains the universal Muslim aversion to Western schools and Western forms of learning in the period before the reformist efforts of Jamal-ad-Din al-Afghani and his collaborator, Shaikh Muhammad ʿAbduh. The secularization of life under colonial rule was most evident in those areas where the Islamic jihadists had made some breakthroughs and had convinced some of the families to accept the Shariʿa as the supreme law of the land. What colonial rule did was to decelerate the process of Islamization and through missionary schools and colonial administration to encourage the adoption of Western ways.[20]

Another development was the cultivation and adoption of a materialistic philosophy in African Muslim societies.[21] The Muslim Africans whose trade routes had been gradually appropriated and controlled by the colonial powers were soon inundated by European manufactured goods, which were not designed to reinforce their Islamic culture and identity. Unable to change the emerging colonial economic relationships, the Muslims responded to their new conditions in two ways: assimilation and avoidance. Those who chose assimilation rationalized it in the name of Islam; those who tried to avoid assimilation also explained their avoidance in the name of Islam and branded Western imports as *haram*. The adoption of a materialist philosophy was also believed to threaten traditional African values. Indeed, there are parallels between the Muslim resistance to Western materialism and the African negritudist rejection of materialism in its philosophy of African socialism. In Muslim eyes, unbridled materialism leads to decadence and political turmoil, necessitating the emergence of a mujaddid in Muslim lands. Thus, currently, after a relatively long period of foreign domination, African Muslims feel that the time has come to challenge their colonizers' cultural domination and to reinstate their old Islamic values.

The estrangement of the African Muslims from their brethren elsewhere in Dar al-Islam (the Abode of Islam) was made possible by the loss of Muslim political power and the redirection of Muslim trade routes from the Sahara to the coastal zones controlled by the European powers. Thus, the African Muslims soon found themselves cut off from Muslim intellectual and cultural trends. If one is to understand the contemporary Islamic revivalism and the contemporary Muslim Africans' effort to forge closer ties with other Muslims, this sense of separation must be addressed. Although the bonds were not completely severed during the colonial period, contacts between the African Muslims and other Muslims were closely watched by the colonial powers and no expression of Muslim solidarity—which was thought detrimental to British or French interests—was tolerated. Nevertheless, Muslim merchants and scholars still traveled, the Islamic shaikhs of the Maghreb visited their flocks in the western Sudan, and exchanges of ideas and materials took place.

The developments listed above changed the nature and direction of most African societies and weakened traditional institutions. One of the most important consequences of the colonial presence was the emergence of a Westernized elite whose membership was no longer confined to the original descendants of slaves and mulattoes living in the coastal towns and villages established by the colonial powers. In the context of Muslim Africa, the late adoption of Western education limited the number of Muslims in this category of Africans. The pattern that developed during the colonial period was that Muslim leaders and their families tried to live in isolation from the Christians. Where possible, they maintained their cultural niches and made do with whatever opportunities colonial powers allowed them. Consequently, in many Muslim areas, the Muslims used their Qur'anic schools as the agencies for the social mobilization of their children. Many resisted the encroachments of missionary workers. In the urban areas to which some of them later migrated, they often tried to establish their own neighborhoods. In cases where ethnicity and religion reinforced each other, an urban phenomenon like the *zongos* emerged. Conversely, in predominantly Muslim areas, non-Muslim migrants working for the colonial masters created their own cultural niches, called the *Sabong Gari*, in northern Nigeria.

The colonial powers responded differently to varying Muslim challenges. In the French empire in Africa there were some minor concessions to the Muslims insofar as religion was concerned. Freedom of religion was guaranteed but no extra effort was made to encourage Islam. In British Africa the situation was slightly different. The colonial power at least theoretically respected Muslim sensitivities insofar as religious practices and feelings were concerned. This would help explain why Shari῾a courts existed in Muslim Africa and why *qadis* (Muslim judges) were on the payroll of the colonial administration in Muslim Africa under British rule. But in comparing and contrasting the different methods of rule of the two major European colonial powers, it is important to point out that, though the French were less sensitive than the British insofar as tolerance of Islamic ways is concerned, they still worked out a modus vivendi with their Muslim colonial subjects.

These developments not only affected Muslim attitudes toward colonial rule; they also created, and to some extent still create, the climate for the growth and development of fundamentalist thought in West Africa. Since colonial rule resulted in the loss of political and economic power for the Muslims, it has been a foregone conclusion that the state of depression among the Muslims of colonized Africa could lead to some flare-ups. Dissatisfied with the state of things in the colonies and determined to maintain their Islamic identity, many of the Muslim leaders felt the need to change their conditions and to lead the *umma* (community) back to its traditional ways. In their view, the only way to do so was to eradicate foreign elements introduced into Dar al-Islam by the agents of colonial rule.

During the transitional period, Islamic revivalism suffered a major setback. After having been defeated or forced to compromise by the military superiority of the European powers, Muslim leaders in Africa began to adjust to new realities. No longer strong enough to make their bid for power and realistic enough to work out a modus vivendi with the colonial powers, the descendants of former jihadists returned to the politics of quietism. However, this attitude of accommodation was not accepted by all Muslims in West Africa. There were some dissidents. Unimpressed and unintimidated by the maxim gun of the colonizer, these Muslims began to rediscover the teachings of the old masters of the jihadic tradition, and soon began to talk about the evil ways of the invader and the danger he posed to Muslim society in Africa.

The Muslim leaders who resisted colonial rule and tried hard to reassert their Islamic identity found the colonial masters very suspicious and repressive. The Nigerian experience aptly illustrates how Islamic fundamentalist ideas were effectively stifled by the colonial power. In the early nineteenth century, after the Shehu, ῾Usman dan Fodio, conquered Hausa lands and established his Islamic state, his relatives and descendants began to govern an Islamic society. When this area came under British jurisdiction, the colonial rulers decided to clip the wings of the Muslim princes and to introduce their own legal system, even though some accommodations with Islam were made. In the Senegambian region, the French fought bitterly against Muslim fundamentalists who were linked to al-Haj ʿUmar and his sons. They also brought tremendous pressure on Maba Jahu Ba. They opposed very strongly the moves of Muhammad Lamin Drame.

But regardless of what the colonialists did, the fact still remains that African Muslims resisted colonial rule. During this period of transition, when African rule, Muslim or otherwise, was being gradually replaced by foreign domination, some of the Muslim leaders saw salvation in the Sufi brotherhoods. Rather than use the brotherhoods as political and military vehicles for the dissemination of jihadist ideas and for the prosecution of a holy war against the unbelievers, they focused on the rituals and meditative exercises of these brotherhoods. But even the Muslim leaders of Sufi brotherhoods who had great appeal and charisma became suspect and were persecuted by the colonial powers, as illustrated by what happened to Shaikh Ahmadu Bamba, the Senegalese religious leader who established the Muridiyya brotherhood early in this century. A learned scholar with deep roots in the Sufi tradition, Bamba started out as a reformer and called Africans to embrace Islam and to return to religion of piety and good works. Many among his contemporaries saw in him marks of the reformer destined to change men from their evil ways and to lead them down the path of righteousness. This image of the Senegalese sage was looked upon with great disfavor by the French colonizing forces. Determined to brush away the "Islamic menace" and committed to a policy of spreading the French civilization among the Africans, French colonial officials saw Bamba as a dangerous man. They spied on his activities and employed agents from rival brotherhoods to report on his activities and to track his movements. When Bamba's activities became too overwhelming and intimidating, the French colonial power acted immediately. Bamba was taken to Gabon, where he remained for many years in exile. Later he went to Mauritania and spent some more years under the watchful eyes of Muslim ʿulama loyal to France. When the French discovered that the Muridiyya leader was harmless and his movement could be effectively harnessed to serve the French policy of cultivating peanuts in the Senegal territory, the colonial administration in Senegal released him.[22]

## The Post-Independence Period

The post-independence African leaders inherited the instruments of power of their colonial masters, and their primary concern was the building of nations out of the variegated ethnic groups in their respective countries. Coming to power at a time when the colonial powers had already destroyed or compromised the power of religious leaders, whether Islamic or traditional, African political leaders had little difficulty working with religious groups within their countries.

A careful examination of the available evidence shows that at the time of decolonization, with few exceptions, the maraboutic elements were also co-operating with colonial authorities. The history of the maraboutic relationship with colonial authorities reveals an interesting picture of co-optation and collaboration which was later inherited by many of the post-independence political leaders, such as President Leopold Sedar Senghor of Senegal.

In post-colonial Africa, Muslim forces were hemmed in by the inherited colonial machinery. As a result Islamic revivalism did not develop in the manner in which it now manifests itself in the Arab world. The first manifestation of confrontation between the revivalist Muslim groups and the state occurred when the returning African Muslim students trained in Arab universities began to press their claims for jobs and attention. Returning to countries run by culturally Westernized elites, these Arabized Africans soon learned that the system did not recognize their education and that the marabouts in the countryside perceived them as a threat to the social order. Thus, rejected by the Westernized elites and scorned by the marabouts, these young men began to seek a niche for themselves in the urban centers of the newly independent African states using Islam.

In the case of Senegal and a few other Sahelian countries, these young men started to agitate a decade or two before independence. The efforts of the Senegalese organization Fraternité Musulman deserves some attention. Founded in 1935, this group of Senegalese Muslims addressed itself to the Islamic cultural needs of the growing urban Muslim populations. Fearful of the corrosive and corrupting influences of the urban secular culture and the Catholic missionary schools, the Fraternité members promoted Qur'anic schools. Their efforts were supported by other Muslim cultural groups that flourished in the 1930s. According to René Luc Moreau, the people of the cities were the main beneficiaries, and the organizers of this revivalist movement were primarily the members of the Tijaniyya Sufi Brotherhood and the disciples of El-Haj Malik Sy of Tivaouane.

One of the earliest groups identified by Moreau was the Brigade of the Fraternity of Good Muslims. Established under the ordinance of 1901, this Muslim cultural organization sought to eliminate primitive elements in the religion of the urban Muslims of Senegal and to preach true Islam based on the Qur'an and the Shariᶜa. This pattern of renewing Islam among the urban Muslims of Senegal did not threaten the colonial power although ultimately it constituted a grave danger to the so-called Black Islam of the colonial anthropologists. These early Islamic cultural groups defended the demarcation lines between Dar al-Islam and the colonial realm of the French Christians, but were materially impoverished compared to the missionaries.[23]

This material imbalance between the Muslim reformists and the Christian missionaries would remain a sore point up to the time of independence. The coming to power of Muslim rulers in many of these predominantly Muslim states did not change the situation, for two reasons. First, many of the Muslim leaders, such as President Sekou Toure of Guinea and President Modibo Keita of Mali, were revolutionaries and did not find Islam very useful in their politics of development. Second, working on the assumption that the nation-building efforts of the New Africa called for an ideology of Africanism, they subordinated religion to the dictates of the reformist rhetoric of pan-Africanism, negritude, and African socialism.

The ideology of pan-Africanism and negritude captured the minds of the first generation of African leaders because they felt that neither tribal loyalty nor religious affiliation could help them in forging a new identity for their peoples. Condemned to build nations out of building blocks drawn from Africa's diverse ethnic groups and determined not to leave an opening for external forces to prey on African disunity, these leaders played down religion and ethnicity and promoted such slogans as "Africa for the Africans," "One Nation, One People, and One Leader," and "We Are All Africans."[24]

Pan-Africanism, which has its origins in the Black Diaspora of the New World, did not necessarily contradict the pan-Islamism of the Muslim revivalists, but its emphasis on African consciousness and identity proved parochial and therefore un-Islamic. Yet the universalism that the Islamic revivalists see in their religion also proved inadequate and unsatisfactory to the negritudists like Senghor, who then argued for the recognition of the existence of the Negro-African civilization for sub-Saharan Africa and an Arab-Berber civilization for the northern part of the continent. This Senghorean dichotomization of Africa was translated into policy when Senegal organized the festival of Negro arts in the mid-1960s. Though Arab states were welcomed by Senegal and other sub-Saharan states to the founding of the Organization of African Unity (OAU), their presence at the Dakar festival was questioned by the Negritudists. This attitude led to a confrontation between Senegal and Nigeria before the opening of the Lagos Festival of Black and African Arts (FESTAC) in 1976–1977. The Senegalese secretary-general, the late Alioune Diop, opposed North African participation and representation on negritudist grounds just as Senghor had done in the 1960s. President Yacobu Gowon of Nigeria, on the other hand, ignored the negritudist stance of the Senegalese and pressed for a pan-Africanist solution, which called for representation of all OAU member states.

In light of the above discussion, one can understand why secular regimes in Africa have made limited concessions to Islamic leaders. Their use of the reformist Muslims was evident only in instances when the marabouts of the Sufi brotherhoods were found to be impediments to their rule. And the conservative character of some of the governments in the predominantly Islamic societies of Africa south of the Sahara made them unwilling to antagonize the French and the Westernized Christian minorities. Because their concept of the African identity transcended religion, the first generation of African leaders in predominantly Muslim states in both the northern and sub-Saharan areas encouraged a subtle form of competition between the traditional Muslim leaders and the reformist groups established or emerging in their urban centers.

For sub-Saharan Africa, and particularly French-speaking Africa, a group whose emergence had great significance and impact was the Muslim Cultural

Union. Founded in 1953 by Senegalese activist Cheikh Toure, a graduate of Ben Badis Institute of Constantine, Algeria, this organization soon established branches in Mauritania, Guinea, Ivory Coast, Mali, Upper Volta, Northern Benin, and even Nigeria. According to some scholars, the organization spread to other parts of West Africa largely because of the *ojulas* (traders). The first declaration of intentions of the Muslim Cultural Union was in a brochure that demonstrated its commitment to the kind of reformism identified with Shaikh Muhammad ʿAbduh of Egypt. In this publication, Cheikh Toure quoted the Egyptian reformer and then added Qur'anic verses. A careful examination of this document reveals a Muslim mind that is set on creating a society of believers who are interested in becoming the lieutenants of Allah on earth. In the rhetoric one detects elements of the thoughts of al-Maghili and Shaikh ʿUsman dan Fodio. Actually what distinguished this body of Muslims in preindependence days was its double opposition to "maraboutic Islam," scornfully labeled "colonial Islam," and colonial rule. The former was opposed because it reinforced the ignorance and superstitions of the masses; the latter was opposed because it led to the distortion and disarticulation of the Islamic culture.[25]

The leaders of this organization tried to participate effectively in the education of the masses for development and nation-building. They pressed for government employment of Arabic-speaking graduates in the education system. Through such efforts they hoped to affect the education policy of the independent states of West Africa. Because of their efforts and those of others in the region, the Senghor government encouraged the formation of a federation of Muslim cultural groups in Senegal. Thus in 1962 a National Federation of Muslim Cultural Associations came into being. This federation brought under its umbrella such groups as the Muslim Cultural Union, the Arabic Teachers Movement, and the Islamic Educational Association.

To carry out its work, it established a national council of 130 members drawn from the constitutive groups. This central body was headed by Shaikh ʿAbdul ʿAziz Sy, a son of the khalifa-general of the Tijaniyya brotherhood. This young member of the Sy family provided a useful link between the Muslim reformist groups and the Senghor regime. Since the family at this time was very much in support of President Senghor, the reformists within the federation found it necessary to press their claims for greater government support for the *Arabisants* (Arabic-speaking students graduated from Arab universities). One of the most militant groups within the federation was the Arabic Teachers Movement, which came into being in 1957. At its second congress, held almost five months after the formation of the federation, its leadership called for the extension of the teaching of Arabic to all primary schools after kindergarten. It also asked the government to integrate these recruited teachers in the pool of primary school teachers. This was a major demand and it had great implications for the rise and spread of revivalist ideas among the young Muslim graduates of Arab universities. What made these Arab university graduates dangerous at the time was not only their clamor for recruitment into the national education ministry but also their links to the maraboutic families. Whereas previously, those who agitated in the urban areas were not necessarily linked to the marabouts, in the post-colonial period many of these agitators for change in the treatment of Islam and the Arabic-speaking graduates were themselves from the maraboutic families.[26]

The Arabic-speaking graduates in Gambia were hired as Arabic teachers in the primary schools. The Gambian government also introduced Qur'anic studies in all schools, including the missionary schools. This measure was bitterly resisted by the Christian institutions in the country. The Guinean government of President Sekou Toure adopted a policy similar to that of Senegal in the sense that it soon began to recruit many of these graduates into the education ministry and Islamic education became an area of greater government concern. This was most evident in Toure's last eight years (he was president from 1958 to 1982). During this final period he himself wrote and spoke more about Islam. A ministry responsible for religious affairs was created to facilitate this process of incorporating the Arabisants into the Guinean cultural scene. The Malians who graduated from Arab universities also pressed their claim. In sum, the union played an important role in asserting the rights of the Arabisants to seek jobs in government and to be respected by the Westernized elites. This claim for recognition was echoed in the Ivory Coast as well. According to René Luc Moreau, in the Ivory Coast the members of the Muslim Cultural Union run the televised Islamic program "Allahu Akbar" (God Is Great).

In the Republic of Niger, the Muslim Cultural Union pursued the same line of action. Its representatives tried to combat the negative image of the Muslim ᶜulama created by the adventurous marabouts. They also pressed for more government support for the Arabisants, and, capitalizing on the Arab drive to establish diplomatic and cultural ties with the newly independent African states, they pressed for and received scholarships to study in North African and Middle Eastern universities. This drive to promote a revivalist Islam was not widely favored by the civilian leadership of President Hamani Diori, although it should be noted that from 1969 to 1974, when his regime was overthrown by the military, his regime established official links with such international bodies as the Organization of Islamic Conference (OIC).[27]

Efforts at revivalism became more evident after the coup d'etat of 1974. In that year, the Islamic Association of Niger was founded and it established branches in the provinces. The organization took a new direction in 1978 when a guiding ideology was propounded by Diallo Hassan Abdoulaye in an article on Islam in Niger. In that piece he referred to Colonel Seyai Kountche's speech, which stressed the Nigerian belief in Allah, Muhammad, and the Holy Qur'an. This new emphasis on Islam was identified with the "New Niger" ushered in by the coup d'etat.

What is interesting about the Islamic Association of Niger is its involvement in national development and its pursuit of many of the activities previously identified with the Muslim Cultural Union of Cheikh Toure. One striking similarity has been its educational campaign against *marabouts cognac* (marabouts who consume alcohol). These fake marabouts are often poorly educated opportunists who prey on the ignorance of the rural masses and some of the urban poor who seek their services.

The activities of the Islamic Association of Niger also resulted in the decision of the OIC to establish the Islamic University of Say. This is one of two universities that the OIC agreed to found ten years ago. The other is to be located in Kampala, Uganda.

Writing on the dynamics of Islam in West Africa south of the Sahara, French scholar Guy Nicolas demonstrated that what is happening in Niger is part of a much broader pattern of thought and strategy that has evolved in African countries with substantial Muslim populations over the past quarter of a century. In his view, in the Muslim search for autonomy and a broader range of associations at the international level, these states have naturally turned to interstate and nonstate affiliations with states and organizations of the Muslim world.[28] These international connections are beneficial to both political and religious leaders. Organizations like the OIC are committed to the restoration of Sahel's Islamic culture, and for this and other related reasons the Muslim revivalists find them useful allies in the contemporary world.

But did the Arabisants' gains constitute a breakthrough for the forces of Islamic reformism in Africa south of the Sahara? One can argue that the postcolonial African state has not allowed this to happen. When the Senegalese Arabic Teachers Movement pressed for the universal instruction of Arabic in primary schools throughout the land, the Inter-Ministerial Committee headed by President Senghor ruled that the teaching of the language must be done in the context of Franco-Arabic studies, that it must not be obligatory, and that, though Arabic is a great language of civilization, it must not be an instrument of adventure. In other words, the instruction of Arabic must be carefully supervised lest it become a dangerous weapon in the wrong hands. The Senegalese leadership was willing to accommodate the Arabisants but it still refused to provide the fertile ground for the cultivation of Islamic reformism or fundamentalism. But if the reformists from the Arab universities were successful in securing jobs for themselves and their kind in the Senegalese government, they failed to convince the government to pursue more Islamically oriented programs. Though the record throughout West Africa shows that the governments did not respond favorably to all the demands of the reformists, it should be stated that Mamadou Dia, while serving as prime minister under Senghor, did project an image acceptable to the reformists. During his brief tenure he raided the hideouts of prostitutes and tried to rid Senegalese society of all elements identified by the reformists as dangerous to the moral well-being of the Muslim umma.

The experience of English-speaking Muslim Africans resembled that of the French speakers. In Ghana, the Muslims have always been on the edge of the power centers. During the Nkrumah era, the Arabisants were not allowed to mobilize. Given the radical political ideology of the ruling Convention People's Party and the traditional role of the Muslim minority in Ghana, Islamic reformism never received government support. The Arabisants began to assert themselves only in the early 1970s, when some of them graduating from Arab universities began to get employment in the civil service. This was made possible largely because many of them had relatives in the armed forces who had climbed up the ladder of political power. Added to this were the growing ties between the government of Ghana and Arab states such as Libya under Muᶜammar Qadhafi.

Another factor which indirectly affected the forces of Muslim reformism in Ghana was the activities of the African Studies Center in Legon University. Here were many Arabists and Islamic studies scholars who helped train Ghanaians, both Muslims and Christians.

In Nigeria, Islamic reformism predated independence. The establishment of Bayero College (1954) was to facilitate the development of a more sophisticated Islamic culture in northern Nigeria. But from the wider perspective of Nigerian Muslim history, the idea of reformism must be traced to developments in the coastal regions of Nigeria, where the variegated Muslim groups in Lagos struggled to maintain their own brands and interpretations of Islam. Divided into various factions but responsive to the Westernization drive of the Europeans along the coast, these Muslims soon began to adjust to the challenges of modernization and the Western cultural presence. As a result, they built schools and participated in the emerging colonial economy. Their positive response to modernization soon made them the propaganda target of the heretical Muslim group from India, the Ahmadiyya of Ghulam Ahmad, the man from Qadian (India) who claimed to be a modern reformer in the guise of Mahdi. Though some of the Lagos Muslims gravitated toward the Ahmadis, the fact remains that the overwhelming majority in western Nigeria developed the skills needed to compete with both the Christian missionary and the Qadiani propagandist, who preached a reformed Islam that was unacceptable to many of the traditionalist Muslims.[29]

The Gambian experience was not very dissimilar from the others. During the first two decades of the twentieth century, the Gambian Muslims tried to adjust to the realities of colonial rule. The Muslim leaders who were quite resistant to Western education began to call for the establishment of a Muhammadan School in the capital city, fearing that the missionaries would steal their children.

Thus, the Muslims soon began to give Western education a try. By 1921, the Muhammadan School was the center where many children of prominent Muslim families were learning Western subjects. It was indeed out of these batches of students that the founders of the Young Muslim Society (founded in 1929) emerged. Later, in the 1950s, the Young Muslim Society would transform itself into the Gambia Muslim Congress. The platform of this party was to promote and protect the interests of the Muslim community, to assure the Muslims greater access in the government and civil service, and to use the electoral process in order to gain a foothold in the colonial society. But the Gambia Muslim Congress lost its claim to leadership in the Gambian political arena largely because the Gambian electorate proved to be more ethnically than religiously motivated.[30]

## Recent Trends

In the past two decades, two factors have contributed to the development of a Muslim sense of solidarity and the rise of Islamic revivalism in West Africa. The first was the result of the limited but successful Naserite drive to contain Israeli activities in Africa and to win and influence the people of Africa south of the Sahara. The second was the result of the Saudi-led Gulf effort at establishing ties with African peoples, following the dramatic rise in oil prices in the mid-1970s.

These two developments serve as important points of reference whenever we discuss the rise of Islamic revivalism. By opposing the Israelis in the African continent the Naserites hoped to accomplish what they had done at the Bandung Conference, where Israel was denied admission into the Afro-Asian community of states. But this Egyptian dream of isolating Israel did not work fully. In fact, the record shows that the Israelis were able to hold the Egyptians at bay, and during the 1957–1973 period they managed to establish diplomatic relations with over thirty countries.

But if Naser's campaign against Israel drove him to some variety of pan-Islamism, in the form of scholarships and cultural aid to Africans, the oil price increase of 1973 and the greater involvement of Arab states in African development led to the rise of Islamic revivalism in certain parts of Africa south of the Sahara. The oil price increase catapulted into prominence countries like Libya under Qadhafi and Saudi Arabia under King Faisal.[31] In their own way these men helped sensitize African Muslims to their Islamic foundation and Muslim identity. Qadhafi used Islam in the early 1970s as a political and ideological weapon in his bid for power in the Arab and Muslim world. He managed to identify Islam with Third World radicalism, an important development that was not seriously examined by scholars until the Iranian revolution erupted. As a result of his activities, there are now many Islamic groups in sub-Saharan Africa that are directly or indirectly linked to Libya's Islamic Call Society (Daʿwatul Islamiyya). This organization is committed to the spread of Islam, not as a moribund belief system that collaborates with Western governments, but as a battering ram aimed at the heart of the problem of Muslim alienation in the contemporary world.[32]

In the world view of this kind of Islamic revivalist fundamentalism, Islam must stand for the rights of the downtrodden and demonstrate its difference from both the capitalist and the communist models of society. Islam, according to this school, is a third alternative and its prescription for mankind is the best. Since May 13, 1972, when the Libyan Revolutionary Command Council formed the Islamic Call Society, it has tried to influence fellow Muslims in Africa and

beyond. The first effort in this direction was the involvement of Libya with the
Moro Liberation Movement in the Philippines, where the Muslim group has
been engaged in guerrilla warfare with the government.

Qadhafi's involvement with Islamic fundamentalism is paradoxical in the
sense that at home he is hated by the fundamentalists just as his hero Naser
was in Egypt. In fact, the Libyan revivalists' distrust of the Qadhafi regime led
to a failed fundamentalist bid for power in Libya in 1986. But if Qadhafi is
unpopular with fundamentalists at home, he has been able to win some converts
in certain African circles. His brand of Islamic fundamentalism has been embraced by certain groups south of the Sahara. Its most vocal advocate has been
Shaikh Ahmed Niasse, the so-called Ayatullah of Kaolack. His militancy has
led to his denunciation of Senghor and to his call for the establishment of an
Islamic state. A group of Gambians who were deceived by Ahmed Niasse
through the offer of employment opportunities in Libya later revealed the real
plan of the Senegalese marabout. His plan was to recruit these young men to
serve in the Islamic Legion, Libya's response to the French Legion.[33] Here
one sees a parallel between the Islamic Legion of Libya and al-Murabitun, the
Islamic religio-military force organized by Abdullah Ibn Yasin in the eleventh
century.

In analyzing recent trends in Muslim societies in Africa, one can therefore
argue that in addition to the traditional Islamic revivalism, there are the Libyan
variety and the Islamic fundamentalism which Nigerian journalists have identified as the Maitatsine movement. The Islamic fundamentalism of Qadhafi is
actually a reaction to both an internal and an external situation. The internal
situation necessitated some form of Islamic militancy to check the remnants of
the old Sanusiyya loyalists and the advocates of the old teachings of the Ikhwan
al-Muslimin philosophy. The external situation that gave rise to Libya's pursuit
of a militant Islamism was the presence of the state of Israel in Africa and the
legacy of Naserite rivalry with the House of Saud for African opinion and support. Since Qadhafi sees himself as the true inheritor of Naser's legacy, he finds
it very important to fight the Israelis with the weapon of Muslim solidarity and
to convince the radical Africans that Muslim advocates of pan-Islamism in the
African context are as radical as anybody. This was the message of Naser to the
generation of Nkrumah, Sekou Toure, and Modibo Keita. Qadhafi cannot be
different when he addresses his collaborators Thomas Sankara of Burkino Faso
and First Lieutenant Jerry Rawlings of Ghana.

In addition to Ahmed Niasse, there were other African Muslims whose organizations decided to collaborate with Libya's Islamic Call Society. According
to a recent study on Libyan activities in Africa, the Daʿwatul Islamiyya has
provided money for the restoration of mosques, the establishment of schools,
and other activities. A large number of scholarships have been offered to African
students from at least thirty-one countries.[34]

Besides the Daʿwatul Islamiyya, there is also the Green Book Center in
Tripoli, charged with the promotion and distribution of the political-philo-
sophical ideas contained in the *Green Book*, Qadhafi's counterpart to Mao's

*Red Book.* The two organizations have friends and allies in Africa south of the Sahara. Currently, there are several Green Book Centers in Africa; the most active ones are in Ghana under Rawlings, in Burkino Faso under Sankara, and in Sierra Leone and other countries.[35]

What makes these centers appealing to some African youths, especially the unemployed, is that they provide money and reading materials. But most importantly, they make it possible for some of these young men to go to Libya for job opportunities or some form of training. Owing to its strong anti-Western stance, the Libyan brand of Islamic revivalism appeals to young Africans with leftist tendencies who feel uncomfortable with what some West African Muslims call maraboutic Islam or reactionary Islam.

The third brand of Islamic revivalism is the Maitatsine movement. According to a recent study on this movement, this group took its name from the derisive nickname given to its founder, Mallam Muhammad Marwa. The story goes that he obtained the name because he tended to frequently use the Hausa phrase "Wanda ba ta yarda ba Allah tatsine" (May God curse whoever disagrees with me). Mallam came to Nigeria from Cameroon and during his long sojourn, gained a wide following. Building his movement on the centrality of the Qur'an, he began to preach against "corrupting elements" in Nigerian society. He was opposed to the consumption of alcohol, dancing, gambling, and the private ownership of what one scholar described as "diabolical creations [which included] bicycles, refrigerators, radios, and buttons."[36]

Many scholars have tried to explain the Maitatsine phenomenon. Some have given economic reasons for its development. Others have maintained that political conditions in northern Nigeria were responsible for the uprising. Regardless of the causes of the first bloodbath of 1980, the fact still remains that Muhammad Marwa fits many patterns identified by social scientists looking into these kinds of sociological problems. He can be identified with the Mahdist motif, as Allan Christelow suggested; he can be perceived as a system challenger who saw modernization and corruption in Nigerian society as an obscenity that deserved to be wiped out for good; he can be viewed as a Muslim heretical leader who abused his followers' fidelity and loyalty.

But all these explanations notwithstanding, the question still remains: what makes the Maitatsine different from the traditional Muslim groups in West Africa? Based on all available evidence, one can argue that the Maitatsine followers are a heretical sect. They reject the notion of compulsory prayer and the Muslim tradition of facing toward the Qiblah (i.e., Makka's Kaʿaba), and they have substituted Muhammad Marwa for the Prophet Muhammad.[37]

In view of the heretical nature of the movement and its tendency to violence, contingency plans have been made by the government to deal with possible future problems caused by the movement. It was thought that the death of the group's leader would lead to its total collapse. But the violent eruptions at Bulunakutu in Maidugur in October 1982 invalidated this optimism.

The result of the revivalist movements, heretical or not, has been a greater willingness on the part of the Nigerian government to re-Islamize the society.

The Yan Izala group, whose members were at one time accused of collaborating with Marwa, has thus become very active in promoting an unadulterated Islam. They, and other groups such as the Muslim Student Association of Nigeria, have been clamoring for the introduction of the Shari⁻a courts in the Nigerian federal system and in the states. This issue was debated without satisfactory resolution in the Constituent Assembly prior to the presidential election of 1979, which brought Shehu Shagari to the Nigerian presidency. But the most significant flare-up since the Maitatsine uprisings of the early 1980s is the issue of Nigeria's membership in the OIC. This was done secretly without adequate debate. As a result, it has shocked most of the Nigerian Christians and has become a major political controversy. However, the OIC issue is only symbolic of much deeper psycho-cultural issues facing Nigeria and its leadership. First of all, Nigerian leaders and peoples have yet to reconcile themselves to the fact that there are many clashing visions of Nigeria at the political and religious levels. Those Nigerians who, like Ibrahim Suleiman, the prolific Muslim activist from northern Nigeria, feel that Islam is now taking its rightful place in that country and that Nigeria's admission into the OIC has "brought together the Muslim north and the Muslim south," do not accept the Western sociologists' notion of religious pluralism. To them, "Nigeria belongs to Islam" and "Christianity in Nigeria is a child of colonialism."[38] On the opposite end of the political spectrum are the Nigerian Christians who have not realized that the association of Christianity with colonialism has indeed given them certain privileges that could not have been otherwise secured. To Nigerians searching for a middle ground, opinions of men like Ibrahim Suleiman and his Christian counterparts could only create a climate of hostility among Nigerians. Yet, one cannot deny the popularity of Suleiman's views among Muslims who believe that their Islamic culture and way of life is being challenged and polluted by the forces of Western secularism.

Writing on what he described as "the solution" to Nigeria's identity problem, Ibrahim argued in a recent article that in the debate on the political future of Nigeria, Muslims "now insist that Islam has to occupy its rightful seat in the political life of the nation, namely the front seat, and that if anything has to go, it certainly is not Islam, but the colonial legacy."[39] This position of Suleiman's is echoed in other parts of the continent. Though aspects of his brand of Islamic fundamentalism resemble Qadhafi's, their sources of inspiration seem to be different. Whereas Qadhafi identified with Naser and the school of thought generally labeled Arab or Islamic socialism, Suleiman traces his roots back to Shaikh ⁻Usman dan Fodio and his collaborators.

But if Suleiman's writings give us the impression of an Islamic activist who is strongly committed to the restoration of the Sokoto caliphate, the literary efforts of his Senegalese contemporaries seem to be less so. In Senegal, Muslim activist Latif Gueye, *Djamra* editor-in-chief, promotes the Islamic revival through moral exhortation. As a result of newspaper and magazine campaigns by Gueye and some of his fellow journalists against Senegalese women who are perceived to be deviating from Islam, there has developed a state of hostility between these Muslim advocates of Islamic revivalism and the women's liberationists in Senegal. Known as the Yewwu Yewwi, this Senegal women's group, whose name means, in Wolof, "liberation through consciousness," has decided to face up to the challenges of the Arabisants who are sexist in their interpretations of Qur'an, Hadith, and Sunna.[40] Though it is too early to know what the outcome will be, it is fair to say that in the coming years the increase in the number of educated women will make it more difficult to suppress women's rights.

## Conclusions

What emerges from the above is that the history of Islamic revivalism is as old as the history of Islam in West Africa. The idea of jihad and of the role of the mujaddid have captured the imagination of African Muslims south of the Sahara since the Almuravid movement. Islamic revivalism has been an effective vehicle for the precolonial Muslim leaders who felt that either waging a jihad or creating Islamic organizations could enhance their status and change their living conditions in the region. During the colonial period, Islamic revivalism was not allowed to develop because the colonialists saw it as a politically dangerous element that could pull down the whole structure of colonial society. Despite the colonial opposition, however, the majority of West African Muslims fought hard to keep their Islamic identity and traditions and refused assimilation within the colonial culture. In the post-colonial era, Islamic forces found better opportunities to organize and to extract social, economic, and political concessions from their governments. However, the strength of secular modernizing forces in post-independence Africa and the prevalence of ethnic links and loyalties prevented Islam from becoming a strong political force. African Muslim revivalism in the post-colonial period has largely been, and still is, a cultural phenomenon and a reflection of West African Muslims' desire to regain their cultural autonomy and to eliminate remnants of colonial cultural domination. Islamic revivalism in West Africa by and large has not been a politically destabilizing factor. Nigeria, however, is an exception. In Nigeria, the emphasis on Islamic identity and culture could create new patterns of political alignments that could lead to either greater unity or a breakdown in the political process, depending on the political sagacity of the Nigerian leadership. Nor is there any evidence that revivalist forces in West Africa could successfully challenge the existing political structure.

At the level of Africa's international relations, there is a growing sense that revivalist efforts to reassert West African Muslims' Islamic identity have led to a great interaction between West African Muslims and other Islamic, and especially Arab, countries. However, the Islamic element in these interactions, although important, should not be exaggerated. In fact, these contacts and links had begun to develop in the 1950s and 1960s when secular political trends were dominant both in West Africa and in the Arab world. They, indeed, derive more from a desire on the part of many Third World countries to form alliances that would strengthen their position vis-à-vis the great powers. In fact, part of Qadhafi's appeal to African youth is that he has incorporated many ideas of Third World radicalism into his version of Islamic revivalism.

Islamic revivalism in West Africa appears to be a deviation from the Middle Eastern pattern. Whereas in the Middle East, Islamic revivalism is seen by some analysts as a clear confirmation of the failure of pan-Arabism, in Africa the evidence does not support the contention that Islamic revivalism is a re-action to the failure of pan-Africanism. Indeed, there is evidence from the African nationalist literature that Islam provided a source of inspiration for some nationalist leaders in their fight against colonialism. This was particularly true of the Islamized areas of the French empire in West Africa. Pan-Africanism, one can argue, is an ideology that created an overarching unity for Muslim and non-Muslim Africans who felt at the time of decolonization that they belonged to a community of suffering and shared a common landmass called Africa. Thus, the pan-Africanism that propelled African leaders to form the Organization of African Unity (OAU) differs from pan-Arabism because, unlike the latter, it did not identify Islam and the Arabic language as vital building blocks for the edifice of African unity. Its focus has been on Africa the landmass and on the community of colonial suffering brought about by European rule in Africa.

Islamic revivalism in post-colonial Africa also owes much to African Muslims' reaction to secularism in their societies. Forced to adjust to changes brought about by external forces and determined to assert their cultural identity, African Muslims see in revivalism a stone that kills two birds simultaneously. It re-assures the Muslim of his identity in a changing world while providing him with the means of meeting his religious and cultural needs.

In sum, the current Islamic revivalist wave in Africa derives from the same social, political, economic, and, most importantly, cultural factors as in the rest of the Muslim world. But its origins and evolution very clearly bear the marks of West African Muslim countries' specific conditions.

# NOTES

1. Aziz Batran, *Islam and Revolution in Africa* (Brattleboro, Vt.: Amana Books, 1984), p. 9.
2. Ibid.
3. See Philip D. Curtin, "Jihad in West Africa: Early Phases and Interactions in Mauritania and Senegal," *Journal of African History*, Vol. 12, No. 1, pp. 11–24.
4. See M.A. al-Hajj, "The Thirteenth Century in Muslim Eschatology: Mahdist Expectations in the Sokoto Caliphate," *Research Bulletin*, CAD, Vol. 3, No. 2 (1967), pp. 100–115.

5. Omar Jah, "Sufism and Nineteenth-Century Jihad Movements: A Case Study of al-Hajj Umar al-Futi's Philosophy of Jihad and Its Sufi Bases," Ph.D. thesis, McGill University, 1973.

6. Aziz Batran, "The Nineteenth-Century Islamic Revolutions in West Africa," unpublished paper, p. 5ff.

7. According to Batran, Sidi Muhammad al-Kunti b. Sidi ᶜAli b. Yahya b. Uthman b. Duman (ᶜUmar) b. Yahs (ᶜAbd Allah) b. Shakir b. Ya'qub b. al-Aqib b. Uqba al-Mustajab b. Nafi' was the son of Sidi ᶜAli and his spouse, the daughter of Muhammad ᶜAlim b. Kunta b. Zam, the leader of the Sanhaja ᶜAbd-u-kal. Following the custom frequently practiced among Saharan Arabs, Sidi Muhammad inherited the name of his maternal grandfather. Hence, it is this Sanhaja name that Sidi Muhammad's descendants adopted and still bear to the present day. For more details on the Kunta ethnic group, see Batran, "The Kunta, Sidi al-Mukhtar al-Kunti, and the Office of Shaykh al-Tariqa al-Qdairiyya," in John Ralph Willis, ed., *Studies in West African Islamic History*, Vol. 1, *The Cultivators of Islam* (London: Frank Cass, 1979), pp. 113–146.

8. Muhammad b. ᶜAbd al-Karim b. Muhammad al-Maghili al-Tilimsani was allegedly initiated, along with his disciple Sidi ᶜUmar al-Shaikh, into the Qadiri tariqa by ᶜAbd al-Rahman al-Suyuti while visiting Cairo. He and his disciple have been credited with spreading the tariqa in the western Sahara. For details on al-Maghili, see Willis, *Studies*, Vol. 1, chaps. 1 and 4. See also Peter B. Clarke, *West Africa and Islam* (London: Edward Arnold, 1982), pp. 61–64, in which we get a brief but informative account of al-Maghili's activities in what is now Kano state in Nigeria.

9. Shaikh Ahmad Lobbo was a Muslim scholar who, with his militant Islamic reform movement, put an end to the Rari dynasty, threw off Bambara overlordship, and turned Masina into an Islamic state. Inspired to a degree by the reform movement in Sokoto, Shaikh Ahmad defeated the combined resistance of the Rari and their Bambara allies, routing them finally at the battles of Nokouma and the Geri. For details on the jihad efforts of Shaikh Ahmad, see Clarke, *West Africa*, pp. 128–131.

10. Al-Haj ᶜUmar Taal was a Torobe Muslim scholar and a charismatic leader who waged a jihad against both the unbelievers and the ᶜulema al-su in Western Sudan. He conquered the Bambara kingdoms of Segou and Kaarta in the nineteenth century. For more details about his activities and his writings, see John Ralph Willis, "Jihad fi Sabil Allah: Its Doctrinal Base in Islam and Some Aspects of Its Evolution in Nineteenth-Century West Africa," *Journal of African History*, Vol. 8, No. 3 (1967), pp. 359–415.

11. ᶜUsman dan Fodio, a Fulbe scholar, was the leader of the jihad against the rulers of Gobir in what is now Niger. For details on his life and activities, see Mervyn Hiskett, *The Sword of Truth* (Oxford: Oxford University Press, 1973).

12. See Nehemia Levtzion, "Abdullah B. Yasin and the Almuravids," in Willis, *Studies*, Vol. 1.

13. Quoted in ibid.

14. See Omar Jah, "Islamic History in the West Sudan," *Bulletin of the Islamic Center of Washington, D.C.*, Vol. 7, No. 1 (May 1978), p. 24. Reprinted from the *Journal of the Muslim World League* (January 1978).

15. See n. 10.

16. Maba Jahu Ba was a Torobe Muslim scholar and a charismatic leader who waged a jihad in the Gambia. Born in Baddibu on the north bank of the Gambia River, this Muslim warrior raised the flag of Islamic statehood against the Mandinka rulers of Baddibu, who refused to abandon what were known as *jahiliyya* ways. For details about his life and activities, see Charlotte Quinn, "M'aba Diakhou and the Gambian Jihad, 1850–1890," in Willis, *Studies*, Vol. 1, pp. 233–259.

17. Muhammad Lamin Drame, better known as Shaikh al-Hajj Mahmadu Lamin (Muhammad al-Amin), was born into a Sarahuli family in 1835. He was a well-known scholar, and thousands of students from all parts of Serahuli country traveled to learn from him. He waged jihad in that part of the present Republic of Senegal called Senegal

Oriental. For details on his life and activities, see Ivan Hrbek, "The Early Period of Mahmadu Lamin's Activities," in Willis, *Studies*, Vol. 1, pp. 211–232.

18. Samori Toure was a Mande-speaking Muslim warrior who waged jihad in Mande country in what is now the Republic of Guinea and parts of the Ivory Coast. Born in 1830, he obtained Islamic education and in later life promoted Islam through conquest. For details of his activities, see Yves Person, "Samori and Islam," in Willis, *Studies*, Vol. 1, pp. 259–277.

19. This was true among all Muslim communities during the colonial period.

20. On the role of Christianity in the Westernization of Africans, see my "Christianity and Westernization in Africa," *Current Bibliography on African Affairs*, Vol. 18, No. 1 (1985–86), pp. 43–54.

21. Sulayman S. Nyang, "Islam and Politics in West Africa," *Issue* (Journal of Opinion of the African Studies Association), Vol. 13 (1984), pp. 20–25.

22. For biographical data on Ahmadu Bamba, see Lucy Behrman Greevy, in Willis, *Studies*, Vol. 1. See also Donal Cruise O'Brien, *The Mourides of Senegal* (London: Oxford University Press, 1971).

23. On this movement, see René Luc Moreau, *Africaines Musulmans* (Paris: Presence Africaines, 1982), pp. 266ff.

24. Ali A. Mazrui, "On the Concept 'We Are All Africans,' " *American Political Science Review*, Vol. 57, No. 1 (March 1963).

25. Moreau, *Africaines Musulmans*.

26. Ibid.

27. Ann Dunba, "Islamic Values, the State and 'Development of Women': The Case of Niger," unpublished paper (1985). See also Jean-Louis Triaud, "L'Islam et l'état du Niger," *Le Mois en Afrique* (December 1981–January 1982).

28. Guy Nicolas, *Dynamique de l'Islam au sud du Sahara* (Paris: Publication Orientalistes de France, 1981), p. 213.

29. On the Nigerian situation, see Clarke, *West Africa and Islam*; idem, "Islamic Millenarianism in West Africa: A Revolutionary Ideology," *Religious Studies* 16 (1980), pp. 317–339; idem, "Islam and Change in Nigeria, c. 1918–1960," in Ralph Willis and A. Ross, eds., *Religion and Change in African Societies* (Edinburgh: Edinburgh University Press, 1979), pp. 97ff.

30. On Islam and politics in the Gambia, see my "Local and National Elites and Islam in the Gambia: An African Case Study," *International Journal of Islamic and Arabic Studies*, Vol. 1, No. 2 (1984), pp. 57–67.

31. For Saudi Arabia's role in Africa, see my "Saudi Arabia's Foreign Policy towards Africa," *Horn of Africa*, Vol. 5, No. 2 (1982), pp. 3–17.

32. On Libya's role in Africa, see Mohamed O'Bai Samura, *The Libyan Revolution: Its Lessons for Africa* (Washington, D.C.: International Institute for Policy and Development Studies, 1986). This is the work of a Sierra Leonean political scientist sympathetic to Libya's role in Africa. No serious treatment of Libya's activities in Africa has come out yet.

33. Shaikh Ahmed Niasse is such a controversial figure in Senegalese politics that his activities became the target of a government probe. For news reporting on his activities, see accounts provided in *West Africa* and *Jeune Afrique* in 1980 and 1981.

34. See Samura, *Libyan Revolution*, p. 90.

35. On Sierra Leoneans supporting or opposing Qadhafi, see Samadu Sesay's account of a demonstration by members of Sierra Leone's Green Book Center, "Sierra Leone: For and against Gaddafi," *African Concord*, May 8, 1986, p. 12.

36. On the Maitatsine movement, see Allan Christelow, "The 'Yan Tatsine Disturbances in Kano: A Search for Perspective," *The Muslim World*, Vol. 75, No. 2 (April 1985), pp. 69–84; M. Adeleye Ojo, "The Maitatsine Revolution in Nigeria," *American Journal of Islamic Social Sciences*, Vol. 2, No. 2 (December 1985), pp. 297–306.

37. See Christelow and Ojo. See also Allan Christelow, "Religious Protest and Dissent

in Northern Nigeria: From Mahdism to Quranic Integralism," *Journal of the Institute of Muslim Minority Affairs*, Vol. 6, No. 2 (July 1985), pp. 375–393.

38. Ibrahim Suleiman, "The OIC Debate," *Inquiry* (London), May 1986, pp. 21–23.

39. Ibrahim Suleiman, "The Solution," *Africa Events*, December 1986, pp. 184ff.

40. On this problem, see El-Hadj Momar Wade, "Feminisme contre intégrisme," *Africa International*, November 1986, p. 39.

# Part V

# Islamic Revivalism in Asia

# XIV

# PAKISTAN

## Mumtaz Ahmad

The Pakistani experience of the interaction of religion and politics is unique in that it is integrally related to the idea of a separate homeland for Indian Muslims, which emerged in the late 1930s. Since then, and particularly after Pakistan's creation in 1947, its political development has been, in one way or another, influenced by Islam and is likely to remain so in the future.

### Forms of Islamic Revival

Islamic revivalism in Pakistan has appeared in various areas of collective life in recent years. In politics, both the Islamic parties and the government have denied the legitimacy of Western parliamentary democracy and have sought instead to introduce a political system based on Islamic principles. One such effort was a national referendum, which sought a mandate for further Islamization and, by implication, the extension of the tenure of the president for five more years, along with nonparty elections for the national and provincial assemblies.[1]

In economics, Islamic revivalism has expressed itself in such measures as the compulsory collection of *zakat* and *ushr* taxes, introduction of an interest-free banking and investment system, legal restrictions on the appropriation of private property, and denationalization of certain business and industrial enterprises. In the legal sphere, revivalism has meant the reintroduction of Islamic penal laws and the Islamic law of evidence. Further ordinances have provided for the establishment of a Federal Shariʿa Court as well as local Qazi Courts to hear criminal and civil cases under Islamic law. The Federal Shariʿa Court, in its original and appellate jurisdictions, rules on whether or not existing laws are in accordance with Islam.

Cultural expressions of Islamic revivalism have included the banning of dance clubs, the imposition of strict sexual morality, the observance of Islamic moral standards in the production and screening of TV programs, the revision of school and college textbooks to express an Islamic bias, increasing allocations for Arabic and Islamic instruction, the establishment of an international Islamic university in Islamabad, declaring Friday as the weekly holiday instead of Sunday, instituting obligatory prayer breaks during working hours in government and private offices, emphasizing the Urdu language and national dress in government offices, and the expression of a kind of moral aversion, at least theoretically, toward Western culture. International Islamic cultural exchanges have increased, and Islamic religious festivals and holidays are celebrated more enthusiastically.

Although most of these "revivalist" measures were introduced during the military regime of President Zia-ul-Haq, they are rooted in the period of Zulfiqar ᶜAli Bhutto's rule. Indeed, it was Bhutto who first unleashed the revivalist forces while bargaining with his opponents in the religious right. Although the "Islamic" measures introduced by Bhutto were piecemeal and peripheral to the core of his socioeconomic policies, they had great impact on subsequent developments. By incorporating extensive Islamic provisions in the 1973 constitution, and later in 1974 declaring the Ahmadis—a heretical group founded by Mirza Ghulam Ahmad in the early years of this century—as non-Muslims, Bhutto helped raise the religious parties' expectations and prepared the ground for a full-grown movement for Islamization during Zia's regime.

Nevertheless, these circumstantial contingents of the Bhutto era were not the major determinants of Islamic revival in Pakistan. Islamic revival, or, more specifically, the increasing politicization of Islam since the middle 1970s in Pakistan, is intimately related to certain important historical and social factors as elaborated below.

### Pakistan as an Islamic State

The establishment of Pakistan in 1947 in itself was a prime religious and political expression of Islamic revival. The Pakistan movement's call for a separate homeland for the Indian Muslims was to enable them to live individually and collectively according to Islam, undisturbed by the Hindu majority. The demand for Pakistan was articulated in terms of national self-determination.[2] The nationalist elements of this demand, however, were anchored in the Islamic consciousness of the Muslim masses.[3] The Muslim League's slogan, "Islam is in danger," politically mobilized the masses. The Two-Nation Theory of the Qaid-i-Azam Muhammad ᶜAli Jinnah further reinforced the Islamic basis of this nationalist movement. It is important to note that Jinnah did not define *nation* in terms of shared language or common territory, history, culture, and customs; rather, he stated that Islam and Hinduism are not religions in the strict sense of the word but are in fact distinct social orders and thus cannot evolve into a single nationality.

Both the poet-philosopher Muhammad Iqbal and Jinnah perceived Islam at three interrelated levels: (1) Islam as a *faith* and as a religious system whose cardinal beliefs identify its adherents as Muslims; (2) Islam as a *culture* and a way of life that would integrate Muslims into a nation-state; and (3) Islam as a *politico ideological system* whose set of values could socialize Muslims into a separate political community.[4]

To many Pakistani intellectuals, Islam constitutes the very raison d'être of the Pakistani state and the only reason that justifies its separate existence from India.[5] This interpretation of the Islam-Pakistan relationship was first articulated in the Objectives Resolution passed by the first Constituent Assembly of Pakistan in 1949, and later became an ideological preamble to all of its subsequent constitutions. The Objectives Resolution clearly established that the state in Pakistan will not be a neutral observer, wherein Muslims may be merely free to profess and practice their religion. Rather, as the country's first Prime Minister, Liaqat ᶜAli Khan, put it, "such an attitude on the part of the state would be the very negation of the ideals which prompted the demand for Pakistan."[6] The state in Pakistan, he said, will have to play a positive part in directing and guiding "the activities of Muslims in such a manner as to bring about a new social order based upon the essential principles of Islam. . . . "[7]

The relationship between Islam and state as formulated in the Objectives Resolution has assumed the status of such an orthodoxy that even avowedly secular and socialist parties do not hazard to challenge it. The existence of a broad consensus on the inseparability of Islam and Pakistan—popularly known as "Pakistan ideology"—has thus helped religiopolitical groups to press their demands for a greater public role for Islam.

### Islam and the Legitimation of Power

From Pakistan's beginnings, its rulers have used Islam to legitimize their authority, which was generally based on coercion. Most of these regimes came to power through extraconstitutional means and their legitimacy was dubious when judged by conventional political norms. Consequently, they became dependent on Islam as a convenient and malleable source of legitimacy. Thus, the early chaotic parliamentary regimes, Ayub Khan's development-oriented dictatorship and Yahya Khan's wayward dictatorship, Bhutto's populist corporatism, and General Zia's conservative authoritarianism all relied on the same social forces and shared more or less the same ideological bases of legitimacy. They all invoked Islamic ideology to legitimize their authority, to sanctify their policy goals, and to control their opponents. The use of Islam by the state helped Pakistan achieve a degree of political stability, at least in the short run.[8]

The early parliamentary regime used a "liberal-modernist Islam," Ayub Khan a "developmentalist Islam," Yahya Khan a "nationalist Islam," and Bhutto a "socialist-populist Islam." Most recently, Zia's military regime has used a "revivalist-fundamentalist Islam" to legitimize its rule.

The Zia government has sought the moral commitment of the people by propagating an ideology that links the destiny of both Islam and Pakistan with the continuity of the military regime. The original formulation of Pakistan ideology, as articulated by the Jama‘at-i-Islami, the main component of the Islamic revivalist movement in Pakistan, emphasized only the essential relationship between Islam and Pakistan, i.e., that "Pakistan came into being in the name of Islam and it could exist in the name of Islam alone." General Zia added another element to this formulation by maintaining that the then-existing political establishment (the military rule) was equally vital for the preservation of Islam and Pakistan. Thus, according to this new formulation, the trinity of Islam, Pakistan, and the military regime became one and the same thing.[9]

When a regime equates itself with both the state and religion and then presents a particular version of religion as official dogma, any deviation from the official interpretation of the ideology inevitably becomes both a religious heresy and treason against the state. When the state assumes a theocratic character and loyalty to the state becomes identical with loyalty to religion, political rebellion and religious dissent become indistinguishable. It is in this context that one should read the following statement by President Zia:

> Pakistan and Islam are the names of one and the same thing and any idea or action contrary to this would mean hitting at the very roots of the ideology, solidarity, and integrity of Pakistan.[10]

The crux of Zia's case against his opposition has been that since the opposition elements are secular and leftist, they ipso facto lack legitimacy to claim power in an Islamic state. President Zia and his colleagues have quite frequently emphasized the "binding relationship" between the ideological basis of the state and the ideological orientation of the government. In 1980, addressing the councilors of Multan district, President Zia declared:

> Pakistan was achieved in the name of Islam, and Islam alone could provide the basis to run the government of the country and sustain its integrity. . . . The present government would provide opportunity to others to serve the country after it achieved its objective . . . [but] no un-Islamic government would be allowed to succeed the present regime."[11]

The use of Islam has thus made the regime's religious interests indistinguishable from purely political interests and need for legitimacy.

The Zia government has used another ingenious argument to legitimize its power, namely, the ideological affinity between, and the undifferentiated structural character of, the ruling institutions in an Islamic polity. According to this argument, the armed forces should not be considered a separate corporate group since the ideological affinities that run through various ruling institutions and govern their relationship with the rest of the society transcend artificial institutional boundaries. If all the "load-bearing pillars" of the society are motivated by the same ideological considerations and adhere to the same Shari‘a, which is the "guiding and controlling spirit" of every section of the population, including the armed forces, the normative distinction between civilian and military rule does not arise. Hence, the argument continues, one does not witness any military rule in the communist polities as the party, presidium, executive, and military are all united in the single ideological structure of communism. Since the Islamic state by definition is an ideological state, the military—adhering to the same ideology—should also be considered as an indissoluble part of the ruling structures and should fulfill its sacred religious duty to defend not only the physical but also the "ideological frontiers" of the Islamic state of Pakistan.[12]

But the instrumental use of Islam was not limited to legitimizing the regime and delegitimizing the leftist and secular political forces, especially the Pakistan Peoples Party (PPP); it was also used to seek political and moral support from the religious political parties and to generate support among the religiously motivated lower middle class of the Punjab, urban Sind, and the Northwest Frontier Province (NWFP). It is this stratum that participates most enthusiastically in the officially sponsored religious festivals and rituals, in the newly created religious institutional network of zakat and ᶜushr and the *islah-i-mu-ᶜashra* (reformation of society) committees, and in government-organized religious gatherings.[13] President Zia, through both his policies and his rhetoric, seemed to have responded positively to the religious sensibilities and economic interests of this stratum, whose support was regarded as critical to the stability of the regime. His promise to protect the sanctity of *chador* (literally, the veil) and *chardivari* (literally, the four walls of a house), both symbols of women's honor and private property, touched the vital spot in the priority structure of middle- and lower-middle-class values.

Similarly, other actions of the government noted earlier have all reinforced the regime's claims to political legitimacy on the basis of its commitment to Islam. As a result, a large number of both nonpolitical ᶜulama (religious leaders) and those with political affiliations have become ardent supporters of President Zia and his policies. The ᶜulama have also benefited, both politically and financially, from government patronage in the form of memberships in various official and elective institutions. By introducing Islamic reforms in consonance with the priorities of the ᶜulama, the regime over the past eight and a half years has achieved considerable success in institutionalizing the participation of the religious sector in the state-sponsored Islamization. It has succeeded in mobilizing the nonpolitical ᶜulama and bringing them inside the orbit of the state in order to counterbalance the influence of the politically organized ᶜulama.

## Islam and Sociopolitical Protest

Like any other ideological system, Islam is a double-edged sword. The most outstanding example of the delegitimizing role of Islam in Pakistan is the 1977 Nizam-i-Mustafa (System of the Prophet Muhammad) movement, as a result of which a militant alliance between the Jamaᶜat-i-Islami and certain conservative ᶜulama groups overthrew the secular regime of Bhutto. The Pakistan

National Alliance (PNA), which was formed by the various religiopolitical groups at the time of the 1977 elections, campaigned on the central theme of the introduction of Nizam-i-Mustafa and stirred up an unprecedented religious enthusiasm during and after the elections. The underprivileged stratum of both the traditional and modern sectors of society constituted an important part of the forces that challenged Bhutto, and formed the backbone of the Islamic revivalist movement. The movement used the Islamic ideals of democracy, fairness, justice, accountability, and accessibility to political power in order to dislodge what it described as an anti-Islamic and authoritarian regime.

The use of Islamic revivalist ideals and symbols by certain discontented groups of society whose religious concerns and material interests converged in the umbrella ideology of Islamic revivalism proved very effective, although Bhutto also had tried to use the same symbol to maintain his power.

Bhutto's failure in turn raises an important question, namely, who uses Islam most effectively and under what conditions? Prime Minister Bhutto enjoyed enormous advantages, including control of the mass media and the educational institutions, which enabled him to publicize widely the Islamic orientation of his government and the services he had rendered to the cause of Islam. He also used the government's financial resources to co-opt the religious establishment. But the fact that the power to confer Islamic legitimacy was in the hands of those whose vital economic, status, and ideological interests he had earlier so vehemently challenged proved to be a great debilitating factor in Bhutto's search for Islamic credentials. Yet, even his success in winning over the orthodox religious establishment would not necessarily have conferred on him Islamic legitimacy, since the challenge came from the lay lower-middle-class Islamic activists and not from the ᶜulama. As Michael Hudson has pointed out, given the relative lack of a structural hierarchy in Islam, incumbents have severe limitations in playing the Islamic "card."[14] A Muslim ruler who has successfully incorporated the "professional" religious establishment into state structures may still be vulnerable to opposition by equally legitimate lay and popular Islamic forces. The relative success of General Zia in establishing his Islamic legitimacy can be explained in part by his strategy of seeking certification for his Islamic authenticity from both the "professional" religious establishment as represented by the ᶜulama and the *mashaikh* (Sufi leaders) and the popular, lay Islamic forces as represented by the Jamaᶜat-i-Islami.

### Islam and National Integration

The political salience of Islam in Pakistan is also related to the role of Islam as a major source of national integration in a society marred by immense ethnic, linguistic, and cultural diversity. It was believed that the emphasis on Islam in official pronouncements and the incorporation of Islamic values in public policies, especially in the fields of education, culture, and mass communications, would help weaken the parochial loyalties of ethnicity and language, and would unify the new state.

East Bengal—later renamed East Pakistan and now Bangladesh—was seen as a test case to demonstrate the efficacy of ideological bonds in a situation where the differences in ethnicity, language, ecology, demography, and culture were relatively acute. The two wings of the country, which were separated by over one thousand miles of hostile Indian territory, shared very little with each other except Islam.[15]

The emphasis on the role of Islam as the major integrative factor increased even more in the 1960s when Pakistan witnessed a marked assertion of centrifugal fissiparous forces based on ethnic identities and regional demands. The emergence of separatist tendencies was seen as further reason to promote Islamic ideology as a basis for national solidarity.[16] But as was evident from subsequent developments, emphasis on the religious aspect to the exclusion of other more tangible ones could not ensure national unity.[17] As Nural Huda, then finance minister of East Pakistan, put it, "it would be unfair to expect that our spiritual bonds through Islam will be so strong . . . that we shall forget all our disparities and will still remain united . . . as a nation."[18] The secession of Bangladesh in December 1971 clearly demonstrated that Islam, although necessary for the creation of Pakistan, was not a sufficient factor for sustaining its unity in the absence of other policy measures. The failure of the national political, intellectual, social, and geographical elite to relate Islam to more mundane issues such as the equitable distribution of economic resources, and to enfranchise the politically alienated sectors of society, led the deprived regions to perceive Islam as an instrument of exploitation. Before the separation of East Pakistan, it was the fear of the country's disintegration which had acted as a propellant for Islam. After the separation, the faith in the efficacy of Islam to maintain national unity has intensified.

The traumatic events of the 1971 civil war and Pakistan's humiliating defeat by India had psychologically unsettling effects on the people. After absorption of the initial shock, a period of introspection and soul-searching followed.[19] A renewed quest for authenticity and national identity plus self-criticism caused by the Bengali separatist movement and defeat at the Indians' hands reaffirmed Islam as both a personal succor and a national ideology. The Islamic groups seized upon the opportunity and pointed out that East Pakistan was lost only because the Pakistanis disregarded Islam in their individual and collective lives. The secession of East Pakistan was, therefore, not Islam's failure but that of the rulers' un-Islamic policies and conduct.[20] The experience of East Pakistan thus became a rallying cry to return to Islam as an ideological remedy to counteract similar developments elsewhere in Pakistan and to cultivate a new sense of religious rejuvenation. This post-1971 rediscovery of Islamic identity in Pakistan resembles Egypt's experience after the 1967 war with Israel.[21] In both cases, humiliating defeats resulted in a return to Islamic roots and renewed public commitment to Islamic ideals.

## Islamization, Social Cohesion, and Political Stability

Coming in the wake of worldwide resurgence of Islamic consciousness, President Zia's Islamization measures were hailed by the Islamic groups as important steps toward relinking Pakistan with its original ideological referent. Opinions differed, however, on the priorities, methods, scope, and effectiveness of Islamic reforms. Critics from within the Islamic groups thought that these reforms were not effective, extensive, or fast enough. They also expressed their skepticism about the sincerity and Islamic commitment of the implementing agencies.[22]

Despite these reservations, the ʿulama have remained convinced of President Zia's personal commitment to Islam. A distinction has thus been made between President Zia and the rest of the government officials, who are suspected of secretly conspiring to sabotage the president's Islamic programs.[23] Furthermore, criticism from within the religious sector has generally been limited to issues that are peripheral to the regime's legitimacy and stability.[24]

Other critics of the regime saw the whole process of Islamization as a cynical attempt by the military to exploit the religious sentiments of the people. They have accused General Zia of manipulating the Islamic symbols and institutions in order to perpetuate his power and to control his opponents.[25]

It is rather premature to make an objective assessment of the long-term consequences of Zia's Islamization policies. Thus far, however, Islamization has not noticeably changed the Pakistanis' lives. Because of the growing gap between expectation of the masses and the outcome of the Islamic reforms, the early enthusiasm has dissipated. Introduction of zakat, ʿushr, and interest-free financial systems, for example, has not led to a more equitable income distribution. The institution of *ihtisab* (accountability) in the form of ombudsmen has not solved the problem of the bureaucracy's corruption and its authoritarian style of dealing with the people. Nor has the enforcement of Islamic penal law solved the problem of crime, which has been on the rise since 1979.[26] Consequently, both the credibility of the sponsors and the authenticity of the Islamization process have been seriously questioned.

Islamization has also become associated with the increasing sectarian tensions in Pakistan.[27] For example, the introduction of zakat and ʿushr and the enforcement of other Shariʿa laws have again brought to the surface the old juristic and doctrinal differences between the Shiʿas and the Sunnis. Thus, the question as to which interpretation of the Islamic law should form the basis for public policy has become a major source of conflict between the Sunni and Shiʿa ʿulama and between the government and the Shiʿa community.

The controversy over the divergent interpretations of Shariʿa has also filtered down to the popular level, causing frequent violent incidents as illustrated by Shiʿa-Sunni riots in Karachi during February and March 1983.[28] Similar incidents have also occurred in Baluchistan and the Punjab. There are, of course, clear manifestations of Shi°a militancy, represented by the pro-Khumaini Im-amiya Students' Federation of Karachi. But the highly inflammatory anti-Shi°a speeches and writings of some prominent Sunni °ulama and the desultory Is-lamization measures of the government have further aggravated the tense sec-tarian situation. Some °ulama, mostly of the Deobandi persuasion, are now demanding that Pakistan be declared a "Sunni state" and restrictions be imposed on the public display and observance of Shi°a religious rituals.

But Islamization—or, more accurately, "Shari°azation,"since the emphasis in Pakistan has been on the enforcement of Shari°a laws rather than on the implementation of cardinal Islamic principles of democracy, freedom, equality, tolerance, and social justice—has also exacerbated disagreements among the various Sunni groups.

One can argue, therefore, that revivalist Islam, with its emphasis on legalistic changes, has created dissensions among various Islamic sects more than it has unified different social strata of Pakistani society. A different set of priorities, signifying freedom and tolerance and concern for social equality, economic justice, and political participation, would have certainly received much more enthusiastic popular response and would have enhanced social harmony and national integration. Furthermore, since the repressive martial law regulations and Islamization policies have come from the same source, Islam and coercion have increasingly been perceived as identical. The regime's practice of justifying all its acts in Islamic terms has also helped identify Islam with policies that were primarily intended for the regime's perpetuation.[29]

Moreover, when the twice-scheduled general elections were postponed in October 1979, Islamization issues came to be overshadowed by demands for the lifting of martial law and the restoration of democracy. This further split the country politically into three dominant groups: (1) those who wanted the Islamization process to continue under martial law regime; (2) those who wanted Islamization of society in a democratic framework; and (3) those who wanted neither martial law nor Islam. The first group was represented by the majority of the traditional °ulama, who had no love lost for the niceties of democratic procedures and feared that the Islamization agenda would be relegated to a lower priority once the elections were held and representative governments were formed.[30] The second group consisted of the Jama°at-i-Islami and some elements from the Jam°iyyat-i-°Ulama-i-Pakistan, a populist religious group of Brelvi persuasion, and reflected the consensus that had been obtained during the 1977 movement for Islam *and* democracy. The third group represented the views of secular forces and the left-wing faction of the PPP.

However, the role of Islam in maintaining political stability during martial law proved critical. The major Islamic political parties remained firm in their opposition to any anti-martial law agitation, if not in their resolute support of the regime. Although these parties shared a demand for the lifting of martial law and the holding of general elections, they also shared General Zia's fear that these elections might result in the political rehabilitation of secular and socialist elements represented by the PPP. Thus, the regime was able to separate these parties from the agitation group and to use their tacit support as a basis for its popularity.

In fact, by using the normative appeal of Islamic symbols and institutional structures, the government defined its goals and objectives in terms of Islamic revivalist ideals and the ideological origins of the Pakistani state. In the process, the corporate interests of the military became indistinguishable from the normative demands of national ideology. The event that epitomized this modus operandi of sustaining political stability was the 1984 referendum, which deftly linked the popular approval of the Islamization process with the continuation of General Zia as the president of the country for five more years.

Since the partyless general elections in March 1985 and the lifting of martial law and the restoration of democracy in January 1986, the course and content of political debate in Pakistan is changing somewhat. Even before the return from self-exile in April 1986 of Benazir Bhutto, acting chair of the PPP after her father's execution in 1979, and the subsequent resurgence of PPP in the country's political process, Islam and Islamic issues were gradually receding to the periphery of political debate. The immediate problems facing the country, such as unemployment, absorption of Middle East returnees, Afghanistan, law and order, and provincial autonomy, had tended to elbow out the "Islamic issues."

The "intrusion" of Benazir Bhutto further strengthened this trend. Both the elected government of Prime Minister Muhammad Khan Junejo and the main opposition forces were struck by a PPP demand for midterm elections on a party basis and with more serious threats from regional political groups, which sought to redefine the center-province relations in a new framework of a nominal federation. Interestingly, all these issues were being debated without any reference to Islam. This was quite unlike the 1970s and the early 1980s, when Islam constituted the basic referent for all political, economic, social, and foreign policy debates.

There could be many explanations for this development. First, one can argue that the regime had already exhausted the instrumental use of Islam and thus no longer found it useful as a main source for its legitimacy. Pakistani nationalism, the Afghanistan situation, and programmatic goals of socioeconomic development seemed to have replaced Islam as a basis of legitimacy for the new civilian government. Second, even the Islamic political parties had exhausted their agenda of Islamic demands. For most of these groups, Islamization had meant the introduction of zakat, interest-free banking, and the Islamic penal laws—the three things on which President Zia obliged them without much delay. The religious parties therefore had nothing substantial to demand from the government except that the newly instituted Islamic measures should be implemented earnestly and effectively. Finally, the PPP resurgence in the summer of 1986 reopened the "mundane" issues of politics, economy, and national integration that had been put aside during the eight-year euphoria over Islamization.

This does not mean, however, that Islam will cease to be a major force in Pakistan's political process in the short or long term. Even if the Zia government left the scene and the PPP, alone or in coalition with other parties, came into power, it is difficult to imagine that the newly created Islamic institutions and legal apparatuses could be dismantled. Not legislating Islamic laws is not being a good Muslim, but abrogating them once they are legislated is blasphemy and will provoke the wrath of the ᶜulama and the Jamaᶜat-i-Islami. Also, zakat and some other Islamic institutions, with more than a hundred thousand functionaries, have now developed a constituency of their own that is intimately linked with the power structures at the local levels.

One must also add that the emerging political conflict in Pakistan should not be seen as one between the government and the PPP only; there is also involved in the conflict a third party—the Jamaᶜat-i-Islami and the ᶜulama. The opponents of PPP may be divided among themselves, but as a "free-floating" legacy of the 1977 movement against Bhutto they have generally rallied behind President Zia whenever the prospect of PPP comeback seemed real. There is no doubt that the PPP constituency has stayed intact during the difficult years of martial law, but so has the constituency of its opponents. President Zia and his colleagues may leave the political scene, but the Jamaᶜat-i-Islami and the ᶜulama will still be there to continue to agitate for Islam.

## Why There Is No Islamic Radicalism in Pakistan

Compared with its Iranian, Egyptian, and Lebanese counterparts, the Islamic movement in Pakistan—despite some degree of militancy in its rhetoric—has been accommodationist in its ideological orientation and evolutionist in its methodology of change. The revivalist Jamaᶜat-i-Islami is a reformist party that has always upheld constitutional and legal methods to achieve its Islamic objectives. It has publicly disapproved the violent methods adopted by some of its ideological kin in the Middle East and has advocated a policy of peaceful transition from the existing state to an Islamic one. According to Khurshid Ahmad, a prominent theoretician of the Islamic movement in Pakistan, Islamically oriented social change involves the "least friction and disequilibria": it is a "planned and co-ordinated movement from one state of equilibrium to a higher one, or from a state of disequilibrium towards equilibrium." As such, he believes, the Islamic movement will work for a change that is "balanced and gradual and evolutionary."[31] Mawlana Mawdudi, the founder of the Jamaᶜat-i-Islami, eschewed violence and was a great believer in the ultimate triumph of Islamic forces through democratic elections. He hoped that if the Islamic movement kept on educating people and striving patiently, it would one day succeed in bringing righteous men to power.[32] Changes of political leadership brought about through street demonstrations, palace revolutions, coup d'etats, and assassinations, according to Mawdudi, were not only Islamically unjustifiable but also detrimental to the prospects for a permanent and lasting Islamic change. He emphasized that both the ends and the means must be "clean and commendable" in order that a healthy and peaceful Islamic order could take shape.[33]

This "soft" approach toward Islamization can also be explained with reference to Pakistan's political culture. Despite periodic military coups and prolonged periods of martial law, the normative appeal of the British legacy of constitutional democracy and the rule of law, including an independent judiciary, political parties, and free press, has not diminished.

Even during the martial law regimes, political groups of all persuasions have continued to operate, albeit under some restrictions, and have taken advantage of the freedoms available to them under the constitution. Thus, when the Jamᶜat-i-Islami was banned by Field Marshal Muhammad Ayub Khan in 1964, the Supreme Court of Pakistan came to the party's rescue and declared the government's action null and void. Although Pakistani regimes have been against both the right- and left-wing radical groups, they have never been as repressive and vindictive as were the regimes of the Shah in Iran and Naser in Egypt. One can argue that it is usually the repressive policies of the governments and the total absence of freedom to pursue normal political activities that tend to drive religious political groups to radicalism and violent methods of change. Another explanation—related to the political culture theory—could be that the state in Pakistan, unlike the states in Iran and Egypt, is officially designated as Islamic. It could not therefore possibly ban Islamic groups that claimed to derive their political legitimacy from the ideological foundations of the Pakistani statehood.

Moreover, unlike the Takfir wal-Hijra group of Egypt and Saudi dissidents who seized control of the Kaᶜaba in 1979, the Pakistani Islamic groups do not exist on the fringe; rather, they are very much in the mainstream of Islamic religious thought and hence do not suffer from the rejection complex that often drives the minority-based, peripheral movements to adopt violent means.

Finally, the reformist and nonmilitant approach of the Islamic groups in Pakistan can also be related to their social bases of support. As has been shown elsewhere,[34] the rank and file of the Islamic parties consists of the lower sections of the new middle classes and the traditional petite bourgeoisie. These groups react with equal resentment against social and economic deprivations at the hands of upper social classes and government bureaucrats, on one hand, and against the increasing militancy of the lower classes, on the other. What is important to note here is that these groups are neither against capitalism nor against the state per se. In line with the programs of the Islamic political parties, they are primarily seeking reform, improvement, and "purification" of the institutions in order to facilitate their own entry into them. It is in this context of making the system more open, fair, and honest rather than in that of demolishing the existing system of social rewards that the thrust of the struggle of these groups and their Islamic spokesmen should be understood.

## Islamic Revivalism and the West

While Islamization in Pakistan has witnessed a notable surge in Islamic aware-ness and a search for Islamic alternatives in intellectual thought and socioeco-nomic practices, it has not, in any significant way, resulted in hostility to, and outright rejection of, the West. Islamic revivalist experience in Pakistan, unlike its counterparts in Iran and Egypt, has followed the philosophical positions of Muhammad Iqbal (d. 1938) and Abul al-ᶜAla Mawdudi (d. 1979), founder of the Jamaᶜat-i-Islami Pakistan, rather than those of Sayyid Qutb (d. 1966) and Aya-tullah Khumaini. Although Mawdudi was not oblivious to the impact of external factors (such as British rule in India and European colonialism in the Arab World), his primary emphasis remained on the failure of the Muslim elite to divert the destiny of their people toward Islam. Mawdudi's and Iqbal's major targets of attack were the Muslim kings, the ᶜulama, the Sufis, and the nobility—whom they castigated for their political intrigues, intellectual stagnation, spiri-tual bankruptcy, and worldliness—and not the West.

Mawdudi and Iqbal did not see any fundamental contradiction between Islam and the West. On the contrary, they saw that the intellectual, scientific, and technological progress of the modern West represented only an extension of the very principles first propounded by Islam.

It is because of this philosophical tradition that, in Pakistan, at the levels of both governmental policies and the ideological orientations of major Islamic groups, it is not the West but the Soviet Union and its communist ideology that are perceived as principal adversaries. Thus, Islamic revivalism in Pakistan has not been accompanied by any significant signs of anti-Westernism. On the contrary, Islamic revivalism in Pakistan has coincided with renewed friendship and long-term economic and military relations with the United States. As is evident from several survey data, despite differences with the United States on its policies on the Arab-Israeli conflict and Pakistan's nuclear program, relationships with Washington have enjoyed a fairly high degree of public sup-port among the Pakistanis.

As a matter of fact, a nationally representative survey with a sample of sev-enteen hundred scientifically selected households across Pakistan indicated that support for economic and military relations with the United States was sub-stantially higher among Islamic revivalist groups than among the general popu-lation in 1984 (table 1).

Although support for relations with the United States can be linked with the developments in Afghanistan, it would not be correct to maintain that it is entirely "a direct outcome" of the Afghanistan situation.[35] A survey of seventy-five ᶜulama in Pakistan in 1975 showed that despite their strong criticism of American social and cultural life and its influence on Muslim societies, the Pakistani religious leaders preferred relations with the United States six times more than relations with the Soviet Union (table 2).

TABLE 1.
**Attitudes toward Pakistan's Military
and Economic Relations with the United States, 1984**

| Group | Percent of respondents | | |
| --- | --- | --- | --- |
| | Support | Oppose | Don't know |
| All Pakistan | 60 | 9 | 31 |
| Muslim League voters | 78 | 12 | 10 |
| Jamaᶜat-i-Islami voters | 81 | 6 | 13 |
| Jamᶜiyyat-i-ᶜUlama-i-Pakistan voters | 74 | 11 | 15 |
| Jamᶜiyyat-i-ᶜUlama-i-Islam voters | 80 | 5 | 15 |
| Pakistan Peoples Party voters | 49 | 17 | 34 |

Source: Pakistan Institute of Public Opinion National Survey.

Thus, general perceptions based on Iran or Lebanon where anti-Americanism is rooted primarily in the intimate involvement of the United States in the domestic and foreign affairs of these countries, are exceedingly misleading.[36] In most of the Muslim world, the extent to which revivalist movements are anti-United States is directly related to U.S. policies toward the Arab-Israeli conflict. However, these movements are not as a rule anti-Western; nor is anti-Americanism an integral part of their ideologies. Thus, for example, in Pakistan, the Sudan, Malaysia, Turkey, Saudi Arabia, and the Gulf states, mainstream revivalist movements are cooperating with the current pro-Western and pro-U.S. regimes.

## Conclusions

Among Muslim societies, the Pakistani case of Islamic revivalism is unique in many respects. First of all, because Islam is the very raison d'être of the Pakistani state, a built-in revivalist potential has always been there. Second, Islamic revival in Pakistan came about as a result of an alliance between the state and the religious sector and not in the form of a confrontation between the two. Third, although the religious sector is divided into various factions because of sectarian and juristic differences, the dichotomy between what is described in the context of Egypt and the Gulf states as "establishment Islam" and "popular Islam"—the latter being the source of Islamic militancy—does not exist in Pakistan. Fourth, unlike the revivalism in Iran, Islamic revival in Pakistan has not come about through a sociopolitical revolution but in the wake of a military coup d'etat—although the military takeover was preceded by a broad-based Islamic movement. Fifth, the state-sponsored Islamization consisted mainly of legal and institutional changes in certain selected areas of public life and has not significantly affected the distribution of economic resources

TABLE 2.
Attitudes of ᶜUlama toward Pakistan's Relations
with the United States and the Soviet Union, 1975

| | Percent of respondents | | | |
| | Favor U.S. | Favor USSR | Favor neither | Don't know |
| --- | --- | --- | --- | --- |
| All ᶜulama | 64 | 10 | 22 | 4 |
| Jamaᶜat-i-Islami-ᶜulama | 72 | 2 | 26 | 0 |
| Jamᶜiyyat-i-ᶜUlama-i-Pakistan ᶜulama | 68 | 8 | 21 | 3 |
| Jamᶜiyyat-i-ᶜUlama-i-Islam ᶜulama | 52 | 25 | 19 | 4 |
| Nonpolitical ᶜulama | 64 | 5 | 22 | 9 |

Source: Author's survey.

and political power in society. Sixth, the state-sponsored Islamization preempted the demands for more radical changes and prevented the Islamic activists from taking independent initiative. Seventh, the conservative resta-bilization of sociocultural life in the wake of Islamization was not met with any significant resistance by the liberal-modernist groups in society, despite Pa-kistan's rich tradition of liberal-modernist Islamic thought. Moveover, many of the well-known liberals of yesteryear have now become the arch champions of today's conservatism. Eighth, although Islam has helped legitimize the military regime and has contributed to the maintenance of a degree of political stability, the Islamization programs have also created sectarian tensions and interjuristic group rivalries.

Finally, in the main, Islamic revivalism in Pakistan has been concerned with domestic issues; its foreign policy agenda has been limited to Afghanistan, which, in effect, became a major issue linking Islamic resistance to the Soviet occupation of a fellow Muslim country with the worldwide resurgence of Islam. Despite a social conservatism and a kind of moral-psychological alienation from the Western cultural symbols and institutions, however, both the government of President Zia-ul-Haq and the major Islamic revivalist groups have tended to define Pakistan's growing relations with the Islamic world on one hand and with the United States on the other in harmonious rather than conflictual terms.

# NOTES

The author wishes to acknowledge Professor Mohammad Umar Memon and Bany Lerner for their helpful comments during the preparation of this chapter.

1. See Mumtaz Ahmad, "Parliament, Parties, Polls and Islam: Issues in the Current Debate on Religion and Politics in Pakistan," *American Journal of Islamic Social Sciences*, Vol. 1, No. 3 (April 1985), and Leonard Binder, *Religion and Politics in Pakistan* (Berkeley: University of California Press, 1961).

2. See Hafeez Malik, *Moslem Nationalism in India and Pakistan*, 2d ed. (Lahore: People's Publishing House, 1980), pp. 228–267 and pp. 293–300.

3. On the critical role of Islam in the Pakistan movement, see Ishtiaq Hussain Qureshi, *The Struggle for Pakistan*, 2d ed. (Karachi: Maʿarif, 1977); Khalid Bin Sayeed, *Pakistan: The Formative Phase*, 1857–1948, 2d ed. (Karachi: Oxford University Press, 1968), Part 1; and Sharif al Mujahid, *Ideological Orientation of Pakistan* (Islamabad: National Committee for the Birth Centenary Celebration of Qaid-i-Azam Mohammad Ali Jinnah, 1976). For a brief and perceptive critique of this approach, see C.M. Naim, Afterword, in Naim, ed., *Iqbal, Jinnah and Pakistan: The Vision and the Reality* (Syracuse, N.Y.: Syracuse University, Maxwell School of Citizenship and Public Affairs, 1979), pp. 177–188.

4. Sharif al Mujahid, *Ideological Orientation*.

5. Ibid., p. 152.

6. *The Constituent Assembly of Pakistan Debates*, Vol. 5, No. 1, pp. 1–7, quoted in William Theodore de Bary, ed., *Sources of Indian Tradition*, Vol. 2 (New York: Columbia University Press, 1958), p. 294.

7. Ibid., p. 295.

8. Mumtaz Ahmad, "Class, Power and Religion: Some Aspects of Islamic Fundamentalism in Pakistan," paper presented at the Conference on Islamic Revival, Center for Middle Eastern Studies, University of Chicago, May 28–31, 1980, pp. 27–30; and Mumtaz Ahmad, "Islamic Revival in Pakistan," in Cyriac K. Pullapilly, ed., *Islam in the Contemporary World* (Notre Dame, Ind.: Cross Roads Books, 1981).

9. See General Muhammad Zia-ul-Haq, *Interviews to Foreign Media* (Islamabad: Ministry of Information and Broadcasting, n.d.), Vol. 1, pp. 18–21, 67–70, 117–124, and 200–205.

10. *Dawn* (Karachi), Oct. 27, 1982.

11. *Muslim* (Islamabad), June 10, 1980.

12. For specific references to this argument by General Zia, see *Dawn* (Karachi), July 4, 1980, and Aug. 26, 1980; and *Muslim* (Islamabad), June 10, 1980. For a more sophisticated and subtle formulation of this, see Brig. (Retd.) A.R. Siddiqi, "Need for a New Civil-Military Equation," *Dawn* (Karachi), Sept. 6, 1980. Justice (Retd.) Qaderuddin Ahmed also agreed with the broad outlines of this argument. See his article, "The Form of Government People Desire," *The Universal Message* (Karachi), Vol. 4, No. 12 (May 1983), p. 13. A somewhat different formulation, which also tended to legitimize the military rule in Islamic terms, was presented in an editorial comment in a Jamaʿat-i-Islami publication.

13. *Dawn* (Karachi), Jan. 1, 1980, and *Muslim* (Islamabad), Feb. 2, 1980.

14. Michael C. Hudson, "Islam and Political Development," in John L. Esposito, ed., *Islam and Development* (Syracuse, N.Y.: Syracuse University Press, 1980), pp. 16–18.

15. Muhammad A. Quddus, *Pakistan: A Case Study of a Plural Society* (Columbia, Mo.: South Asia Books, 1982), p. 17.

16. Khalid Bin Sayeed, *The Political System of Pakistan* (Boston: Houghton Mifflin, 1967), pp. 182–193.

17. Quddus, *Pakistan*, pp. 17–18. Sayeed, *Political System*, pp. 183–184, reported a survey of Pakistani university students in the mid-1960s which showed that 87 percent of West Pakistani students regarded Islam as an effective bond of unity between the eastern and western wings of the country.

18. *Dawn* (Karachi), July 1, 1965, quoted in Sharif al Mujahid, "Bangladesh: Was It a Failure of Ideology?" *Impact International* (London), July 12–Aug. 8, 1974, p. 9.

19. For a penetrating study of the attitudes and responses of the Pakistani creative writers to the 1971 national disaster and its emotional and moral significance for the intelligentsia, see Muhammad Umar Memon, "Pakistani Urdu Creative Writing on National Disintegration: The Case of Bangladesh," *The Journal of Asian Studies*, Vol. 42, No. 1 (November 1983), pp. 105–127.

20. The first public reaction of the Islamic parties and their student organizations after the fall of Dacca in December 1971 was to demand a ban on alcoholic drinks since, according to them, liquor was responsible for this national tragedy and humiliation. One could see posters with the slogan "What broke up the country? Liquor!" everywhere on the walls in the big cities. It was obviously a reference to President General Yahya Khan's "un-Islamic" personal life and his reputation as a drunkard.

21. For a comparative study of Pakistani and Egyptian experiences, see Ali E. Hillal Dessouki, "The Resurgence of Islamic Organizations in Egypt: An Interpretation," in Dessouki and Alexander S. Cudsi, eds., *Islam and Power* (Baltimore: Johns Hopkins University Press, 1981), pp. 113–116; John Waterbury, "Egypt: Islam and Social Change," in Philip H. Stoddard et al., eds., *Change and the Muslim World* (Syracuse, N.Y.: Syracuse University Press, 1981), pp. 54–56; Yvonne Haddad, "The Arab-Israeli Wars, Nasserism and the Affirmation of Islamic Identity," in Esposito, ed., *Islam and Development*, pp. 107–121; G.H. Jansen, *Militant Islam* (New York: Harper and Row, 1979), p. 121; and John L. Esposito, *Islam and Politics* (Syracuse, N.Y.: Syracuse University Press, 1984), pp. 153–155.

22. See two recent editorial articles, in al-e-Hadith group's weekly magazine, *Al-Islam* (Lahore), Nov. 22, 1985, and in the Deobandi group's monthly magazine, *Al-Bayyanat* (Karachi), November 1985. Also see the editorial in the monthly organ of the Jama°at-i-Islami, *Tarjuman-al-Quran* (Lahore), November 1985.

23. See, for example, the speech of the president of Jama°at-i-Islami, Mian Tufail Mohammad, at a gathering of Pakistani workers in Saudi Arabia as reported in *Jasarat* (Karachi), Feb. 24, 1983.

24. The °ulama have mostly protested against the non-observance of certain Islamic moral rules, especially those pertaining to segregation of sexes. See the editorial in a Deobandi magazine, *Al-Khair* (Multan), November 1985.

25. See, for example, chapters by Aijaz Ahmad, Hasan N. Gardezi, and Zia-ul-Haq in Hasan Gardezi and Jamil Rashid, eds., *Pakistan: The Roots of Dictatorship* (London: Zed Press, 1983), and Tariq Ali, *Can Pakistan Survive?* (London: Penguin Books, 1983), pp. 133–162.

26. Murder and attempted murder cases increased from 10,760 in 1979 to 13,952 in 1984. See Government of Pakistan, Statistical Division, *Monthly Statistical Bulletin*, Vol. 28, No. 6, June 1980, p. 96, and Vol. 33, No. 10, October 1985, p. 163.

27. *Economist* (London), Mar. 26, 1983, p. 40.

28. Mumtaz Ahmad, "The Military and Search for Legitimacy in Pakistan," unpublished manuscript, 1985, p. 9.

29. It is no wonder that when some military courts ordered public flogging of certain criminals and political workers—a carry-over from British rule—the Western media were quick to describe these incidents as evidence of "Islamic justice."

30. See the editorial note in a *Deobandi* magazine, *Al-Haq* (Akora Khatak-Peshawar), November 1985, in which the editor, Maulana Sami-ul-Haq—himself a senator from the Northwest Frontier Province—expresses his irritation over "the time-consuming" parliamentary procedures causing delay in the passage of the Shari°a bill.

31. Khurshid Ahmad, "Economic Development in an Islamic Framework," in Ahmad, ed., *Studies in Islamic Economics* (Leicester, England: Islamic Foundation, 1980), p. 177.

32. Khurshid Ahmad and Zafar Ishaq Ansari, "Mawlana Sayyid Abul A°la Maududi: An Introduction to His Vision of Islam and Islamic Revival," in Ahmad and Ansari, eds., *Islamic Perspectives* (Leicester, England: Islamic Foundation, 1979), pp. 378–380.

33. Ibid, p. 381.

34. Ahmad, "Class, Religion, and Power," pp. 11–25.

35. Ijaz S. Gilani, *The Four "R"s of Afghanistan: Refugees, Resistance, Regime, Russia* (Islamabad Pakistan Institute of Public Opinion, n.d.), p. 24.

36. For example, the perceptions of Daniel Pipes, *In the Path of God: Islam and Political Power* (New York: Basic Books, 1983).

# XV

# MALAYSIA AND INDONESIA

## Fred R. von der Mehden

A review of much of the foreign reporting and government rhetoric of the past half-dozen years could easily mislead the outside observer as to the character of the Islamic revival in Malaysia and Indonesia. Newspapers and news magazines from both within and outside of the region have made references to "Islamic extremism" or "another Iran?" and have heavily publicized acts of violence associated with religious tensions. On their part, the authorities in Jakarta and Kuala Lumpur have also given considerable publicity to violent incidents in an effort to control more moderate Muslim opponents by tainting some aspects of religious activism with extremism, sedition, and violence. This reporting has all too often treated what has come to be called the Islamic revival as of one cloth, rather than recognizing the variations within the movement. This chapter will concentrate on the varied character of the changes taking place in the Islamic world of Malaysia and Indonesia and the factors responsible for their development. But first, there will be an assessment of the political and religious environment.[1]

### Political Setting

While Islam is the majority religion of both Malaysia and Indonesia, considerable differences exist between the two. In the former, Islam is the faith of approximately half the population and is closely associated with Malay ethnicity. Almost all Malays are Muslims, with a scattering of Muslims among other indigenous people, and some Chinese converts plus those of Arab and Pakistani descent. The rest of the population is primarily Chinese (approximately 35 percent) and Indian. Malaysian Islam is more homogeneous than Indonesian Islam, with a high level of conservatism and emphasis on the ritualistic elements of the faith. Until recently, extreme regional theological influences have been less significant in Malaysian Islam, giving it a certain parochialism. Finally, there has always been a substantial animist substratum of belief affecting attitudes or behavior among Muslims; Buddhist and Hindu elements have not been particularly strong.[2]

Indonesia's population is approximately 90 percent Muslim, but this apparent homogeneity hides considerable variation. On one level there is the division between the more orthodox strains of Islam and a strain more conditioned by Javanese mystical elements arising out of pre-Islamic influences (sometimes called *santri* and *abangan*). This *agama Java* or *kepercayaan* belief system is accepted by the majority of the people of Java (who compose about two-thirds of the nation's population). Other divisions reflect differences between modernist and traditional schools and those local practices and beliefs rooted in the great cultural mosaic of the islands. Indonesians have long been active participants in the *hajj* (pilgrimage to Makka). Thus, the impact of Middle Eastern intellectual currents has been stronger there than elsewhere in Southeast Asia.[3]

The political environment also deeply influences the Islamic revival in these two states. Malaysia is a limited competitive democracy ruled since independence by a multiracial coalition (now called the National Front), which in turn has been dominated by its Malay partner, the United Malays National Organization (UMNO). The pluralist character of the Front, composed as it is of Malay, Chinese, and Indian parties, demands a delicate balance of policies so as to maintain stability within the coalition. Its opposition comes from Chinese who see the Front's Chinese partners, the Malaysian Chinese Association (MCA) and Gerakan, as compromising their people's interests and from the Partai Islam Se-Malaysia (PAS), a Malay Muslim party that wants greater support for their ethnic-religious interests. It is therefore incumbent upon the UMNO leadership to both react to the demands of its Malay-Muslim constituency within and outside of the party and to retain the delicate balance in the coalition.

In these circumstances, the Islamic revival presents the government with a difficult set of problems. It is necessary for UMNO to placate the rising sense of religious consciousness among Muslims if it is to continue to garner the majority of Malay voters and hold off its Malay-Islamic opposition. However, by expressing solidarity with Islamic activism other issues arise. To the extent that the government is perceived by other communal elements as too strongly Muslim, it can endanger their support of the Front as well as exacerbate religioethnic tensions. There is also the possibility that by actively supporting the growing Islamic movement it may strengthen those Muslim forces that demand even stricter adherence to the Islamic cause. Until the last election, no such difficulties faced the Front's Chinese and Malay opposition. Since neither belonged to an intercommunal coalition, there was no need to compromise with other groups and a more purely ethnic or religious program was possible. On the other hand, every move to reinforce the pluralist nature of the coalition is further grist for PAS and can increase Muslim self-consciousness.

In Indonesia, by contrast, the government controls the electoral and party structure and is not as encumbered by the intricacies of a competitive democratic state. Also, the ruling military-bureaucratic elite largely adheres to the Javanese interpretation of Islam and feels little need to placate the orthodox Islamic minority. The latter is divided politically and religiously and does not pose a serious challenge to the present regime's power and thus has been the object of coercive rather than co-optive policies. The Islamic revival is thus viewed as a potential danger to the authorities because it could solidify the orthodox community and present a view of Islam contrary to that of the government. Meanwhile, violent actions by Muslim radicals enable Jakarta to control moderate Muslims on the pretext of eliminating religious extremism.

## Manifestations of Revivalism

Assessments of the many manifestations of the Islamic revival will focus on five major aspects: (1) radical groups, (2) *dakwah* and religious expression, (3) international influences, (4) changing personal practices and attitudes, and (5) political tensions. Many of these elements simultaneously tend to reinforce and undermine the revivalist cause.

### The Radicals

The manifestations of the recent Islamic revival in Southeast Asia have centered on a series of violent acts allegedly involving radical elements of the movement. The extensive coverage given these events has resulted only in part from their inherent dramatic aspects. Both the Malaysian and Indonesian authorities have given considerable attention to these acts of violence or conspiracies to undermine the state. Many Muslim moderates have charged that this emphasis has been part of a concerted effort, particularly in Indonesia, to discredit the Islamic revival by tainting it with extremism.

There is no doubt that in the last decade the number of violent activities seemingly related to Islamic activists has increased. Meanwhile the movement's leaders have been accused of conspiracies that are hard to prove. In Malaysia, the three major cases involving radical Muslim groups took place in 1978, 1980, and January 1985. In the first instance, a group of primarily Indian Muslims was caught and tried for their depredation of Hindu temples. In 1980 there was an attack on a rural police station by a small party of white-robed individuals led by Muhammad Naser, who said that he was attempting to cleanse the country of evil and establish an Islamic state. In the process, eight members of the assault group were killed and a number of civilians were injured. This was a fringe group with ties to Cambodian Muslims.[4] The most recent and violent event involved a police attack on an "extremist" Muslim leader and his followers, resulting in eighteen deaths. There were charges and countercharges regarding what precipitated the action.[5] None of these cases seriously endangered the government's stability.

Indonesia has also experienced a series of violent acts allegedly carried out by generally isolated Muslim organizations, with at least one case with considerable public involvement. An early dramatic incident was the hijacking of an Indonesian passenger plane, which ended with the storming of the aircraft in Bangkok by Indonesian commandos. This was perpetrated by an organization calling for an Islamic state and the ending of "yellow culture" in the country. Another group, the Gerakan Pemuda Islam (Islamic Youth Movement), was accused of destroying a shopping center and there have been a number of arson attacks on shopping centers since. In 1984 Muslim extremists were accused of placing bombs in the historic Buddhist Borobadur monument outside the city of Jogjakarta. The most dramatic event, known as the Tanjung Priok riots, occurred in September 1984.[6]

During 1984 there had been an increase in Islamic activity in the North Jakarta area with religious teachers emphasizing themes such as morality, the importance of following religious laws, and the duty to fight unbelievers. Of particular interest to the government were attacks on vice, official corruption, and efforts by authorities to enforce the government's Pancha Sila ideology on the Islamic community.[7] During the early part of the month, officials had entered a prayer house in the district looking for illegal leaflets and reportedly threatening the people. Following an incident in which several alleged activists were arrested, the local preachers began to increase their cries for the protection of Islam and freeing of the detainees. This culminated in a march on the local police and military subcommand headquarters with the crowd continually chanting "God is great." At this point, there is a difference of opinion as to who started the violence, but government forces fired on the crowd, reportedly killing some sixty-three persons, and wounding severely another one hundred. Some Muslims accused General Murdani of the Operational Command of leading the attack and being a Christian and Zionist out to destroy the Islamic community. These events were followed by other criticisms from Muslim leaders and a series of trials for sedition.

The Indonesian situation differs from the Malaysian in several respects. The radicals' activities appear to be more widespread and enjoy broader popular support. Rhetorical attacks have been targeted more directly on government acts and policies. In Malaysia, demands have been primarily in terms of the need to establish an Islamic state and the purification of the society, with relatively less antagonism expressed against the government in power. Here I am viewing as different in character the small radical groups and the political party PAS, an organization that does castigate the government on religious grounds. Indonesian radicals have sought goals similar to their Malaysian counterparts, but have also focused on alleged transgressions of the Suharto government and specific policies perceived as inimicable to Islamic interests. Preachings criticizing corruption, tyranny, and the Pancha Sila have been frequent in contemporary Indonesia. In part, this can be explained in terms of the two governments' different approaches toward the Islamic movement: Kuala Lumpur seeking accommodation and Jakarta opting for confrontation.

## Dakwah and Religious Expression

A second manifestation of the religious revival has been an apparent expansion of dakwah activities and religiopolitical expression in terms of preaching, leaflets, and other publications. The dakwah movement, particularly in terms of earlier Muhammadiya activities in Indonesia and contemporary organizations in Malaysia, has been amply documented elsewhere.[8] Broadly speaking, there have been three types of dakwah movements in postwar Indonesia and Malaysia. The first has been the large-scale organization primarily committed to reinforcing Islamic identity among the faithful, increasing their knowledge of their religion, and providing a bridge between the modern world and fundamental Islamic values. While there may be some interest in the conversion of non-Muslims, this has not been the major task. The two most notable examples of such organizations have been the Muhammadiya and the Angkatan Belia Islam Malaysia (ABIM). The former is a product of the modernist movement of the prewar era and is illustrative of the existence of elements of an Islamic revival that predate present patterns. The Muhammadiya was and is an officially non-political organization intent on expanding the horizons of Indonesian Muslims through educational, social, and cultural programs. It has organized and maintained schools, orphanages, clinics, and other social action programs, as well as attempting to synthesize religious values and modernization. While formally nonpolitical, it allied itself with anticolonialism during the Dutch period and with liberal causes after independence. In recent years it has been at odds with the Suharto government over the independent operation of its schools and has reacted negatively toward making the Pancha Sila Indonesia's ideology. While essentially nonviolent, it has allied itself with other organizations attempting to maintain and expand Islam's role in Indonesian society.[9]

ABIM has been the largest Islamic youth group in Malaysia, claiming some thirty thousand members and large numbers of supporters. It has concentrated on educational and social programs, although it has been involved in ill-fated entrepreneurial activities. While it also is supposedly nonpolitical, ABIM has become involved in many issues characterized as political by the government. For many years its policies reflected its charismatic leader, Anwar Ibrahim.[10]

As president of the organization, Ibrahim espoused a multiethnic and multireligious Malaysia but sought to enhance the Muslims' Islamic identity. He argued that Islam does not simply mean adherence to ritual but stands for such fundamental beliefs as democracy and social justice. While he denied that he was a religious socialist, his rhetoric sounded much like that of Islamic socialists in postwar Indonesia. He briefly supported the Iranian revolution, visited Iran, and expressed his admiration for certain changes.[11] But he came to deny the validity of imitating Iran and criticized some Iranian policies. In fact, he was often privately appalled by what he perceived as overly narrow thinking among Middle Eastern revivalists and commented that Malaysia's multicommunal citizenry would not allow the kind of Islamic political and social environment envisioned by these spokesmen. He also flirted with a political career with the opposition, but UMNO co-opted him and he became minister of education and a likely prime minister. Since then, ABIM has adopted a more conservative and less pluralist approach to Malaysia's communal situation and has been severely challenged on campus by PAS.

The second type of dakwah organization has been more proselytizing. While a number of moderate and conservative Muslims in both countries have called for a totally Muslim society or attacked Christian influence, missionary activists have generally not sought such goals.[12] The Malaysian dakwah association best known for its proselytizing efforts is PERKIM (Islamic Welfare and Missionary Association), which originated from the Malayan Prime Minister's Office.[13] Although Perkim is involved in other dakwah activities, it receives its greatest publicity from its proselytizing campaigns on the Islam Chinese, Indians, and tribal peoples. Often claiming major coups in conversion, PERKIM has been moderately successful because its campaigns and publicity have raised fears among the nation's nonIslamic populations that Islam will become a requirement for being Malaysian; and it has been accused by competing dakwah groups of seeking numbers rather than real commitment. Be that as it may, the considerable attention shown PERKIM is a further illustration of the Malaysian government's interest in expanding Islam's place in the society.

Finally, there is a variety of smaller nongovernmental organizations catering to particular groups or interpretations of Islam. These have grown in number and prominence over the past decade. Examples would be the now weakened Darul Arqam, known for its commune and school in Malaysia as well as its involvement in economic programs and its traditional-modern clinic. Darul Arqam is viewed as a conservative movement expressed through the traditional patterns apparent in its educational philosophy, medical practices, dress, and ascetic manners. It also displays strong Malay chauvinism and suspicions of foreign influences, including Chinese economic interests. Another relatively exclusionist dakwah organization is the Jama'at Tabligh, whose past and present Indian character has been diluted by efforts to carry its message to the Malay community. A loosely structured, all-male association, it lacks a sharp ideological focus.

Informal meetings and transitory associations seeking to bring their messages to the people have also proliferated in Indonesia and in Malaysia, and entail religiopolitical ramifications. In Indonesia, groups centering on mosques and prayer halls have become the main critics of the Suharto regime's policies. Recent sedition trials have targeted individuals and associations on Java, Sumatra, and even parts of the outer islands, charging them with the publication and distribution of leaflets and the preaching of seditious or "deviant" sermons.[14] Without accepting the government's definition of sedition, it appears obvious that the number of such activities has grown and a network among Muslim organizations seeking to publicize their positions has developed. *Ceramahs* (religious lectures with political overtones) have become popular and are finding their way in printed form or cassette to wider audiences.[15]

Similarly, in Malaysia the government is concerned with ceramah and religious publications. Traditionally, in Malaysian politics, local ᶜulama have been involved in UMNO-PAS politics and ceramah and speeches frequently have been employed to aid local candidates. This partisanship has reached such levels that the authorities have found it necessary to attempt to halt the practice of ᶜulama, calling opponents *kafir* (unbeliever) and withholding their services from such "infidels." More recently, there have been fears that ceramahs have been used to propagate deviant religious views and that local religious leaders have been misleading the faithful.

An example of this type of development was the so-called Memali incident and its aftermath.[16] In late 1985, a politicoreligious leader and teacher, Ibrahim Mahmud, called "Libya," had gathered around himself a relatively large number of followers. Ibrahim had a warrant against him and was suspected of "deviant" religious teachings. He had established a school in a poor rural area of Kedah that was a stronghold of PAS, the more radical Muslim party opponent of UMNO. Some two hundred police attacked his compound, only to be met by villagers prepared to resist. The result was the death of fourteen villagers, including Ibrahim, and four policemen; twenty-nine people were injured and 160 villagers arrested, including women and children as young as eleven years old (the villagers were later released). Fearing that ceramah would be used by PAS to stir up the people against the government, the authorities banned ceramah temporarily in all or part of six states. The issue of how and why the events of November 1985 happened remains a point of religious and political contention and illustrates how volatile the mixture of politics and differing religious interpretations has become.

## International Activities

When asked by an American colleague whether it was possible to visit Malaysia during an international Islamic meeting, a prominent Malaysian cabinet minister facetiously remarked, "That's easy, we have one a week." This was an exaggeration, but no doubt international contacts of Malaysian and Indonesian Muslims have greatly increased. There has been a major increase in private interaction, while the number of Muslims from both Malaysia and Indonesia taking the hajj has increased markedly during the postwar era, reaching some 70,000 by the 1980s.[17] Malaysian pilgrims have almost tripled, from 5,229 in 1965 to 14,846 in 1980.[18] There has also been an expansion of contacts between Southeast Asian scholars, religious leaders, politicians, and colleagues and their Islamic counterparts.

Involvement in regional and international Islamic organizations has also become commonplace. The Malaysian government has both been represented in international conferences abroad and hosted them in Kuala Lumpur. There has been Southeast Asian representation and often leadership in such organizations as WAMY (the World Assembly of Muslim Youths), Islamic Call Society, Asia-Pacific Mosque Council, Regional Islamic Daᶜwa Council of Southeast Asia and the Pacific, and a wide variety of economic, social, and political associations dealing with Islamic issues. Tenku Abdul Rahman, Malaysia's first prime minister, and Anwar Ibrahim have been particularly active in Islamic international organizations.

There has also been more interest in and a greater reaction to events in the rest of the Islamic world. An interest in developments in the Middle East is not new. In fact, during World War I, Indonesian loyalty to the Caliphate was thought to be serious enough to worry Dutch authorities and after the war there were efforts to become involved in the Caliphate movement and pan-Islamic organizations.[19] However, this was generally an elite preoccupation and only recently has extended into the general population. Issues and events in the Middle East such as the Palestinian cause, the attack in Makka, and the invasion of Afghanistan are widely covered, often generating high emotions, demonstrations, and considerable discussion.

Finally, foreign governments have attempted to influence Muslims in Southeast Asia. In some cases this has been acceptable, as with Middle Eastern support of the new International Islamic University recently established on the outskirts of Kuala Lumpur. It has also been pictured as undesirable, as with the charges of Libyan and Iranian interference in the domestic affairs of Indonesia or alleged efforts to export the Iranian revolution to the region. In the former case, authorities in Jakarta have alleged that radical groups have sought Libyan support. There are frequent rumors, usually unproven, of Libyan money being employed to aid Muslim causes in the region. No doubt the increased religious interests and international contacts of Southeast Asian Muslims make them an attractive target.

## Personal Behavior

For frequent visitors to Southeast Asia during the past two decades, there are obvious outward changes reflecting a greater sense of Islamic identity. In Malaysia, there has been a marked increase in more conservative dress among Malay women and some dakwah groups have taken to Arabic ways. The government initially encouraged conservative attire but has recently criticized an overemphasis on the emulation of Middle Eastern traditional dress. In both countries, observers have commented on the increased numbers, especially of young people, appearing at Friday prayers or joining Islamic organizations.[20] The population also seems to have become more observant of religious rituals. In Indonesia, there has been a trend away from more mystical Javanese interpretations of Islam and toward orthodoxy.

Demands for the purification of individuals' life-styles and attacks on immoral Western ways have increased. This is nothing new, and mosque sermons for many years have warned of the dangers of foreign influences. It would appear, however, that there are more attacks on "yellow culture." It is difficult to assess the extent of these sentiments. In Indonesia, however, many devout Muslims' alienation from the present regime reflects their disapproval of their leaders' Western life-styles.[21]

In Malaysia, government policies to propagate Islam have contributed to this trend. In television programming, for example, more attention is given to religious subjects, including prayer times, sermons, Arabic films, and Koranic reading contests. The official rhetoric includes more references to Islam, and government representatives are more likely to be present at Islamic functions. A greater effort is made to ensure the correct observance of religious rituals. There are constant references to the dangers of deviant beliefs and behavior, more attention has been given to the religious education of Muslim youth, and efforts are made to make Islamic religious holidays national in scope.

In the Indonesian case, by contrast, the government's confrontational policies have reinforced a sense of Islamic identity.

## Political Reactions

As might be expected, this Islamic resurgence has been viewed by both governments with some concern.[22] To understand the regional political interactions, it is useful to analyze four elements of the Islamic revivalist movement: the radicals, fundamentalists, revivalists, and traditionalists.

The radicals are those relatively small groups intent upon immediate and fundamental change in the direction of an Islamic state and the purification of the society. The Malaysian and Indonesian authorities have tended to lump together these activists with those sympathetic to extensive change but not committed to violence. The Indonesian regime has been particularly active in targeting those held responsible for preaching, publishing, and distributing material defined as seditious. Both governments have met the radicals' violent acts by force and stiff sentences. Nonviolent deviationism and sedition have been dealt with through a combination of warnings and arrests, with the Indonesian courts recently meting out prison sentences of ten to fifteen years or longer. Also the two governments have used these groups in order to limit the activities of the more moderate forces.

Those classified as fundamentalists here are the religiously conservative activists who look toward strengthening traditional Islamic values and ultimately establishing an Islamic state. They are somewhat suspicious of modernization and lack tolerance toward other faiths. In Indonesia, the backbone of this category tends to be the conservative ᶜulama, madrasa, religious colleges, and elements within the Nahdatul ᶜUlama party. While the government may characterize these individuals and organizations as seditious or deviationist because of their criticism of its policies, activists in this category do not generally support violence or revolutionary change. However, for some of them, conservative religious values may go hand in hand with a penchant for radical economic and social solutions.

PAS in Malaysia reflects this combination of religious conservatism and more radical demands for change, particularly under its new leadership.[23] While PAS has recently called for an opening to other communal elements in the nation and wavered on the issue of special rights for the Malays, it has also attempted to mix social justice issues with its Islamic goals. Its leaders have decried government economic policies as creating a rich Malay class in league with Chinese capitalists and stated that within an Islamic state all would be treated equally. Party president Haji Yusof Rawa proclaimed at a recent youth rally that the nation needed an Islamic constitution and that UMNO misunderstood Islam. He queried, "Have they forgotten that Islam is not for one race but for all on earth?"[24]

Those in control of the Malaysian government have perceived the fundamentalists in general and PAS in particular as serious political challenges to their authority. Yet, their efforts to expand the role of Islam in the society also create an environment propitious to those who wish to move faster toward establishing an Islamic society than they do. PAS has attempted to attract local religious leaders by becoming involved in protests against government actions; that was the case in its expression of sympathy for those attacked in the Memali incident. However, the 1986 parliamentary elections continued to show UMNO strength at the polls and PAS was badly defeated, in part because of an electoral alliance with the largely Chinese DAP.[25]

The third group involved in the Islamic revival is composed of what might be called the revivalists. These are Muslims interested in expanding the role of Islam in society, but achieving this within a modern context. They see the real challenge to Islam to be both to develop within Muslims an understanding of what a commitment to Islam really is and to educate the people as to how that faith can deal with contemporary economic, social, and political issues. Examples previously provided of organizations reflecting these goals would be the Muhammadiyya and ABIM. They present problems to those in political authority in terms of their programs and membership. Arguments that Islam means more than ritual and also includes social justice and egalitarian economic policies are seen as criticism of government policies. For example, individuals within this group have been at the forefront of those questioning the equity of Suharto's development policies. Prime Minister Mahathir is somewhat less vulnerable to such criticisms, given his own recent attacks on the undesirable role of money in UMNO politics and comments that Islam means more than slogans and trifling religious prohibitions. However, the development of a Malay-Muslim capitalist class under the government's New Economic Policy and the alleged collusion of this class with Chinese entrepreneurs have made easy targets for critics of UMNO.[26]

The leadership and membership of the revivalist movement must be a particularly difficult challenge to both governments. These are not poorly educated rural ᶜulama or old-line politicians. Their stands on religion and contemporary issues are especially attractive to the educated youth of both countries and have found fertile ground on local campuses and among students studying abroad. These are individuals who know how to deal with organization, communications, and technological questions. Admittedly, at times they have difficulty in interacting with rural religious leaders and have made rather naive mistakes, but they seem to be learning. Although they tend to define themselves as non-political, they are deeply interested in contemporary problems and there is always the potential for their formal entrance into political life.

These fundamentalist and revivalist challenges have been met differently in Indonesia and Malaysia. In the former there has been the tendency to confront both elements as part of the general orthodox Islamic opposition to the Suharto regime. The government has used its judicial powers and the Pancha Sila as a means of controlling their movements. The government's demand that the Pancha Sila be the sole ideology of the Indonesian people has been perceived by both groups as a direct attack on their fundamental religious beliefs and has probably driven many moderates toward more extreme positions.[27]

In Malaysia the government has tended to use the carrot and stick: it has warned of the dangers of deviationist thinking and threatened to use the force of law, including the sedition act; it has also criticized the imitation of Middle Eastern thoughts and life-styles; and it has countered the fundamentalists' and revivalists' challenge by claiming to be the protector of Islamic values.

Finally, there are the traditionalists, the great majority of Muslims who are not politically and socially active but who want to protect Islam and have become more religiously conscious. They are the targets of the fundamentalists, the reformists, and the governments.

## Factors behind the Revivalist Movement

The factors that have driven the Islamic resurgence in Malaysia and Indonesia are reasonably obvious, including the interaction between tradition and modernity, international influences, and political tensions.

Both countries have been passing through a process of major economic and social development during the past two decades. Malaysia now prides itself on a per capita GNP of over $2,000, literacy of almost 75 percent, and secondary school enrollment of over 50 percent of age group, and an increasing urban population. Although considerably poorer than Malaysia on a per capita basis, Indonesia has now entered the ranks of the middle-income countries. In part, these changes reflect the two governments' commitment to modernization and development, which has in turn fueled the Islamic revival.

Modernization has brought previously traditional and largely rural people in closer contact with Western culture and the modern economic sector. At times, this has produced negative reactions to what is perceived to be a challenge to traditional religious values, with Western culture portrayed as immoral and un-Islamic; hence the ᶜulama's attacks on "yellow culture." With increased communications and mobility, traditional populations have seen their leaders practice life-styles considered questionable—a factor in criticism of the Jakarta-based elite of the Suharto regime.

The efforts of the Malaysian government to upgrade the education of Malay students, bringing a growing number of youths from rural areas to the universities at home and abroad, further exacerbates the situation. At local institutions dakwah organizations such as ABIM and PAS campus organizers attempt to recruit students to their cause. Abroad, Muslim groups are also active and the student confronted by unfamiliar cultures often tends to seek identity within his or her religion.

In the economic realm a somewhat similar pattern exists. The rural Muslim encounters an unfamiliar economic system often controlled by non-Muslims. In urban centers the Chinese, Indians, and Europeans tend to play a dominant role, seemingly validating the charges that the governments have sold out to foreign interests. Rural areas have also been invaded by modern economic investment, often by non-Muslims, which has coalesced the interests of the poorer farmer and the previously more dominant Muslim landowners and entrepreneurs.

As Ruth McVey has observed,

> rural reaction has been blurred by agrarian changes accompanying the spreading capitalist transformation of agriculture and investment in the land by the urban elite: rural religious notables begin to appear less as exploiters of the village poor and more as fellow victims of an urban, capitalist assault on peasant livelihood and values.[29]

This pattern reinforces the revivalists' position of combining religious causes with those of equity and social justice, thereby making the revival even more attractive. For its part, the Malaysian government has attempted to emphasize the interrelationship of modernization and the strengthening of Islam. Mahathir and others have argued that it is essential for Malay Muslims to be able to compete in their own country. Thus they must learn to handle modern technology, managerial tools, and communications. Opponents argue that this only enriches those in power and weakens traditional values.

International influences on the Islamic revival in Southeast Asia are derived from both reactions to events elsewhere and external efforts to influence domestic activities in the area. In the first instance, the religious consciousness of Malaysian and Indonesian Muslims has been raised by events abroad. There is pride in the important role now being played by the oil-rich Islamic world. Better communications allow for greater knowledge of external events and Islamic identity is enhanced in response to what are seen as attacks on other Muslims in the Middle East and Afghanistan.

Foreign governments and international Islamic organizations have also tried to influence Muslims in Southeast Asia. There has been actual and alleged Libyan involvement in the Philippines and Indonesia, and allegations of Iranian propaganda efforts. The Saudis have openly aided missionary and educational programs. The extent to which such activities have influenced the region is open to question and charges of state-planned Libyan or Iranian campaigns in

Indonesia and Malaysia are tenuous. More important has been interaction through membership in international and regional Islamic associations.

The political tensions outlined in this chapter have assuredly been factors in advancing the Islamic revival. In Indonesia, the rising tension between the Suharto regime and orthodox Muslims has intensified the latter's sense of religious identity. Many of these Muslims feel endangered by government actions such as the marriage bill, amalgamation of Muslim parties into one closely watched political organization, the Pancha Sila campaign, and sedition trials against Muslim leaders. Arguably, the government's politics of confrontation may strengthen rather than weaken the Islamic revivalist movement.[30]

In Malaysia, Islamic consciousness has been heightened by the political competition between UMNO and PAS. This is nothing new as both have been active in displaying themselves as the true protectors of Islam and the Malay community for decades.[31] What has changed has been the spread of the Islamic revival, which has come at a time of increased racial tensions because of government plans to implement its New Economic Policy in order to improve the Malays' socioeconomic conditions. This, in turn, has increased the sense of communal identity. UMNO and PAS have attempted to capture this ethnic-religious consciousness and have accelerated their public support for the faith. PAS has always identified itself with the Malay Muslim, as have many UMNO local organizations and parliamentary backbenchers. What is new is that the national leadership and the UMNO elite have become more articulate in their support of Muslim causes. Consequently, the increased religious tone of the rhetoric and implementation of such symbolically important programs as the Islamic Bank, International Islamic University, Koranic reading contests, and Islamic pawnshops have all enhanced Islam's role.

In sum, the political environment of both countries appears to presage the continuation of the Islamic revival. While it is highly doubtful that the radicals and fundamentalists will be able to achieve their goals, it is probable that we will see continued sporadic violence by frustrated activists. More important, the differing policies of Malaysia and Indonesia have helped increase the sense of Islamic identity and this will have long-term influences on their political systems.

# NOTES

1. Fred R. von der Mehden, "Malaysia: Islam and Multiethnic Politics," in J. Esposito, *Islam in Asia* (London: Oxford University Press, 1987), pp. 177–201, and "Political and Social Challenge of the Islamic Revival in Malaysia and Indonesia," *Muslim World*, Vol. 76 (July–October 1986), pp. 219–233.

2. See C. Geertz, *The Religion of Java* (Glencoe, Ill.: Free Press, 1960); R. Winzeler, "Malay Religious Society and Politics in Kelantan," Ph.D. diss., University of Chicago, 1970.

3. See J. Vredenbregt, "The Haddj," *Bijdragen Tot de Taalland en Volkenkunde* 118 (1962), pp. 91–154, and J. Peacock, *Muslim Puritans: Reformist Psychology in Southeast Asian Islam* (Berkeley: University of California Press, 1978).

4. *Far Eastern Economic Review*, Oct. 24 and 31, 1980, and *Asia Week*, June 8, 1979.

5. *Far Eastern Economic Review*, Dec. 5, 1985, and Jan. 16, 1986.

6. For a lengthy account sympathetic to the Muslims, see the political supplement in *Indonesia Reports*, Jan. 15, 1985.

7. The Pancha Sila was the ideological foundation of the Sukarno regime and was later adopted by the Suharto government. Its five principles related to nationalism, internationalism, democracy, social justice, and belief in God. The last point does not refer to Islam specifically and is considered agnostic by many orthodox Muslims.

8. See, for example, J. Nagata, *The Reflowering of Malaysian Islam* (Vancouver: University of British Columbia Press, 1984); B. Boland, *The Struggle of Islam in Modern Indonesia* (The Hague: Nijhoff, 1971); Alfian, "Islamic Modernism in Indonesian Politics: The Muhammadijah during the Dutch Colonial Period (1912–1942)," Ph.D. diss., University of Wisconsin, 1969; and Fred R. von der Mehden, *Religion and Modernization in Southeast Asia* (Syracuse, N.Y.: Syracuse University Press, 1986).

9. Interviews with Muhammadiyya officers, 1984.

10. Some of this information comes from interviews with Anwar Ibrahim, 1981, 1982, and 1984.

11. *Bintang Timur*, May 8, 1979.

12. For example, the then chief minister of Sabah was alleged to have used the powers of his office to convert people to Islam, and former Prime Minister Tengku ᶜAbdul Rahman seemed to support such efforts as a means of bringing unity to the society. See ᶜAbdul Rahman, *Looking Back* (Kuala Lumpur: Pustaka Anatara, 1977). There have also been comments critical of Christian activities by people as varied as officers of the Muhammadiya and writers in *Al-Nahdah*, the magazine of the Regional Islamic Daᶜwa Council of Southeast Asia and the Pacific.

13. See Nagata, *The Reflowering*, pp. 168–174.

14. See *Indonesia Reports*, January 1985 to January 1986.

15. For examples of such talks, see *Indonesia Reports*, August and September 1985.

16. See the *Far Eastern Economic Review*, Dec. 5, 1985, and Jan. 16, 1986, for details of the incident.

17. For a good review of the prewar period, see Vredenbregt, "The Haddj." Later data taken from Saudi Arabia, *Statistical Yearbook*, 1981, and Indonesia, *Statistik Indonesia*, 1980 and 1981 (Jakarta: Biro Pusat Statistik).

18. Saudi Arabia, *Statistical Yearbook*, 1965 and 1981.

19. See Fred R. von der Mehden, *Religion and Nationalism in Southeast Asia* (Madison: University of Wisconsin Press 1963), p. 161.

20. *Christian Science Monitor*, Jan. 2, 1986. Clifford Geertz is said to have commented, "I was amazed. It's strange to me, but true. The younger generation of *abangan* [nominal Muslims] are becoming *santri* [devout Muslims]."

21. See R. McVey, "Faith as the Outsider: Islam in Indonesian Politics," in James P. Piscatori, ed., *Islam in the Political Process* (Cambridge: Cambridge University Press, 1983), pp. 199–225.

22. For more detail, see von der Mehden, "Political and Social Challenge of the Islamic Revival."

23. For a provocative analysis of PAS's history, see C. Kessler, *Islam and Politics in a Malay State: Kelantan 1838–1967* (Ithaca: Cornell University Press, 1978). Also see N. Funston, *Malay Politics in Malaysia* (Kuala Lumpur: Heinemann Educational Books, 1980).

24. For variations in current PAS positions, see *The Star* (Penang, Malaysia), July 16, Sept. 28, and Oct. 7, 1985.

25. *Far Eastern Economic Review*, Jan. 2, July 24 and 31, and Aug. 14, 1986.

26. *The Star*, Sept. 22 and 23, 1985.

27. See various editions of *Indonesia Reports* and M. Morfit, "Panchasila: The Indonesian State Ideology according to the New Order Government," *Asian Survey* Vol. 21, No. 8 (August 1981), pp. 838–851.

28. *The Star*, Sept. 16, 1985.

29. McVey, "Faith as the Outsider," p. 210.

30. See E. Utrecht, "The Muslim Merchant Class in the Indonesian Social and Political Struggle," *Social Compass*, Vol. 31 (1984), pp. 27–55.

31. See Fred R. von der Mehden, "Religion and Politics in Malaya," *Asian Survey*, Vol. 3, No. 12 (December 1963), pp. 610–612.

*Part VI*

# XVI

# ISLAM IN POWER
## THE CASE OF IRAN

### Shireen T. Hunter

The rise of militant Islam dramatically illustrated by the Iranian revolution in 1979 has generated widespread anxieties in the Western world regarding the future of the West's relations with the Islamic countries in the event of the victory of militant forces in other countries. Yet it is very difficult to assess how the West's relations with the Islamic world would be affected if the militant Muslims were to gain power in other parts of the Islamic world.

It is, however, clear that the mere restructuring of Muslim societies along an Islamic model is not the real threat to Western interests. For example, Pakistan's Islamization program under President Zia-ul-Haq has not affected Pakistan's friendly relations with the West. The same is true of Saudi Arabia and the Persian Gulf Arab states, whose societies are based on Islam.

Of course, it could be argued that Saudi Arabia, the Persian Gulf Arab states, and Pakistan represent that brand of Islam which has been variously labeled "moderate," "traditional," or "establishment," and that this would not be true of the militants.[1]

This is a valid argument. It also points to the central issue in the West's relations with the militant Muslims, namely, that it is not the militants' domestic Islamization agenda that is the real cause of Western concern, but rather their world view and what could be called their foreign policy agenda.[2]

Since, however, the militants thus far have not gained power, except in Iran, it is very difficult to predict their international behavior. For example, would they, once in power, apply their ideological principles irrespective of its costs, or would they be willing to make pragmatic compromises?

It is in this context that a study of Iran's Islamic experience is a useful exercise that can shed some light on the future behavior of other militant groups should they gain power. A survey of the Iranian experience will show how the Muslim militants in Iran have had to adapt their Islamic ideology to the existing national, regional, and international environments. It will also show how Iran's geo-political, historical, and cultural realities have affected the militants' behavior, a process likely to be experienced by other militants in case of their access to power.

Iran's experience will further show that militant Islam once in power is as vulnerable to the vagaries of political life, including popular criticism and rejection in the case of failure, as are other ideologies. In fact, the militants' victory may have in it the seeds of an anti-Islamic backlash, since if the Iranian example is any guide, even Islam cannot easily resolve the Islamic world's mammoth social and economic problems.

### Islamic Political System in Iran

In March 1979, by a national plebiscite, Iran's political system was changed from an hereditary monarchy to an Islamic republic. In August 1979, an elected council of experts drafted a new constitution, which was approved by another plebiscite in November 1980.

This new constitution reflects the views of Ayatullah Ruhullah Khumaini on the nature of government and leadership in Muslim societies, and is based on the concept of the *Vilayat-e-Faqih*, or the guardianship of the supreme religious leader. Although Khumaini has been credited with developing this concept, its roots are in the Shiᶜa theory of political legitimacy and the concept of *Imamat*. According to this theory, ᶜAli (Prophet Muhammad's cousin and son-in-law) and his descendants from his union with Fatima (the Prophet's daughter) are the true guardians of Islamic faith and the Muslims' rightful spiritual and political leaders.

After the Prophet's death, ᶜAli and his descendants were denied leadership. Thus the Shiᶜas came to view the Muslim rulers as usurpers, lacking legitimacy and unworthy of their allegiance. As long as the Imams lived among the Shiᶜas they guided their attitude toward the ruling authorities. When the infant son of the eleventh Imam disappeared from view in the ninth century A.D., the Shiᶜa community entered a period of waiting. During the first part of this period, the Lesser Occultation, four representatives *(Vakil)* who were in direct communication with the Hidden Imam guided the Shiᶜas. The last Vakil, however, died without appointing a successor and thus the Shiᶜa community entered the period of the Greater Occultation, which will last until the return of the hidden Imam as the Mahdi.

In this new period the Shiᶜas adopted a passive attitude vis-à-vis the ruling authorities. They refrained from open opposition but denied them legitimacy and allegiance. In spiritual matters they sought guidance from their ᶜulama, or religious leaders and teachers. Thus the ᶜulama, in a sense, came to represent the Imam and became the guardian (Vali) of the Shiᶜa tradition.

As long as the Shiᶜas were ruled by the Sunnis, the question of political legitimacy—or, rather, illegitimacy—was clear-cut. When in the fifteenth century A.D. the Safavids established a Shiᶜa empire in Iran, the issue of the legitimacy of secular leaders was once again raised. A compromise was worked out on the basis of which the true leadership of the Shiᶜas continued to rest with the hidden Imam, and in his absence the ᶜulama exercised spiritual leadership. The secular leaders, as long as they ruled according to the Shiᶜa law and under the ᶜulama's supervision, acquired a limited legitimacy. A nineteenth-century Iranian ᶜalim, Mirza Abul Hasan Shirazi, captured the essence of this compromise:

> If you see the ᶜUlama at the gates of the kings, say they are bad ᶜUlama and bad kings. If you see the kings at the gates of the ᶜUlama, say they are good ᶜUlama and good kings.[3]

By the mid–nineteenth century, influenced by growing contacts with the West, the Iranian government began a process of secularization and modernization. Even the early timid efforts of modernization were viewed by the ᶜulama as threatening to Iran's Islamic character, and thus they began to slowly erode the basis of this historic and tacit compromise between Iran's spiritual and temporal leaders.

The question of political legitimacy and the right type of government for Iran became a burning issue during Iran's constitutional revolution. It divided the secular leaders and the clerical establishment and caused rifts within the ranks of the religious leadership. Some clerics such as Shaikh Fazalullah Nuri, a hero of Iran's current Islamic regime, and their followers demanded the establishment of a *Hokumat-e-Mashrua'*, or, literally, government based on the Shariᶜa. The secular nationalists, by contrast, asked for a *Hokumat-e-Mashruta*, or constitutional government. A number of religious leaders supported the idea of constitutional government provided there were sufficient guarantees that Iran's Islamic character would be maintained and that all legislation passed by the new Parliament would conform to the Shariᶜa.

Finally, this view prevailed and a new compromise reflected in Iran's 1906 constitution was reached between the country's secular and religious elites.[4] The Pahlavi dynasty, which came to power in 1925, totally disregarded the 1906 constitution and embarked on an aggressive policy of secularization and modernization, which was carried out in an arbitrary and authoritarian manner, thus destroying the basis of the new secular-religious political compromise. A fundamental breach between the secular leadership and the religious establishment thus ensued. For a variety of reasons, despite unhappiness with the new secularizing policies, the religious establishment did not mount a frontal attack against the government for a long time.[5] June 1963 marks a turning point in this regard. Serious disturbances led by some clerical personalities, notably Khumaini, occurred in opposition to the Shah's so-called White Revolution. It took Khumaini, however, until the early 1970s to develop his idea of an Islamic state based on the concept of the Vilayat-e-Faqih, and to declare the monarchical system as inherently un-Islamic.[6]

In the context of Khumaini's Islamic government, sovereignty belongs to God and all the necessary laws are given in the Shariᶜa. The duty of the people is, therefore, to apply God's laws and to live by them. From this premise, it then logically follows that those fit to govern are those who understand God's laws, and in the absence of the Imam these people are the ᶜulama. Thus within Khumaini's Islamic government, the ᶜulama become both the Guardians (*Vali*) and the interpreters and executors of God's law. And such a government becomes a just and truly Islamic government.[7]

The principle of the guardianship of the supreme religious leader—in the absence of one recognized leader, a group of leaders—is institutionalized in article 7 of Iran's constitution, which bestows on the leader or leaders the exercise of "governance and all the responsibilities arising therefrom." All other organs of the government, including the presidency, are only the executors of the Shariᶜa laws according to its interpretation by the supreme *Faqih*.

Although the Parliament cannot legislate but, as Khumaini has put it, can only formulate programs, the constitution provides for a twelve-member Guardian Council to ensure that the laws passed by the National Consultative Assembly comply with the Shariᶜa.

Political parties are permitted to function, provided they are committed to the Islamic Republic and to its constitution. This is natural since popular will is not the source of law, sovereignty, or power in the Islamic government, in which sovereignty belongs to God and Shariᶜa is the source of law. Thus, in Khumaini's Islamic government, popular participation in political life has a different and limited definition, and only permits voicing of views and grievances regarding specific government programs or the performance of its officials. As a result, currently in Iran the only effective political party is the Islamic Republican Party.[8]

A large number of high governmental positions, including the presidency, are occupied by the clerics, which reflects Khumaini's views on the relationship between politics and religion.[9]

Khumaini and his militant followers have succeeded in reshaping Iran's political system according to their ideas. But their views have not been accepted either by all of the people or by the totality of the religious establishment. Rather, differences persist between the militants' views and those of the more traditional ᶜulama. There are even considerable differences of view within the leadership of the current government. For example, Ayatullahs Shariᶜat Madari, who died in 1986, Taba-Tabai Qomi, and Khu'i, who resides in Najaf (Iraq), oppose the concept of the Vilayat-e-Faqih and the clergy's involvement in politics, for both doctrinal and practical reasons. They maintain that according to the Shiᶜa theory, since the disappearance of the Twelfth Imam, the Islamic world has been without a legitimate and just leader. Until his return, there can be no legitimate and just leader and thus no legitimate and just government. Khumaini's version of an Islamic government based on the concept of the Vilayat-e-Faqih with presumed qualities of justice and legitimacy goes against this basic Shiᶜa theory. These ayatullahs also fear that the clerics' involvement in politics would make them subject to public scrutiny and wrath should they fail, and thus would erode the clerics' special position and might even create an anticlerical backlash.

Indeed, there is evidence that this has been happening to some extent.[10] Even among the supporters of the ruling clerical regime itself, a group identified as the Hujatiya, which has been muzzled in the past few years, favors a less visible political role for the clerics.[11]

In sum, in Iran the militant Muslims who have gained power have proven as politically intolerant of dissent as their secular predecessors. The changes they have brought about have been done in an arbitrary fashion and have been based more on repression than on consensus building, as illustrated by the government's efforts to eliminate all opposition groups. Thus many of these changes are even now being challenged by many groups. Iran's experience has shown that the Muslim militants take a narrow view of democracy, freedom, and political participation despite their opposition to such attitudes on the part of secular leaders. Based on the Iranian experience, a victory of Muslim militants in other countries is unlikely to resolve the problem of political repression and lack of adequate popular participation within the Muslim societies. Such a victory is more likely to lead to political repression of another kind and thus generate in due course negative popular reactions toward the militants. In fact, in Iran's case, it is not at all clear whether, without the charismatic leadership of Khumaini, Iran's Islamic government as presently structured could survive for long without significant changes.

### Iran's Islamic Sociocultural Reorganization

Since the establishment of the Islamic government, Iran has undergone a profound and extensive social and cultural transformation.

Iran's judicial system is now based on the Shari<sup>c</sup>a and its prosecutor general is a cleric. At the Ministry of Justice, religious judges preside with lay judges in order to ensure the compatability of all decisions with the Shari<sup>c</sup>a.

The educational system has been even more deeply affected. Khumaini and his followers believe that in order to create an Islamic society and government, the Iranians must be purged of un-Islamic influences and turned into true Islamic men and women. Thus, since the revolution, school books have been rewritten, Iran's history has been reinterpreted, and great attention has been paid to religious instruction and the teaching of Arabic. The universities have been heavily purged, and since 1980 a seven-member Council for Cultural Revolution has been set up and has become the decision-making body of Iran's higher educational system. Students wanting to go to universities are systematically and thoroughly screened and are accepted on the basis of their attitudes toward the Islamic revolution and their knowledge of Islamic history and precepts.[12]

In addition, radio and television programming has changed and the discussion of religious matters has acquired high priority. Traditional Iranian music has been replaced by military-sounding patriotic songs exalting the Iranians' sacrifices in the war with Iraq.

Frequent poetry contests are still being held, but instead of the traditional romantic subjects of Persian poetry, religious subjects and revolutionary themes are emphasized. The same applies to painting. The filmmaking industry has flourished, but again with emphasis on revolutionary and Islamic themes. In general, the regime's position on the arts is that no art form should encourage corrupt and anti-Islamic behavior, and all art form should advance the revolution's objectives.[13] Cultural revolution has also meant the denigration of Iran's pre-Islamic heritage and its representatives. For example, during the early days of the revolution, Iran's pre-Islamic historic monuments were attacked.

Poets such as ᶜUmar Khayyam and Firdowsi, who in his epic work *The Book of Kings (Shahnameh)* resurrected the Persian language and Iranian history after three centuries of Arab domination, were particularly vilified.

The Islamic government also tried to change the pre-Islamic names of the months in the Iranian solar calendar and actively discouraged the celebration of Now Ruz, Iran's pre-Islamic and mythical New Year. It also began a campaign against the use of non-Islamic Iranian first names. However, negative popular reaction and the war with Iraq forced the government to come to terms with Iran's national culture and, indeed, to tap nationalist symbols in order to bolster its war efforts. Thus the attacks on pre-Islamic sites and certain literary figures were stopped, the calendar remained unchanged, and the government itself began celebrating Now Ruz.

The Iranian government has even discovered the virtues of the Persian language and its contribution to the expansion of Islam, particularly in the Indian subcontinent.[14] The government has also imposed a strict Islamic moral code, including the obligatory Islamic dress for women. Popular groups have been organized to ensure strict adherence to the Islamic code of conduct. But here, too, the government's actions have met with some resistance, and on occasion the government has had to moderate its actions.[15]

In sum, the Islamic militants have had to make some concessions to external realities, including Iran's cultural and historical realities. Whether or not this will still be necessary once the present generation, which is being reared according to Islamic principles, comes of age is not clear. Most probably, however, those aspects of Iran's cultural heritage that have become part of its national folklore will survive. However, if popular disenchantment with Islamic experience were to deepen and a widespread anti-Islamic backlash were to develop, Iran's pre-Islamic heritage could very well reemerge with even greater force.

## Accommodating Nationalism

The Islamic militants in Iran have had to contend with the forces of nationalism. It is generally assumed that nationalism and Islam are inherently incompatible. Before accepting or refuting this assertion, however, it is important to know what is meant by nationalism.

If by nationalism one means love of the homeland (patriotism), then Islam does not object to it.[16] But if nationalism is defined as an ideology based on the assertion of a nation's separateness or even superiority over others and on making the nation the only source of legitimacy and focus of allegiance, then a conflict with Islam, which is an eternal universalist message demanding the full allegiance of its adherents, emerges. It is to nationalism in this sense that Islamic revivalists object.[17]

Since the mid–nineteenth century, when the Islamic world came into contact with the West, the tension between nationalism and Islam has existed as illustrated by the tension between pan-Arabism and pan-Islamism in the Arab world.[18]

In the case of Iran, this problem has been exacerbated by the fact that by the time of the Arab-Islamic invasion, Iran had existed as a nation and a culture for nearly two thousand years. Also, unlike many other countries, Iran was never Arabized and its pre-Islamic heritage has proved tenacious, even after its Islamization, and has greatly affected its cultural development in the post-Islamic era.[19] Thus, despite their Islamization, most Iranians maintained their ethnic pride and their sense of separateness. These feelings were strengthened at an early stage by Iran's new Arab Muslim rulers' practice of favoring Arabs over other Muslims.[20]

The Iranians' embrace of Shiᶜism, particularly after the Safavids, which once more unified Iran, further intensified their sense of distinctiveness. More importantly, after the establishment of a Shiᶜa state in Iran, the territorial confines of Iran also became those of the true realm of Islam. Thus, with the fusion of Iranian nationalism and Shiᶜa Islam, the Iranians, including the Shiᶜa ᶜulama, did not feel any conflict between Islam and Iranian nationalism.[21]

The situation began to change in the nineteenth century when Iran's decline accelerated and it increasingly came under foreign domination. In trying to discover the roots of their decline, many Iranians saw the contamination of their culture by foreign, especially Arab and Turkish, elements as a main cause.[22] Given Islam's Arab origins, many also blamed Islam and the Muslim clerical establishment for Iran's decline.[23] Their solution was the resurrection of Iran's pre-Islamic past and the purging of the Iranian culture of foreign influences.[24]

When the Pahlavis came to power, they made the consolidation of a new brand of Iranian nationalism based on the glorification of Iran's pre-Islamic past state policy, and thus began the rift between the new nationalists and the Muslim ᶜulama. For nearly forty years, however, the ᶜulama did not attack nationalism frontally for two reasons: (1) the strength of nationalist forces and their popular appeal; and (2) the fact that no major legislation contrary to Islamic law was passed and the prerogatives of the ᶜulama were not seriously endangered. Fear of Communist inroads also played a role. However, after the 1960s, Muhammad Riza Shah's wide-ranging policies for changing Iran's socioeconomic

structure seriously threatened the ᶜulama's prerogatives. His efforts to legitimize his rule by promoting Iran's pre-Islamic culture and the institution of
kingship also totally broke the 400-year tacit agreement between the Shiᶜa
establishment and the Iranian kings on the basis of which the ᶜulama granted
the latter a limited and qualified legitimacy. The Shah's efforts also led for the
first time in Iran's modern history to open and explicit attacks on Iran's pre-
Islamic culture and on nationalism by the Shiᶜa ᶜulama.[25] It is, however, important to note that the dichotomy between nationalism and Islam in Iran is
mainly an elite phenomenon and is directly related to efforts by the elite to
maintain, gain, or regain power. The Pahlavis manipulated nationalism in order
to establish their legitimacy and the current regime is doing the same with
Islam. Yet the majority of Iranians see no conflict between their attachment
to Iran and its past and their devotion to Islam, and they oppose any excess in
emphasizing either aspect of their national culture and identity.

The excesses of the Pahlavi regime, particularly its cult of monarchy and its
downplaying of Islam's role in Iran, created an antinationalist backlash. However, this backlash partly stemmed from the Iranians' dissatisfaction with the
results of the Pahlavis' socioeconomic policies and their autocratic style of rule,
and Iranian nationalism suffered because of its identification with the Pahlavis.

There is some evidence that the same is happening in regard to Islam. When
the Muslim militants took power in Iran, they embarked on a systematic campaign against what they termed *Meligaraei* (national tendencies) and their manifestations.

References to the Iranian nation (*Melat-e-Iran*) were dropped and the Ayatullah Khumaini addressed the Iranians as the *Ummat-el-Islam* (Nation of Islam).
The traditional view that in Islam there is no room for nationalism and the
more recent argument that nationalism is a Western creation to divide the
Muslims were impressed upon the population. There was even some talk of
changing the name of the Persian Gulf to the Islamic Gulf to prove that for
true Muslims boundaries did not matter. As with other efforts, however, these
acts were very badly received by large segments of the population and had to
be stopped. Iraq's invasion of Iran and the Baᶜthists' characterization of the
Iranians as fire-worshipping Persians also strengthened nationalist feelings.[26]
Many Iranians who were told by the government about brotherhood among
the Muslims and the virtues of Arabic language and culture were shocked into
realizing that the other side did not share these feelings. Expulsion of large
numbers of Iranians from Iraq and Kuwait and the general Arab support for
Iraq further weakened the government's cause. Of course the government has
argued that current Arab regimes are not truly Islamic, hence their anti-Iranian
behavior. But the government's case is weakened by the fact that the only
country supporting Iran has been the secular nationalist government of Syria.
Consequently, the government has had to somewhat relent on its antinational
campaign. Now the Islamic government's authorities do refer to the "Iranian
nation" although they qualify it as Islamic. Some of them even betray latent

nationalist tendencies.[27] The Gulf has remained Persian; the Iranian authorities' statements regarding Iran's role in the Persian Gulf bear a striking resemblance to those of the Shah, and the war communiques of the Iranian armed forces refer to the Shat al-Arab by its Persian name, Arvand Rud. In sum, nationalism, especially cultural, has proved a tenacious rival and, together with regional pressures, has forced the government to moderate its anti-nationalist campaign.

Admittedly, Iran is a special case in that it is unique among Muslim countries by virtue of its rich, long, and still relevant pre-Islamic culture. In Muslim Africa, too, pre-Islamic African traditions and cultures have proven a serious rival for Islam. In fact, if early Islamic history itself is any guide, militants in other countries, once in power, would have to deal with problems of ethnic and regional particularism. Thus nationalism is unlikely to totally disappear as a political force in the Muslim world should the militants gain power. Nor is it likely that a united Islamic *umma* (community) would be created in case of the militants' victory in other countries. Rather, old rivalries would continue to divide the Muslims, although they might be cast in Islamic terms.

### Economic Reform, Social Equality, and the Islamic Republic's Record

Economic and social factors played an important role in Iran's Islamic revolution. Iran's Islamic opposition succeeded largely because it promised social and economic prosperity and equality to the deprived classes, especially the peasants and the shanty town dwellers of Tehran.[28] In fact, for more than a decade, certain religious leaders (e.g., Ayatullah Mahmud Taleghani of Iran and Muhammad Baqer as-Sadr of Iraq) and religiously inclined lay intellectuals (e.g., Abol Hasan Bani-Sadr and ʿAli Shariʾati) through their work had tried to portray Islam as an egalitarian system and as a viable alternative to both capitalism and socialism.[29]

Taleghani's and Bani-Sadr's Islamic alternatives give the state vast powers to organize economic life in order to ensure social justice and equality. Khumaini, by contrast, has not focused much on the economics of his Islamic government. The underlying theme of his vision of society is that it is divided into two categories: the oppressors (*mustakbarin*) and the oppressed or the disinherited (*mustadʿafin*). He also believes that the primary purpose of the Islamic government is to protect the latter.

The official rhetoric of Iran's Islamic government has reflected these themes. Beyond this essential vision of society, the Muslim militants' economic outlook and program have included the establishment of interest-free Islamic banking, an emphasis on rural development, the elimination of economic dependence on foreigners, and the encouragement of a simpler and less consumption-oriented life-style. Many of the latter ideas, however, are or have been popular in non-Muslim Third World states and are not specifically Islamic.

Once in power, the militants began to translate their theories into concrete policies. Massive nationalizations of industry, banking, and trade took place. Private properties—including agricultural land—were confiscated and distributed among the poor. Later, interest-free Islamic banking was established. Some emphasis was given to rural development.

Despite these efforts, the Islamic government has failed in its promise of bringing economic prosperity and social equality to the majority of the Iranians, and Iran's economic conditions have steadily worsened under Islamic rule. Not all of Iran's economic ills can be blamed on the government's policies, as external factors, especially the war with Iraq and a dramatic fall in oil prices in the past few years, have also contributed to these problems. But ideological differences within the regime, ideological rigidity of some of the regime's members, and bad management have caused serious damage.

For example, ideological differences—some deriving from diverging interpretations of Islamic laws of property—have prevented the government from deciding on a land reform policy, which has hurt agriculture and has perpetuated dependence on agricultural imports. Nor has there been a clear policy on the role of the private sector in the economy, because of divisions between those favoring total state control over the economy and those willing to recognize a role for the private sector. The result has been conflicting signals from the leadership. However, aware of the economic and political power of the Bazar (merchant community), Ayatullah Khumaini has interfered in favor of some role for the private sector.[30] The living conditions of the majority of people have worsened, although some urban poor, especially in Tehran, have benefited. Government employees have been forced to take pay cuts and, with the economy stagnant, job opportunities for Iran's growing and young population have decreased. Real cumulative inflation since the revolution has reached triple-digit figures and shortages of all kinds have become part of the daily life.

Meanwhile, governmental corruption and a reputation for profiteering by those close to the regime have remained high, forcing Ayatullah Khumaini to periodically call on the clergy and the government to be examples of probity and honesty.

Social and economic distinctions have remained pronounced, and a new rich class made up of those who have profited from the black market caused by the war and related shortages has emerged.

In sum, thus far the Islamic government has not been able to resolve Iran's economic problems, improve the living conditions of the majority of the people, eliminate socioeconomic disparities, or end corruption. The result has been mounting popular disenchantment with the Islamic model. Of course, Iran has had to wage a foreign war, which has sapped its economic resources, but other factors have also been important. If the Iranian experience is any guide, however, other Muslim militants, once in power, are unlikely to rapidly resolve the mammoth socioeconomic problems of other Muslim countries by simply applying the so-called Islamic principles, and thus, in all likelihood, in due course popular disenchantment with the Islamic alternative will also mount.

## The Islamic Republic's International Relations

Important as the domestic policies of Iran's Islamic republic have been, the government's international behavior and what it could imply for the behavior of other Muslim militants are more significant from the perspective of other countries. Since the revolution, Iran's foreign relations have undergone significant changes. Some of these changes have directly resulted from the new regime's Islamic nature and the impact of the views of Khumaini and his followers.

Other changes, however, have derived from factors with deep roots in Iran's history and political culture as well as views and theories that are dominant in the Third World in general. Differences of view that have characterized the regime's domestic policies have also impacted on its foreign policy. Thus, the same element of ambiguity and contradiction and the tension between ideological purity and the need to accommodate and respond to external environment have characterized Iran's international behavior.

### Khumaini's World View

Khumaini's world view is dominated by the same duality that characterizes his interpretation of Iran's internal conditions. In his view, the world, like Iranian society, is divided into two categories: the mustakbarin and the mustadᶜafin.

The worst of the oppressors are the two superpowers, which, according to Khumaini, are motivated only by greed and lust for power. Their goal is to dominate other countries economically, politically, and culturally so as, in his words, to plunder their resources. They achieve their purpose through the intermediary of corrupt leaders.[31]

According to Khumaini, the world as currently structured is made up of those who are dominated by one or the other superpower. Thus the world is divided into two camps, East and West, respectively dominated by the Soviet Union and the United States. Khumaini does not think much of the nonaligned countries even though they proclaim independence, since even if not politically dominated by the two superpowers, they are culturally and ideologically dominated by them and follow either the Eastern or Western path. Yet both Eastern and Western ways are inherently corrupt since they are based on human laws. The only true and right way is that of Islam because it is based on divine law.

Thus, Khumaini believes that the Muslims should forsake the corrupt ways of both East and West and follow the path of Islam. From this belief comes the Islamic republic's slogan, "Neither East nor West," which is echoed by other militant revivalist movements.

The duality of Khumaini's world view corresponds to the basic Islamic view, which divides the world into the Dar-al-Islam (realm of Islam or peace and belief) and Dar-al-Harb (realm of war and disbelief). But this view also betrays the impact of more recent experiences and the essentially bipolar nature of the post-1945 international system.

The slogan "Neither East nor West" is indeed appealing to the vast majority of Iranians largely because of Iran's historical experience of having been the battleground for two competing great powers. Moreover, essentially the same idea had in the past been advanced by Iran's secular nationalist leaders, as illustrated by Dr. Muhammad Mossadeq's theory of "negative equilibrium." Similar ideas had also been the main inspiration for the nonaligned movement. This aspect of Khumaini's world view has had a significant, but by no means determining, impact on Iran's relations with the two superpowers. Other factors have also been important. For example, Iran's relations with the United States have suffered more because of the latter's association with the Shah and the belief on the part of Iran's current leaders that the United States is intent on unseating them. The USSR, by contrast, has not had this handicap. Iran's geopolitical conditions, especially its geographical proximity to the Soviet Union, the USSR's overwhelming power, and Iran's dependence on its trade routes, have argued against overly hostile relations with the USSR.

Iran's new international outlook has led to its active support for what the Iranians call movements of the world's oppressed people. Thus Iran has become outspoken on African problems, especially apartheid, and has established warm relations with such countries as Nicaragua and Zimbabwe. This aspect of Iran's policy, however, is inspired by what could be called militant Third Worldism rather than Islam. The determined efforts to expand Iran's political, economic, and cultural relations with Third World countries also derive from this factor. In fact, Islamic ideological considerations have played no role in Iran's establishing relations with these countries, or with Syria and South Yemen. Rather, pragmatic considerations, particularly animosity toward common enemies, Iraq and the United States, has been the principal reason behind these relations.

Similar practical considerations, especially economic necessity, have led to the continuation of Iran's economic and political relations with the close associates of the two superpowers. In fact, Iran's trade and economic relations are still dominated by a few West European countries and Japan. However, cultural contacts and reliance on technical experts from these countries have been reduced, although it is not clear how far this has reflected the general decline in economic activity. Khumaini's world view also emphazises Islamic unity. He believes that the Islamic world's fragmentation and disunity is caused by the big powers' past and current policies and the fact that the Muslims no longer follow the Qur'an.

For example, Khumaini believes that the Ottoman Empire collapsed because the imperialist powers, Russia, Britain, and Austria, saw this united Islamic state as a hindrance to their plans to control the Muslim countries' resources. Thus, they divided the Ottoman realm and created Israel as their agent in the region.[32] He also attributes the Muslims' falling off the Islamic path to their cultural contamination by foreign ideologies.

In his view, in order to correct this situation, Islamic governments on the Iranian model should be established, and Iran as the only true Islamic government should encourage such development. This is a central point in Khumaini's view and has had a tremendous impact on the most controversial aspect of Iran's international behavior, namely, its exporting of its revolution.

This point has even been embodied in principle 11 of Iran's constitution:

> Islamic Republic of Iran is to base its overall policy on the coalition and unity of the Islamic nation. Furthermore, it should exert continuous effort until political, economic and cultural unity is realized in the Islamic world.[33]

However, Khumaini believes that this aim should be carried out through peaceful means and propaganda. Consequently, since the revolution the Ministry of Islamic Guidance has established a program to spread Iran's message by such means as sponsoring visits of Islamic clergy to Iran, offering scholarships for young Muslims to study in Iran's religious institutions, and propaganda through radio and written material.

There is, however, evidence that Iran has also used less peaceful means, such as training and financing subversive groups.[34] However, most of these activities have been related to Iran's war with Iraq, which was caused by Iraq's aggression, an act only partly prompted by Iran's efforts to export its revolution.[35]

This ideological imperative to export revolution has also caused a split within the Iranian regime between the pragmatists and the more ideologically oriented elements. The first group believes that the blind pursuit of ideology is isolating Iran and generating responses from outsiders that are harming Iran, and thus Iran should behave more in accordance with international rules of conduct. In fact, this group believes that Iran will be more successful in spreading its revolutionary message if it becomes an active member of the international community. The others, by contrast, demand ideological purity irrespective of costs.

The ideological contest within the regime is not over, but the pressure of external realities has led Iran to become increasingly more pragmatic in its foreign policy. Thus, despite ideological differences, Iran maintains political and economic relations with a vast group of countries as well as with international organizations. Meanwhile, it continues some ideologically motivated activities that give its international behavior a contradictory character at times highly confusing to its partners.

## Conclusion

Although Islamic revolution has led to significant domestic changes in Iran as well as in its international behavior, the new regime has also had to come to terms with a variety of internal and external forces. Externally, the revolution has not totally transformed Iran's relations with the outside world. In fact, in many respects Iran's foreign policy entails considerable continuity with the past, especially if one looks beyond the Iranians' inflammatory rhetoric. For example, Iran's relations with the Western world, especially Europe and Japan, have remained extensive, particulary in economic fields. Thus, Iran's experience seems to warrant the prognosis that in the case of a victory of militant Muslims in other countries, their domestic and foreign policies will be determined by their national peculiarities and historical experience as well as by Islam. Moreover, they, too, in time will have to take into account external factors and adapt themselves to them. This means that in the case of a victory for other militant forces, a total rupture of the Muslim states' relations with the West will not occur and that current Western anxieties about such a rupture may prove to have been exaggerated.

# NOTES

1. See James Bill, "Resurgent Islam," *Foreign Affairs*, Vol. 63, No. 1 (Fall 1984).
2. See Shireen T. Hunter, "Islamic Fundamentalism: What It Really Is and Why It Frightens the West," *SAIS Review*, Vol. 6, No. 1 (Winter/Spring 1986).
3. Quoted in Hamid Algar, *Religion and State in Iran 1785–1906* (Berkeley: University of California Press, 1969), p. 22.
4. Article 5 of the 1906 Constitution provides that five eminent religious leaders should sit in the Parliament in order to ensure that legislation conformed to the rules of the Shariᶜa.
5. See Sharoug Akhavi, *Religion and Politics in Contemporary Iran* (Albany: State University of New York Press, 1980).
6. In fact, Khumaini wrote in 1943: "The Ulama never wanted to destroy the foundations of the government. . . . They have never to this day opposed the principal foundations of the monarchy. . . ." Quoted in Farhang Rajaee, *Islamic Values and World View: Khomeini on Man, the State and International Politics* (New York: University Press of America, 1983), p. 57.
7. For details, see Rajaee, *Islamic Values*, pp. 51–72.
8. For a brief period, the Communist Tudeh Party, which supported the Islamic government, was allowed to operate. But in 1983 the Tudeh was disbanded and its leadership imprisoned. Ex-Prime Minister Mehdi Bazargan's freedom movement has also been allowed a very limited and sporadic freedom to operate.
9. According to Khumaini: "This slogan of the separation of religion and politics and the demand that islamic scholars should not intervene in social and political affairs has been formulated and propagated by the imperialists. . . ." See *Islam and Revolution: Writings and Declarations of Imam Khomeini*, trans. and annotated by Hamid Algar (Berkeley, Calif.: Mizan Press, 1981), p. 38.
10. Profiteering by the clerics and charges of corruption and irregularities in organizations run mostly by the clerics, such as the Foundation of the Deprived, have generated considerable anticlerical and anti-Islamic sentiments. Some Iranians, including devout Muslims from lower classes, have been giving up observance of Islamic rules.
11. See Shahrough Akhavi, "Clerical Politics in Iran since 1979," in *The Iranian*

Revolution and the Islamic Republic, ed. Nikki R. Keddie and Eric Hoaglund (The Middle East Institute and the Woodrow Wilson Center for Scholars, 1982).

12. See Farhang Rajaee, "The Islamic Cultural Revolution and Postrevolutionary Iranian Society," in Shireen T. Hunter, ed., *Internal Developments in Iran*, Significant Issues Series, Vol. 7, No. 3 (Center for Strategic and International Studies, Georgetown University, 1985), pp. 55–56.

13. See the interview with ᶜAli-Akbar Hashemi Rafsanjani, speaker of the Iranian Parliament, in *Keyhan-e-Hawai*, May 15, 1985, p. 15.

14. See the interview by the Tehran daily *Jomhuri-e-Islami* with the director general of the Office of Cultural Agencies, in which he said:

> through the Persian language, Islam was transmitted to the Indian subcontinent. Considering the high percentage of Muslims interested in Persian language and writing, the important and valuable role of Persian language can be understood in transmitting the Islamic culture in that area. For this reason, attention to these two issues is the main duty of the agencies. Cultural agencies try, as the case requires, to offer cultural and propaganda issues through various exhibitions and competitions or to establish educational and other classes in the form of art. They also make an effort to spread Persian language by establishing Persian language classes for beginners and holding seminars to re-train Persian language professors abroad.

Reprinted in Joint Publications Research Service, June 25, 1986, p. 76.

15. In part to prevent the actions of these groups from unduly antagonizing the population, Khumaini issued an eight-point program designed to protect certain essential rights and liberties. For the text of the program, issued in December 1982, see Farhad Kazemi, "The Iranian Revolution Seven Years Later," *Middle East Insight*, Vol. 5, No. 1 (1987), pp. 16–17.

16. The Prophet Muhammad is said to have praised patriotism (*Hubb-al-wattan*) as a sign of faith. In Khumaini's view, too, if nationalism means "To love one's fatherland and its people and to protect its frontiers," then it is acceptable. See Algar, *Islam and Revolution*, p. 302.

17. The militants, including Khumaini, believe that this type of nationalism is a stratagem concocted by foreigners to divide the Islamic world.

18. However, many Arabs have managed to square this circle by equating Arabism with Islam, and by making the revival of Islam dependent on the resurgence of the so-called Arab nation. See Hamid Enayat, *Modern Islamic Political Thought* (Austin: University of Texas Press, 1982), pp. 111–120.

19. See Henry Corbin, *En Islam Iranian*, 4 vols. (Paris: Editions Gallimard, 1972).

20. For example, early Shiᶜa sources report that ᶜUmar prohibited marriage between Arabs and Iranians. By contrast, ᶜAli is reported to have treated them equally. See Enayat, *Modern Islamic Political Thought*, p. 33. Also see ᶜAli-Akbar Khan Mohammadi, "Shoubiyeh va Tasir An Dar Adb va Farhang-e-Iran va Arab" (Shoubiyeh and its impact on the literature and culture of Iran and the Arabs), *Keyhan-e-Farhangi*, No. 9 (Azar 1364/November–December 1985), pp. 22–26.

21. Quite the contrary, prominent Shiᶜa clerics such as Mohammad Baqir Majlesi produced Hadith that ascribed to the Iranians superior qualities. See Enayat, *Modern Islamic Political Thought*, p. 33.

22. Ironically, the Arabs believe that the pure teachings of Islam were corrupted after the Arabs came into contact with the Persian and Byzantine empires and acquired their imperial ways.

23. See Fereydoun Adamyat, *Andisheh-e-Taraqi va Hukumat-e-Qanun* (The idea of progress and the rule of law) (Tehran: Kharazmi, 1351/1973).

24. Even in this period, however, there were many Iranians who thought that Iran's salvation was in an even stricter application of Islam. See Shireen T. Hunter, "Iranian Perceptions and a Wider World," *Political Communication and Persuasion*, Vol. 2, No. 4 (1985), pp. 408–409.

25. See Enayat, *Modern Islamic Political Thought*, p. 123.

26. See, for example, *Le Monde*, Mar. 6, 1984.

27. Note the following statement by Foreign Minister Velayati to the outgoing Chinese ambassador to Iran: "Relations between Iran and China are several thousand years old, and works of culture, art, literature and religion which stem from an ancient civilization can be seen in both countries." Foreign Broadcast Information Service, Dec. 9, 1982, p. 18. Needless to say, the civilization the foreign minister is referring to predates Islam by two millennia and is referred to by the militant Muslims as the era of ignorance and corruption.

28. Rich bazaar merchants for a variety of reasons also supported the Islamic opposition and through their financial assistance contributed to its success. See Shaul Bakhash, *The Reign of the Ayatollahs* (New York: Basic Books, 1984), pp. 190–192.

29. Ayatullah Taleghani's main work on Islamic economics is *Eslam va Malekkiyat* (Islam and property) and Bani-Sadr's is *Eghtesad-e-Towhidi* (The economics of divine harmony). See ibid., pp. 167–173.

30. See Bakhash, *Reign of the Ayatollahs*. Also see various issues of the *Middle East Economic Digest*.

31. See Rajaee, *Islamic Values*, pp. 73–92.

32. Ibid., pp. 86–87.

33. See Iran's Islamic constitution.

34. See Robin Wright, *Sacred Rage: The Wrath of Militant Islam* (New York: Simon and Schuster, 1985).

35. Iraq's principal motives were to establish itself as the leading power in the Gulf and the Arab world and to separate Khuzistan, toward which the Arabs have a long-standing irredentist claim, from Iran.

# CONCLUSION

## Shireen T. Hunter

A number of broad conclusions emerge from the foregoing survey of revivalist movements across the Islamic world. Some of these conclusions confirm widespread perceptions about Islam and the revivalist movement. Others, by contrast, demonstrate the invalidity of these perceptions.

For example, the study once more confirms an important view about the nature of Islam: its role as the most important component of most Muslims' identity and culture, combined with its all-encompassing nature, goes a long way toward explaining both the periodic emergence of revivalist movements in the Muslim world and Islam's current political vitality.

The study also shows, however, that as a focus of political and cultural identity and loyalty, Islam is not without rivals. For some countries, such as Pakistan, Islam is indeed their only raison d'être and the basis of both their individual and their collective self-identities. In the case of others, however, notably Iran and to a much lesser extent Egypt and some Muslim African countries, a strong non-Islamic culture competes with Islam as the focus of popular identification and allegiance. But no matter how important the impact of non-Islamic factors in determining those countries' perceptions of their self-identity, Islam remains an extremely important component of their self-image, their culture, and their perceptions of the outside world.

The study also confirms the view that both historically and at the present time, certain underlying characteristics of Islam have contributed to its social and political vitality. But it also makes clear that throughout the Muslim world, factors other than the peculiarities of Islam and of the Muslims have been responsible for generating the current revivalist movements and for producing their political vitality. The study shows that a major contribution to this revivalist wave has been the failure of secular governments in many Muslim countries during the past sixty years to recognize the importance of Islam's place in the socioeconomic, political, and cultural fabric of their respective societies, and their arbitrary actions to weaken this role.

These actions, over time, have created among the Muslims a sense of threat to Islam and its influence in society, which in turn has contributed to the revivalist movements. The early perception of threat and reaction to it, however, has generally been limited to the religious establishments, whose interests were directly and strongly affected, and to those segments of society whose fortunes were closely linked to those of the religious establishments.

By contrast, the growth of the movements' popular appeal and the expansion of their support bases have depended on the convergence of a wide range of social, economic, and political factors, rather than on the mere perception of a vague threat to Islam. Moreover, even in the case of the religious establishments, the tangible negative impact on their economic and power positions has been a strong factor in their early reaction to efforts they have perceived as undermining Islam.

Among the socioeconomic factors that have acted as spurs to revivalist movements, the particularly important ones have been an increasing popular intolerance toward social and economic disparities, a demand for greater social equality, rising expectations, and the popular perception that existing governments and political systems are either unwilling or unable to satisfy demands and aspirations.

As most scholars have emphasized, the disillusionment of Muslims with the results of the modernization and development inspired by foreign models and ideologies, the resultant socioeconomic disruptions of this process, and the unequal manner in which its benefits have been distributed have no doubt been among the primary causes of the revivalist movements. But the evidence presented in this study shows that, to a great extent, the movements have also resulted from the success of many aspects of the development and modernization process in the Islamic countries.

For example, the rise of revivalist movements has been aided by the expansion of education to those layers of society that have most tenaciously maintained their Islamic roots, and education has raised their social and political consciousness. These movements have also been aided by the large influx of rural populations to the cities, a development that has led to what Professor Sonbol in chapter 2 called the "villagization of the cities." A third factor aiding these movements has been the resultant erosion of the traditional elites' position and the emergence of mass politics. Moreover, the social and economic content of the revivalist movements in most countries clearly reflects the phenomenon of rising expectations, itself a creature of the development experience. Thus, the current revivalist movements have been both an outcome and a reaction to the development experience.

Nor is there any evidence that the revivalist movements imply a rejection of material development or modernization altogether. Rather, their opposition is to the socioeconomic, political, and indeed cultural and moral contexts within which material development has so far taken place.

The study also makes clear that other significant contributors to the rise of revivalist movements include a widespread feeling among Muslims that they are not yet in control of their own destiny, a strong desire for independence and autonomy, and a widespread belief that today's ruling elites in Muslim countries are dominated by foreign powers and ideologies and thus have become alien to their own countries and cultures. But it is also important to note that this quest for autonomy, including cultural autonomy or authenticity, is not limited to Muslim societies nor to Islamic groups in these societies.

Indeed, this quest is widespread throughout the Third World, where traditional cultures feel threatened by the spread of foreign cultures, itself often a result of political domination. Themes such as national and collective self-sufficiency, including cultural self-sufficiency, were common in Third World parlance long before the emergence of Islamic revivalist movements.

Another conclusion which emerges from this study, and which thus far has received relatively less attention, is that specific actions of Muslim governments, at both national and international levels, have contributed to the revivalist wave. The early efforts of modernizing elites to arbitrarily weaken Islam were noted before. Also important have been the limitations imposed on political debate by Muslim governments and active manipulation of Islam as a counterforce to ideas perceived as radical or revolutionary. In the process, Islam has become the only medium for articulating popular grievances. Also, many followers of other (particularly leftist) ideologies have tried to use Islamic symbolism to convey their own messages. What is highly interesting and clearly emerges from the study is that manipulation of Islam by governments as a political counterforce has continued after the rise of revivalist movements. In fact, by co-opting certain symbols of the revivalist movements and by adopting some of their social and cultural agenda, governments have tried to control these movements and, in particular, check the influence of their militant flank. But since these actions have not been accompanied by fundamental socioeconomic and political reforms, their impact has been limited.

Meanwhile, by encouraging Islamic tendencies, governments have paradoxically created a more congenial and receptive environment for the militants' views. This is particularly so since, while competing with the revivalists in co-opting Islam and using it to their own advantage, Muslim governments continue to muzzle and repress other political forces and groups.

The study also makes clear that the revivalist wave is not a monolithic phenomenon. Not only do the characteristics of the various movements, their histories, and their evolution reflect the specific conditions of their respective countries, but also there are ideological differences between and within the different movements. Thus, these differences are not limited to those between the so-called traditionalists and the militants but also exist within the militant organizations. Yet, despite significant differences the revivalist movements share certain underlying views and objectives, as well as certain causes for their emergence. The greatest unifying themes derive from social, economic, and political concerns and reflect widespread yearning for social and economic justice and political and cultural autonomy.

This fact also means that, so long as the basic grievances of Muslim populations remain unanswered, Muslims will find, even under repressive conditions, some means—including, at times, violent means—of articulating these grievances. Thus, those in the Muslim world who now feel threatened by the Islamic revivalist wave must realize that the existing orders will be challenged so long as social and economic underdevelopment and injustice and political repression exist in the Muslim world, and so long as the Muslims continue to view their international condition as one of political and economic dependence. If the Islamic movements were to fail, then a different medium of articulating Muslim grievances would be found with similar effects.

Therefore, the best way for today's Muslim governments to deal with the revivalist movements is to tolerate a greater degree of open debate and to show more sensitivity to popular views, rather than either to resort to repressive measures or to engage in a competition with the revivalists in the race to see who represents Islam best. It is also important to note that not all revivalist movements oppose existing governments or advocate violent action to bring about political changes. Quite the contrary, the nonviolent and gradualist groups are the largest groups within the revivalist wave. These groups are willing to cooperate with existing governments provided they agree to en- courage greater Islamization of the society.

It is quite clear from this study that the anti-Western or, more specifically, the anti-American dimension of the revivalist movement is not caused by the so-called inherent incompatibility of Islam with the West. On the contrary, this opposition derives basically from three factors. First, there has been a general tendency among Third World states to be suspicious of the superpowers and great powers, largely because of memories of domination, plus the feeling that the superpowers help maintain an international order that the smaller states view as unfair. For this reason, the revivalist movements are suspicious not only of the West but also of the Soviet Union and reject the Soviet—or, as they call it, the Eastern—model of socioeconomic and political organization and close alliance or identification with the Eastern bloc. Second, individual countries, based on experience, view the great powers as supporters of au- thoritarian regimes or potential sources of security threats. And third, many identify the West, and especially the United States, with Israel, which, rightly or wrongly, is perceived as the enemy of Islam.

If the Iranian experience is any guide, the victory of revivalist movements would create certain difficulties in the relations of the Muslim countries— particularly those in the Middle East—with the Western world, but it would not result in a break in all economic, commercial, or political relations. Nor would it drastically weaken the Western position, if the West is defined to mean not just the United States but also Western Europe and Japan.

Again, if the Iranian experience is any guide, once in power the revivalists would have to adapt their ideologies to their domestic, regional, and interna- tional conditions. Thus they would often have to follow pragmatic rather than ideologically determined policies. Also, Islam and the revivalists, once in power, would be judged by the same criterion as today's secular governments. This criterion is the ability to satisfy the social and economic needs and political aspirations of the people. Thus, in the case of failure, the revivalists would lose their appeal. Since the Muslim world's socioeconomic problems do not lend themselves to easy solutions, it is safe to say that the appeal of Islamic revivalism would diminish once its proponents assumed political power and responsibility.

The study clearly illustrates that while there are transnational links among revivalist groups, in particular among militant organizations, there is no firm evidence of the existence of an elaborate global militant revivalist network directed or financed by one or two countries such as Libya or Iran. There is, however, evidence that certain countries such as Iran extend assistance to some militant revivalist groups in specific regions. But there is also evidence that nonmilitant revivalists—such as branches of Muslim Brethren—receive assistance from those Muslim countries which themselves feel threatened by the militant revivalists.

But perhaps the most significant conclusion, which goes against the existing widespread perceptions, is that, with a few exceptions, the revivalist movements are not yet in a position to successfully challenge the existing political orders and power structures. This, of course, does not imply that they may not be able to do so at some future time. Their success or failure, however, would depend greatly on how effectively the Muslim governments would be able to deal with their problems and to maintain or restore their people's confidence and allegiance.

Finally, it becomes clear from this study that irrespective of what happens to the current revivalist wave, Islam will remain an important social, cultural, and political force in the Muslim world for the foreseeable future. It will, however, not be the only, or in some cases even the most important, force. Rather, it will interact with other forces such as those of ethnic particularism, nationalism, and other ideologies and political theories. In the process it will acquire new dimensions and new interpretations. It will be used, manipulated, and at times abused by many actors in their competition to control Muslim societies and to shape the direction of their future evolution. This will be so until a new sociopolitical order founded on a fairly broad-based consensus emerges in the Muslim countries and replaces the traditional patterns of social and political life which have been disrupted by the process of modernization. Such an order will include a new consensus on the sources of the legitimacy of political power. Whether or not Islam will be the core component of such an order cannot be ascertained at this time, but no doubt Islam and the diverse forces it represents will be major players in this dynamic interplay of forces in the Muslim world.

Thus, given this outlook for Islam's political future, the only constructive way for the West to deal with the revivalist phenomenon is to place it within the broader context of the Islamic world's social, political, and economic evolution. The West must see the phenomenon as the outcome of many specific factors and actions, rather than as purely an outcome of the pecularities of the Muslim faith and the Muslims' basic idiosyncracies.

The West should also realize that, so long as the underlying problems of the Islamic world remain unresolved, the danger that militant political movements will emerge periodically will remain, even if militant Islamic revivalism were to fade. Viewed in this way, the Western world could find it possible, through its policies, either to affect the evolution of Muslim societies in ways that would prevent Islamic revivalism from acquiring an overly militant or anti-Western character, or to help promote the emergence of alternative forces. For example, a Western policy on the Arab-Israeli conflict that took into account Muslim sensitivities and interests as well as Israel's security would go a long way toward diminishing the anti-Western dimensions of the revivalist movements.

Similarly, Western assistance in resolving the Muslim countries' economic problems, the encouragement of more genuinely participatory political systems, and willingness to engage in sincere efforts to reform the most discriminatory aspects of the international system would help take the edge off the militancy of the revivalist movements and decrease the chances that other militant movements would emerge.

Western-Muslim relations, like those between all states, will always be a mixture of conflict and cooperation. The challenge for the future is to minimize conflict and to maximize cooperation.

# SELECTED GLOSSARY

**Allah**—The Arabic name for God used by all Muslims and by Arab Christians.

**ᶜAmal**—Arab word meaning hope; also the acronym of the Shiᶜa militia established by Musa as-Sadr in Lebanon and headed by Nabih Berri.

**ᶜAshura**—The tenth day of the month of Muharram in the Islamic lunar calendar; a day of mourning, sacred to Shiᶜa Muslims especially, commemorating the martyrdom of the Prophet's grandson, the Imam Husain.

**Ayatullah**—Literally, reflection or sign of God, used especially in Iran to refer to Shiᶜa religious leaders elevated to this rank by the consensus of the religious establishment.

**Caliph**—Successor to Muhammad's temporal, but not spiritual, authority over the Muslim community. The Caliphate (Islamic domain ruled by the Prophet's successor) no longer exists.

**Deobandi**—A Sunni Muslim group in Pakistan, known to support such Islamic fundamentalist groups as the Jamᶜiyyat-i-ᶜUlama-i-Pakistan and the Jamaᶜat-i-Islami.

**Druze**—An offshoot of Shiᶜism; its members are not considered Muslims by orthodox Muslims or themselves. Their origins can be traced back to the eleventh century A.D., to a Turkish shaikh named al-Darazi and a Persian named al-Hamza. The Druze faith is a closed religion; converts are not sought and a distinction between initiates and outsiders is preserved. The members of the closely knit Druze community adhere to a rigorous moral code and put a great emphasis on loyalty and cohesion. Roughly 250,000 Druze live in Lebanon, while other Druze communities can be found in Syria, Israel, and the United States.

**Faqih**—Religious jurisconsult.

**Fath** (al-Fatah)—Arabic word meaning conquest; also the acronym for the mainstream Palestine Liberation Organization (PLO) faction under the leadership of Yaser ᶜArafat.

**Fiqh**—The jurisprudence of Islamic law.

**Hadith**—The traditions and sayings of the Prophet, consulted as a source of doctrine on matters not made clear by the Qur'an.

**Hajj**—The pilgrimage to Makka, which all Muslims are obliged to make once in their lives, if they are able.

**Hizb**—Party, as in Hizbullah, Party of God.

**Husain**—The second son of ᶜAli, who succeeded his older brother Hasan as the leader of the Shiᶜas. He and a small group of his followers were slain near Karbala by a superior Umayyad force on the 10th of Muharram 61 (Islamic lunar calendar), or October 10, A.D. 680.

**Ijtihad**—The attempt, when faced with a new situation, to establish a ruling through creative scholarly effort and reasoning based on the recognized fundamental principles of Islam.

**Imam**—Leader of worship, spiritual leader of a community, or, in Shiᶜa Islam, the divinely inspired successor to the Prophet.

**Islam**—Submission to the will of God; used in reference to the "nation" of believers and their faith.

**Jihad**—Holy war or struggle, a term sometimes used generally, but also specifically, to designate either a war waged in accordance with the Shariᶜa in defense of the faith, or the personal struggle to overcome one's imperfections and baser impulses in order to become a better Muslim.

**Ka<sup>c</sup>aba**—A square structure in the central courtyard of the Grand Mosque in Makka; said to have been built by Abraham, it encases the "black stone"; recognized as a shrine, it is the point toward which Muslims turn to pray and the focal point of the hajj.

**Kafir**—Irreligious, unbelieving, infidel (pl., kuffar).

**Karbala**—A city in present-day Iraq sacred to the Shi<sup>c</sup>as, where the decapitated body of the Prophet's grandson Husain was interred. A celebrated place of pilgrimage for Shi<sup>c</sup>a Muslims.

**Madina**—The city in present-day Saudi Arabia to which Muhammad and his followers immigrated in A.D. 622, when the message of Islam was rejected by the inhabitants of Makka; Muhammad died and was buried in Madina.

**Madrasa**—Religious school, where one studies the Qur'an, Islamic law, and related subjects.

**Makka**—City in Saudi Arabia, Muhammad's birthplace and the site of the Ka<sup>c</sup>aba.

**Marabout**—Folk religious leader in Muslim Africa, active mainly in the countryside.

**Maronites**—Arabic-speaking members of an Eastern Christian church having communion with the Vatican, with their center in Lebanon. There are an estimated 600,000 Maronites in Lebanon, while others reside in Israel, Egypt, Syria, Cyprus, and the United States.

**Mujahid**—Holy warrior, one who undertakes jihad (pl., mujahidin).

**Mujtahid**—Independent legal interpreter of a school of law.

**Mullah**—A religious teacher or preacher.

**Muslim**—A person who submits to the will of God; an adherent of Islam.

**Najaf**—A city in present-day Iraq, where, according to tradition, <sup>c</sup>Ali was buried, and which ever since has been a place of pilgrimage.

**Qur'an**—The book of recitations of the Word of God as revealed to the Prophet Muhammad; the holy book of Islam.

**Ramadan**—The ninth month of the Islamic lunar calendar. It is the month of fasting; no food or drink may be consumed from first light to last light.

**Riba**—Interest, usury.

**Shaikh**—Religious teacher, respected leader, or tribal chief.

**Shi<sup>c</sup>a (Shi<sup>c</sup>ite)**—Partisans of <sup>c</sup>Ali; the branch of Islam whose adherents hold that <sup>c</sup>Ali, the Prophet Muhammad's cousin and son-in-law, was Muhammad's successor; they accept the spiritual authority of a divinely inspired Imam descended directly from <sup>c</sup>Ali and his wife Fatima, the daughter of Muhammad; now found principally in Iran, Iraq, Yemen, Afghanistan, and Pakistan.

**Sunni (Sunnite)**—A follower of the tradition (Sunna), an "orthodox" Muslim; the branch of Islam whose adherents recognize no divinely guided heir to Muhammad's spiritual authority; they accept the temporal authority of caliphs and elected leaders and now comprise about 85 percent of all Muslims.

**Tawhid**—Belief in the unity of Allah, as opposed to belief in ascribing "partners" to the godhead. The term also refers to the name of the Islamic Unification Front (IUF) of Lebanon, a Sunni political party headed by Shaikh Sa<sup>c</sup>id Shaban, which advocates Islamic unity.

**<sup>c</sup>Ulama or <sup>c</sup>ulema**—Religious leaders (sing., <sup>c</sup>alim).

**Umayyad dynasty**—Established by the fifth caliph, Muawiya; endured less than a century, from A.D. 661 to 750; however, the events during this period determined the fate of Islam.

**Umma**—The community of Muslims, Islamic polity, worldwide.

**<sup>c</sup>Ushr**—The tenth or tithe levied for public assistance.

**Wahhabism**—An ultraconservative puritan reform movement within Sunni Islam, named after its founder, Muhammed ibn <sup>c</sup>Abd al-Wahhab, a legal scholar of eighteenth-century Arabia. Wahhabism, which is characterized by strict application of Qur'anic laws, is the prevalent form of Islam in Saudi Arabia.

**Waqf**—A religious charitable foundation, operated by the state or by private associations (pl., awqaf). These foundations often control vast wealth and large expanses of real estate, used to support various charitable and social welfare activities.

**Zakat**—A tithe or tax; compulsory almsgiving for the poor, one of the essential duties of all Muslims.

# SELECTED BIBLIOGRAPHY

## Books

Abd-Allah, Umar F. *The Islamic Struggle in Syria*. Berkeley, Calif.: Mizan Press, 1983.

Abrahamian, Ervand. *Iran between Two Revolutions*. Princeton, N.J.: Princeton University Press, 1982.

Achour, Y. Ben. "Islam perdu, islam retrouvé." *Le Maghreb musulman en 1979*. Paris: CNRS, 1981.

Ahmad, Aziz. *Studies in Islamic Culture in the Indian Environment*. London: Oxford University Press, 1964.

Ahmad, Aziz. *Islamic Modernism in India and Pakistan*. New York: Oxford University Press, 1967.

Ajami, Fouad. *The Vanished Imam, Musa al-Sadr and the Shia of Lebanon*. Ithaca, N.Y.: Cornell University Press, 1986.

Akhavi, Sharoug. *Religion and Politics in Contemporary Iran*. Albany: State University of New York Press, 1980.

Algar, Hamid. *Religion and State in Iran 1785–1906*. Berkeley: University of California Press, 1969.

Algar, Hamid, ed. *Islam and Revolution: Writings and Declarations of Imam Khomeini*. Berkeley, Calif.: Mizan Press, 1981.

Ali, Tariq. *Can Pakistan Survive?* London: Penguin Books, 1983.

Arjomand, Said, ed. *Contemporary Social Movements in the Near and Middle East*. Albany: State University of New York Press, 1982.

Arkoun, Mohammad. *Critique de la raison islamique*. Paris: Maisonneuve-Larose, 1984.

Bakhash, Shaul. *The Reign of the Ayatollahs*. New York: Basic Books, 1984.

Bashir, Mohamed Omar. *Terra Media: Themes in Afro-Arab Relations*. London: Ithaca Press, 1982.

Batatu, Hanna. *The Old Social Classes and the Revolutionary Movements of Iraq*. Princeton, N.J.: Princeton University Press, 1978.

Batran, Aziz. *Islam and Revolution in Africa*. Brattleboro, Vt.: Amana Books, 1984.

Bechtold, Peter K. *Politics in the Sudan: Parliamentary and Military Rule in an Emerging African Region*. New York. Praeger, 1976.

Beling, William A., ed. *King Faisal and the Modernization of Saudi Arabia*. Boulder, Colo.: Westview Press, 1980.

Binder, Leonard. *Religion and Politics in Pakistan*. Berkeley: University of California Press, 1961.

Bin-Sayeed, Khalid. *The Political System of Pakistan*. Boston: Houghton, Mifflin, 1967.

Boland, B. *The Struggle of Islam in Modern Indonesia*. The Hague: Nijhoff, 1971.

Braudel, F. *La méditerranée, l'espace et l'histoire*. Paris: Flamarion, 1985.

Burki, Shahid Javed. *Pakistan under Bhutto, 1972–1977*. New York: St. Martin's Press, 1980.

Clarke, Peter. *Islam and West African History*. London: Edward Arnold, 1982.

Cohen, Amnon. *Political Parties in the West Bank under the Hashemite Regime, 1949–1967*. Ithaca, N.Y.: Cornell University Press, 1980.

Collins, Robert O. *The Southern Sudan in Historical Perspective*. Tel Aviv: Shiloah Center, 1975.

Crone, Patricia, and Cook, Michael. *Hagarism: The Making of the Islamic World*. London: Cambridge University Press, 1977.

Curtis, Michael, ed. *Religion and Politics in the Middle East.* Boulder, Colo.: Westview Press, 1981.

Daniel, Norman. *Islam and the West: The Making of an Image.* Edinburgh: Edinburgh University Press, 1958.

Daniel, Norman. *Islam, Europe and Empire.* Edinburgh: Edinburgh University Press, 1966.

Dawisha, Adeed, ed. *Islam in Foreign Policy.* Cambridge: Cambridge University Press, 1983.

Dekmejian, R. Hrair. *Islam in Revolution: Fundamentalism in the Arab World.* Syracuse, N.Y.: Syracuse University Press, 1985.

Dessouki, Ali E. Hillal, ed. *Islamic Resurgence in the Arab World.* New York: Praeger, 1982.

Dessouki, Ali E. Hillal, and Cudsi, Alexander S. *Islam and Power.* Baltimore: Johns Hopkins University Press, 1981.

Enayat, Hamid. *Modern Islamic Political Thought.* Austin: University of Texas Press, 1982.

Esposito, John L. *Islam and Politics.* Syracuse, N.Y.: Syracuse University Press, 1984.

Esposito, John, ed. *Islam and Development: Religion and Sociopolitical Change.* Syracuse, N.Y.: Syracuse University Press, 1980.

Esposito, J.L., ed. *Voices of Resurgent Islam.* New York: Oxford University Press, 1983.

Fischer, Michael M.J. *Iran: From Religious Dispute to Revolution.* Cambridge, Mass.: Harvard University Press, 1980.

Funston, N. *Malay Politics in Malaysia.* Kuala Lumpur: Heinemann Educational Books, 1980.

Geertz, C. *The Religion of Java.* Glencoe, Ill.: Free Press, 1960.

Granguillaume, G. *Arabisation et politique linguistique au Maghreb.* Paris: Maisonneuve-Larose, 1984.

Hamid, Mohammed Beshir. *The Politics of National Reconciliation in the Sudan: The Numayri Regime and the National Front Opposition.* Washington, D.C.: Center for Contemporary Arab Studies, Georgetown University, 1984.

Harris, Christina Phelps. *Nationalism and Revolution in Egypt: The Role of the Muslim Brotherhood.* The Hague: Mouton, 1964 (published for the Hoover Institution on War, Revolution, and Peace, Stanford, Calif.).

Hasan, Yusuf Fadl. *The Arabs and the Sudan, from the Seventh to the Sixteenth Century.* Edinburgh: Edinburgh University Press, 1969.

Heikal, Mohamed. *Autumn of Fury: The Assassination of Sadat.* New York: Random House, 1983.

Hermassi, Elbaki. *Etat et société au Maghreb: Etude comparative.* Paris: Anthropos, 1974.

Holt, P.M. *The Mahdist State in the Sudan, 1881–1898.* 2d ed. Oxford: Clarendon Press, 1958.

Holt, P.M., and Daly, M.W. *The History of the Sudan from the Coming of Islam to the Present Day.* 3d ed. Boulder, Colo.: Westview Press, 1979.

Ismael, Tareq Y., and Ismael, Jacqueline S. *Government and Politics in Islam.* New York: St. Martin's Press, 1985.

Jansen, G.H. *Militant Islam.* New York: Harper and Row, 1979.

Kaba, Langine. *The Wahabiyya: Islamic Reform and Politics in French West Africa.* Evanston, Ill.: Northwestern University Press, 1974.

Keddie, Nikki. *Roots of Revolution: An Interpretative History of Modern Iran.* New Haven, Conn.: Yale University Press, 1981.

Kepel, Gilles. *Le Prophète et pharaon: Les mouvements islamistes dans l'Egypte contemporaine.* Paris: Editions La Decouverte, 1984.

Kessler, C. *Islam and Politics in a Malay State: Kelantan 1838–1967.* Ithaca, N.Y.: Cornell University Press, 1978.

Laroui, Abdallah. *La crise des intellectuels arabes: Traditionalisme ou historicisme?* Paris: Maspero, 1974.

Lewis, I.M., ed. *Islam in Tropical Africa.* London: Oxford University Press, 1966.

Malik, Hafeez. *Moslem Nationalism in India and Pakistan.* 2d ed. Lahore: People's Publishing House, 1980.

Malwal, Bona. *The Sudan.* New York: Thornton Books, 1985.

Marr, Phebe. *The History of Modern Iraq.* Boulder, Colo.: Westview Press, 1985.

Martin, B.G. *Muslim Brotherhoods in 19th Century Africa.* New York: Cambridge University Press, 1976.

Mawdudi, S. Abu al-ᶜAla. *A Short History of the Revolutionary Movement in Islam.* Lahore: Islamic Publications, 1963.

McCall, D.F., and Bennett, N.R., eds. *Aspects of West African Islam.* Boston: Boston University Press, 1971.

Mortimer, Edward. *Faith and Power: The Politics of Islam.* New York: Random House, 1982.

Munson, Henry, Jr. *The House of Si Abd Allah: The Oral History of a Moroccan Family.* New Haven, Conn.: Yale University Press, 1984.

Nagata, J. *The Reflowering of Malaysian Islam.* Vancouver: University of British Columbia Press, 1984.

Ochsenwald, William. *Religion, Society, and the State in Arabia: The Hijaz under Ottoman Control, 1840–1908.* Columbus: Ohio State University Press, 1984.

O'Fahey, R.S., and Spaulding, J.L. *Kingdoms of the Sudan.* London: Methuen, 1974.

Parker, Richard. *North Africa: Regional Tensions and Strategic Concerns.* New York: Praeger, 1984.

Peacock, J. *Muslim Puritans: Reformist Psychology in Southeast Asian Islam.* Berkeley: University of California Press, 1978.

Pipes, Daniel. *In the Path of God: Islam and Political Power.* New York: Basic Books, 1983.

Piscatori, James P., ed. *Islam in the Political Process.* Cambridge: Cambridge University Press, 1983.

Quandt, William. *Saudi Arabia in the 1980s: Foreign Policy, Security, and Oil.* Washington, D.C.: The Brookings Institution, 1981.

Quddus, Muhammad A. *Pakistan: A Case Study of a Plural Society.* Columbia, MO.: South Asia Books, 1982.

Qureshi, Ishtiaq Hussain. *The Muslim Community in the Indo-Pakistani Sub-Continent.* The Hague: Mouton, 1962.

Qureshi, Ishtiaq Hussain. *A Short History of Pakistan.* 4 vols. Karachi: University of Karachi Press, 1967.

Qureshi, Ishtiaq Hussain. *The Struggle for Pakistan.* 2d ed. Karachi: Maarif, 1977.

Rabinovitch, Itamar. *Syria under the Baᶜth, 1963–1966.* New York: Halstead Press, 1972.

Rahman, Fazlur. *Islamic Modernism.* Chicago: University of Chicago Press, 1982.

Rajaee, Farhang. *Islamic Values and World View: Khomeini on Man, the State and International Politics.* New York: University Press of America, 1983.

Said, Edward. *Orientalism.* New York: Vintage Books, 1978.

Salem, Norma. *Habib Bourguiba, Islam and the Creation of Tunisia.* London: Croom Helm, 1984.

Sivan, Emmanuel. *Radical Islam: Medieval Theology and Modern Politics.* New Haven, Conn.: Yale University Press, 1985.

Soulié, Jean-Louis, and Champenois, Lucien. *Le Royaume d'Arabie Saoudite.* Paris: Michel, 1978.

Souriau, Christiane. *Le Maghreb musulman en 1979.* Paris: CNRS, 1983.

Tibawi, A.L. *A Modern History of Syria.* London: Macmillan, 1969.

Van Dam, Nicholas. *The Struggle for Power in Syria: Sectarianism, Regionalism and Tribalism in Politics, 1961–1978.* New York: St. Martin's Press, 1979.
Vernier, Bernard. *L'Irak d'aujourd'hui.* Paris: Armand Colin, 1963.
Voll, John Obert, and Voll, Sarah Potts. *The Sudan: Unity and Diversity in a Multicultural Society.* Boulder, Colo.: Westview Press, 1985.
von der Mehden, Fred R. *Religion and Modernization in Southeast Asia.* Syracuse, N.Y.: Syracuse University Press, 1986.
von der Mehden, Fred R. *Religion and Nationalism in Southeast Asia.* Madison: University of Wisconsin Press 1963.
Waardenburg, J.D. *L'Islam dans le miroir de l'Occident.* Paris: Mouton, 1963.
Wai, Dunstan M., ed. *The Southern Sudan: The Problem of National Integration.* London: Frank Cass, 1973.
Williams, John Alden, ed. *Themes of Islamic Civilization.* Berkeley: University of California Press, 1971.
Wright, Robin. *Sacred Rage: The Wrath of Militant Islam.* New York: Simon and Schuster, 1985.
Yasin, Abd al-Slam. *La revolution à l'heure de l'Islam.* Marseille: Les Presses de l'Imprimerie du College, 1979.

## Articles

Abd-al-Monein, Said Aly and Wenner, M.W. "Modern Islamic Reform Movements: The Moslem Brotherhood in Contemporary Egypt." *The Middle East Journal,* Vol. 36, No. 3, Summer 1982.
Ahmad, Mumtaz. "Parliament, Parties, Polls and Islam: Issues in the Current Debate on Religion and Politics in Pakistan." *American Journal of Islamic Social Sciences,* Vol. 1, No. 3, April 1985.
Ansari, Hamied. "The Islamic Militants in Egyptian Politics." *International Journal of Middle East Studies,* Vol. 16, No. 1, March 1984.
Batatu, Hanna. "Iraq's Underground Shiʿa Movements: Characteristics, Causes and Prospects." *The Middle East Journal,* Vol. 35, No. 4, Autumn 1981.
Batatu, Hanna. "Syria's Muslim Brethren." *MERIP Reports,* Vol. 12, No. 9, November–December 1982.
Bechtold, Peter K. "The Contemporary Sudan." *American-Arab Affairs,* No. 6, Fall 1983.
Bengio, Ofra. "Shiʿis and Politics in Baʿthi Iraq." *Middle Eastern Studies,* January 1985.
Bill, James. "Resurgent Islam in The Persian Gulf." *Foreign Affairs,* Vol. 63, No. 1, Fall 1984.
Cristelow, Allan. "Religious Protest and Dissent in Northern Nigeria: From Mahdism to Quranic Integralism." *Journal of the Institute of Muslim Minority Affairs,* Vol. 6, No. 2, July 1985.
Cristelow, Allan. "The Yan Tatsine Disturbances in Kano: A Search for Perspective." *The Muslim World,* Vol. 75, No. 2, April 1985.
Dekmejian, R. Hrair. "The Anatomy of Islamic Revival: Legitimacy Crisis, Ethnic Conflict and the Search for Islamic Alternatives." *The Middle East Journal,* Vol. 34, No. 1, Winter 1980.
Dekmejian, R. Hrair. "Fundamentalist Islam: Theories, Typologies, and Trends." *Middle East Review,* No. 4, Summer 1985.
Drysdale, Alisdair. "The Asad Regime and Its Troubles." *MERIP Reports,* Vol. 12, No. 9, November–December 1982.

Drysdale, Alisdair. "The Syrian Political Elite, 1966–1976: A Spatial and Social Analysis."
    Middle Eastern Studies, Vol. 17, No. 1, January 1981.
Etienne, Bruno. "L'Islam à Marseille ou les tribulations d'un anthropologue." Les Temps
    Modernes, No. 452–454, March–May 1984.
Haddad, Yvonne Yazbeck. "The Qur'anic Justification for an Islamic Revolution: The
    View of Sayyid Qutb." The Middle East Journal, Vol. 37, No. 1, Winter 1983.
Heller, Mark, and Safran, Nadav. "The New Middle Class and Regime Stability in Saudi
    Arabia." Harvard Middle East Papers, Modern Series, No. 3, 1985.
Hinnebusch, Raymond A. "Political Recruitment and Socialization in Syria: The Case
    of the Revolutionary Youth Federation." International Journal of Middle East
    Studies, Vol. 11, No. 2, 1980.
Hinnebusch, Raymond A. "Syria under the Baᶜth: State Formation in a Fragmented
    Society." Arab Studies Quarterly, Vol. 4, No. 3, Summer 1982.
Humphreys, R. Stephan. "Islam and Political Values in Saudi Arabia, Egypt and Syria."
    The Middle East Journal, Vol. 33, Winter 1979.
Hunter, Shireen T. "Iranian Perceptions and a Wider World." Political Communication
    and Persuasion, Vol. 2, No. 4, 1985.
Hunter, Shireen T. "Islamic Fundamentalism: What It Really Is and Why It Frightens
    the West." SAIS Review, Vol. 6, No. 1, Winter/Spring 1986.
Ibrahim, Saᶜad ad-Din. "Anatomy of Egypt's Militant Islamic Groups: Methodological
    Notes and Preliminary Findings." International Journal of Middle East Studies,
    Vol. 12, No. 4, 1980.
Ibrahim, Saᶜad ad-Din. "Egypt's Islamic Militants." MERIP Reports, No. 103, February
    1982.
Jamali, Fadil. "The Theological Colleges of Najaf." The Muslim World, Vol. 50, January
    1960.
Kechichian, Joseph. "The Role of the Ulama in the Politics of an Islamic State: The Case
    of Saudi Arabia." International Journal of Middle East Studies, Vol. 18, No. 1,
    February 1986.
Kelidar, A.H. "Religion and State in Syria." Asian Affairs, Vol. 61 (New Series Vol. 5),
    part 1, February 1974.
Lawson, Fred H. "Social Basis of the Hama Revolt." MERIP Reports, Vol. 12, No. 9,
    November–December 1982.
Lewis, Bernard. "The Return of Islam." Commentary, Vol. 61, No. 1, January 1976.
"The martyred Imam Sayyid Muhammed Baqer as-Sadr" [in Arabic, no author given].
    Tariq al-Haqq (London), Vol. 2, No. 12, February 1982.
Mazrui, Ali A. "On the Concept 'We Are All Africans.'" American Political Science
    Review, Vol. 57, No. 1, March 1963.
Morfit, M. "Panchasila: The Indonesian State Ideology according to the New Order
    Government." Asian Survey, Vol. 21, No. 8, August 1981.
Munson, Henry, Jr. "Islamic Revivalism in Morocco and Tunisia." The Muslim World,
    Vol. 76, No. 3–4, July–October 1986.
Munson, Henry, Jr. "The Social Base of Islamic Militancy in Morocco." The Middle
    East Journal, Vol. 40, No. 2, Spring 1985.
Nasr, Salim. "Roots of the Shiᶜi Movement." MERIP Reports, No. 133, June 1985.
Ochsenwald, William. "Saudi Arabia and the Islamic Revival." International Journal of
    Middle East Studies, Vol. 13, No. 3, August 1981.
Paul, Jim. "States of Emergency: The Riots in Tunisia and Morocco." MERIP Reports,
    Vol. 14, No. 8, October 1984.
Perera, Judith. "The Shifting Fortunes of Syria's Muslim Brothers." The Middle East,
    May 1983.
Rabinovitch, Itamar. "The Islamic Wave." The Washington Quarterly, Vol. 2, No. 4,
    Autumn 1979.

Ramazani, R.K. "Iran's Islamic Revolution and the Persian Gulf." *Current History*, Vol. 84, No. 48, January 1985.

Seddon, David. "Winter of Discontent: Economic Crisis in Tunisia and Morocco." *MERIP Reports*, No. 127, October 1984.

Tessler, Mark. "Politics in Morocco: The Monarch, the War, and the Opposition." *American Universities Field Staff Reports*, No. 47, 1981.

Thompson, William R. "Delineating Regional Subsystems: Visit Networks and the Middle Eastern Case." *International Journal of Middle East Studies*, Vol. 13, No. 2, May 1981.

Utrecht, E. "The Muslim Merchant Class in the Indonesian Social and Political Struggle." *Social Compass*, Vol. 31, 1984.

Voll, John O. "Reconciliation in the Sudan." *Current History*, Vol. 80, No. 47, December 1981.

von der Mehden, Fred R. "Religion and Politics in Malaya." *Asian Survey*, Vol. 3, No. 12, December 1963.

Wimberly, Dale W. "Socioeconomic Deprivation and Religious Salience: A Cognitive Behavioral Approach." *The Sociological Quarterly*, Vol. 25, No. 2, Spring 1984.

# ABOUT THE AUTHORS

MUMTAZ AHMAD, formerly a senior instructor at the National Institute of Public Administration in Karachi and a fellow at the Brookings Institution, is now a private consultant in Washington, D.C. His publications include *Bureaucracy and Political Development in Pakistan*, Karachi, National Institute of Public Administration, 1974; *The Kashmir Dispute*, Lahore, Mihrab Publications, 1968; *Studies in Local Government and Rural Development in Pakistan*, Karachi, Aziz Publications, 1975; and *Islam, Politics and the State*, Indianapolis, American Trust Publications (forthcoming).

MOHAMMAD ARKOUN is a professor at the Sorbonne in Paris and acting director of its Institute of Arab and Islamic Studies. Professor Arkoun has also been a visiting professor at UCLA (1969) and Princeton University (1985). In 1986–87, Professor Arkoun was a fellow at the Institute for Advanced Study in Berlin. He has published extensively on Islam, including *Critique de la raison Islamique*, Paris, 1986, and *L'Islam dans l'histoire*, MAGHREB/MACHREQ, 1984.

AMIRA EL-AZHARY SONBOL is a visiting assistant professor of history at Georgetown University in Washington, D.C.

R. HRAIR DEKMEJIAN is chairman of the Political Science Department at the University of Southern California, Los Angeles. Dr. Dekmejian's many publications include *Islam in Revolution*, Syracuse University Press, 1985.

JOHN L. ESPOSITO is professor and chair, Department of Religious Studies, College of the Holy Cross, Worcester, Massachusetts. His many publications include *Islam and Politics*, Syracuse University Press, 1984, and *Islam and Development* (ed.).

RAYMOND A. HINNEBUSCH is associate professor of political science at the College of St. Catherine in St. Paul, Minnesota. He is the author of numerous articles on Syria and of a book, *Egyptian Politics under Sadat*, Cambridge University Press, 1985.

SHIREEN T. HUNTER is deputy director of the Middle East Project at the Center for Strategic and International Studies in Washington, D.C. Her many publications include *OPEC and the Third World: The Politics of Aid*, Indiana University Press, 1984, and "Islamic Fundamentalism: What It Really Is and Why It Frightens the West," *SAIS Review*, Winter/Spring, 1986. Her articles have also appeared in *The Middle East Journal*, *The Washington Quarterly*, and *Foreign Policy*.

JOSEPH KOSTINER is a lecturer in the Middle East and African Studies Department at Tel Aviv University. Dr. Kostiner has published extensively on issues related to the Gulf region and the Arabian Peninsula, especially North and South Yemen. His latest book is *Struggle for South Yemen*, 1984.

CHIBLI MALLAT, an attorney, is completing a doctoral thesis on the work of Imam Muhammad Baqer as-Sadr at the School of Oriental and African Studies, University of London.

HENRY MUNSON, JR., is assistant professor of anthropology at the University of Maine. His publications include *The House of Si Abd Allah: The Oral History of a Moroccan Family*, Yale University Press, 1984, and *Islam and Revolution in the Middle East*, scheduled for publication by Yale in spring 1988.

SULAYMAN S. NYANG is associate professor of government and acting director of the African Studies and Research programs at Howard University, Washington, D.C. His publications include *Islam, Christianity and African Identity*, Amana Books, Brattleboro, Vermont, 1984. His articles have also appeared in *Presence Africaine*, *The Middle East Journal*, *Muslim World*, and *Islamic Culture*, among others.

*About the Authors* 297

WILLIAM OCHSENWALD is professor of history at Virginia Polytechnic Institute and State University at Blacksburg, Virginia. He is the author of *The Hijaz Railroad*, Charlottesville, University Press of Virginia, 1980, and *Religion, Society and the State in Arabia: The Hijaz under Ottoman Control*, Columbus: Ohio State University Press, 1984; and the co-editor of *Nationalism in a Non-National State: The Dissolution of the Ottoman Empire*, Columbus: Ohio State University Press, 1977.

EMILE F. SAHLIYEH is associate professor of Middle East at Bir-Zeit University and a visiting lecturer at North Texas State University. He was a fellow at the Brookings Institution (September 1985–July 1986) and at the Woodrow Wilson Center for Scholars (March 1985–August 1985). His many publications include *The PLO after the Lebanon War*, Westview Press, 1986, and *Political Trends among West Bank Palestinians: The Post 1967 Era*, Woodrow Wilson International Center for Scholars, 1986.

NORMA SALEM is a researcher at the Institut Québequois de recherche sur la culture (igre). Her many publications include *Habib Bourguiba, Islam and the Creation of Tunisia*, Croom Helm, 1984.

FRED R. VON DER MEHDEN is a professor at Rice University in Texas. His many publications include *The Challenge of Islamic Revival in Malaysia and Indonesia*, Boston University Press, 1986, and *Islam in Public Life in Malaysia*, Oxford University Press (forthcoming).

ROBIN WRIGHT, a journalist, is a senior associate at the Carnegie Endowment for Peace. She is the author of *Sacred Rage: The Wrath of Militant Islam*, Simon and Schuster, 1985.

# INDEX